Max Duncker

The History of Antiquity

Vol. V

Max Duncker

The History of Antiquity

Vol. V

Reprint of the original, first published in 1881.

1st Edition 2023 | ISBN: 978-3-36863-707-1

Verlag (Publisher): Outlook Verlag GmbH, Zeilweg 44, 60439 Frankfurt, Deutschland
Vertretungsberechtigt (Authorized to represent): E. Roepke, Zeilweg 44, 60439 Frankfurt, Deutschland
Druck (Print): Books on Demand GmbH, In de Tarpen 42, 22848 Norderstedt, Deutschland

THE HISTORY OF ANTIQUITY.

THE

HISTORY OF ANTIQUITY.

FROM THE GERMAN

OF

PROFESSOR MAX DUNCKER,

BY

EVELYN ABBOTT, M.A., LL.D.,

FELLOW AND TUTOR OF BALLIOL COLLEGE, OXFORD.

VOL. V.

LONDON:

RICHARD BENTLEY & SON, NEW BURLINGTON STREET,

Publishers in Ordinary to Her Majesty the Queen.

1881.

Bangay:

CLAY AND TAYLOR, PRINTERS.

CONTENTS.

BOOK VII.

THE ARIANS OF EASTERN IRAN.

CHAPTER I.

CHAPTER II.

CHAPTER III.

CHAPTER IV.

CHAPTER V.

CHAPTER VI.

CHAPTER VII.

CHAPTER VIII.

CHAPTER IX.

CHAPTER X.

BOOK VIII.

THE EMPIRE OF THE MEDES AND PERSIANS.

CHAPTER I.

CHAPTER II.

CHAPTER III.

CHAPTER IV.

CHAPTER V.

BOOK VII.

THE ARIANS OF EASTERN IRAN.

EASTERN IRAN.

CHAPTER I.

THE LAND AND THE TRIBES.

BETWEEN the valley of the Indus and the land of the Euphrates and Tigris, bounded on the south by the ocean and the Persian Gulf, on the north by the broad steppes which the Oxus and Jaxartes vainly attempt to fertilise, by the Caspian Sea and the valley of the Aras, lies the table-land of Iran. Rising to an average height of 4000 feet above the level of the sea, it forms an oblong, the length of which from east to west is something more than 1500 miles. The breadth in the east is about 1000 miles, but at the narrowest point, from the Caspian Sea to the Persian Gulf, it is not much more than 500 miles; while the western edge, reaching from the Persian Gulf to the mountains of Aderbeijan, again extends over a distance of about 750 miles.

In this seclusion, neither penetrated by bays of the sea nor traversed by mighty rivers, the region exhibits a certain similarity to the highlands of Arabia. The centre of the Iranian land, like that of Arabia, is occupied by a great desert where only nomadic life is possible. But the soil of Iran is more diversified in regard to

elevation and depression. The northern half of the
land is higher than the southern, the centre is hollowed
out in the form of a trough, so that in the east, at any
rate, the waters from the inner slopes of the mountainous rim fall into the depression, and collect in
fructifying lakes. The oases and fertile valleys are
more numerous and extensive than in Arabia, and
though the rivers of the inner table-land, like the
streams of the northern edge, which flow to the north,
are lost in the sand or end in unimportant lakes, they
nevertheless render agriculture possible over wide
tracts of country.

The northern side is more diversified and superior
in formation to the south. The southern edge, which
sinks down to the ocean, closely resembles Arabia
in the climate and the nature of the country; the
mountains of the north, on the other hand, exhibit
green pastures and splendid forests where Arabia has
nothing but bare peaks: in the Hindu Kush, and
Elburz on the Caspian Sea, as well as in Aderbeijan,
they rise into vast Alpine districts. The eastern edge,
extending over a distance of 900 miles, rises like a
steep wall out of the valley of the Indus; a few long
and difficult passes lead from the Indus to the high
ground, which on the north commences with cold bare
flats, and on the south with slopes still more desolate
and barren, and at the same time intolerably hot. Only
the terraces of the valley of the Cabul, which flows
down into the Indus, allow a convenient exit towards
the north, and present a soil to a great extent so
fertile that three harvests can be reaped in the year.
The western edge of Iran, on the other hand, is formed
by parallel ridges running from the north-west to the
south-east, between which, beside extensive mountain
pastures, lie narrow and well-watered valleys. In the

north-west the low-lying regions are rich in meadows
and forest ; while those between the abutting ridges of
the western and southern edge are warm, and even hot,
in climate, rich and luxuriant in vegetation.

On this table-land the heat is softened, though not
entirely, by the elevation of the soil. After violent
storms in the spring, no cloud darkens the sky from
May to September ; the atmosphere is peculiarly dry
and clear, and through the fine air can be seen, bright
and sharp, the outlines of the mountains and the whole
country, while at night the star-lit sky almost replaces
the light of day. The changes in temperature are
sudden and severe. From cold, snow-covered terraces,
8000 feet in height, we suddenly descend to the
glowing heat of the plains, lying barely 2000 feet
above the sea. In the north-east oppressive heat
alternates with great cold ; the north suffers from a
severe winter, with heavy falls of snow and icy storms,
blowing over the Caspian Sea and the broad steppes ; in
the south the air is filled with the dust of the desert,
here extraordinarily fine, and the hot winds give the
heaps of sand the appearance of changing waves, and
roll masses of it to the sky.[1]

As far back as our information extends, we find the
table-land of Iran occupied by a group of nations
closely related to each other, and speaking dialects
of the same language. On the edges of that great
desert, which occupies the centre of the land, are
tracts of pasture, and further inland, treeless steppes,
which, however, are watered here and there by
brackish pools, and produce a salt vegetation barely
sufficient to provide buffaloes and camels with sustenance, until the soil becomes entirely barren. In the
western part of these steppes wandered a pastoral

[1] Ritter, "Erdkunde," 7, 231—240; 8, 721.

people, whom Herodotus calls Sagartians. They were horsemen, but, according to the historian's statement, carried no weapons of attack beyond a dagger and a rope of twisted straps, at one end of which was a loop. In this they placed their confidence in battle ; they threw it over men and horses, and so dragged them down and strangled them. In the inscriptions of the Achæmenids this nation is called *Açagarta*.[1]

Close to the Indus, and beyond the bare, hot, treeless shores of the ocean, the southern part of the plain consists of sandy flats, in which nothing grows but prickly herbs and a few palms. The springs are a day's journey from each other, and often more. This region was possessed by a people whom Herodotus calls Sattagydæ, and the companions of Alexander of Macedonia, Gedrosians.[2] Among the nations of the East who were subject to them, the inscriptions of the Achæmenids mention the "*Thatagus*," which the Greeks understood as Sattagush and Gadrush. Neighbours of the Gandarians, who, as we know, dwelt on the right bank of the Indus down to the Cabul, the Gedrosians led a wandering, predatory life ; under the Persian kings they were united into one satrapy with the Gandarians.[3] To the south of the Gedrosians, on the coast, there dwelt, according to the Greeks, a miserable race, eaters of fish and tortoises, who built

---

[1] Herod. 1, 125 ; 7, 85 ; Lassen, "Z. D. M. G." 6, 55. Herodotus reckons the Paretaceni among the tribes of the Medes (1, 101) ; the Sagartians, whom he represents as armed partly like Persians, partly like Pactyans, with the Carmanians, he places among the Persians. Yet the nomad Sagartians seem rather to have had relations with the Medes than the Persians ; for, according to the inscription of Behistun, a rebel obtains a following among the Sagartians by giving himself out to be a descendant of Cyaxares, the Median king. Ptolemy places the Sagartians in Media ; cf. Plin. "Hist. Nat." 6, 29.

[2] Arrian, "Anab." 6, 22 ff. ; "Ind." 25, 26 ; Curtius, 9, 10, 5.

[3] Behistun, 1, 6 ; Persep. 1, 17 ; Herod. 3, 91.

their houses of the bones of whales thrown up by the
sea. They wove their nets from the bark of palms,
and their weapons were javelins hardened in the fire.[1]
The edge on the south allows no streams of any size
to flow to the sea, so that even to this day this coast
presents only a few small fertile spots. About equally
distant from the northern and southern edge of the
table-land, to the east of the desert of the interior, lies
a considerable lake, now called Hamun, but known
to the Greeks as Areios. It forms the centre of a cultivated district, though the storms from the west often
drive the sand of the desert to its shores. This basin
is formed by and receives important streams flowing
from the inner slopes of the northern and eastern edge.
From the southern spurs of the Hindu Kush comes
the Hilmend, the Haetumat of the Avesta, *i. e.* rich
in bridges, the Etymandros of the Greeks, which has a
course of about 400 miles, and before falling into the
lake is joined by the Arghandab. The Lora, which
flows from the east, but further to the south, does not
now reach the lake. From the north flow the Harut
and Chashrud. Round this lake, and on the banks of the
Hilmend, the Arghandab, and the Lora, lies a fruitful
region ; higher up the walls of the valleys are covered
with forests, until towards the east the upper course of
the rivers is enclosed by bare cliffs. On the shores of
the Hamun, and in the valley of the Hilmend, dwelt a
people whom the inscriptions of the Achæmenids call
Zaraka, i. e. dwellers on the lake. A lake in Old
Persian is *Daraya;* in the ancient language of the East,
Zarayanh ; in modern Persian, *Zareh*. Hence we
understand why Herodotus calls this nation Sarangians, the later Greeks, Zarangians and Drangians.
According to the Greeks the Zarakas were a warlike

[1] Strabo, p. 711; Arrian, "Ind." 25, 26; "Anab." 6, 23.

nation, armed with Median bows and spears, unsurpassed in battle on horseback; and a tribe of them which lived under good and equitable laws bore the name of Ariaçpians.[1] The ruins of cities and works of irrigation testify to the former prosperity of this region. East of the Zarakas, up the valley of the Arghandab, dwelt the Arachoti. In the inscriptions of the Achæmenids they are called *Harauvati;* in the Avesta, *Harahvaiti,* i. e. the rich in water. These names the Arachoti received from the river on which they were settled, the older name of which was Arachotus (*Sarasvati*).[2] Herodotus does not designate the Arachoti by this name derived from the river of their land, but by the tribal name of Pactyes; he tells us that they wore peculiar bows, daggers, and skins.[3] The Afghans, who in ancient times occupied the region from the Suleiman mountains on the east as far as the Arghandab on the west, Shorawak on the south, the Cabul and the range of the Sefid-Kuh on the north, and in the middle ages forced their way to Cabul and Peshawur, still call themselves Pashtun and Pakhtun, or Rohilo, *i. e.* mountaineers. They still speak their old rough mountain language, which is closely

---

[1] Arrian, "Anab." 3, 27; Diod. 17, 81; Strabo, p. 724.

[2] Vol. IV. p. 33.

[3] The city of Kapisakani, which Darius, according to the inscription of Behistun (3, 9, 1), conquered in the land of the Arachoti, is no doubt the Capissa of Pliny, in the district of Capissene; "Hist. Nat." 6, 25. Pliny speaks of the city and river of Cabul as belonging to the Arachoti. The inhabitants of the southern slope of the Hindu Kush are known to the Greeks as Paropanisadæ. The explanation of the name by Paropanisos (Paropamisus), Paropanishadha, given by Lassen, is quoted in Vol. IV. p. 21, *n.* 2. In the Babylonian text of the inscription of Behistun, the Gandaras of the Persian text are called Parupanisana. In the narrower sense the name denotes the south-western part of the range of the Hindu Kush, the group which forms the cradle of the Herirud and Hilmend, the modern Ghuristan, to the west of the plateau of Ghasna.

connected with the dialects of the Arian tribes on the Indus.[1]

Eastward of Elburz, the point where the northern edge of Iran again rises into a lofty range to the west (Demavend is more than 18,000 feet in height), and then sinks down to the Caspian Sea, lay the Hyrcanians. In the inscriptions of the Achæmenids their land is known as *Varkana*; the modern name is Jorjan. Here, according to the Greeks, the mountains were covered with forests of oaks, where swarms of wild bees had their hives; in the valleys vines and fig-trees flourished, and the soil down to the sea was so luxuriant that corn grew from the fallen grains without any special sowing.[2] The description is hardly exaggerated. The waters pouring from the heights and snow-fields of Elburz water the soil of the coast so thoroughly, that a tropical growth flourishes in Jorjan, Taberistan, and Ghilan, the luxuriance of which is assisted by the volcanic heat of the earth. The lagunes of the coast are succeeded by marsh forests; higher up are fields of rice and plantations of sugar-cane, and beyond these fertile meadows, above which splendid forests of oaks, planes, and elms clothe the heights of Elburz. There is abundance of water fruits, figs and mulberries, olives and oranges, and the vigorous creepers of the vines run even to the summits of the trees.[3] Nevertheless, these favoured regions

---

[1] Lassen, "Indische Alterthumskunde," 1, 428. Fr. Müller ("Ueber die Sprache der Afghanen") is of the opinion that the Afghan does not come between Indian and Persian, but belongs to the Iranian stem, and the Afghan has preserved the old Bactrian relations of sound more faithfully than the Persian, and thus shows itself to be a direct descendant of the old eastern dialect of Iran. Trump proves that Afghan is an ancient independent language of strong Indian type. "Z. D. M. G." 21, 10 ff.

[2] Strabo, pp. 508, 514, 724; Plin. "Hist. Nat." 6, 29; Diod. 17, 75.

[3] Ritter, "Erdkunde," 8, 425 ff.

have a darker side. Frequent earthquakes disturb the soil; in the winter furious north winds blowing over the Caspian rage along the walls of Elburz, and even on the outlying spurs the snow falls to the depth of several fathoms; the rain-clouds, hemmed in by the mountain ranges, often burst in water-spouts, which lay the land far and wide under water, and roll as torrents down the gorges; the marsh air blanches the inhabitants, while in the summer the hot and moist climate breeds deadly fever.

Further to the east, where the Caspian Sea ends and the mountains of Iran descend towards the desolate, pathless steppes of the Oxus, is a wild, hilly country. In the depressions, and there only, the region of the Parthians (*Parthava* in the inscriptions of the Achæmenids[1]) exhibits fruitful lands, and, further eastward still, agriculture is favoured by the long, narrow valley of the Areios (Herirud). Springing from the southern slope of the Hindu Kush, the river flows towards the west along the inner edge of the table-land, till it bursts through the northern barrier in order to lose itself in the sand of the steppes. In this valley the district of the modern Herat, lay the Areians, who are called *Haraiva* in the inscriptions of the Persian

[1] Isid. "Charac. Mans. Parth." 10–14. The Parthians rose with the Hyrcanians against Darius; Parthians and Hyrcanians formed one satrapy. The Parthians are the Pahlav of Moses of Khorene, the Pehlew of later writers. The mention of them in the inscriptions of Darius proves that they are not a later immigrant Scythian, *i. e.* non-Arian, nation, as Justin, Strabo, and others maintain. The cities which the inscription of Behistun mentions in Parthia (2, 95; 3, 4), Viçpauzatis and Patigrabana, we cannot fix more definitely; Ammian (23, 6) mentions Patigran in Media. Parthunisa, with the graves of the Parthian kings, mentioned in Isidorus, "which the Greeks call Nisæa," is Parthava-Niçaya, and must be sought for near the modern Nishapur. It must be the Niça which the Vendidad places between Mouru and Bakhdhi. Justi, "Beitrage," 2, 6 compares Isidorus' Βατζιγράβαν, ὅ ἐστι τελώνιον.

kings. The name points to the possession of water. To
the north of the Areians, in the valley of the Margos
(now Murghab), which rises in the northern edge of
the table-land, and flows to the north-west, where it
also ends in the sands of the desert, in Margiana (Old
Persian, Marghush ; Bactrian, Mouru ; modern Merv),
lay the Margiani, in a well-cultivated region, rich in
vineyards, with numerous cities and a large population. But the fertility only extends so far as the soil
can be watered from the Margos and the neighbouring
streams.

At the foot of the mountain barrier, towards the
northern steppes, and on the edge of the steppes of
the Oxus, to the north of the Hyrcanians, Parthians,
and Margiani, in a land which only partially admits
of agriculture, lay the Chorasmians, a people partly
stationary and partly migratory — the *Uvarazmiya*
of the Achæmenids, the *Hvairizem* of the Avesta.
Further to the east, where the edge rises to the lofty
Hindu Kush, there lies on its northern slope a favoured
district in the region of the Upper Oxus. That river
flows from the table-land of Pamire, which lies more
than 15,000 feet above the sea, exactly at the point
where the Hindu Kush abuts on the Belurdagh, the
western edge of the central table-land. On the banks
of the river, which flows in a north-westerly direction,
extend broad mountain pastures, where support is found
in the fresh mountain air for numerous herds of horses
and sheep, and beneath the wooded hills are blooming
valleys. On these slopes of the Hindu Kush, the
middle stage between the table-land and the deep
plain of the Caspian Sea, lay the Bactrians—the *Bakh-
tri* of the Achæmenids, the *Bakhdhi* of the Avesta.
Curtius, following the accounts of the companions of
Alexander, tells us of the land of the Bactrians that it

was much diversified in character; in one part were pastures, another was rich in beautiful fruit-trees and vines,
and frequent springs watered the rich soil, on which
corn was cultivated. These districts supported a large
number of oxen and horses. Under the range of
Paropanisos (*i. e.* on the slope of the Hindu Kush) lay
the city of Bactra, on the river of the same name,
which washed its walls. But a great part of the country
was covered with waste tracts of sand. If the winds
blew from the Caspian Sea, they swept the sand into
high hills, under which not only did every trace of
the road disappear, but travellers were at times over-
whelmed ; and, as if voyaging by sea, it was necessary
to guide the course by the stars.[1] Strabo remarks,
after Apollodorus of Artemita, that Bactria was the
best part of East Iran (Ariana). In ancient times the
Bactrians were hardly distinguished from nomads ;
but their land was extensive, and produced fruits of all
kinds, with the exception of the vine. The fertility
of the land enabled the Hellenic princes to make great
conquests. Their cities were Bactra, traversed by the
river of the same name, Darapsa, Aornus (*ararana,
i. e.* protection), Kariata, and many others, and besides
these cities, the Bactrians had citadels on lofty rocks.[2]
According to Strabo, Bactra was also called Zariaspa,
and Pliny asserts that at any rate in earlier times it
was called by that name. In Arrian Zariaspa is the
largest city of Bactria, while Ptolemy places Zariaspa
to the north of Bactra, on the bank of the Oxus.
Zariaspa means golden horse. A river might possibly
be known by such a name, but hardly a city, unless it
belonged to a tribe of the name of Zariaspians, and

[1] Curt. 7, 4.
[2] Strabo, pp. 118, 516, 682 ; Arrian, " Anab." 3, 29. On Aornus, cf.
Vol. IV. p. 395.

was inhabited by them. In fact Ptolemy places the tribe of the Zariaspians in his Zariaspa.[1]

The air on these north-western terraces of the Hindu Kush is warm, and the soil sufficiently vigorous, under irrigation, to produce rice and southern fruits. Eight leagues below the snow-fields of the mountains, which resist even the hottest months of the year, two good leagues to the north of the place where the Dehas, after forcing a passage through the last heights, reaches the plains, lies the city of Balkh, on the banks of that river. At this day it is a town only partially inhabited; but the ruins of the ancient city are said to cover a circuit of several leagues. The adjacent soil is now well cultivated; the fields are thickly planted with trees, and beside old water-courses, now dried up, and extensive ruins of yet older aqueducts, eighteen channels still convey their rills to fields under active cultivation.[2]

North of the Bactrians, beyond the Oxus, on the western slope of Belurdagh, in the valley of the Polytimetus (Zarefshan, i. e. strewing gold), which flows towards the Oxus from the east, but, instead of joining it, ends in Lake Dengiz, lay the Sogdiani of the Greeks, the *Suguda* of the Old Persian inscriptions, and *Çughdha* of the Avesta, in the region of the modern Sogd. As the Oxus in its upper course separates the Bactrians from the Sogdiani, the Jaxartes, further to the north, separates the latter from the Scyths. According to Strabo, the manners of the Bactrians and Sogdiani were similar, but the Bactrians were less rude.[3] Maracanda (Samarcand), the chief city of the Sogdiani, on

---

[1] Ptolem. 6, 11 ; 8, 7 ; Strabo, pp. 514, 516 ; Arrian, " Anab." 3, 29 ; 4, 1, 16, 22 ; Plin. " Hist. Nat." 6, 17, 18 ; Steph. Byz. *sub voc.* Firdusi mentions a hero Zarasp.

[2] Elphinstone, " Kabul," 2, 213, 214.　　　[3] Strabo, *loc. cit.*

the Polytimetus, is said to have had a circuit of 70
stades in the fourth century B.C. The soil is not
without fertility, but the climate varies between great
heat and severe cold.

Herodotus observes that the Bactrians, who carried
bows of reed and short lances, closely resembled the
northern Indians in armour, clothing, and mode of
life, and then informs us that the Areians, Parthians,
Sogdiani, and Chorasmians resembled the Bactrians.
All these tribes of the east, according to the account
of Herodotus, carried the Indian bow of reed; the
Areians alone used the Median bow, which Herodotus
states to have been in vogue not only among the Medes,
but also among all the nations of Western Iran. He
adds that in ancient times the Medes were called
Areians by all men. Strabo uses the name Ariana for
the land of all the nations of Iran, except that of the
Medes and Persians, i. e. for the whole eastern half
of Iran.[1] In Diodorus also the nations of Eastern Iran
are Arians.[2] The Avesta, which, as we shall show,
belongs to the east of Iran, calls its native land *Airyao
Dahvyu*, i. e. abode of the Airyas; or *Airyao Danhavo*,
i. e. land of the Airyas, in contrast to the *Anairyao
Danhavo*, i. e. the non-Arian lands.[3] In his inscriptions king Darius styles himself "a Persian, son of a
Persian, an Arian (*ariya*) of an Arian tribe,"[4] and therefore the name must have held good of the west of Iran
also, and have included all the nations of Iran, though
afterwards it continued in use more especially for the

---

[1] Herod. 7, 62; Strabo (pp. 516, 517, 724) includes in Ariana,
Gedrosia, Arachosia, Drangiana, Paropanisus, Aria, Parthia, and
Caramania. Cf. Pausan. 2, 3, 8.

[2] Diod. 1, 94. Damascius ("De Primis Principiis," p. 384) speaks
of the Μάγοι δὲ καὶ πᾶν τὸ ἄριον γένος.

[3] "Vendid." 19, 132; "Mihr Yasht," 4, 13; "Tistar Yasht," 9, 56, 60.

[4] Naksh-i-Rustem, a., 14.

tribes of the east. The inhabitants of the modern
Persian kingdom call their kingdom by the general
name of Iran. Iran is only the regular new Persian
form of the old name, which in the west was pronounced Ariyana, and in the east Airyana.

We remember that the ruling nation of India called
themselves Arya, and this name compared with Airya
and Ariya shows us that the nations of Iran assumed
the same title with very little difference. Among the
Greeks Ariya and Airya became Areioi and Arioi, and
the name of the land, Ariyana and Airyana, became
Ariana. We have learnt the meaning of the names
Aryas, Ariyas, Airyas; they signify "the noble or
ruling people" (IV. 8). Much the same is the sense
of the name Artæans,[1] which, according to the assertion of Herodotus, was the title by which the Persians called themselves; it signifies "the exalted," or
"mighty." The Persians may have assumed it after
they became the ruling people in Iran and Hither
Asia.

These distinctions show us that the Aryas whom we
found on the Indus and in the Panjab, and who forced
their way from thence to the conquest and colonisa-
tion of the valley of the Ganges, and then extended
their dominion over the Deccan, and imported their
religion and their civilisation into those wide regions,
were closely connected with the group of nations which
occupied the table-land of Iran. It is obvious that
this relationship was most strictly maintained and
most strongly marked where the intercourse between
the neighbouring nations was most lively, i. e. among
the nations of Eastern Iran. The conclusion drawn
from the common title of the two nations on the west
and east of the Indus, and from the statements of

[1] Herod. 7, 61. Cf. Steph. Byz. 'Αρταία.

Herodotus about the manners of the eastern and the name of the western nations of Iran, is confirmed by the examination of the existing remnants of the ancient languages of Iran, whether spoken in the east or the west. This evidence derived from the names and the language is confirmed yet further by the coincidence in certain traits of religion and worship.

We are not in a position to fix the place from which and the time when the Arian tribes entered the table-land of Iran and peopled it. That Iran was not their native country is clear from the divergence of the Arian stock from the common stem of the Indo-Europeans (IV. 4). Still less can we decide whether the Arians found an older population already settled in Iran. So far as the ancient monuments of east and west allow us to form an opinion, there exist no elements of an alien language from which we could deduce the existence of an earlier population, which the Arians conquered. Yet we cannot deny that tribes of an alien origin and character were settled on the western spurs of the mountain wall of Iran, in the north no less than in the south.[1] The foreign elements which the later forms of the language of Iran have adopted are due to the influence which the Semitic neighbours of the Arians on the west, and the dominion of the Arabs, exercised on Iran. As to the direction in which the Arians entered Iran, we can only conclude, from their close relationship to the Arians of India, that they peopled the east of Iran before the west. If the Arians of India came into the Panjab, as we assumed, soon after 2000 B.C., the Arians of Iran entered the eastern part of that country at a date certainly not later. According to the list of dynasties

[1] On the tribe of the Brahuis in the south-east, on this side of the Indus, cf. Vol. IV. p. 10.

furnished by Berosus, the Arians about 2500 B.C. were
not only settled in Iran, but already possessed the
western part of the country. He represents the Medes
as conquering Babylonia in 2458 B.C., and from this
date down to 2224 B.C. mentions eight Median kings
as ruling over Babylon (I. 241, 247).

In spite of their cruel treatment, the nucleus of the
ancient Arian population of Iran has not succumbed to
the alien dynasties, the Seleucids, Arabs, and Mongols
who have invaded the land since the fall of the Achæmenids; and the ancient territory has been maintained, with some losses, even against the incursions
and immigrations of the Sacæ, Yuëchis, and Turkish
hordes. As in the vast regions of the Indus and the
Ganges, so in Iran the ancient language still lives
on the lips of the modern population. Yet the
changes have been great. Under the Arsacids the Old
Persian passed into Middle Persian, which at a later
time was known by the name of the Parthians, the
tribe at that time supreme in Persia. Pahlav and
Pehlevi mean Parthian, and, as applied to language,
the language of the Parthians, i. e. of the Parthian era.[1]
In the west this older Middle Persian grew up out of
the Old Persian, in the east out of the Old Bactrian.
In the latest period of the dominion of the Sassanids,
the recent Middle Persian or Parsee took the place of
Pehlevi. When the kingdom of the Sassanids succumbed to the Arabs, and Arabic became the language
of the ruling people in Iran, the reaction which took
place in the eastern districts of the country against the

[1] Haug, "The book of Arda Viraf," p. xxv. Mordtmann has shown
on the coins of the Arsacids and Sassanids the stages between the
older forms and the language of Firdusi; "Z. D. M. G." 4, 84 ff., 8,
9 ff. On the forms of the Old Bactrian on the coins of the Græco-
Bactrian and Indo-Scythian princes: Lassen," Indische Alterthum."
2², 831 ff. Spiegel, "Parsigrammatik," s. 116 ff.

dominion of the Abbasids brought about the formation
of the new Persian, which was finally completed
when the national reaction broke out in the beginning
of the eleventh century of our era.   Beginning from
Merv, Balkh, and Sejestan (the ancient Haetumat), that
rising found its strongest point in Ghasna and Cabul.
It did not preserve the religion, but it saved the
language, nationality, and independence of Iran.   The
change from the Middle Persian to the modern began
with the north-eastern dialects ; in the south-east the
Afghans and Beluchees still speak in ancient forms,
closely akin to the dialects of the peasants of the Panjab.
To this day the greater part of the entire population
of Iran consists of the descendants of the Arians, in
spite of all the distress and ruin which the land has
suffered,[1] though the residuum of foreign elements is
larger here than beyond the Indus, especially in the
north-west, in Aderbeijan, and above all in Bactria and
Sogdiana, in the north-east.   The descendants of the
Arians are still recognised by the formation of their
bodies, which appeared so striking to Western nations
in antiquity—the slender growth, the semicircular,
united eyebrows, and the yellow skin, which becomes
browner towards the east.   The Persians and Afghans
still possess a sound judgment, a keen intelligence, and
lively sense of poetry—characteristics which, as we
saw, belonged in a pre-eminent degree to the Arians
of India.

[1] It has been recently proved that the inhabitants of the mountain
country between Cabul and Herat, the Aimaks and Hazares, speak
Persian.

CHAPTER II.

THE KINGDOM OF THE BACTRIANS.

AMONG the ruins of the residence of the kings of
Asshur at Chalah, on the confluence of the Greater Zab
and the Tigris, was discovered the obelisk which
Shalmanesar II., who reigned from 859 to 823 B.C. over
Assyria, erected in memory of his successes. In the
tribute offered to him we find the rhinoceros, the
elephant, the humped ox, and the camel with two
humps (II. 320). This species of camel and the yak are
found in Bactria, on the southern edge of the Caspian
Sea, and in Tartary, and we afterwards find elephants
in the possession of the rulers of Bactria.[1] Hence, in
order to obtain these animals for tribute, the armies of
Shalmanesar must have advanced as far as the eastern
tribes of the Iranian table-land. From the inscriptions of Tiglath Pilesar II., it is clear that he advanced
along the same table-land as far as the Hilmend
and the Arachoti, if not as far as Bactria. Among
the lands subjugated in 745 B.C., he enumerates Nisaa,
Zikruti, and Arakuttu. In Nisaa we cannot mistake
Nisæa in the east of Media (p. 31). The Zikruti were
no doubt the Sagartians of Herodotus, the Açagarta
of the old Persian inscriptions.[2] Arakuttu represents

---

[1] Polyb. fragm. 34 f.; below, p. 26.

[2] Above, p. 6; Vol. III. p. 3, "Zikruti in rugged Media I added to
the land of Assyria;" ib. p. 4.

in a Semitic form the name of the Arachoti, the
Harauvati of the Achæmenids (p. 8). So far as we
can at present judge from inscriptions, the successors of
Tiglath Pilesar did not carry their campaigns further
to the east of Iran, and we can assert with certainty
of both the sovereigns who raised the power of Assyria
to its summit, Esarhaddon and Assurbanipal (681—
626 B.C.), that they made no conquests in this direction.

If the inscriptions of the Assyrians leave us in
almost total darkness about Bactria, the Medo-Persian
epic poetry can give us full information about the
country. When Ninus, king of Assyria, had subjugated
all the nations of Asia as far as the Nile and the
Tanais, he made an attempt upon Bactria, but without
success. The entrance into the land was difficult, the
number of warriors great, and they knew how to fight
bravely. Then Ninus collected an army of two mil-
lions of soldiers, which was opposed by Oxyartes, the
king of the Bactrians, with 400,000 men. When the
Assyrian army came in detachments out of the passes,
Oxyartes attacked and drove them back into the
mountains with the loss of 100,000 men. The army
of Ninus then combined, outnumbered and overcame
the Bactrians, and scattered them into their cities,
which Ninus took with little trouble. But Bactra,
where was the palace of the kings, was large and well
supplied, and had a very strong citadel in a high
position, while the city extended over the plain. It
resisted for a long time, till Semiramis ascended the
citadel, and Ninus was enabled to take possession of
the treasures of gold and silver which were in Bactra.
At a later time Semiramis collected her vast army
for the invasion of India in Bactria, and returned
to Bactra after she had been defeated on the Indus,
and had lost two-thirds of her army (II. 10). Such

are the descriptions given by the epic poetry of the Medes and Persians, in the account of the rise of Assyria and subjugation of Bactria. The Bactrians are again brought forward in the narrative of the overthrow of Assyria, which was the proper theme of these poems. When Sardanapalus has already thrice defeated the Medes and Babylonians, a strong force comes to his assistance from Bactria. The leader of the Medes determines to attack this first, if it would not join in the contest for freedom against Assyria. The Bactrians joined the Medes, the power of Assyria was broken, and Nineveh destroyed (III. 253).

From these poems it follows that in the first half of the sixth century B.C., in which the Medo-Persian epic attained its original form, the tradition, or at any rate the opinion, existed among the minstrels of Media that a powerful kingdom and large metropolis once existed in Bactria, the situation of which is correctly described. This kingdom possessed a strong citadel and abundant treasures, and could put in the field a large army of brave warriors. Without such a conception they could not represent the first attack of the Assyrians on Bactria as a failure, the second as successful only after considerable time and trouble had been spent, and the conquest as the last and greatest achievement of Ninus, the mightiest sovereign of Assyria, which he only performed with the aid of Semiramis.

The inscriptions of the Assyrians have already informed us that no dominion of Assyria over Eastern Iran existed in the earliest period of the kingdom; on the contrary, even when her power was at the highest Assyria could only carry on temporary excursions into that region. The western part of the country was first trodden by the armies of Shalmanesar II.; his inscriptions mention tribute of the Medes, and

from the inscriptions of his successors it is distinctly
clear that only the nations of Western Iran were
tributary dependants of the kings of Asshur from
the period of Tiglath Pilesar, *i. e.* from the middle of
the eighth century B.C., till the period of Phraortes and
Cyaxares of Media, *i. e.* till the middle of the seventh
century B.C.[1]

The conquests of Cyrus, who overthrew the power
of the Medes, founded the Persian empire, and extended
it to the east, would give us more accurate information
about Eastern Iran if connected accounts of these were
in existence. Herodotus contents himself with stating
that Cyrus, after subjugating the Lydians, determined to
march against the Bactrians and Sacæ. He conquered
all the nations of Upper Asia, one after the other,
without omitting any.[2] Ctesias relates that the Bactrians after a doubtful battle submitted voluntarily
to Cyrus. According to the account of Xenophon, the
Hyrcanians, Cadusians, and Sacæ joined Cyrus, and in
the fragments of Nicolaus also the Hyrcanians, Parthians, and "the other nations" passed over to Cyrus
immediately after the conquest of the Medes. However this may be, there is no doubt that the east of
Iran was subject to Cyrus. He marched through the
land of the Arachoti, entered into relations with the
Ariaçpas (p. 8), and subjugated the Gandarians on
the south of the Cabul. He is also said to have
imposed tribute on the Açvakas to the north of the
river (IV. 384). The Sogdiani, in any case, were his
vassals. On a stream which flows into the Jaxartes
he built a fortress called by his own name, known to
the Greeks as Cyreshata (*ultima Cyra*, or with others
Cyropolis), *i. e.* the furthest Cyrus. The walls and
citadels were strong and spacious, and in the neigh-

[1] Vol. III. p. 77.　　　　[2] Herod. 1, 153, 177, 201, 204.

bourhood were six other citadels.[1] The value placed
by Cyrus on the regions of Eastern Iran is not only
clear from these fortresses, but may be deduced from
the statement that his second son Bardya, whom the
Greeks call Smerdis, was intrusted with the government of Bactria, if indeed the statement is genuine.[2]

The nations and condition of Eastern Iran can be
ascertained more clearly from the inscriptions of
Darius. According to his inscription at Behistun,
his empire in that direction comprised the Parthians,
Sarangians, Areians, Chorasmians, Bactrians, Sogdiani,
Gandarii, Sattagydæ, Arachoti, and Sacæ; and to these
the Idhus, i. e. the Indians on the right bank of the
upper course of the Indus, are added in the inscriptions of Persepolis and Naksh-i-Rustem.[3] Further
information is preserved by Herodotus with respect
to the tribute imposed by Darius on these nations.
As these statements are undoubtedly derived from
Persian tribute lists, they serve to throw a side light
on the state of civilisation existing in the east of Iran
at the division of the sixth and fifth centuries B.C.
The Sarangians, who, as we have seen (p. 7), inhabited the fertile land round Lake Areios (Hamun),
together with the Sagartians and some neighbouring nations on the south, paid yearly 600 Babylonian
talents into the treasury of the king. The Areians
(Haraivas), Parthians, Sogdiani, and Chorasmians, who
formed the sixteenth satrapy of the Persian empire,
had to pay 300 talents; the Gedrosians and Gandarians together paid 170 talents; the Caspiani (i. e.
no doubt, the Tapurians and other tribes on the
southern shore of the Caspian Sea) and the Sacæ, who

[1] Strabo, p. 517; Arrian, "Anab." 4, 23; Plin. "H. N." 6, 18;
Ptolem. 6, 12.
[2] Ctes. fragm. Pers. c. 12.
[3] Behist. 1, 6; Persep. 25; Naksh-i-Rustem, 12—14.

traversed the steppes of the Oxus, *i. e.* the fifteenth
satrapy, paid 250 talents; and the Bactrians, the
twelfth satrapy of the empire, paid 360 talents.[1]
These sums, which do not include the whole of the
burdens of the provinces, but are only the land taxes
which they had to pay,—in addition, tolls were levied
and contributions in kind to the court of the king and
the satraps, as well as for the maintenance of the army,
—show that at the time of Darius agriculture and
wealth had proceeded far beyond the earliest stages
in the eastern districts of Iran. The Babylonian silver
talent amounts to more than 2000 thalers (6000
shillings).[2] If a sum of more than 1,200,000 thalers
(£180,000) could be raised every year in land tax
from the districts round Lake Hamun, extensive
though they were, and 720,000 thalers (£108,000) in
a similar manner from the land of the Bactrians, the
gardens, fields, and pastures of these regions must have
been considerable in breadth, and of great fertility.

Beyond this indication of the state of the civilisation
in these districts, we learn but little of their fortunes
under the dominion of the Persians. Darius (521—485
B.C.) informs us, at the beginning of his reign, that his
father Hystaspes (Vistaçpa), his viceroy in Persia, the
native land of the kingdom, and with him Vivana the
Persian, the satrap of Arachosia, and Dadarshis the
Persian, the satrap of Bactria, had quelled the re-
bellions of the Parthians, Hyrcanians, and Margiani;
that the Mede Takhmaçpada had conquered the rebellious Sagartians, and captured their leader, Chit-
ratakhma, whom he, Darius, had crucified at Arbela.
The army of the second Pseudo-Smerdis, which attempted to gain possession of Arachosia, Vivana had

[1] Herod. 3, 91, 92.
[2] Vol. I. p. 285. The amount is about 2096 thalers.

defeated at the fortress of Kapisakani, in Arachosia,
and the leaders, with their chief associates, had been
captured in the fortress of Arsada and put to death.
Hystaspes had slain 6560 men of the Parthians and
Hyrcanians, and taken 4182 of them captives.   Dadarshis had subjugated the Mardians by slaying 4203
of them in battle, and taking 6562 of them captive.[1]
Xerxes, the successor of Darius, successively intrusted
two of his brothers, Masistes and then Hystaspes,
with the government of Bactria.[2]   In the great campaign against Hellas, the Bactrians, like all the other
nations of the kingdom, had to furnish their contin-
gent; and when Mardonius had to select the best troops
in the army in Hellas, in order to winter with them in
Thessaly, he retained, besides the Persians and Medes,
the infantry and cavalry of the Bactrians, Sacæ,
and Indians.[3]   The Bactrians, under their viceroy
Hystaspes, revolted against Artaxerxes, the brother
of Hystaspes.   The first battle was not decisive; in
the second Artaxerxes conquered, "because the wind
blew in the face of the Bactrians," and subjugated
the land.[4]   To the army of Darius III. with which
he met the Macedonians in Assyria, the Bactrians
contributed 30,000 cavalry ; and in the battle of
Arbela they fought with the Arachoti on the left wing.
Accompanied by Bactrian horsemen, Darius escaped
from the field of battle to Media, and sought afterwards to maintain his position in their country.   The
Caspian gates, the pass of Damaghan, were gained,
when the satrap of Bactria got possession of the king,
and put him to death before he reached Bactria.   The
satrap hoped to establish an independent power
there,[5] but without success.   Though Alexander at

[1] Behist. 2, 14—16 ; 3, 10—12.   [2] Herod. 7, 64, 82 ; 9, 113.
[3] Herod. 8, 93.   [4] Diod. 11, 69; Ctes. Pers. ccl. 31.
[5] Arrian, "Anab." 3, 21.

first overcame the Bactrians, who were astonished at his rapid approach, he soon found a stubborn resistance in Sogdiana and Bactria, which occupied him for two years.[1] Not till then could he make his preparations in Bactria for the invasion of India, and collect at Bactra the army intended for the subjugation of that country, in order to pass over the Hindu Kush into the valley of the Cabul.

In the contests which the successors of Alexander carried on for the supremacy after his death, the valley of the Euphrates and Tigris, and the table-land of Iran, finally fell to the lot of Seleucus. But in the middle of the third century (256 B.C.), Arsaces in Parthia and the satrap Diodotus in Bactria rebelled against the second successor, Antiochus Theos. The descendants of Arsaces not only succeeded in maintaining their independence against the Seleucids, in spite of severe reverses, but Mithridates I., the sixth Arsacid (174—136 B.C.), united all Iran under his dominion. The Greeks lost their supremacy, and Iran again became subject to native princes.

Meanwhile Diodotus had founded an independent supremacy in Bactria. His son, of the same name, was succeeded by Euthydemus, against whom, towards the year 200 B.C., Antiochus III. marched, in order to force Bactria to submission. Euthydemus was defeated at the river Areios (p. 10), and fled to Zariaspa. By the surrender of his elephants he obtained an established recognition from Antiochus. Demetrius and Eucratides, the successors of Euthydemus (after 180 B.C.), extended the sphere of their dominion to the east over the land on the Cabul to the Indus. The kingdom of Chandragupta, Vindusara, and Açoka, which, as we know, included the east of Iran, and has left

---

[1] Arrian, *loc. cit.* 3, 29.

us inscriptions at Peshawur (IV. 525), fell to pieces under Açoka's grandsons. Apollodorus of Artemita told us above that the fertility of the Bactrian soil enabled the Greek rulers to make important conquests (p. 12); he informs us that Eucratides founded the city of Eucratideia in Bactria, and subjugated a thousand cities in India. We may assume that Bactria under these princes was not merely powerful, but prosperous. According to the statement of Justin, a thousand cities were at that time enumerated in Bactria,[1] and we possess satisfactory evidence that these rulers and their courts, and the Greek settlements which Alexander founded in the distant East, were able permanently to establish the style and art of Hellas. The coins of these princes, who are designated in Greek as "kings," "great," "invincible," rival the best work which proceeded from Greek mints. The faces present the heads of the princes, in characteristic and individual portraits; the reverses exhibit Heracles, Athena, Apollo with a crown of rays, the Dioscuri on horseback, lance in hand. But by degrees the national types of the East are again employed on these coins. The reverse presents the galloping horse, the animal of Bactria, the elephant, and the humped ox.[2] The head of Demetrius, who first conquered territory in India, and that of some of his descendants, is covered by a helmet adorned with the tusks and trunk of an elephant. Besides the round, numbers of rectangular coins have also been found, from which we can discover the native traditional form of the Bactrian coinage.

[1] Justin. 41, 4.

[2] As was shown in Vol. IV. p. 278, the Vishnu Purana represents the sacrificial horse of Pushpamitra, who sat on the throne of Magadha between 178 and 142 B.C. (Vol. IV. p. 550), to have been carried off by an army of Yavanas on the right bank of the Indus, and then restored. The dominion of the Græco-Bactrian princes in the East existed from 200 to 150 B.C.

After the reign of Eucratides these rectangular coins present on one side Greek inscriptions, which are repeated in other characters on the reverse. To the inscriptions of king Açoka at Kapur-i-Giri, and to these coins, together with those of the Græco-Indian kings, and some later coins belonging to the Arsacids and the Indo-Scythian princes, we owe the information that the east of Iran possessed a peculiar alphabet and mode of writing, while the Medes and Persians of the west borrowed their earliest letters from the Assyrio-Babylonian cuneiform writing, and afterwards, from about the fourth century B.C., adopted the cursive character of the Aramæans.

Although, as we may conclude from these indications, the Greek sovereigns of Bactria resolved to pay a certain respect to the civilisation of their subjects, their kingdom was short-lived. The nations of the steppes of the Oxus, themselves under pressure, began to advance to the south (after 160 B.C.); in the west the Parthians rose into power. Mithridates I. of Parthia incorporated Bactria in his kingdom about 140 B.C., and Bactria subsequently became a part of the Parthian empire. Heliocles, the son of Eucratides, was thus limited to the land of the Cabul and Indus, but on the borders of India the power and influence of the Greeks remained unbroken. Greek captains—Menander, and after him Apollodotus, who had previously no doubt been subject to the Bactrians — issued from the southern slope of the Hindu Kush in the last decades of the second century B.C., and conquered the land of the Indus as far as the mouth of the river, and the Panjab. They advanced to the Yamuna, and reduced Surashtra (Guzerat) and Cashmere to dependence. Even at the end of the first century B.C. coins of these princes were current on the coast of

Surashtra, and they are still found on the banks of the Yamuna.[1]

On the western coast of India, from the Gulf of Cambay to Bombay, we find from one hundred to one hundred and fifty thousand families whose ancestors migrated thither from Iran. The tradition among them is, that at the time when the Arabs, after conquering Iran and becoming sovereigns there, persecuted and eradicated the old religion, faithful adherents of the creed fled to the mountains of Kerman. Driven from these by the Arabs (in Kerman and Yezd a few hundred families are still found who maintain the ancient faith[2]), they retired to the island of Hormuz (a small island close by the southern coast, at the entrance to the Persian Gulf). From hence they migrated to Diu (on the coast of Guzerat), and then passed over to the opposite shore. In the neighbourhood of Bombay and in the south of India inscriptions have been found which prove that these settlers reached the coast in the tenth century of our era.[3] At the present time their descendants form a considerable part of the population of Surat, Bombay, and Ahmadabad; they call themselves, after their ancient home, Parsees, and speak the later Middle Persian (the Parsee, p. 17). Their worship and life they regulate by the rules given in certain scriptures which they brought with them from their ancient home. These

---

[1] Strabo, p. 516. I need not prove that Ἰωμάνης must be read here for Ἰσάμος, or that Σαραόστου παραλία is Surashtra; cf. Wilson, "Ariana antiq." p. 281. Apollodotus, Apaladata on the Arian legends of his coins, is no doubt the Bhagadatta of the Mahabharata, just as the Dattamitra there mentioned is Demetrius; Vol. IV. p. 80, n. Among the Indians Menander appears in the form Milinda.

[2] In the year 1843 there were about 1000 Guebre families in Yezd, and a hundred in Kerman. Westergaard, "Avesta," 1, 21: the persecution of 1848 considerably reduced their numbers.

[3] Haug, "Pahlavi-Pazand Glossary," pp. 80, 81.

are fragments of a much larger whole, part of a book of law, and a collection of sacrificial songs and prayers. The Parsees no longer speak or understand the language of these scriptures (the Avesta), and even the priests, who use them every day, ascertain the meaning through an accompanying translation into the later language.

That these scriptures arose in the east of Iran is clear from the language of the Avesta. It exhibits a close relationship with the forms of the Veda and Sanskrit, the ancient language of the Arians in India. If, on the other hand, we compare the language of the Avesta with the ancient language of Western Iran as we possess it in the inscriptions of the Achæmenids, we find that both are merely different dialects of one language, but they differ in such a manner that the language of the inscriptions of Darius and Xerxes is less closely connected with Sanskrit than the language of the Avesta. This language then we may regard as the ancient speech of Eastern Iran, and this assumption is raised into evidence by the contents of the Avesta. These prove that the Avesta arose in the east of Iran, with even greater certainty than the songs of the Rigveda prove that that collection arose in the land of the Indus and the Panjab. The Avesta entirely ignores the west of Iran. No mention is made of Ecbatana and Pasargadæ, the abode of the Median and the Persian kings, though they reigned over the whole of Iran and Hither Asia; nor even of the nations of the west, the Medes and Persians. It speaks of the land of the seven streams, i. e. India (IV. 12), and the heat which prevails in that land;[1] it mentions the beautiful Harahvaiti (Arachosia) and Haetumat (afterwards Sejestan[2]): the latter is extolled

---

[1] "Vendid. 1," 73—76.   [2] "Vendid." 1, 46.

as a beaming, glowing, brilliant country.[1] The knowledge of the Avesta is most accurate in the north-
east. Here we find Airyana Vaeja, *i. e.* home or canton
of the Airyas,[2] Çughdha (Sogdiana), Bakhdhi (Baktra),
Mouru (Margiana, Merv[3]), Niça, between Bakhdhi
and Mouru, Haraeva (Haraiva in the inscriptions;
Herat, the land of the Arcians), and Vehrkana, *i. e.*
land of wolves (Hyrcania).[4] The furthest point known
to the west is Ragha in Media, which, according
to the Avesta, consists of three citadels or tribes.[5]
These statements carry us very distinctly to the east
of Iran, the region from Ragha to the Indus. Mouru
is "the high," "the holy," and Bakhdhi's "high
banner" is extolled. In this way this city was no
doubt marked out as the seat of an important dominion,
the centre of a kingdom.

If we might assume that in these fragments of the
sacred books of the Parsees we have not only the
ancient language, but also the ancient religion of
Eastern Iran before us, we might also hope that we
should meet in them with remnants of the tradition,
with native accounts of the fortunes of the country,
enabling us to supplement the scanty information
which we could glean from the inscriptions of the
Assyrians and Darius, and the accounts of Western
writers. Leaving out of sight for the present the

---

[1] "Vendid." 19, 130 ; 1, 50.

[2] Burnouf, " Jour. Asiat." 1845, pp. 287, 288. It seems to me doubtful
whether we should look for Airyana Vaeja on the sources of the Oxus.
The statement in the Bundehesh that Airyana Vaeja was situated beside
Atropatene is, however, of very little weight against the fact that the
Arians of East Iran are nearest to the Arians of India. I shall return
to this point below. The remark in Stephanus, "'Αριανία, a nation
among the Cadusians," would be of some importance if it were
taken from Apollodorus of Artemita, and not from the grammarian of
that name. The district of Arran on the Kur may possibly be meant.

[3] "Vendid." 1, 14—18.   [4] "Vendid." 1, 30, 42.

[5] "Vendid." 1, 60.

question, At what period did these writings come into existence ? we may collect what we can find in them on the early history of Iran.

In the Avesta the god Haoma says, Vivanghana was the first who crushed out the juice of the Haoma. As a reward there was born to him the brilliant Yima, the lord of the nations, the most famous of all who have seen the sun. While Yima Kshaeta (Yima the king) reigned there was neither cold nor excessive heat, neither age nor death, nor envy, caused by the evil spirits : fathers and sons equally had the vigour of men of fifty years. Yima caused the means of support for mankind to be inexhaustible ; he liberated the waters and trees from drought, and the herds from death.[1] In an invocation to the goddess Ardviçura, the giver of water, to whom Yima sacrifices a hundred horses, a thousand oxen, and ten thousand head of small cattle on Hukairya, the summit of the divine mountain, he prays, "Grant to me, Saviour Ardviçura, that I may be the sovereign of all lands, that I may carry away from the Daevas (the evil spirits) increase and health, fodder and herds, joy and glory." To the goddess Ashi vanguhi, Yima also offers a prayer "that he may bring food and flocks to the creatures of Mazda, and immortality, and may remove hunger and thirst, age and death, the hot wind and the cold from the creatures of Mazda for a thousand years." And the morning wind, Vayu, is entreated that "Yima may be the most merciful of all creatures, and that under his dominion he may make cattle and mankind immortal, that the waters and trees may never dry up and wither." In the fragments of the book of the law in the Avesta, Zarathrustra inquires of Auramazda to whom he (the god) had first revealed the true doctrine.

[1] "Yaçna," 9, 4.

Auramazda answers, "I spoke first with Yima, the excellent one. I said to him, Yima, thou beautiful son of Vivanghana, be thou the preacher and bearer of my doctrine. But Yima answered, I am not fitted to be the preacher of the doctrine. Then I, Auramazda, spoke and said, If thou wilt not obey me, Yima, to be the bearer of my law, yet make my world fruitful; be the keeper of my earthly creatures, their protector and lord. And Yima, the excellent one, answered, I will cause thy creatures to prosper and increase; I will be the keeper, protector, and lord of them. Therefore I, Auramazda, gave to him two instruments, a golden staff and an ox goad adorned with gold, and three hundred years passed by. And the land was full of herds and beasts of draught, of men, and dogs, and birds, and red flaming fires. And there was no more any room for the flocks, and men, and beasts of draught. Then I warned Yima: O Yima, excellent one, son of Vivanghana, there is no more any room for the herds, and beasts of draught, and men. And Yima went forth to meet the stars and the path of the sun (i. e. towards the east). He struck with the golden staff upon the earth, and smote it with the goad, and said, Çpenta Armaiti (O holy earth), arise, part thyself asunder, thou bearer of animals and of men. And Yima pushed the earth asunder so that it was a third part greater than before. Then the flocks found a home, the beasts of draught, and men, according to their wish and desire." Again three hundred years passed, and there was no more any room for herds, beasts, and men; and at Auramazda's command Yima again caused the earth to stretch asunder, and it became two-thirds greater than before; and after another three hundred years Yima caused the earth to become as large again as

before.[1] Then a thousand years passed, and Auramazda
said to Yima, " Bitter cold and sharp frost will fall upon
the earth, and the snow will lie deep on the summits
of the mountains and in the clefts of the valleys. Make
an enclosure (vara) of the length of a horse's course on
each of the four sides. Bring into it a stock of herds
and beasts of draught, of men and dogs, and birds and
red flaming fires, and make the enclosure to be a
dwelling for men and a stall for the cattle. Carry
water thither, and build houses and tombs, and a fortification and palisade round about, and drive them with
the golden staff into the citadel, and shut to the door.
And Yima made a citadel of the length of a horse's
course. Thither he brought a stock of all men and
women who were the tallest, best, and most beautiful
of earth, and a brood of all animals which were largest,
best, and most beautiful, and the seeds of all fruits and
growths which were best and most beautiful. And he
provided that a pair were ever together. There was no
evil speaking there, nor strife, nor injury, nor deception, nor meanness ; nothing crooked, no mal-formation
of teeth, no crippled form, nor any other of the signs
which are the signs of Angromainyu. In this enclosure
which Yima made men lived the happiest life. A
year was a day, and every forty years two children,
a male and a female, were born from each pair of
human creatures, and so also of each kind of animal."[2]

In an invocation in the Avesta we are told that
the bright gleaming majesty in the form of the bird
Varaghna had passed from Yima when he began to
love lying speech. Yima fell terrified to earth, and
Mithra, the lord of wide pastures, seized the majesty.

---

[1] " Vendid." 2, 1—21, after Karl Geldner's translation. [Cf. Darmesteter's translation in M. Müller's ' Sacred Books of the East,' Vol. IV.]
[2] " Vendid." 2, 21—43.

When it passed a second time from Yima, Thraetaona seized it, and when it passed a third time, Kereçaçpa seized it.

The second who crushed the juice of the Haoma was Athwya. Hence there was born to him a son, Thraetaona, in the land of Varena. The evil spirit Angromainyu had created a wicked being, "with three heads, three throats, six eyes, and a thousand strengths"—the Azhi dahaka, i.e. the biting serpent, which swallowed horses and men, and threatened to desolate the world. But Thraetaona sacrificed a hundred horses to Ardviçura, a thousand oxen, and ten thousand head of small cattle, and called on the goddess, and with bound bundle of rods, on Vayu on his golden throne, with golden footstool and golden canopy, to grant that he might smite the strong Druj, which Angromainyu had created as the strongest to bring death upon the pure world ; and he overcame the monster, because Verethraghna was with him, the most victorious of mortals.[1] And Thraetaona obtained the splendour of the dominion when it departed a second time from Yima. In the prayers of the Avesta, Thraetaona, who has slain the great serpent, is invoked as helper against the "pain which is caused by the serpent," against fever and sickness.[2]

The third who crushed the juice of the Haoma for the sacrifice was Thrita, of the race of Çama. Thrita was the first who by skill in medicine kept back sickness and death from the bodies of men. He wished for means to withstand the pains, the sickness, the death, the hot and cold fever which Angromainyu had created for the bodies of men. "Then I, Auramazda, caused healing plants to grow by hundreds, by thousands,

[1] "Aban Yasht," 9; "Farvardin Yasht,' 131; "Bahram Yasht," 40; "Ram Yasht," 23.   [2] "Farvardin Yasht," 131 ff.

by tens of thousands around the one Gaokerena." And
in reward for his offering of Haoma two sons were
born to Thrita—Urvakshaya, who put in order the law,
and Kereçaçpa (i. e. having slim horses), the youth
of beautiful form, the bearer of the weapon Gaeçu.[1]
Kereçaçpa smote the poisonous green serpent Çruvara,
on which flowed poison to the thickness of a thumb,
and it swallowed men and horses. Afterwards, after
he had sacrificed to Ardviçura on the shore of Lake
Piçano (i. e., no doubt, in the valley of Pishin in Sejestan), he smote the giant Gandarewa, who dwelt in Lake
Vourukasha, and the descendants of the nine robbers,
and Çnavidhaka, who had attempted to overcome
Auramazda and Angromainyu. And when his brother
Urvakshaya had been slain by Hitaçpa, Kereçaçpa
besought the wind, who works on high, to grant to
him to slay Hitaçpa in revenge for the death of his
brother. And he conquered him, and yoked him to
his chariot. When for the third time the majesty
departed from Yima, Kereçaçpa seized it, the strongest
of men after Zarathrustra. In the prayers of the
Avesta, Kereçaçpa's help is invoked against robbers
and hostile hosts.[2]

Yima, Thraetaona, Kereçaçpa, and the forms which
are genealogically connected with them, Vivanghana,
Athwya, Çama, Thrita, and Urvakshaya, are collected
by the Avesta under the name *Paradhata*, i. e. those
who first exercised dominion.[3] Indications in our
fragments show that other names were also included

---

[1] "Yaçna," 9, 30; "Vendid." 20, 11 ff.
[2] "Vendid." 20; "Yaçna," 9, 32, 39; "Ram Yasht," 7, 28;
"Farvardin Yasht," 136; "Zamyad Yasht," 41 ff. According to the
"Mainyo-i-Khard," Kereçaçpa, besides slaying the serpent Çruvar,
slew the wolf Kapod, the water demon Gandarsi, the bird Kamak, and
kept back much oppression from the world. West, "Mainyo-i-
Khard," c. 27.   [3] Justi, "Handbuch," s. voc.

in them. Thraetaona's son was Airyu, and Airyu's son
was Manuschithra.[1] These most ancient sovereigns were
followed by a second group, whose distinguishing mark
is the surname *Kava*. The first of these Kavas, whom
the Avesta mentions merely as the wearer of the
divine majesty, is Kava Kavata.[2] He is succeeded by
the agile, brilliant Kava Uça, who sacrifices to Ardviçura on Mount Erezifya in order to obtain the
dominion over all lands, over Daevas and men, wizards
and Pairikas, and this favour the goddess granted him.
After Uça the royal majesty united itself, to use the
phrase in the Avesta, with the beautiful pure body of
Kava Çyavarshana. He died by a violent death.[3]
His son was Kava Huçrava, "the brave uniter of the
Arian lands into one kingdom," as the Avesta tells us,
which then goes on to relate that he was without sickness
or death. He had to contend against the destructive
Franghraçianas, the Turanians (*tura, tuirya*). He besought Ardviçura that it "might be granted to him to
put an end to the long dimness, and bind the Franghraçianas in their abundance and pride." This prayer
the goddess granted. Haoma himself desired "to bind
the destructive, murderous Franghraçiana and carry
him away as a captive of the king Huçrava, and that
Kava Huçrava should slay him behind the lake Chac-
chaçta, the deep lake with broad waters."[4] Kava
Huçrava was followed by king Aurvataçpa, the son of
Naotara, the son of Manuschithra, the son of Airyu;
and Aurvataçpa was succeeded by his son the strong
and warlike Vistaçpa.[5] Of the twenty-nine sons of this

[1] "Farvardin Yasht," 131.
[2] "Farvardin Yasht," 132; "Zamyad Yasht," 71.
[3] "Gosh Yasht," 18; "Ashi Yasht," 38.
[4] "Aban Yasht," 49; "Gosh Yasht," 18; "Ashi Yasht," 38; "Afrin
Zartusht," 7; "Zamyad Yasht," 77; "Ram Yasht," 32.
[5] "Aban Yasht," 76, 98; "Ashi Yasht," 46; "Farvardin Yasht,"
102; "Ram Yasht," 36.

king, the Avesta mentions the strong Çpentodata, and
informs us that Frashaostra and his brother Jamaçpa,
of the race of Hvova, were men of importance with the
king. Like Huçrava, Vistaçpa had to contend with a
Turanian, Arejataçpa, *i. e.* the winner of horses, who
sacrificed to Ardviçura in order to obtain the victory
over Kava Vistaçpa and the warrior on horseback,
Zarivairi (the brother of Vistaçpa). The goddess heard
him not, but heard Vistaçpa when he sacrificed to her
behind the water of Frazdana, in order to overcome
the hostile Arejataçpa, born of darkness, skilled in
evil, who sought to smite the lands of the Arians.[1]
But Zarathrustra, the son of Pourushaçpa, of the
race of Haechataçpa, sacrificed to Ardviçura that
he might unite with the mighty Vistaçpa, the son of
Aurvataçpa, and to Drvaçpa, " that he might unite
with Hutaoça, and she might impress on his memory
the good law."[2] Zarathrustra proclaimed a new
law, the law of Auramazda. The heroes and kings
before him were known in the Avesta by the name
Paoiryotkaesha, i. e. the men of the earliest custom,
the earliest law.

These are all the traits and pictures of the antiquity of East Iran, of any importance, which can be
gathered from the remaining fragments of the Avesta.
Of the antiquity and genuineness of the narrative
there is no doubt. The close relationship and coincidence which they exhibit with the form and views of
the Veda are proved on both sides. As we saw, the
Veda distinguishes the sacrificers and sages of the
ancient time, the earlier time, and the present (IV. 29.)

---

[1] " Aban Yasht," 109, 117 ; " Farvardin Yasht," 38 ; " Gosh Yasht,"
29, 30; " Ashi Yasht," 50, 81 ; " Zamyad Yasht," 87.

[2] " Aban Yasht," 104 — 106; " Farvardin Yasht," 142; " Gosh
Yasht," 26 ; " Ram Yasht," 36.

The god Haoma is the well-known god Soma of the Arians in India, the variation in the name being due to the change of sounds which distinguishes the Old Bactrian from the language of the Veda. Here, as there, he is the sacrificial libation, and at the same time the god who pours the libation, and is its power. The great heroes Yima, Thraetaona, Kereçaçpa and Zarathrustra were born to their fathers as a reward for offering the libation of Soma. King Yima (Yima Kshaeta) in the Avesta is no other than the Yama (Yama Rajan) of the Veda. Yama is the son of Vivasvat, the brilliant, the shining, the giver of light ; and in the Avesta Yima is the son of Vivanghana. In the Veda he is the assembler of the people, the first king, the first mortal who shows to men the way which leads from the depths to the height of heaven ; who first experiences death, but returns into heaven as the son of the god of light, where he gathers round him the brave and pious for new life in imperishable joy (IV. 61). Yima is also the assembler of men, the first king; he rules with the golden staff; he founds the religious worship, a merit which in the Veda belongs to Manu. Under Yima the earth is filled with red-glowing fires ; he worships Vayu and Ardviçura. He is the representative of the golden age ; in his reign there is neither heat nor cold, age nor death, hate nor strife ; and his dominion continues a thousand years. It was the first happy period of the world, which men passed under the dominion of the son of the god of light. At what an elevation Yima must have been placed in the oldest form of the mythus of East Iran is clear from the fact that creative acts and the triple extension of the earth are ascribed to him. After the close of this golden period, winter comes upon the earth, heat and cold, strife, sickness, and death. The happy life of

the golden age only continues within certain limits, in
the enclosure of Yima, where he carries on the blessed
and immortal life with selected men, trees, animals, and
food. Here Yima is to live till the end of all things,
when his companions will again people the earth. As
in this garden of Yima the sun, moon, and stars shine
together,[1] it must be sought in the sky, or at any rate
on the bright, divine mountain Hukairya, where there
is neither night nor gloom, and which is at the same
time described as Yima's place of sacrifice.

If the Indians have placed the old Arian legend of
a golden age on earth in the days of Yima's reign,
they have also, after their manner, depicted his heavenly kingdom with brighter colours, while among the
Iranians this part of the legend is combined with the
heavenly garden into which Yima receives the men he
has selected as the best. Nevertheless, a reminiscence
of Yima's garden has remained beyond the Indus in
the story of the Uttara Kurus, who dwell beyond the
holy mountains to the north.[2]

The most striking variation from the common Arian
myth in the Avesta is the statement that Yima is
subordinate to a deity, Auramazda, of whom the Arians
of India knew nothing. The old legend is thus brought
within the sphere of new views, which must have exer-

---

[1] "Vendid." 2, 39, 40.
[2] Vol. IV. 21 n. Spiegel, "Avesta," 3, Einl. s. 58. The favourite
comparison of the enclosure of Yima with the deluge of the Hebrews
appears to me anything but apposite. Iran, and still more Bactria, is
unsuited to give rise to the legend of a flood. Nor is there any question of the destruction of evil men (if there had been, Yima would have
been the most guilty and the least deserving of pardon), but of the end
of the golden age, as is shown in the Vendidad, the Yaçna, and the
Yashts: the earth becomes more thickly peopled, men and animals do
not grow old or die. If we must bring together things which have
really no relation to each other, it would be more apposite to compare
the paradise of the Hebrews. The reason for the end of the golden age
is the guilt of Yima. [Cf. Kuenen, "Religion of Israel," 3, c. 9, E. T.]

cised still further influence upon it. It is Auramazda
who places in the hand of Yima the control, superintendence, and protection of animals and men. It is
not through Yima's own desire, as was certainly the
case in the old-legend, but at Auramazda's bidding,
that the enclosure is made, and the selected men,
animals, and trees brought into it. The main reason
for this change was the necessity of giving an answer
to the question, Why did not the golden age continue? and if, long after Yima, Zarathrustra proclaimed
a new and better law, why had not Auramazda revealed
this law to the favoured Yima? In order to answer
this riddle, the Avesta represents Auramazda as asking
Yima to become "the preacher and bearer of his
doctrine," and Yima refuses to accept this mission.
Hence Yima becomes guilty of a fault, and a reason is
given why the golden age, the thousand years of the
reign of Yima, came to an end. Without the good
doctrine, the invasion of evil spirits, and with them
of heat and cold, sickness and death, strife and blight,
could not be kept back from the earth. This trait of
the guilt of Yima, which is entirely unknown to the
earlier legend, is carried out still further. According to the prayer in the Avesta (p. 34) blessing and
immortality continued in the kingdom of Yima, "till he
began to love lying speech." When he had rejected
Auramazda's law he cannot himself resist the seduction
of evil spirits. The first offence brings on the second,
and this causes the triple loss of majesty, which at
length ends in the fall and violent death of Yima, an
incident already indicated in the Avesta.[1] How this
form of the legend allowed the garden of Yima to be
placed on the divine mountain, and whether the

1 "Zamyad Yasht," 46.

contradiction was removed or not, our fragments do
not enable us to decide.

In the Veda it was Indra who had to contend
against Vritra and Ahi, *i. e.* the serpents, and the
black spirits, which desired to drink up the water of the
sky and veil its light. In Iran, as we shall see, this
office is transferred to other spirits, and also to Thraetaona. The Azhi dahaka of the Avesta is the Ahi
of the Veda. Ahi and Azhi are the same word, with
the same meaning; the addition *dahaka* refers to the
destructive power of this demon. Verethraghna, *i. e.*
the slayer of Vritra, stands in the Avesta at the side
of Thraetaona in his struggle with Azhi (p. 35), and
the morning wind supports him just as in the Veda
the winds assist Indra against Ahi and Vritra. Among
the Indians, Traitana is a spirit of the air, who
dwells in the remotest regions of the sky, who hews
off the head of a giant from his shoulders, and in the
Veda, Trita, the son of Aptya, drinks the draught of
Soma, in order to win strength for the slaying of
Vritra; he slays the snake with three heads and seven
tails; with his iron club he splits the hollows in the
rock in which the demons have hidden the cows of the
heaven (the rain clouds).[1] In the Veda, Aptya is the
father of Trita; in the Avesta, Athwya is the father
of Thraetaona. Of Trita, whom it represents as sprung
from Çama, the Avesta declares that he was the first
physician; in the Veda we are told of Trita he knew
how to heal sickness as the gods had taken his sickness
from him; that he bestowed long life.[2] The two
figures of Trita and Traitana gradually unite in the

---

[1] "Rigveda," 1, 158; 10, 8, 5.
[2] Westergaard in Weber's "Ind. Studien," 3, 413 ff., 426 ff. Kuhn
combines Trita with Triton and Tritogeneia; Hofer's "Zeitschrift," 1,
276, 289.

Veda; in the Avesta, Thrita and Thraetaona remain separate persons. The Kereçaçpa of the Avesta seems to correspond to the Kriçaçva of the Indians, whom we first find in the Epos, where he is celebrated as a warlike Rishi.[1]

If the Paradhatas, Yima, Athwya, Thraetaona, Thrita, and Kereçaçpa in the original conception are spirits of the sky, if the monsters with which Thraetaona and Kereçaçpa struggle are not to be sought on earth but in the heavens, if in these dragons we find once more the cloud-serpents, against which Indra and his company have to contend—we do not at once set foot upon earth, when we come to the Kavanians. According to the later tradition of Iran, Kava Kavata was fetched from the divine mountain in order to reign over the country; two white falcons bring him a golden crown. The Rigveda mentions Kavya Uçanas, i. e. Uçanas, the son of Kavi, who brings the cows of the sky, i. e. the clouds, to the pasture.[2] In the Avesta, Kava Uça sacrifices not only to rule over the whole earth but also over the spirits. According to a later tradition this sovereign — now called Kai Kaus—causes beautiful castles to be built on the divine mountain by the demons, and is then carried by four eagles into heaven. Kava Huçrava, for whom in the Avesta the god Haoma contends, is without sickness and death (p. 37). In the later tradition, in which he is known as Kai Chosru, he begins a pilgrimage to heaven after conquering and slaying his opponent the Turanian Franghaçiana, like the sons of Pandu in the Mahabharata after their victory over the Kurus and their happy reign. Like them also, Kai Chosru climbs the mountains and disappears from his companions at a well. Against

---

[1] Haug, "Essays," pp. 235, 236.
[2] Kuhn, "Beiträge," 4, 44; Haug, "Essays," pp. 235, 236.

his command they seek him in the mountains, and are all buried in a great snow-storm. From the name Manuschithra (p. 37), *i. e.* scion of Manu, we may conclude that the twin brother of Yama, "father Manu," was not unknown to the Arians of Iran. But the genealogy in which the Avesta has preserved these names has no greater claims to historical value than the figures which have passed in review before us. Airyu is the son of Thraetaona; *i. e.* from the mightiest hero, the slayer of the great dragon, are sprung the sovereigns and the nation of the Airyas; the son of Airyu is Manuschithra; from whose son, Naotara, are derived the two last Kavas, Aurvataçpa and Vistaçpa.

If the coincidence of the forms from Yima to Kava Huçrava with the Veda is a proof of the antiquity and genuineness of the tradition of the Avesta, the gain for history becomes less instead of greater. No one would take mythical persons for historical. Yet the style and form in which we find these traditional statements in the fragments of the Avesta supply certain guides for the lost history of Eastern Iran. The splendour of the royal majesty is so often and so distinctly brought into prominence, that the conclusion forces itself upon us, that the regions in which the Avesta arose, *i. e.* the north-east of Iran, must have been acquainted with a powerful and highly-respected monarchy. The ancient spirits of the sky are changed in the Avesta into mighty warriors and far-ruling kings, a circumstance in favour of the supposition that an empire once existed here, the image of which is reflected on prehistoric times. It is in Epic poems that the spirits of the first sky become heroes, and Epic poetry only arises in and follows on periods of war and conflict. The fact that the forms of

the spirits thus changed into heroes by Epic song are
turned into the forefathers of the kings and progenitors of the nation, further establishes the conclusion
that a military monarchy must have been in existence
here ; only warlike princes could appear as the heirs
of heroes. Moreover, the Avesta extols the high
banner of Bakhdhi and speaks of the neighbouring
regions as favoured ; the later tradition of Iran marks
out Bactria very clearly as the abode of Aurvataçpa
and Vistaçpa ; in the third century B.C. Bactria
supplied its princes with means not merely to achieve
their own independence, but to maintain it against
the great kingdom of the Seleucids and to subjugate
the land of the Indus (p. 25 ff.) ; and if, in addition to
these facts, we bear in mind the conceptions found in
the Median poems of the great power of the kings of
the Bactrians, their treasures in gold and silver, their
fortified city, the conquest of which was the greatest
achievement of Ninus—we may venture to assume
that before the days of the Medes, *i. e.* before the
year 650 B.C., there must have existed an important
monarchy in the north-east of Iran.

With the assistance of the Avesta we may go
a step further. We saw that Kava Huçrava no less
than Vistaçpa is represented as fighting against the
Turas or Tuiryas. Who were these enemies ? In
Old-Bactrian the word means the enemy, the op-
pressor. Strabo speaks of a region of Turuia in the
north of Parthia, towards the steppes of the Oxus.[1] In
the later tradition of Iran the Turanians are the
constant and most dangerous enemies of the kings of
Bactria. The steppes of the Oxus and Jaxartes were
inhabited by nations to whom the Persians gave the
collective name of Sacæ, while the Greeks called them

----

[1] Strabo, p. 517. [Τοριοὔαν is a *v. l.* for Ταπυρίαν.]

Scythians. They found but scanty pasture on the steppes, and it was natural that they should look with longing eyes on the more fertile regions of Bactria and Sogdiana. It has already been mentioned how careful Cyrus was to protect these countries, when he had conquered them, against the nations of the steppes. At a later time, from the middle of the second century B.C. downwards (p. 28), we have definite information of the pressure of these nations on Parthia, Margiana, and Bactria. When freed from the attacks of the Seleucids on the west, the Arsacids had to defend the east of the kingdom. Phraates II. and Artabanus II. fell in battle against the nomads; Mithridates II. succeeded in protecting Parthia, but about the year 100 B.C. the Sacæ were able to force a way through Bactria. They possessed themselves of the best land in the east of Iran, the valleys of the Hilmend (p. 7), bequeathed their name to the country (Sikashtan, Sejestan), and from the valley of the Cabul extended their dominion beyond the Indus. The white Huns, or Yuëchis, followed the Sacæ; and they also reached the Indus. Is there any reason to doubt the Avesta that even before the Medes and Cyrus the princes of Bactria and Sogdiana were occupied with beating back the tribes of the steppes?

In ancient times, as Strabo tells us, the Bactrians and Sogdiani were little removed from wandering shepherds. The Avesta exhibits them in close connection with horses. The names compounded with açpa (horse) are common; Kereçaçpa, Aurvataçpa, Vistaçpa, Haechatapça, Jamaçpa, Pourushaçpa. Of Zariaçpa and the Zariaçpians we have already spoken. The most important source of wealth must have consisted in horses, for which the mountains supplied ample pasture. The horse-sacrifice is the chief sacrifice of the

Avesta. One hundred horses were equal to 1000 oxen, and 10,000 head of small cattle. We found that Bactria could furnish the last Darius with 30,000 cavalry, and the horse was the symbol of Bactria on the coins of the Greek princes of the land (p. 27).

From all these indications we may assume that when the Arians had settled in Margiana, Bactria, and Sogdiana, and agriculture became of importance beside the breeding of cattle, the necessity of protection against the migratory tribes of the endless plains stretching to the north, created among the Arians a warlike nobility who took upon themselves the duty of defence. The valley of the Zarefshan (Sogdiana), the terrace of Bactria, the region of Merv, became in the hands of the Arians advanced posts of civilisation in the desert. If Western Iran was protected in the north by the Alps of Aderbeijan and the Caspian Sea against attacks from that quarter, Eastern Iran lay open to the nomads of the steppes, and had nothing but arms to defend its cultivated lands. We have already seen that Bactria even in the sixth century had passed beyond the earliest stages of civilisation (p. 24). But even a less degree of prosperity was sufficient to excite the sons of the desert to invasion. Hence we may assume that the incursions and raids of the nomads of the steppes began with the increase of the flocks and the prosperity of agriculture in the valleys of Merv, Bactria, and Sogdiana. The increasing severity of these attacks compelled the Bactrian soldiery to collect their forces for more successful resistance, and to place the best warriors at the head of the community. Thus it was not by spontaneous development, but rather by the opposition to the nations of the steppes, that the north-east of Iran first outgrew the tribal life, and became transformed into a larger state. Of this king-

dom Aurvataçpa and Vistaçpa became the rulers; in
the Avesta they are distinguished from the Paradhatas
and from Kava Kavata, Kava Uça, and Kava Huçrava,
by a new addition to the name and other peculiar
traits, and form a third group. The progress of our
investigation will show that the formation of this
Bactrian kingdom cannot be placed later-than 1100
B.C.; the date of Vistaçpa must be put about 1000
B.C., and it was the successors of Vistaçpa who sent to
Shalmanesar II. the tribute of camels with two humps,
and yaks (about 850 B.C.), who found themselves
menaced once more by the advances of Tiglath Pilesar
II. to Arachosia in the year 745 B.C., and at length
succumbed to Cyrus. We shall find that this kingdom
was not without its warlike races and priestly families,
that Zariaçpa and Bactria were the centres of it, and
that the sovereigns attained despotic power. Yet the old
warlike families must have preserved a certain importance under the monarchy, unless they regained it when
lost under the viceroys of the Achæmenids. It was
the chieftains of the Bactrians whom Alexander summoned to Zariaçpa, and who with the Sogdiani at their
side took the lead in resistance. The most powerful
of them stubbornly defended their rocky citadels
against the Macedonians.

CHAPTER III.

THE SCRIPTURES OF IRAN.[1]

THE statements of the Avesta concerning the ancient rulers of Eastern Iran were proved to be without historical value, yet we found in them an ancient and genuine tradition, the form of which allowed us to draw certain conclusions about the political condition of that region in a period for which we have no other records except the poetry of Western Iran. But what the Avesta tells us of the rulers of ancient days is of secondary importance for the book, which comprises the doctrines and ordinances of the faith proclaimed by Zarathrustra, and the rules of life which he is said to have laid down. May we assume that we possess these in a genuine and unaltered form in the Avesta, though they have only come down to us in fragments?

A book of the Parsees of India, which tells the story of their flight from their ancient home, relates that Iskander (Alexander of Macedon) burned the revealed scriptures, and the faithful were persecuted for 300 years. When Ardeshir (the first Sassanid) ascended the throne, the true faith was restored, under the superintendence of Arda Viraf. After this the true religion was again suspended till king Shapur (Shapur II.) rose and once more made the faith famous, and Aderbat Mahresfant girded his loins in the good cause. The same account is given in the Book of Arda Viraf, also

[1 Cf. Darmesteter, "Zend-Avesta," Introduction, c. iii.]

a book of the Parsees of India. From this we learn
that the religion received by the pious Zarathrustra
lasted for 300 years in purity. Then the evil one stirred
up Iskander Rumi, so that he spread war and devastation over Iran, and slew the rulers of the land. The
Avesta which was preserved at Stakhar Papakan (Persepolis), written on cow-skins with golden ink, he burned,
and put to death many priests and judges, pillars of the
faith, and spread hatred, strife, and confusion among
the people of Iran. They had now no lord, guide,
and high priest, who knew their religion; they were
full of doubts and had different modes of belief and
worship of various kinds, and different laws prevailed
in the world till the time when Ardeshir came to the
throne and listened to the words of the holy Arda
Viraf and believed him. But after Ardeshir's death
a schism broke out, and more than 40,000 souls
fell away from the true faith, till the day when the
holy Aderbat Mahresfant arose.[1] An older writing
of the Parsees, the Dinkart (composed under the
Sassanids), tells us, apparently on the ground of a
proclamation of the Sassanid Chosru Parvez (590—
627 A.D.) that king Vistaçpa of Bactria had commanded
that all books which were written in the language of
the Magians should be collected, in order that the faith
of the worshippers of Auramazda might have some
support, and all men were to go to Frashaostra (whom
the Avesta mentions as a companion of Zarathrustra)
to be instructed in the faith. And Darai, the son of
Darai (Darius Hystaspis is meant), commanded that
two copies of the entire Avesta, precisely as Zarathrustra had received it from Auramazda, should be
preserved, the one in the treasury at Shapikan, and
the other in the city of scriptures. Then Valkosh

[1] Haug, "The Book of Arda Viraf," p. 142 ff.

(Vologeses), the descendant of Ashkan (Arsaces), gave orders that so much of the Avesta as had escaped destruction and the ravages of Iskander and the warriors of Rum, and existed in fragments or in oral tradition, should be sought out and brought from every city. And king Artakshatr (Ardeshir) summoned the Herbedh (*i. e.* the priest)[1] Tosar with the holy scriptures, which were scattered, to his residence, and when Tosar came he gave command to the other priests that everything, which differed from that which was now considered to be knowledge and wisdom, should be suppressed. The son of Artakshatr, Shapuhar (241—272 A.D.), the king of kings, gave command that all writings on medicine or astronomy or other subjects in Hindostan, Rum, and other lands, should be collected, and again united with the Avesta, and that an exact copy should be deposited in the treasury of Shapikan. Lastly Atropat (Aderbat) in the reign of Shapuhar (Shapur II, 309—379 A.D.), the son of Auharmazdi, purified the sayings of Zarathrustra and enumerated the Nosks (chapters) of the sacred scriptures.[2]

In the rivayats of the Parsees in India, *i. e.* in the collections of the sayings of the priests on their doctrine, we find an enumeration of these sections of the scriptures. At each book this list notes how many chapters were re-discovered "after Alexander." According to this enumeration the scriptures of Iran consisted of twenty-one books.[3] The first book contained the songs of praise to the supreme spirits in 33 chapters; the second (22 chapters) treated of good works; the third (22 chapters) of the sacred word; the

---

[1] Herbedh is the old Bactrian *athrapaiti.*
[2] Haug, "Pahlavi-Pazand Glossary," p. 144, 146.
[3] It is found in the so-called "Great Rivayat."

E 2

fourth (21 chapters) of the gods ; the fifth (22 chapters)
of the earth, of water, of trees, of wild animals ; the
sixth (35 chapters) of the heavens and the stars ; the
seventh (22 chapters) of pure and impure kinds of
food, and of the celebration of the great festivals ; the
eighth (50 chapters) of the kings and priests, of pure
and impure animals ; the ninth (60 chapters) of the
laws according to which the kings and judges were to
give sentence ; the tenth (60 chapters) of virtue and
wisdom ; the eleventh (60 chapters) of the reign and
conversion of king Vistaçpa ; the twelfth taught agriculture in 22 chapters, the planting of trees, the duty
of the priests and laity, and treated of the orders ; the
thirteenth (60 chapters) was occupied with the sacred
sciences, the teachers and pupils, and the miracles
which Zarathrustra worked ; the fourteenth book (22
chapters) spoke of the life of men from birth to
death ; the fifteenth (17 chapters) contained songs of
praise ; the sixteenth (54 chapters) laid down rules for
what was permitted and what was not ; the seven-
teenth (64 chapters) contained the doctrines of medicine
and astronomy ; the eighteenth (65 chapters) the
doctrine respecting animals and their treatment ; the
nineteenth (52 chapters) contained the civil and
criminal law ; the twentieth (22 chapters) the rubrics
for the removal of impurity ; the twenty-first gave in
30 chapters the history of creation.[1]

According to this list the scriptures of Iran must
have been of very considerable extent. The Arabian
author Masudi, who lived about the middle of the
tenth century A.D., also puts the number of books at
twenty-one. " Zartusht," he says, " gave the Parsees
the book which is called the Avesta. It consisted of

[1] Vullers, " Fragmente über die Religion Zoroasters," s. 15—42 ;
Haug, " Essays," p. 125.

twenty-one sections, of which each amounted to 200 pages. This book was written in the character which Zartusht invented and which the Magians call the religious character, on 12,000 cow-hides, and these were kept together by bands of gold. It was composed in the old Persian language, which no one now understands."[1] From the list of the books and chapters it is clear that these writings comprised not only the religious doctrine and law, together with the rules for correct conversation, but also the rubrics for the liturgy and ritual. They were at the same time the code of criminal and civic law, and in them was deposited what was known of medicine and agriculture, and the sum total of the science of their authors

Can we assume that writings of this importance, nature, and extent existed in Iran before Alexander of Macedon overthrew the kingdom of the Achæmenids? Herodotus tells us that the Magians or priests of the Persians recited the theogony, i. e. long poems, at their sacrifices. The disciples of the sophist Prodicus are said to have asserted that they were in possession of writings of Zoroaster, who taught the Persians their religion.[2] Hermippus of Smyrna, who wrote in the second half of the third century B.C., and devoted especial attention to the religions of the east, stated that the Magians maintained two principles, a good and an evil deity; the one they called Zeus and Oromasdes, the other Hades and Areimanius.[3] Zoroaster, who founded the doctrine of the Magians, had composed twenty books, each of 100,000 lines, and Her-

---

[1] Quatremère, " Journ. des Savants," 1840, p. 413.

[2] Clemens Alex. " Strom." p. 598.

[3] Diogen. Laert. prooem. The corrupt passage in Athenæus (p. 478) is not a sufficient reason for refusing to accept Hermippus of Smyrna as the author of the treatise on the Magians. Pliny could not quote the Berytian Hermippus.

mippus gave the contents of the various books and
quoted regulations from them. Pliny tells us: "The
doctrine of the Magians prevails to this day among a
great part of the nations, and in the East is supreme
over the king of kings" (i. e. the Arsacids); and
vouches for Hermippus that he had written with great
care about the Magians,[1] from whose work no doubt he
quotes some particulars of the doctrine of Zoroaster.
According to Zoroaster's rule the sowing of the fields
should take place when the moon is in the sign of
Taurus; and it was forbidden to expose the person
before the sun or moon, or to defile a man's shadow.
Pliny also mentions the precious stones, of which
Zoroaster had extolled the brilliance; the herbs, used
by the Magians; and enumerates a number of remedies, which they applied. Finally, he speaks of the
Nyktegertos, a herb growing in Gedrosia, which the
Magians used when making vows.[2] Philo of Byblus
quotes a passage, apparently from "the sacred collection of Zoroaster," on the nature of the deity, and
assures us that the Persian Osthanes maintained the
same in the Octateuch.[3] Plutarch gives us a short
but accurate account of the system of Zoroaster; his
contemporary Dio Chrysostom asserts that Zoroaster
and the sons of the Magians had sung of the balance of
Zeus and the constellation of the day in strains more
sublime than those of Homer or Hesiod;[4] and Pausanias
relates that at the kindling of the sacrificial fire the
invocation was sung by the Magians from a book in a
barbarous language wholly unintelligible to the Greeks.[5]

This evidence from the West confirms the existence

[1] Plin. "H. N." 30, 2.
[2] "H. N." 37, 49, 55, 58; 26, 9; 27, 35; 28, 19, 27; 29, 38; 21, 36.
[3] Philon. Bybl. fragm. 9, ed. Müller.
[4] Dio Chrysost. ed. Dind. 2, 60.   [5] Pausan. 5, 27, 3.

of sacred writings in Iran after the time of Alexander, and also indicates that they existed previously to that date; it contradicts the story of their destruction by the Macedonians. The books must have been in existence when Hermippus could speak of their extent, and quote rules from them; and writings of the kind must have been known when, in the days of Pausanias, the Magians could sing their invocations from a book. From other sources we are sufficiently informed that Alexander's efforts were not directed towards destroying the national character and traditional religion of the Persians. Arrian tells us that Magians no less than Greek soothsayers took part in their festivals.[1] Nor were the Seleucids more desirous than Alexander to effect the destruction of the Iranian nationality; just as the Ptolemies never attempted to set aside the Egyptian religion and life. Even if they had cherished such views, they were far from being strong enough to carry them out, for the Greek empire over Iran lasted in its integrity only eighty years. The Arsacids also, who recovered Iran from the Seleucids, were not averse to the Greek nation. They called themselves friends of the Hellenes, and not only was Greek spoken, but even the tragedies of Euripides were acted at their courts. The scanty remains of the monuments present us with echoes of Greek;[2] their coins, with few exceptions, bear Greek legends like those of the Bactrian princes whom they overcame. But though the influence of the Hellenic character continued under the Arsacids, and at the same time the Aramæan language and manners

---

[1] "Anab." 7, 11, 8.

[2] *E. g.* the bas-relief on Mount Behistun in the winged victory, which refers to the battle between Vardanes and Gotarzes, between 40 and 50 A.D. [Cf. Rawlinson, "Sixth Monarchy," p. 389, where a sketch of the relief is given.]

obtained even greater recognition than Hellenism
during their dominion, the reign of the Arsacids was a
restoration and revivification of the Iranian nationality.
According to the evidence of western writers the
Magians together with the members of the royal race
formed the council of the Arsacids.[1] Pliny has already
told us that these princes obeyed the rules of the
Magians, and we also find that they invoked Mithra
as the Achæmenids had done, and "saluted the sun."[2]
Like the Achæmenids, too, they would not permit
their armies to fight by night, and we are told that
in their time the greatest weight was given to the
love of truth and fidelity, i. e. to the virtues which,
according to Herodotus, the Persians of his time considered the most important, and on which the Avesta
insists above all others.[3] We also learn from western
writers that the founder of the kingdom (Arsaces I.)
was a descendant of Phriapites (Friyapaiti), and with
his brother Tiridates and five others he slew the satrap
of Antiochus Theos, and drove out the Macedonians;[4]
just as Darius with the six Persian princes overthrew
the dominion of Gaumata ; and the Arabs relate that
the Arsacids trace back their stock to Çyavarshana,
the son of Kava Uça, a story which cannot have been
invented in Arabia.[5] In the list of the Arsacids we
also find the name Chosru (108—130 A.D.), the Kava
Huçrava of the old legend (p. 37) ; on the coins we
find a Vologeses and a Phraates before the fire-altar,
the characteristic symbol of the ancient worship of

[1] Poseidonius in Strabo, p. 515; Justin, 42, 1.

[2] Herodian, 4, 30.

[3] Plut. " Crassus," c. 29 ; "Anton." c. 47 ; Joseph. "Antiq." 18, 9,
3 ; Justin (12, 3), and Horace ("Ep." 1, 2, 112), are of another opinion
in regard to the latter point.

[4] Above, p. 26. Arrian, "Parth." 2, ed. Müller ; Eunap. p. 222.

[5] Al Biruni in Droysen, "Hellenismus," 3², 372.

Iran. Just as the old Arian character appears beside the Greek on the coins of the Greek princes of Bactria, the Greek character on the coins of the Arsacids gradually degenerates until at length it gives way to a new Iranian character and language. The tradition sketched in the Dinkart, as we have seen, represents the Arsacid Vologeses (which of the four princes of the name is meant is not clear)[1] as collecting what fragments remained of the holy scriptures in the memory of the priests. The burning of the scriptures by Alexander, as related in the books of the Parsees on their exodus and the Arda Viraf, is merely a transference to him of the conduct of the Moslems on their conquest of Iran. Of the continuance of the ancient religion of Iran under the Arsacids there can be no doubt, though it is true that along with it, in the Greek cities which Alexander and the Seleucids founded, and which were independent within their walls even under the Parthians, Hellenic rites were practised. In these cities Syrian modes of worship were also permitted, and the Aramaic language and culture found entrance into Iran.[2]

In the land of Persia, among the Persians whom Mithridates I. subjugated to the dominion of the Arsacids, reminiscences of the ancient time, of the splendour and glory of the Achæmenids, were naturally more lively than in Parthia, which was formerly subject to the Persians, and now under the Arasacids stood at the head of Iran. In Persia, Artakshatr (Ardeshir), the son of Papaki, the grandson of Sassan, rebelled

[1] Vologeses I. reigned 50—80 A.D. ; Vologeses II. 130—149 A.D. ; Vologeses III. and IV. 149—208 A.D. ; the son of the fourth, also Vologeses, reigned beside Artabanus IV.

[2] " Joseph. "Ant." 18, 9, 1 ; " Bell. Jud." Prooem. 1, 2 ; Ammian. Marcell. 23, 6.

against king Artabanus IV. In three great battles
the Persians contended with the Parthians; the latter
were conquered, and Artabanus fell, and with him the
kingdom of the Arsacids after a continuance of 476
years (225 A.D.). With the reign of Ardeshir began
a more energetic restoration of Iran. He and his
successors after him revered the memory of the Achæmenids, and strove to continue their achievements [1]
We again hear of seven houses, and seven princes who
had the right to wear diadems beside the king, like
the seven tribal princes of the old Persian kingdom; [2]
we find the fire-altar before the tent of the Sassanids
as well as the Achæmenids; and in the army of the
Sassanids, no less than in that of Darius and Xerxes,
was a troop of "immortals." Ardeshir, like the founder
of the Persian empire, caused a portrait of himself on
horseback to be cut in a rock-wall to the north-west
of Persepolis (Naksh-i-Rustem) in remembrance of the
achievements which established his kingdom—the rock
on which 700 years before Darius had marked his
tomb by a portrait and inscription. The inscription
under this portrait (in the Pehlevi of East and West
Iran, with a Greek translation) runs thus: " Portrait of
the worshipper of Mazda, the god Artakshatr (Artax-
ares in the Greek), the king of kings of the Arians
(of the kings of Airan, in the Pehlevi texts), the scion
of the sky (*minu chitri*), the son of the god Papaki,
the king." [3] Ardeshir's son, Shapur I. (241—272 A.D.),
caused his victory over Valerian and his capture of
the emperor to be recorded on the same rock; we see
Shapur on horseback, and Valerian kneeling before
him, a representation which recurs at the old Persian

[1] Ammian. Marcell. 17, 5.   [2] Nöldeke, "Tabari." s. 437.
[3] De Sacy, "Memoires de l'institut Cl. Hist." 2, 162—242. [Raw-
linson, "Seventh Monarchy," p. 70, 606.]

city of Darabgerd. At Naksh-i-Rejeb, between the
rock-wall of Naksh-i-Rustem and Mount Nachmed, on
which abutted Persepolis, the proud citadel of the
Achæmenids, and in the grotto of Haiyabad, we
find in the one case a portrait of Shapur, and
in the other inscriptions which mention this ruler
and king Varahran. At Kermanshah, on the western
side of Mount Behistun, on the eastern side of which
mountain Darius inscribed the proudest memorial of
his achievements, we see king Ardeshir, and beneath
him the corpse of Artabanus ; behind the king is
Mithra with the club which gave him victory, and
before him Auramazda who presents the ring of empire
to Ardeshir. Not far from this portrait Shapur II.
(309—379 A.D.) caused a grotto to be excavated in the
rock. In the sculpture of this cave we see the goddess
Anahita, who presents to the king the ring of empire ;
at some distance are the hunting expeditions of the
king ; a second grotto close to this exhibits the pictures
of king Auharmazdi II., the father of Shapur II., and
of Shapur III. his second successor.[1]

Though the Sassanids sought to restore the kingdom
of the Achæmenids, and immortalise their own achievements beside those of the early kings, the religious
revival which they undertook was far more thorough
than the political. In this direction they went further
than the Achæmenids ; they caused the forms which
the old faith of Iran had retained and forced on the
East, to be current throughout the whole kingdom.
Agathias assures us that Ardeshir was eagerly devoted
to the study of the doctrine of the Magians, who
since his accession had gained an importance such
as they never enjoyed before. The business of the
State was decided upon their advice and predictions ;

[1 Rawlinson, loc. cit. p. 602, 607, 92 ff.]

they assisted individual persons in their private matters
and suits at law, and the Persians did not regard any-
thing as legal and right which was not confirmed by a
Magian.[1] At the head of the Magians, we are told in
another account coming from a western source, a Grand
Magian was placed under the Sassanids,[2] and as a fact
the Magians now received a thorough organisation.
At the head of their caste was the High Magian
(*Magupat*, Mobedh); and over all the High Magians
was the Grand Magian (*Magupatan magupat*); to the
Magians belonged the judicial power; and the Grand
Magian performed the coronation of the king. The
Sassanids erected fire-temples in Persia no less than
in Aderbeijan; their coins always exhibit the fire-
altar, and as a rule two priests before it. They carried
their genealogy beyond Sassan through Çpentodata
(p. 38) to Vistaçpa of Bactria, who is now said to
have established the seven princes; they call themselves by the names of the ancient heroes who met us
in the Avesta; Kavadh (Kava Kavata) and Chosru
(Kava Huçrava). While styling themselves the worshippers of Mazda (Auramazda) like the founders of
their empire, they went so far as to assume the names
of the gods of the Avesta; some even called themselves
after Verethraghna (Varahran, Bahram), others Auharmazdi after Auramazda himself. The numerous Christians on the Euphrates and Tigris as well as in Armenia
had to undergo severe persecutions; especially under
Shapur II., Varahran V., and Yezdegerd II. (438—457
A.D.), whose viceroy declared to the Armenian Christians that the Daevas (Dews) of Ahriman had deceived
them; it was not the good God who had created evil
and death but the wicked spirit. Defection from the
faith of Auramazda was punished with death. In the

[1] Agathias, 2, 26.   [2] Sozomen, "H. Eccl." 2, 10, 12.

treaties of the years 422, 533, and 563 A.D. Theodosius II. and Justinian obtained the concession that the Christians in the kingdom of the Sassanids should not be compelled to conform to the rules of the Magians; they were to be at liberty to bury their dead,[1] whereas the doctrine of Zarathrustra required that the corpses should be exposed.

As such was the attitude of the house of the Sassanids, we may believe the books of the Parsees that Ardeshir eagerly took in hand the revival of the true faith, and that he was assisted in this by competent Magians; by Arda Viraf, according to the book of the Exodus and of Arda Viraf (p. 50); according to the Dinkart, by the Herbedh Tosar. The book of Arda Viraf relates at length how he fell asleep in the assembly of priests before Ardeshir, and his soul was carried by the god Çraosha through heaven and hell. And when the Dinkart represents a standard of true religion as being set up under Ardeshir, there is no reason to doubt the statement. After the reign of Ardeshir, we are told in the Book of the Exodus, the true religion was again suspended, or, as the Book of Arda Viraf tells us, a schism arose. The cause of this division is sufficiently known from other sources. In the reign of Shapur I. (241—272 A.D.) a native of Ctesiphon, of the name of Mani, came forward with a new doctrine which attempted to mingle Chaldæan, Jewish, and Christian elements in the faith of Iran, and to resolve it into abstractions. He found numerous adherents.[2] Varahran II. (276—293 A.D.) allowed him to dispute with the Magians, and then put him to death. Under Shapur II., who succeeded his father Auharmazdi II. as a posthumous child (309—379 A.D.),

---

[1] Menandri Protect. fragm. 11, ed. Müller.
[2 Cf. Rawlinson, "Seventh Monarchy," p. 96 ff.]

in order to check Manicheism and the advance of Christianity, it was necessary to go back to the principles of the old faith, and to invigorate these by the collection and establishment of the sacred scriptures. We may therefore have the fullest confidence in accepting from these three books of the Parsees the facts that Shapur "made the sacred faith to be famous;" that Aderbat, whose work under Shapur is confirmed by Hamza of Isfahan, collected the scriptures, purified the sayings of Zarathrustra, and enumerated the chapters. It is on this redaction of the canon by Aderbat Mahresfant under Shapur II. that the list of the books and chapters rests, distinguishing what were originally in existence and what were then preserved. What was not discovered "after Alexander" means what was not discovered or not accepted at this redaction. Instead of the 815 chapters which the Avesta is said to have previously contained, the new canon amounted to only 348 chapters. That Aderbat was the founder of this canon is clear not only from the epithet which the books of the Parsees give him (Mahresfant, Old Bactrian Manthraçpenta, meaning " the sacred word,") but also from the confession of faith still in use among the Parsees: "I abide in the law which Zarathrustra taught to Vistaçpa, to Frashaostra, to Jamaçpa, and Çpentodata, which came in the succession of generations to Aderbat, who duly corrected and purified it."[1]

It was shown above that the language of the sacred books thus again collected was that of Eastern Iran (p. 30). When Aderbat revised the canon it had long ceased to be spoken. But there were already translations of the sacred books into the later forms which the language of Iran had received in the time of the Parthians, or at any rate such translations

[1] Spiegel, Avesta, 3, 214, 218, 219, 227.

were made after the revision of the canon.[1] Masudi
informed us that the Avesta was composed in the old
Persian language, which at that time (tenth century
A.D.) was no longer understood. Ibn Haukal, who
travelled in Persia in the same century, tells us : " In
Fars three languages are in use ; the Farsi, in which
the inhabitants converse with each other ; the Pehlevi,
which was the language of the ancient Persians, and
in which the Magians wrote their historical books, but
which in our time is no longer understood by the
inhabitants of Fars without a translation ; and the
Arabian.[2] " When Aderbat revised the Avesta in the
middle of the fourth century B.C., the Parsi (Farsi), i. e.
the later Middle Persian, was still in formation ; the
older Middle Persian or Pehlevi was still intelligible,
but translations of the Avesta into this language did
not make clear to every one the meaning of the ancient
language in which the scriptures were composed. In
the time of the Parthian empire the old mode of
writing was given up in the West as well as in the
East of Iran, and exchanged for new methods. In the
West a cuneiform character derived from the writing of
Babylon and Assyria had been adopted ; the East used
the Arian alphabet. Under the Arsacids the Pehlevi
became common. Like the old Persian cuneiform
this is borrowed from a Semitic pattern. The chief city
of the Parthians lay on the Tigris in the midst of a
Semitic population. The cursive character of the
Aramæans, as we find it on the coins of the satraps of
the Achæmenids of the fourth century B.C., with a few
modifications, forms the base of the Pehlevi ; and the
earlier shapes of this character are seen in the coins of

---

[1] Above, p. 17. On the date of these translations, Haug, " Pahlavi-
Pazand Glossary," p. 147.

[2] Quatremère, " Journal des Savants," 1840, p. 412.

the Arsacids of the first century A.D. But it is not
the character which forms the peculiar mark of Pehlevi.
Along with the Aramaic letters the Parthians took the
Aramaic vocabulary; they wrote the Aramaic word
instead of the Persian, and to this they attached the
termination or case-ending of the corresponding Persian
word; the reader must understand Aramaic and substitute the Persian word for the Aramaic when reading.[1] Hence Pehlevi was in reality a secret mode of
writing, intended exclusively for the learned, i. e. for
the priests. It is a proof of the close connection
between the priests of the East and West that this
character, which arose in the West out of the contact
with the Aramaic population on the Euphrates and
Tigris, spread to the East also and was adopted by the
scholars there. Nor was this all. The variations in
the Eastern dialect brought about certain modifications in the forms of the letters, and thus there arose
an Eastern alphabet of Pehlevi beside the Western
alphabet. When Ardeshir destroyed the empire of the
Parthians in the year 226 A.D. these two alphabets were
in existence. The Eastern alphabet finally triumphed
over the Western. It became the royal mode of
writing, and as such was used on the coins. The letters
in the manuscripts of the Pehlevi translation of the
Avesta in the possession of the Parsees agree throughout
with the characters on the legends of the coins of the
Sassanids about the year 600 A.D.[2] The characters

---

[1] Haug, " Pahlavi-Pazand Glossary," p. 120 ff.; 128 ff. [West,
" Pahlavi Texts," part 1. Introd. § 2.

[2] Lepsius, "Zendalphabet, Abh. B. Akad." 1862, s. 338; Lenormant,
" Sur l'alphabet Pehlevi Journ. Asiat. 1er." 6, 6, 180 ff.; Levy, "Beiträge
Z. D. M. G.", 21, 459 ff. From Ardeshir down to Narses, i. e. from 226
to 302 A.D., the writing on the coins agrees with the West Pehlevi of
the monuments of the Sassanids. From 302 to 600 A.D. the character
on the coins is different. From 600 the writing on the coins agrees
with the MSS. of the Parsees; Mordtmann, "Z. D. M. G." 8, 12 ff.

also, in which the text of the Avesta is written in the manuscripts of the Parsees, belong to the later East-Pehlevi alphabet, which, owing to the greater wealth of the old Bactrian alphabet in sounds, especially in vowels, possesses a greater number of letters.[1] The coincidence of the letters in the manuscripts of the Parsees with those on the coins of the later Sassanids, proves beyond contradiction that although the oldest existing manuscripts belong to the fourteenth century of our era,[2] they are nevertheless true copies of the characters in which the Avesta was written in the last century of the empire of the Sassanids.

All that the Parsees of India now possess are some not very extensive remains of the revision of the sacred scriptures made in the reign of Shapur II. The existing part of the laws corresponds in the title, the divisions and their arrangements, with the twentieth book of the text (p. 52). It contains the rubrics for purification, for repelling and removing the evil spirits. The title is the Vendidad, or, in the older form, the Vidaevodata, *i. e.* " given against the Daevas," or evil spirits. Obviously this book was regarded as the most important and valuable part of the law, and to this circumstance it owes its preservation. Besides this we have invocations and prayers, chiefly belonging to the liturgy. They form a considerable collection, known by the title of Yaçna, *i. e.* worship. The remainder of the 348 chapters was lost in the invasion of the Arabs into Iran, owing to their fanatical zeal for conversion.[3]

---

[1] Lepsius, *loc. cit.* s. 306.   [2] Westergaard, " Avesta," 1, 4 ff.

[3] That the author or authors of the Bundehesh,—for the work consists of a collection of fragments of various character,—had before them larger remains of the Avesta, or a commentary which included more than our fragments, may be conceded. The composition of the work cannot be placed before the time of the Arabs, for the whole period of the Sassanid empire is given, and even on an extended scale (p. 82),

Though we were able to establish the fact that these fragments belonged in their language, their contents, and their written character to Eastern Iran, and the evidence of Western writers proved to us that at the time when Alexander of Macedon overthrew the kingdom of the Achæmenids, there were sacred scriptures of considerable extent in Iran—this does not enable us to decide the date of the origin of these scriptures. We have to inquire whether these writings were known in the West of Iran also, before the date of the Sassanids; whether the new collection and revision about the year 350 of our era was satisfied with faithfully representing the old condition of the scriptures, so far as it could be discovered, or whether it altered their contents; whether the influence exercised by Hellenic and Aramaic elements in the time of the Seleucids and Parthians—so obvious in the one case and so searching in the other—affected the contents of the Avesta.[1] This question cannot be set aside, because even under the Sassanids, in spite of their zeal for the Avesta and for Iran, these elements were not unknown. We are aware that Greek and Jewish schools flourished in Syria and Mesopotamia at the date of the Sassanids, that Chosru Nushirvan (531—578 A.D.) gave his protection to Damascius and the Platonists in his kingdom, and caused Greek works to be translated. However much other virtues, required in the Avesta, were extolled in this ruler, such as the foundation of fire-temples, and appointment of sacristans for them, the promotion of agriculture (no temple was to be without cultivated lands) and of marriages—nevertheless sects

mention is made of the empire of the Arabs, and Arabian words occur. Cf. Justi, "Bundehesh," p. ix. ff.; cf. below, p. 73. [West, "Pahlavi Texts," 1, Introd. p. xci. ff].

[1] On the Aramean sketch of the dialectic of Aristotle which was written for Chosru, cf. Renan, "Journ. Asiat." 1852, p. 311.

sprung up within the true religion. Even in official documents of the fifth century we find a certain deviation from the doctrine of the Avesta; under king Kavadh (488—453 A.D.), Mazdak, who proclaimed the community of goods and women, found adherents, and the Arabs speak of sects in Iran which opposed the teaching of the Magians.[1] They mention the Zarvanites, the Gayomarthians, and others, of whom the Zarvanites sought to derive the good and evil deity from some higher abstraction,[2] while the Gayomarthians represented the evil deity as proceeding from the thought of the good deity. Had conceptions of this kind, and other later views which we find in their doctrines, influence on the restoration of the canon? The fact that the sacred writings were composed in a language no longer current, when the canon was restored, is not a complete safeguard against changes and interpolations, for the priests at that time may have understood the language, and therefore may possibly have been able to compose in it.

[1] [Cf. Rawlinson, *loc. cit.* 448 ff.; 342 ff.]

[2] "Sharastani," by Haarbrücker, 2, 281. The son of Mihr Narses is called Zarvandadh.

CHAPTER IV.

THE examination of the difficult questions, whether,
from what period, and to what extent, the Avesta was
known in Western Iran before the time of Alexander,
when the book came into existence, whether its contents have come down uninjured from an ancient
period, or whether it underwent alterations in the
time of the Parthians and the Sassanids, will be best
opened by collecting and testing the accounts which
have been preserved in the West about Zarathrustra
and his work. Herodotus does not mention him, but
Xanthus the Lydian is said to have spoken of him,
before the date of Herodotus. Plato describes Zoroaster as the founder of the doctrine of the Magians,
and calls him a son of Oromazes.[2] With Hermodorus,
a pupil of Plato, Zoroaster is a Persian, the first
Magian.[3] Deinon concludes from the name that he
was a worshipper of the stars. Hermippus of Smyrna
speaks of him as a Bactrian, and is said to have
described him as a pupil of Azonakes (or Agonakes).[4]
Diodorus informs us that Zoroaster gave out among
the Arians that the good spirit had revealed to him
the laws which he published.[5] Trogus Pompeius

[1 Cf. Darmesteter, "Zend-Avesta," Introduct., c. iv. § 40, and c. iii.]
[2] Plato. "Alcib. 1." p. 122.   [3] Diog. Laert. prooem.
[4] Plin. "H. N." 30, 2.   [5] 1, 94.

relates that Ninus finally carried on war with Zoroaster the king of the Bactrians, who discovered the
art of the Magians, and inquired accurately into the
primal forces of the world, and the movements of the
stars; he was slain by Ninus.[1] Pliny observes that
Zoroaster, the founder of the doctrine of the Magians,
smiled on the day of his birth, and beat his head
vigorously as a symbol of his wisdom; for thirty
years he lived in the desert on cheese. Plutarch's
account is that Zoroaster took no other food or drink
all his life but milk, and like Lycurgus and Numa, he
associated with the Divine Being.[2] Dio Chrysostom
tells us that Zoroaster from his love for wisdom and
justice lived remote from men in solitude on a mountain, which had been kindled by fire from above, and
burned continuously, and when the king approached
the mountain with his leading men to offer prayer to
the god, Zoroaster came unharmed out of the fire, and
bade them offer sacrifice for the god had visited the
place. After this Zoroaster did not associate with all
men, but only with those who were most adapted to
receive the truth and converse with the god, whom
the Persians called Magians, i. e. those who have skill
to serve the Divine Being.[3] Kephalion asserted that
Zoroaster the Magian, the king of the Bactrians,
fought with Semiramis and was vanquished by her.[4]
Theon of Alexandria also speaks of the conflict between
Semiramis and the Bactrian Zoroaster. Arnobius is
aware of the battle of Ninus with Zoroaster and the
Bactrians,[5] and in Eusebius Zoroaster, the Magian, the

[1] Justin, 1, 1.
[2] "Numa," c. 4; "Quaest. Sympos." 4, 1. [The reading Ζωροάστρην
is doubtful; cf. Wyttenbach.]   [3] Dio Chrys. 2, 60, ed. Dind.
[4] Euseb. "Chron." ed. Auch. p. 43; cf. Georg. Syncell. p. 167.
Βάτου after Zoroaster should here be changed into Βάκτρου rather than
Μάγου.   [5] Arnob. "Adv. Gent." 1, 5.

king of the Bactrians, fights against Ninus.[1] According to the treatise of Eubulus of Athens on Mithras, Porphyrius related that Zoroaster had consecrated a natural cave, in which were flowers and springs, in the neighbouring mountains of Persia, in honour of Mithra, the creator and father of all, and since that time the favour of the god had been sought in a cave.[2] Ammianus Marcellinus calls Zoroaster a Bactrian, and tells us that Hystaspes, the father of Darius, spread abroad the doctrine of the Magians.[3] Agathias remarks that the Persians of his time asserted that Zoroaster, or Zaradus, as they called him, who gave them their religious doctrine and law, the son of Oromasdes, lived at the time of Hystaspes; but they made the assertion in such a manner that no man knew whether this Hystaspes was the father of Darius or some other of the name. But whatever the date of his life, he changed the earlier forms of worship, and was the discoverer of the doctrine of the Magians.[4] Suidas distinguishes between the Perso-Mede Zoroaster, the chief of the Magians, and the astronomer of the same name, an Assyrian, who lived at the time of Ninus.[5] In Syncellus, Zoroaster is the first of the eight Median kings, who, according to the statement of Berosus, reigned over Babylonia from 2458 to 2224 B.C.[6]

These statements do not amount to much. Yet we find the tradition maintained from the pupils of Plato down to Agathias, that Zoroaster founded the doctrine of the Magians; Diodorus, Plutarch, and Dio mention the intercourse of Zoroaster with the good spirit or the

---

[1] Euseb. loc. cit. p. 35. [2] Porphyr. " De antro nymph." c. 6.
[3] Ammian. Marcell. 23, 6. [4] Agathias, 2, 24.
[5] Suidas, Μάγοι, Ζωροάστρης.
[6] Above, p. 17. Georg. Sync. p. 78, 79. Vol. I. p. 241, 247.

deity. Diodorus calls him an Arian, *i. e.* an inhabit-
ant of Eastern Iran. Hermippus, Trogus Pompeius,
Kephalion, Theon, Arnobius, and Eusebius speak of him
as a Bactrian, and the king of the Bactrians, and
represent him as fighting with Ninus or Semiramis,
which is also asserted by Moses of Khorene.[1] Hence
in the last two centuries B.C. it must have been known
in the West that Zoroaster belonged to the East of
Iran, and thus he was brought into connection with the
most prominent fact known in the history of Bactria,
the contest of the Bactrians against Ninus and Semiramis. This story, as we said, comes from the Medo-
Persian Epos, and moreover the Epos did not authorise
this connection of Ninus and Zoroaster. The opponent of Ninus, who reigned over Bactria, was, according to Diodorus, Oxyartes or Exaortes (p. 20). The
fact that Zoroaster was the most important name in
the antiquity of Iran among western nations obviously
induced Syncellus to put him at the head of the
supposed ancient Median dynasty. If Zoroaster, as
Pliny and Plutarch think, lived only on milk and
cheese, and passed thirty years in the wilderness, these
are merely traits taken from the lives of the Brahman
ascetics. The story in Dio Chrysostom, that Zoroaster
came unharmed from the fire, and the opposite statements of the Chronicle of Alexandria and of Suidas,
that he brought down fire from heaven and was consumed by it, or struck by lightning, contain traits
which have obviously sprung from the importance
which the doctrine of Zoroaster and the Magians
ascribe to the worship of fire, and from the division
between the fire of lightning and earthly fire, of which
we shall speak below. The narrative of Eubulus is
founded on the mysteries of Mithra, which came into

---

[1] Yet with Moses Zoroaster is a Mede, I. p. 87.

the West in the first century B.C.[1] These mysteries are due to the confusion of the Mithra of the Iranians with the sun-god of the Syrians; the mystæ were consecrated in caves, or in places called caves, and there underwent their probation. As the god of light and the soul Mithra slays in the cave, that is in the world of gloom and matter, the bull which is the symbol of matter, as opposed to light, in its creative power, and conveys the soul, the side of man akin to light, out of the gloom of matter through the heaven of the fixed stars, and then through the heaven of the planets, to the light.[2] Ammianus Marcellinus and Agathias have better information about Zoroaster. They are aware that he stands in some relation to Hystaspes. Ammianus, though he expressly describes Zoroaster as a Bactrian, puts Hystaspes the well-known father of Darius, as the supporter of the doctrine of the Magians, in the place of the Vistaçpa of the Avesta, who opens a wide path for the teaching of Zoroaster; Agathias, on the other hand, expresses himself with greater circumspectness; he cannot decide whether the father of Darius or some other Hystaspes is meant.

The result is this: Before the time of Alexander of Macedon, at the latest in the first half of the fourth century B.C., the Greeks were aware that Zoroaster had founded the doctrine of the Magians; in the last centuries B.C. and onwards it was known that he belonged to Bactria and Eastern Iran; but it was not till the fourth century A.D. that he was known to have lived under king Hystaspes; at any rate we have no older evidence on this point.

---

[1] Plut. "Pomp." c. 24.
[2] Cf. Von Gutschmid, "Die Sage vom heiligen Georg;" Sächsische Gesellschaft d. W., 1861, s. 175.

Much more recent in date, and of far less value, is the information derived from the East, with the exception of the Avesta, on Zarathrustra. It does not go back beyond the period of the Arabian empire over Iran. The Bundehesh, written in this period (p. 65, *n.* 3), contains a genealogy, which carries Zarathrustra's origin beyond Pourushaçpa and Haechataçpa, from whom, according to the Avesta, he was sprung (p. 38), through twelve generations to Manuschithra (Minocher). In the Avesta, the soul of the pure Manuschithra, the son of Airyu, is invoked;[1] it has been observed above that the national genealogy in Iran placed Thraetaona, and not Manu, at the head; Airyu, the son of Thraetaona, was the proper progenitor of the Airyas. With the name Manuschithra, *i. e.* scion of Manu, who is now the son of Airyu, this table passed back into the old Arian conception of the father Manu (p. 44). In the Avesta, Zarathrustra is connected by his father, the fourth sacrificer of the Haoma, with the old sacrificers; and by deriving his family from Manuschithra the Bundehesh places him in the closest relation to the progenitors of the Airyas. For the rest this book has little to say about the life of Zoroaster. It informs us that the house of Pourushaçpa lay on a hill on the river Daraja, a river which we cannot identify;[2] the Bundehesh places it in Airyana Vaeja (Airanvij), in a district which we must place in the high region of the Hindu Kush, on the sources of the Oxus (p. 31, *n.* 2), though the Bundehesh informs us that "it lay by the side of Atropatene." According to another passage in the book, Airyana Vaeja lay near the garden of Yima and Cashmere. In a third passage the garden of Yima, which we are compelled by unmistakable indications

---

[1] "Farvardin Yasht," 131.
[2] C. 20 in Justi, [c. 20 ; § 32 West]; cf. "Vend." 19, 15.

in the Avesta, to seek on the divine mountain, lies in
the centre of Iran, under Mount Damkan.[1] Atropatene, as a name for the Alpine land in the north-
west of Iran (now Aderbeijan), came into use in the
time of the Greek empire ; at any rate we cannot trace
it earlier.[2] *Athrapaiti* means " lord of fire " ; *athrapata*,
" one protected by fire " ; in the remote mountains of
this district the old fire-worship was preserved with
peculiar zeal under the Seleucids ; from the time of
Ardeshir the Sassanids venerated the fire-temple Adar
Guçasp (near Takht-i-Soliman), which lay in this region,
above all others, and this was the reason why in the
time of the Arabs it was thought that Airyana Vaeja
must be sought there.[3] In any case it is impossible,
out of regard to the Bundehesh and even later statements of the Moslem period, to place Zarathrustra in
the north-west of Iran in order to represent him as a
foreigner, reforming the religion of the north-east, when
the Avesta, which distinctly places him in the east
and puts him among the sacrificers and heroes of the
east and rulers of Bactria, together with the older
and more important evidence of the West, is on the
opposite side.

The " Book of Zartusht," one of the most recent
books of the Parsees (it dates from the thirteenth
century of our era), can only tell us of the marvellous
preservation of Zarathrustra and the miracles which
he wrought. The first miracle recorded in it is the
fact that Zoroaster smiled at his birth. But the
wicked king Durausarun sought to murder the newly-

[1] C. 30, cf. above, p. 40. [C. 29, § 14, West.]

[2] Strabo, p. 515, derives it from Atropates, whom Alexander made
satrap there.

[3] Still less important than the Bundehesh is the gloss on " Vend."
1, 60. " Many say that Zartusht was from Rak in Atropatan." Ragha
is not in Atropatene.

born child in his cradle. His arm is paralysed, and
he cannot strike the blow home. Then the evil spirits
steal the child, kindle a great fire in the desert, and
throw him into it. But he sleeps peacefully in the
fire, and his mother recovers him without injury. A
herd of cattle are about to trample him on a narrow
path, when the largest one stands over and protects
him, till the herd have passed by. In a similar manner
he is preserved when a pair of wild horses are driven
over him. Even the wolves will not eat him. When
he has reached his thirtieth year these trials are over,
and Zarathrustra emigrates with his followers. On
reaching Iran the good spirit Vohu mano appeared and
conducted him to Auramazda. He had to pass over a
fiery mountain, but the fire did not singe a hair;
molten metal was poured on his breast, and he felt it
not; his entrails were removed and then replaced
without injury to him. Auramazda gave him the
Avesta and commanded him to go to king Vistaçpa
(now Kai Gushtaçp) to Balkh, and proclaim it to him.
In Balkh Zoroaster overcame the sages of the king in
argument, but they maligned him before their master
as a wizard, and he was put in prison. Then the feet
of the king's horse were drawn up into its belly, and
the king bade Zarathrustra heal his horse. He required the king to believe in him and his doctrine;
and when the king had acknowledged the new faith,
one of the horse's feet was restored to it. Zarathrustra
further demanded that Vistaçpa's son Çpentodata
(Isfendyar) should consecrate himself to the defence of
the new faith, that the king's consort should adopt the
law, and those who maligned him should be punished.
When these three requests had been complied with, the
horse recovered all its four feet. After this Vistaçpa
did nothing without the advice of Zarathrustra, and

built fire-altars and fire-temples. And Zarathrustra
showed the king the place he would one day occupy in
heaven, and made Çpentodata invulnerable.[1]

Hence from the Bundehesh we obtain no more than
the genealogical tree of Zarathrustra, which though
characteristic for the place allotted to him, is without historical value ; and from the Zartusht Nameh,
Sharastani, and Mirkhond, which repeat some miracles
more or less similar to those quoted, we gather nothing
beyond certain traits : the smiling at birth, the fiery
mountain, the preservation of Zarathrustra in the
fire, which Pliny and Dio Chrysostom had already
made known to us, and which belong to the ancient
tradition of Iran. In the miracles which take place by
means of oxen and horses, we can merely recognise
the ancient and close relation of the Arians in Iran
to these animals, a relation which has already been
remarked (p. 46). We might perhaps add that Firdusi represents Zarathrustra, whom he puts beside
Vistaçpa, as having been killed at a fire in Balkh when
the city was captured by Turanians. The intercourse of Zarathrustra with Auramazda was known
to Western writers, as we saw, at a far earlier
date.

If we can hardly glean anything worth notice from
these accounts about Zarathrustra's life and work,
we may perhaps gain some information about his
date. The evidence of Ammianus Marcellinus and Agathias, when they represent him as a contemporary of
Hystaspes, in whom we recognise Vistaçpa of Bactria,
carries us no further than the Avesta, which places
him in the closest relation to this prince (p. 38), because his date is equally uncertain. Trogus Pompeius,

---

[1] Spiegel, " Eran," 1, 684 ff.

Kephalion, Theon, and Eusebius make Zarathrustra an opponent and therefore a contemporary of Ninus and Semiramis. But as neither Semiramis nor Ninus ruled over Asshur, and they are to be regarded as the personification of the rise of the power and dominion of that country (II. 23), we must substitute for this king and queen the ruler or rulers of Asshur of whom it is certain that their campaigns reached the east of Iran. We found that so far as we can at present judge from the monuments it was only Shalmanesar II. who received tribute from the Eastern lands, and that the armies of Tiglath Pilesar II. trod the soil of Arachosia (p. 19). If we could assume that the contests of Ninus and Semiramis have taken the place of the achievements of these rulers in the East of Iran, the date of Vistaçpa and Zarathrustra would have to be placed between 860 and 740 B.C. But this supposition is really without any basis.

The more ancient statements of the Greeks carry us much further back than the reasoning of Trogus Pompeius and his successors. If we set Pliny aside, who asserts " that the kind of Magism established by Zoroaster was many years older than that taught by Moses," Hermippus of Smyrna puts Zoroaster 5000 years before the Trojan war. Even before Hermippus, Theopompus of Chios, and Hermodorus, the pupil of Plato, had ascribed the same date to him. Eudoxus of Cnidus, the contemporary of Plato, placed him still higher; he thought that Zoroaster lived 6000 years before the death of Plato. According to Pliny, Aristotle ascribed to him the same antiquity, and, as we learn from Diogenes Laertius, maintained that the Magians were older than the Egyptians. And even in the fifth century B.C., Xanthus the Lydian is said to have

written that from the time when Zoroaster lived to
the march of Xerxes against Hellas a period of 6000
years had elapsed.[1]

Through these statements there runs, beyond all
doubt, a system, the knowledge of which began in the
fifth century B.C. among the Greeks and continued
beyond the time of Alexander. Whether we take
5000 years before the Trojan war, or 6000 years before
Plato's death, we are equally brought back into the
seventh millennium B.C. If the later statements of the
West, which make Zoroaster a contemporary of Ninus
and Semiramis, are the results of combining the most
prominent name in Bactria with the conquest of Bactria by the founder of the Assyrian power, as related
in the Medo-Persian Epos, the fixing of Zoroaster's
date so many thousand years previously must have
been taken by the Greeks from the Persians. In these
dates we seem to be dealing with certain cyclic
periods. We learn from Theopompus of Chios, that
according to the doctrine of the Magians, one of the
two gods Oromazdes and Areimanius would reign and
the other be subject for 3000 years; for another 3000
years they would be in conflict, and one destroy the
works of the other, until at length Areimanius would
succumb and men become happy.[2] From this we
may with certainty conclude that periods of 3000
years were in use among the priests of Iran to denote
certain spaces of time, and that these cycles form the
base of the statements of the older Greeks, if we
can prove the use of such periods in the Avesta or
in the books of the Parsees.

[1] Plin. "H. N." 30, 2. Diogen. Laert. procem. The different read-
ings of 500 years in Suidas and 600 in Diogenes, as compared with
5000 and 6000 in the other MSS., can hardly be maintained against the
uniform evidence of other witnesses.

[2] Plut. "De Isid." c. 47.

In the fragments of the Avesta which have come down to us we find invocations addressed to the " time without beginning," " the time that rules the long periods." [1] But the fact that Yima's reign is fixed at 1000 years shows that the priests of Iran reckoned by long periods, and other expressions in the Avesta (p. 33) prove that triple multiplications were in use,[2] which agrees with the periods given by Theopompus. If, therefore, the Greeks of the fifth and fourth century B.C. relate that Zarathrustra lived about 6000 years before their time, a system must by that time have been current among the priests of Iran in which two cycles of 3000 years were supposed to have elapsed since the time of the prophet, and the third cycle had commenced. A book of the Parsees, the Mainyo-i-Khard, which appears to have been written towards the close of the empire of the Sassanids,[3] tells us that Angromainyu made a compact with Auramazda for 9000 winters, and when these winters were past, Angromainyu would be destroyed, and the creation and all creatures would be as Auramazda had made them.[4] The Bundehesh also speaks of a similar compact, but divides the years in a different manner. All time consists of 12,000 years. In the first 3000 Auramazda reigned alone with the creatures which he had created in an invisible manner ; for the first 3000 of the next 9000 everything went according to the will of Auramazda ; for the second 3000 the will of Auramazda was crossed by that of Angromainyu, but for the last 3000 Angromainyu will be powerless. The Bundehesh goes into yet further detail in these matters : in the first 3000 years the heavenly creation was secure from

---

[1] "Vend." 19, 33 ; Spiegel, "Avesta," 3, 9, 201, 206.
[2] "Ashi Yasht," 17 ; " Vend." 2, 20 ff.
[3] West, "Mainyo-i-Khard," p. x.   [4] West, loc. cit. c. 8.

attack ; in the next 3000 Gayo maretan and the ox,
i. e. the first man and the first bull, came into existence.
After these 6000 years the enemy arose and slew the
first man and the first bull. The reign of Yima is
placed by the Bundehesh in the first millennium of the
new period, but this reign extends only to 716 years,
the first 284 years of the thousand being filled with
creatures prior to Yima. The second millennium of
the period is occupied with the reign of Thraetaona,
Manuschithra, Kava Kavata, Uça, Huçrava, and
Aurvataçpa, and the early part of the reign of Kava
Vistaçpa, whose thirtieth year coincides with the end
of the second millennium.[1] At the beginning of the
third millennium, *i. e.* a thousand years after the death
of Yima, Zarathrustra appears ; and the period of
more successful opposition to the evil spirits begins.
According to the more ancient conception, which may
still be plainly traced in the Avesta, the world began
with the happy age of Yima ; it is owing to later views
formed within priestly circles that earlier creatures
such as the first man and first bull are placed before
this period ; but it will be shown below that these
views existed when the Avesta was written down. A
later book of the Parsees, the Sad-der-Bundehesh, puts
the period of the conflict between the good and evil
deity at 6000 years, and places Zarathrustra exactly
in the middle of it ; he was created 3000 years after
the period of Gayo maretan, and 3000 years before
his own resurrection.[2] Hence it is clear that the
formation of these cycles rose among the priests of
Iran from the necessity of limiting the period of the
old and new law, and of conflict between the good and
evil spirits, and the desire to fix the date of the more

---

[1] Justi, "Bundehesh," c. 1, 3, 34. [Cf. West's commentary on c. 34.]
[2] Spiegel, "Eran," 1, 507.

successful repulse of evil which came in with Zarathrustra. The abbreviation of the period of Yima shows
us that the cycles in the Bundehesh do not throughout
agree with those of the Avesta. But it is sufficient to
establish the fact that periods of 3000 years were in
use, and that Zarathrustra appeared at the beginning
of a new millennium, in order to understand that the
Persians could speak to the Greeks of millenniums in
this sense, and of one or two cycles which had elapsed
since Zarathrustra's time.

The idea and tendency of such a scheme for the
history of the world are easily understood: these
periods of 3000 years, which can be increased or diminished without alteration of the sense, have only a
dogmatic value. We cannot obtain from them any
chronological date for the appearance of Zarathrustra,
nor can we obtain such a date by the attempt to go
back from the chronological statements in recent Parsee
works to the older periods. We may leave unnoticed
the assertion in the book of Arda Viraf that the true
faith had existed in purity for 300 years down to the
time that Alexander came into Iran (p. 50), which would
thus bring Zarathrustra into the seventh century B.C.
The Bundehesh allows 460 years for the reigns of the
Sassanids, 246 for the Askanids, *i.e.* the Arsacids, 16 for
Alexander, before whom come Darai the son of Darai
with 14 years, Darai Chirazatan with 12, Huma (a queen)
with 30, Vohumano with 112, and Vistaçpa with 90,—
all subsequent to the appearance of Zarathrustra.[1] According to this, 996 years elapsed between Zarathrustra
and the fall of the Sassanids, and he would thus, if we
reckon from the battle of Nahavend (640 A.D.), be placed
in the year 356 B.C., in the reign of Artaxerxes Ochus.
But even if we alter the incorrect items in the text of

---

[1] Justi, "Bundehesh," c. 34.

the Bundehesh in accordance with our better knowledge,
we do not arrive at any result which is even apparently
certain. The dominion of the Sassanids, down to the
date of the battle, did not last 460 but only 414 years;
on the other hand, the Arsacids reigned for 476 years,
not for 264.[1] The empire of Alexander, if we add
the reigns of the Seleucidæ to his own, occupied 80
years instead of 14, and if in the place of the 26 years
of the two Darais of the Bundehesh, who represent the
kingdom of the ancient Achæmenids, we put the old
Persian kingdom with 229 years, and add to these
items the numbers given in the Bundehesh for Huma,
Vohumano, and Vistaçpa, after the appearance of
Zarathrustra, which amount to 232 years, Zarathrustra
would have commenced his work 1431 years before the
battle of Nahavend, i. e. in the year 791 B.C. But who
can guarantee that Cyrus, the Persian, overthrew the
empire of the Medes in the year when Huma, the
supposed daughter of Vohumano, died; or that Huma
reigned for 30 years? How could Vohumano, the
grandson of Vistaçpa, and son of Çpentodata (p. 38),
have reigned 112 years, and Vistaçpa himself 90 years
after the appearance of Zarathrustra? Huma is not
merely a doubtful person, she is altogether fictitious.
She is said to have been the mother of Darai Chirazatan, i. e. Darius I., and to have been called Shamirain,
i. e. Semiramis, but her brother was the first Sassan,
the ancestor of the Sassanids. As the later Arabs and
Persians, including Firdousi, are no better informed,[2] we
see clearly that the remembrance of the Achæmenids
had almost entirely died out at the time when these

---

[1] If the rise of Arsaces is put in the year 250 B.C. It makes no
difference in the total if we choose the year 248 B.C. for the beginning
of the Arsacids.

[2] Blau, "Z. D. M. G." 18, 686. Von Gutschmid, ibid.

writings were composed; only the name of Darius remained, and an attempt was made to connect this name with Vistaçpa by two fictitious names, Vohumano, *i. e.* the good spirit, and Huma. Besides Vistaçpa's son Çpentodata (Isfendyar) and Hutaoça, the wife of Vistaçpa, the Avesta mentions a woman, "the pure Huma,"[1] out of whom this queen must have been formed. It is clear that the tradition of the East, like the Avesta, broke off in the generation after Vistaçpa, and that in the Arabian period only the names Darai and Iskander could be placed between Vistaçpa and the Arsacids.

We must attempt to reach the goal by another path. I have already shown what was the condition of the sacred scriptures in Iran at the date of Alexander and the Seleucids (p. 55). Even before Hermippus of Smyrna, Aristotle had taught that the Magians considered that to be the best in the first instance which was first created, and maintained two principles, a good and evil deity, Oromazdes and Areimanius.[2] Theopompus mentioned both these deities and the strife between them, and when he adds that there would one day be a time when the dead would rise again, and men would be immortal and able to withstand everything by their prayers—that after the victory of Oromazdes men would be happy and need no longer any sustenance, and would cast no shadow[3] —it will be seen below how definitely and exactly the doctrine of the Avesta is here reproduced. Hermodorus mentions a series of teachers, who succeeded the first teacher of the Magians, the "Persian Zoroaster," down to the campaign of Alexander of Macedon.[4] With

---

[1] "Farvardin Yasht," 139.
[2] Aristot. "Metaph." 13, 4. Diogen. Laert. prooem.
[3] Theopom. Fragm. 71, 72, ed. Müller.
[4] Diogen. Laert. prooem., cf. Suidas, Μάγοι.

Eudoxus of Cnidus Zoroaster was the founder of the most beneficent wisdom; the pupils of Prodicus claimed to be acquainted with the writings of Zoroaster (p. 53). Plato calls him the son of Oromazdes, and adds that the heir to the throne was instructed in Magism as well as in the duty of being true during the whole of his life.[1] The importance which the Avesta ascribes to truthfulness will become clear hereafter. If the Greeks of the fourth century could speak of Zoroaster as the teacher of the Persians, and put him in the closest relation with Auramazda, if they could repro- duce correctly the names of the good and evil spirits and the main doctrines of the Avesta, it is an inevit- able conclusion that the religion of Zarathrustra must have prevailed in the kingdom of the Achæmenids.

This result is confirmed by all the further informa- tion which we obtain from the Greeks. In Plutarch the last Darius calls on an eunuch, " to tell the truth in reverence for the great light of Mithra"; the eunuch replies that the king has no reason to accuse the evil spirit, and entreats " Lord Oromazdes," " that he may cause the light of the king to shine again."[2] Artaxerxes II. was informed by his mother Parysatis that the Persians had received the law which distinguished good and evil from god. He swears " by Mithra," and Plutarch tells us how some related that when Darius, the eldest son of Artaxerxes, who sought his life, was slain, Artaxerxes went into the court of the palace and cried aloud to the Persians : " Rejoice, ye Persians, and tell it to others, that the great Oro- mazdes has executed judgment on those who imagined crime and wickedness."[3] In Plutarch, Artaxerxes I. says to Themistocles : " May Areimanius ever implant

1 " Alcib. I." p. 121.　　　　2 Plut. " Alex." c. 30.
3 Plut. " Artax." c. 4, 23, 29.

such a disposition in my enemies that they may drive
from themselves their best and bravest men."[1] According to Deinon the Magians prophesied with branches in
their hands, sacrificed under the open sky, and looked
on fire and water as the only symbols of the divinity.[2]
Xenophon represents Cyrus as praising the gods and
sacrificing to them every morning according to the
instructions of the Magians.[3] Though Herodotus does
not mention either the name of Zarathrustra or of
Auramazda, what he says of the rites of the Medes
and Persians agrees exactly with the rules given in the
Avesta. "Temples, images, and altars," he says, "are
not erected by the Persians, because, as it seems to me,
they do not believe like the Hellenes that the gods
have the form and nature of men. They call the
whole circle of heaven Zeus, and offer sacrifice to
him after ascending the summits of mountains. Besides Zeus they have from ancient days sacrificed to
the sun, the moon, the earth, water, winds, and fire,
which among the Persians is a deity :[4] the winds they
also charm by songs. When offering sacrifice they
build no altar and kindle no fire, nor pour libations, nor
make any use of flutes, or cakes, or barley meal. If
any one wishes to offer sacrifice he brings the victim
to an open space, and calls on the god, after crowning
his tiara with branches of myrtle. After cutting the
animal in pieces, and cooking the flesh, he spreads out
the most delicate grass, chiefly trefoil, and lays the
flesh upon it. The Magian who stands by sings the
theogony over it, for such, according to the Persians, is
the nature of the prayer. After some time, the person
who has made the sacrifice carries the flesh away and
uses it for a feast. The Magians, in whose control is

[1] "Themistocl." c. 28.   [2] Dinon, Fragm. 9, ed. Müller.
[3] "Cyri Instit." 8, 1, 21.   [4] Herod. 3, 16.

the worship by sacrifice, make it a great object to kill
ants, serpents, and other creeping winged things : dogs
and men only do they spare. No Persian may pollute
a river, nor even wash in it, nor will they allow any
one else to do so, for they have a great reverence for
rivers. The bodies of the dead may not be burned ; it
is said indeed that the corpse of a Persian cannot be
buried till it has been torn by a dog or a bird, and
among the Magians this is an acknowledged practice.
It is a meritorious act among the Persians to have many
children, and he who can show the most receives gifts
each year from the king. Each man celebrates the day
on which he was born above all other days. What may
not be done, may not be spoken of amongst the Persians:
the most shameful action is lying, and the next to this is
borrowing, for the reason that a man who has debts is
generally compelled to lie. Any one afflicted by the
itch or the leprosy may not come into the cities or mix
with other Persians ; and it is believed that such persons
have sinned against the sun-god. Lepers from foreign
lands are driven out of the country." When Xerxes came
to the Hellespont, and was about to cross the bridge,
Herodotus represents him as praying to the sun-god,
pouring libations from a golden cup, and throwing it
with a golden goblet and a Persian sword into the sea.[1]
We shall see hereafter to what a degree the killing of
noxious animals, the reverence for rivers, the expulsion
of lepers, the delight in life and the increase of life,
the exposing of dead bodies, and singing of the
theogony at sacrifices, correspond to the rules and
doctrines of the Avesta. In one point only is Herodotus mistaken : he states that the Persians worshipped
a female deity called Mithra.

[1] Herod. 1, 101, 131—140 ; 7, 40, 43, 113, 191 ; 3, 84.

From this array of witnesses belonging to the West it follows that the doctrines of the Avesta, and the religion of Zarathrustra, were current among the Persians and in Western Iran at any rate after the beginning of the fifth century B.C., and they must therefore have been in existence in Eastern Iran at a still earlier date. The inscriptions of the Achæmenids prove that the doctrine of the Avesta was maintained among the Persians with even greater clearness and for a period more ancient. Artaxerxes Ochus prays to Auramazda, Anahita, and Mithra for their protection, and in like manner Artaxerxes Mnemon prays to Auramazda and Mithra. In the inscriptions on Mount Behistun, Darius I., the son of Hystaspes, styles Auramazda "the greatest of the gods" (*mathista baganam*). Besides Auramazda, "the rest of the gods" are repeatedly mentioned, and denoted by the name Baga. Of Auramazda, Darius and Xerxes say in their inscriptions : "A great god is Auramazda ; he has created the heaven and the earth ; he has created man and all that is good for men." After crushing in the beginning of his reign the rebellion of nearly all the lands which Cyrus had reduced, Darius repeatedly records his thanks : "that Auramazda had granted him assistance ; that his army had been victorious by the grace of Auramazda." He and his successors acknowledge that they have received their throne and their kingdom from Auramazda ; by his grace they are kings.[1] The reason why Auramazda has assisted him Darius finds in the fact that he has not been a "liar," and has committed no sin. He entreats Auramazda to protect the land against the invasion of hostile armies, against blight, and "the lie" (*dranga*). He asserts that "the

---

[1] Inscription of Darius at Elvend in Spiegel, "Keilinscriften," s. 45, 47.

lie" caused the provinces which had revolted to be rebellious, and declares that the land of Persia, which Auramazda has granted to him, which is beautiful, rich in horses, and well populated, has no fear of enemies owing to Auramazda's grace, and his own. He commends his inscription at Behistun to the protection of his successors, with the words: " If thou destroyest not this tablet then may Auramazda be thy friend ; may thy descendants be numerous, and thy life be long, and whatsoever thou undertakest, may Auramazda cause it to succeed. But if thou destroyest it, may Auramazda smite thee, and thy house perish ; and whatever thou doest, may Auramazda render it of no effect." [1] On his tomb Darius says : " What I have done I have done by the grace of Auramazda. O man, this is the prayer of Auramazda ; think no evil, leave not the right way, sin not." The inscriptions of Xerxes regularly end with the invocation : " May Auramazda protect me, with all the gods ; me, my kingdom, and my work."

As we shall see, the fundamental principle of the religion of Zarathrustra is that a supreme god stands over all gods, and to him is ascribed the work of creation. In entire belief in the power of this supreme deity, whom the Achæmenids invoke by the name which is given to him in the Avesta, "who has created heaven and earth and all that is good for men," Darius ascribes to Auramazda victory in battles, the power of granting or refusing success to the king's undertakings, of protecting the land against hostile invasions, blight, and lies. To those who live according to his commands he grants long life and numerous descendants. The rebellion of the provinces is with Darius the work of the lie, the lie of him who had given

[1] Behistun, 4, 73—80; 56—61; Persep.

himself out to be the son of Cyrus, and the lie of those
who had claimed to be the descendants of Nebuchadnezzar and Cyaxares. We have already observed what
" the lie" meant in the Avesta. In the same spirit—
the spirit of the principal rules of the Avesta—Darius
adjures his Persians to think no evil, and not to leave
the right path.

Nicolaus of Damascus assures us that the Persians
were acquainted with the sayings of Zoroaster. He
and others relate that Cyrus or his father was called
Atradates, i. e. given by fire,[1] and that he had given
to the Areians (p. 11), who provided his famished
army with sustenance, the honourable title of Oro-
sangians, i. e. *Huverezanha* (benefactors). It is in
harmony with the doctrine of the Avesta that Cyrus
should be represented by such a descent or name as the
gift and nursling of fire, and we shall see with what
emphasis the Avesta marks and distinguishes good
thoughts, words, and actions. From these facts and
the inscriptions of Darius there can be no doubt that
Zarathrustra's doctrine was current among the Persians
at the time of Cyrus. But if it was in force in the
West of Iran in the sixth century B. C. the fact that
Herodotus, in his account of the period during which
the Medes obtained the dominion, down to the time of
Cyrus, speaks of no change in religion, either among
the Persians or the Medes, is evidence that this religion existed at any rate before the time of Phraortes.
The statement found in Herodotus that Deioces had
forbidden any one to spit in his presence, reminds
us of the rules of the Avesta, by which no one was
allowed to approach the sacred fire and gods with
uncovered mouth, and on the sculptures of Persepolis
the bearer of the fan stands with covered mouth

---

[1] Strabo, p. 719 ; Nicol. Damasc. fragm. 66, ed. Müller.

beside Darius. The seven walls which Herodotus
represents Deioces as building round Ecbatana, the
seven tribes of the Persians, remind us of the seven
girdles of the earth in the Avesta; the king of the
Persians surrounded by the six tribal princes is the
symbol of Auramazda and the six gods who are about
him.

Hence we may assume that the doctrine of Zarathrustra had reached the West of Iran at the time
when Phraortes united the tribes of the Medes (about
650 B.C.), and was known among the Medes when
they were still living under their tribal chiefs and
paid tribute to Asshur, or, in case of refusal, were attacked by the Assyrian armies, which, as we ascertained
from the inscriptions of the kings of Asshur, was the
case from the time of Tiglath Pilesar II. to the time of
Assurbanipal, *i. e.* from the middle of the eighth to the
middle of the seventh century B.C. A statement in
Herodotus seems to lead us still further back. He
calls the Magians a race or tribe of the Medes. According to his narrative this tribe was in existence
in the time of Deioces, *i. e.* about the year 700 B.C.
Herodotus could only speak of the Magians as a tribe
or family when they had become an hereditary order.
At that time, therefore, there must have been among
the Medes a priesthood who perpetuated in their
families their worship by sacrifice, their doctrine and
wisdom, as well as their social importance. Like
all Greeks, Herodotus ascribes the discharge of the
religious functions among the Persians and Medes to
the Magians, and we find that what Herodotus quotes
of their rites agrees with the rules of the Avesta.
The rise and separation of a peculiar order of priests,
their more or less sharply marked distinction from the
remaining orders, can never be the work of a short

space of time, and such separation can only take place when the worship of the gods requires a knowledge which is not easily accessible or obtainable, when doctrine has obtained a place by the side of belief, when ritual has become developed, and particular duties and rules are prescribed for the life of the priests. When the worship of the gods requires the use of long and definite prayers, the knowledge of complicated usages, on which depends the effect of the sacrifices, and the observation of numerous rules of purification,—such knowledge is only perpetuated in families of hierophants or priests, or in schools which take the place of such families. The formation of a distinct hereditary order on such grounds can hardly have occupied less than a century from the time when the doctrine, on which it is formed, was introduced. Hence we may assume that the doctrine known as Zarathrustra's reached the Medes before the year 750 B.C., *i.e.* before the date of Tiglath Pilesar II. of Assyria.

Let us hold firmly to the facts that the worship of Auramazda was current among the Persians about the middle of the sixth century B.C., that the same worship was in force among the Medes at least a century earlier, about 650 B.C., and that if an hereditary priesthood was in existence about this time among the Medes who performed and conducted the worship, the doctrine which this priesthood represented must have been adopted before the year 750 B.C. In this way we obtain a proof that the doctrine of Zarathrustra was not only in existence in the East of Iran about the year 800 B.C., but was the dominant creed there, and had force enough to penetrate to the West, and win over the neighbouring tribes of the Medes and Persians.

We cannot explain more exactly how the doctrine of

Zarathrustra reached the nations of the West of Iran.
Pliny, it is true, exclaims : " Who knows the Medes,
who were taught by Zoroaster, Apusorus, and Zaratus,
even by hearsay, for no memorials of them are left ?"[1]
According to this the religion of Zoroaster spread
even in the West by the influence of eminent men
among the Medes. But the date of the persons mentioned cannot be fixed, though Porphyry represents
Pythagoras as going to the Chaldæans and Zabratus,
by whom he was purified from the evil of his former
life, and instructed as to the things from which the
disciple should restrain himself, and about the nature
and beginning of all things,[2] and this Zaratus or
Zabratus may be intended for Zarathrustra himself.
Hermodorus tells us that Zarathrustra had been followed by many Magians as teachers, one after the
other, down to the time when Alexander marched
against Persia : these teachers were Osthanes, Astrampsychus, Gobryas, and Pazates.[3] Others also assert
that Zoroaster was followed " by Osthanes and Astrampsychus."[4] Pliny observes that so far as he could
discover, Osthanes who accompanied Xerxes in the
war against the Hellenes, was the first who had written
on the doctrine of the Magians. The second Osthanes,
whom Alexander had received among his followers,
had caused this religion to be of great importance.
From the work of one of these two persons, Philo of
Byblus quotes a passage — the work he calls the
Octateuch—and Pliny notes down apparently some of
the doctrines of the first Osthanes. If then there were
men under the Achæmenids in the West of Iran who
could write on the doctrine of Zarathrustra from the
beginning of the fifth century B.C., we can without

---

[1] Plin. "H. N." 30, 2; 28, 19.   [2] " Vita Pythag." 12.
[3] Diogen. Laert. prooem.   [4] Suidas, Μάγοι.

hesitation believe the statement that long before this time there were prophets and teachers of the doctrine among the Medes and the Persians.

Can we go beyond the result thus gained by our investigation?—that the doctrine of Zoroaster flourished in Eastern Iran about 800 B.C., and advanced towards the West from this period; may we assume that at this date it was already in possession of written monuments, and even that the fragments of the Avesta which still remain were in existence then? We must first answer the question whether the use of writing in Iran, especially in the East, goes back so far.

According to the statements of Herodotus, the West of Iran was not only in possession of the art of writing by the year 700 B.C., but made considerable use of it. He tells us that Deioces required complaints to be sent in to him in writing, and gave out his decisions also in writing. If processes at law were conducted in writing in Media about the year 700 B.C., it cannot be surprising that Herodotus should also inform us that letters passed between Media and Persia about the year 560 B.C.[1] We learn from the Hebrew Scriptures that when Cyrus allowed the Jews, whom Nebuchadnezzar had removed to Babylon, to return to their homes, he gave his permission for the restoration of the temple in writing. This document was afterwards discovered in the archives of Ecbatana.[2] We know it for a fact that Darius I. gave his orders to the satraps in writing, and we are acquainted with the seal of Darius by which they were authenticated. The oldest inscriptions which have come down to us from the Achæmenids, not to mention a seal of Cyrus from Senkereh, belong, if not to Cyrus himself, to Darius, and begin about the last quarter of the sixth century

[1] Herod. 1, 100, 124, 125.   [2] Ezra, c. v., vi.

B.C. It is the cuneiform writing of Assyria and Babylon which forms the basis of the writing in these inscriptions, but with considerable alterations. The highly complicated syllabarium of the Eastern Semites is reduced to a phonetic system; we might almost say to an alphabet of about 40 letters. A change of this kind can hardly have been made at one stroke. If it was after they entered into closer combination with Assyria, *i. e.* after their dependence on the king of Asshur, which began with the accession of Tiglath Pilesar II. (745 B.C.), that the Medes became acquainted with the Assyrian system of writing, this must have been completely mastered before it could be abbreviated and altered, as it was altered by the Medes, whose changes were adopted by the Persians. The cuneiform writing of Western Iran, as we find it in the inscriptions of Darius, can therefore hardly have been established before the year 600 B.C. However this may be, the facts mentioned prove that the writing of the Assyrians in the seventh century B.C. was not unknown in the West of Iran. This would therefore have passed into the East of Iran in its original or simplified form, either at some earlier period, or when the East came under the dominion of the Achæmenids. But it did not, and this is a plain proof that the East, when the cuneiform writing of the West came in that direction, was already in possession of another kind of writing. This Eastern mode of writing, the Arian, which rests on an entirely different basis from the cuneiform, is first known to us from coins and inscriptions of the third century B.C.; but it certainly would not have maintained its ground under the Achæmenids against the writing of the West, and of the rulers, magistrates, and dominant nation, unless it had been in vigorous use before this period. We must therefore assume that the Arian character was in use in the East of Iran a considerable time before the date of Cyrus, and hence we have no reason to deny the existence of it in that region in the eighth century B.C., since we must allow the neighbouring Arians of India to have been in possession of their written characters from the year 800 B.C. at the least (IV. 155).

If we may assume that the Arian character was in use in the East of Iran about the year 800 B.C., the prayers and sayings of Zarathrustra might have been written down about this date, and the doctrine might have passed on to the West supported by written documents. But the fact that the prayers might have been written down is in no way a proof that they were so written.

It is true that at first sight it seems that the part of the law which has come down to us (the Vendidad) leads to the conclusion that it was written down long before the Persians gained the dominion over Iran, and Media became a powerful state under Cyaxares. The book does not mention the name of the Persians or the Medes, of Ecbatana or Persepolis, while Bactria is spoken of as the seat of the empire ; the most westerly district mentioned in the Vendidad is Ragha in Eastern Media.[1] If we add that the book reproaches certain districts in the East, the land of the Arachoti and others, with deviations from the doctrine of Zarathrustra, and that Ragha is indeed Zoroastrian but wavering in its fidelity, we may easily conclude that the Vendidad was written when the doctrine of Zarathrustra had not as yet thoroughly penetrated the East, and was still unknown in the West, when it had just reached, but had not yet completely conquered, the

[1] The Niça of the Vendidad is the Eastern Niça, Parthorum Nisæa, not very far from Merv; above, p. 10, n. 1.

district of Ragha. The Medes were still dependent on
Asshur, living separately according to their tribes, Ecbatana was not yet the centre and metropolis of Media, and
the kingdom of Bactra was still in existence in the East.
This points to a date about 750 B.C. as the time when
this doctrine must have spread widely over Media ; at
any rate to a date before the rise of the Median power,
i. e. before 650 B.C. This conclusion is not, however,
absolutely certain. The silence of the Vendidad and
of the Avesta generally on Ecbatana and Persepolis,
the Medes and the Persians, can be explained in
another though a more artificial manner. The nations
and chief cities of the West were unknown to the
tradition of Eastern Iran, and the royal abodes of the
Medes and Persians were not consecrated by the action
of Zarathrustra. In the accounts given by the Greeks
of the worship of these nations, in spite of much
agreement, points are found at variance with the rules
of the Avesta, and as a fact certain distinctions did
prevail. The doctrine had arisen in the East, and the
priesthood there was in possession of the purer and
more orthodox dogma. If Persia and Media did not
follow this in all respects, it was convenient to be
silent about the differences in the time of the Achæmenids, or if any one desired to brand them, to mark out
the Median Ragha as the seat of heresy, rather than
Pasargadæ or Persepolis. This explanation it is true
is somewhat far fetched. The result that the religion
known by the name of Zarathrustra had reached the
Medes and Persians by the middle of the eighth
century B.C. is in no way weakened by it, though the
assumption that at this period written documents of
this doctrine were in existence, and that the book
of the law of which we have fragments arose in
the first half of the eighth century B.C., is rendered

more doubtful if such a mode of interpretation is admitted.

The forms of language preserved in the Avesta have not survived with sufficient distinctness to assist us in fixing the time at which it was written down. As was shown above (p. 65), the manuscripts date from the later period of the Sassanids; they are written in the later East-Pehlevi character, and at a time when the old forms must have undergone changes owing to the language which had come into use in the mean time, and can in fact be proved to have undergone them. The old sounds are obviously modified and confounded,[1] so that the language of the Avesta, when compared with that of the inscriptions of the Achæmenids, exhibits forms less ancient and fixed, and indeed in some cases it is more recent than the language of the legends of the Græco-Bactrian coins (p. 27). Nor can any certain conclusions be drawn from the condition of political and social life shown in the Avesta. It is only the splendour of regal power in general, the old sacrificers, heroes, and kings that are extolled in it; a sacrificial prayer to Mithra speaks of the abode of the Arians, where "horse-guiding rulers govern noble troops;" for the rest we hear only of lords of villages, of tribes or cantons, and provinces, and of three orders into which the people are divided. The Vendidad, it is true, reckons by winters and nights, not by years and days; the amount of fines and punishments is computed in animals, goats, sheep, oxen, horses, or camels; and these facts point to an ancient period, but they may have been handed down by tradition. We also hear of the value of these animals and of money (shaeta).[2] This is the less surprising as

---

[1] Lepsius, "Ueber das ursprungliche Zendalphabet," Abh. B. Akad. 1862, s. 298, 306, 381.   [2] "Vendid." 4, 120; Astad Yasht, 1.

the Vendidad speaks of palaces and pillars and various
works of art, and mentions smelting-ovens and even
ovens for making glass.   We found that the Greek
princes of Bactria struck square coins, which they
would not have done if this had not been the traditional
form in Bactria (p. 28).   The Achæmenids did not
strike coins of this kind, and this shape must therefore
have come down from a period anterior to them.   The
frequent mention of the physician, on the other hand,
ought not to be regarded as a proof of later composition, for we hear of the physician and his remedies in
ancient poems of the Veda (IV. 35).

In regard to the antiquity of the Avesta, then, we
can only build upon the simple facts that it cannot
have been written down for the first time when the
Buddhists found adherents in Bactria (IV. 542), or
when the kingdom of the Greek princes arose in
Bactria, or when the Seleucidæ and Alexander, before
them, reigned over Iran.   It has been proved that the
Avesta was in existence before Alexander overthrew
the kingdom of the Achæmenids.   The series of the
successors of Zarathrustra, which western writers could
trace backwards from this point—Osthanes II., Pazates,
Gobryas, Osthanes I., Astrampsychus, Apusodorus—
plainly shows that even under the Achæmenids the
West was seriously occupied with religious questions.
As Osthanes I. had written on the doctrine of Zoroaster about the time of Xerxes (p. 92), it is at
least more probable than not that the Avesta was
already in existence at that time.   If in the West
there was a series, and as the Greeks point out, a
continuous series, of priestly teachers, round whom
naturally pupils and schools grew up, and after the
beginning of the fifth century a theological literature,
similar teachers and schools must have existed long

before in the East, and this greatly strengthens the conclusion drawn from the contents of the Vendidad, that
it must have been written down before the rise of the
Medes. But for any more precise determination of the
date of the Avesta between the two limits obtained—the
year 750 B.C., *i. e.* the beginning of the formation of a
priesthood in the West and the contemporary use of
writing in the East, and the year 350 B.C.—we are
confined wholly to internal evidence.

Scriptures of such extent as the Avesta is shown to
have been, by the accounts of the Greeks and Arabs,
and the list of contents (p. 51), and the existing
fragments, could not have been written down at once
or within a brief space of time. We saw (p. 33)
that it set up a religious canon, which not only regulated the doctrine and the worship, the duties of priests
and laity, but also comprised the law, and in a word all
the relations of life. A codification of this kind is
only possible when belief and doctrine, culture and
ritual, have arrived at fixed and complete formulæ,
have been arranged in a system and developed, and
the consequences bearing on life, morality, and law
have been drawn from them by an active and influential priesthood. Hence before the Avesta was written
down and collected there must have been a priestly
order in the East, in the circles of which the doctrine
and practice went through this developing, revising,
and fixing process. Various sketches, lists of prayers
for certain offerings, collections of rules belonging to
this or that priesthood or school, must have been in
existence, and combinations of the traditional material
must have been made, before a canon comprising the
whole wisdom of the priests, and far exceeding in
extent the law of Manu, could have been compiled.

Among the existing invocations of the Avesta we

find sacrificial prayers of a primitive character; but
the greater part of the prayers and thanksgivings are
without religious feeling or poetical power, and very
far removed from the richness and abundance, the
beauty and freshness of conception, which streams
through the majority of the hymns of the Veda.
There are not wanting *naïve* and poetical pieces which
have obviously been handed down and preserved by
their use at sacrifices, but these are frequently spoiled
by later interpolations, and the form of the whole is
generally dry and prosaic. We find but scanty relics
of any vigorous conception of the gods, of a living
mythology; on the whole the mythical element is faded,
and the sacrifice of animals thrown into the background.
The greater part of the prayers receive their value
from a certain system and completeness; the object is
to bring forward all the characteristics of the deity to
which they are addressed, and to invoke him by all
his names. Thus laudations and epithets are repeated
without end. A good many of the prayers are mere
nomenclatures, and repeat the same forms in varying
order. Besides this tendency, which is far removed
from the original simplicity of religious meditation, a
value is ascribed to the repetition of certain prayers.
Some are to be said a hundred, or a thousand times.
In the same way the liturgies are long and full of
detail, and sometimes take the form of responses
between the celebrant and the ministering priest;
they are extremely careful to neglect none of the
heavenly spirits or genii, or to injure them by omission,
or treat them with less respect than others.

Beside the faded colours of the mythology, the
decreasing importance of animal sacrifice, and the
formalism of the prayers, we observe in the five
Gathas, the invocations which alone have preserved the

verse-measure, and present older forms of language
than the rest, a tendency to speculation. Not only
are the good and evil spirits combined under one head,
as is always the case in the Avesta, but the Gathas
attempt to resolve the contrast of the beneficial and
harmful sides of nature, of the good and evil spirits,
into the reciprocal play of two fundamental forces ;
they identify the prosperity and destruction of nature
with moral good and evil, and combine the one with
truth, the other with falsehood. The good spirits are
the truth, the evil are the lie. The life of appearance
and of falsehood is distinguished from the true life,
and the service of truth promises life not in this world
only but in the next. It is in harmony with these
tendencies to abstraction that, according to other passages of the Avesta, heaven is filled with a multitude
of the most lifeless personifications of ideas and real-
ities. Could the doctrine of a new religion in an
early period come forward with such a spiritualised
system, with such elevated moral demands, such abstract conceptions ? Could prayers of such a kind
have been composed or written down in a primitive
age ?

The existing fragment of the book of the law is
composed in the form of a dialogue, and is for the
most part filled with conversations which Zarathrustra
carries on with Auramazda. Zarathrustra inquires
what is to be done in certain cases against the evil
spirits, the Daevas, on the commission of certain sins
and impurities. What must be done when a woman is
in labour, etc., or when any one has made himself impure
by touching a corpse, or has slain a water-dog (otter) ?
Is the rain impure which has fallen on a corpse and
then runs off from it, etc. ? These questions Auramazda answers very precisely, and when it is a matter

for expiation and purification, he fixes the number of stripes with the horse-whip or the whip of the sacred Çraosha (Çraosha-charana) which the penitent is to receive. It is a theory and practice of purity, on a level with the analogous rules in the laws of Manu, and in some points even more subtle and casuistical. The offences have already been brought under definite categories, and in like manner the purifications and punishments fall into a number of distinct classes. Not only are expiations required for all sins and prescribed down to the minutest details, but the offences must also be repented of; certain formulæ of confession and repentance are prescribed.

We need not stop to prove that a book of laws in this form could not have been written down *à priori*. The rules for punishment and purification must have grown up in long practice, before they could be put in the mouth of the deity; difficulties and doubts must have been weighed before solutions could be proposed. The book contains the dialogues and inquiries which were held in the schools of the priests on questions of this kind, the practice which prevailed in the schools and the catechisation of the pupils. The answer is naturally placed in the mouth of Auramazda, for it was the answer which he once gave to the question when asked by Zarathrustra. The fragments of the Vendidad are a catechism, the result of the labour of the priestly schools, a system of rules and regulations which marks and postulates the same stage of development for Iran as was reached for the Indians on the Ganges by the law of Manu. Many periods in the religious life must have been passed through before the religious consciousness was no longer shocked by the fact that the supreme deity in person answered petty questions of ritual, and dictated in the most exact gradation and with regard to every possible variety of circumstance, the number of stripes required for the criminals.

This faded mythology and formalised worship, these speculative attempts and casuistry of law, are accompanied by a completely-arranged scheme of certain abstract categories already established. Throughout the whole Avesta runs the division between this world and the next, between the corporeal and incorporeal world, truth and falsehood, and the triple distinction of thinking, speaking, and acting, of thought, word, and deed. And when we further consider that rewards are attached to the reading of sections of the Avesta, that the "long study" of the "thoughts of the pure man," "the excellent knowledge, thought, and conception" are praised and invoked as divine powers, no one will be inclined to see in the Avesta the product of *naïve* religious feeling, or the deposit of a priestly civilisation which is as yet in its early stages.

Still, if we wish to avoid making any false steps in the conclusions to be drawn from the nature of the Avesta about the time of its composition, we must bear in mind that it contains some conceptions which are the exact opposite of the characteristics just noticed. The myth of Yima, the form of Mithra, the descent of plants, prove older traits in the Avesta than we find in the Veda; the old gods still occupy a large space beside Auramazda and the abstract forms of heaven, and strict unity of system is not yet attained. We must remember also at what an early date the neighbours of Eastern Iran, the Arians of India, arrived at meditation and abstraction; how quickly and entirely they allowed animal sacrifice to pass into the background; with what breadth and detail they developed the rules for purification; how numerous were the daily prayers and repetitions, before the religious feeling became weakened. In the Avesta the time without limit is frequently invoked; among the Indians the gods of light are even in the oldest hymns of the Veda the sons of Aditi, *i. e.* of the Eternal or the Infinite. And if the attitude of the Avesta is for the most part by far more flat and prosaic than that of the Veda, the Arians of Iran were of a more logical nature, and the glow of imagination which the land of the Ganges kindled in their kindred tribes did not exist in Iran. For this reason the consideration of the character of the Avesta can only lead us to the result that a period of several centuries must have elapsed between the rise of the religion named after Zarathrustra and the writing down of the Avesta; that lists of prayers and rubrics must have been in existence about the year 800 B.C.; that the extensive books which then formed the Avesta may have been written in the first half of the period, which we ascribed to them, extending from 750 to 350 B.C. In any case we can maintain that the Gathas were composed, and that the Avesta existed in its essential parts in the East of Iran, before Cyrus put the empire of the Persians in the place of the empire of the Medes, and all the various parts were collected together before the "Enlightened" began to preach on the Ganges, *i. e.* about the year 600 B.C.

We have already remarked the importance which the Achæmenids ascribed to the possession of Bactria (p. 23); and we were able at any rate to guess at the civilisation of that district about the year 500 B.C., from the amount of the tribute imposed upon it by Darius. That the economic civilisation was not behind the material was shown by indications in the Avesta. The kingdom which grew up there, as we saw (p. 47), long before the days of the Medes, and in which about

the year 800 B.C. the doctrine of Zarathrustra was
current, succumbed to Cyrus, the great founder of the
Persian empire. If we place the beginning of the doctrine of Zarathrustra, which first made its appearance
there, before the middle of the ninth century B.C., at
which time the armies of Shalmanesar II. reached the
East of Iran, and assume that it came forward about
1000 B.C., we shall hardly place its rise too high. We
remember that about this time occurred the great
change in the religious conceptions of the Arians in
India, the repression and degradation of the old gods
by Brahman. It was an analogous development when
the good and evil spirits of Bactria were combined into
unities, and placed under leaders, when the chief of
the deities of light was made the creator of the heaven
and the earth, and surrounded with abstract forms,
which contest the traditional place and honour of the
old god. It is the same religious impulse, the desire
to grasp the unity of the divine nature, the same line
of combination that we observed in its beginning and
progress in India, which comes to the surface in the
doctrine of Zarathrustra. We have no reason to contest with the Avesta the fact that Vistaçpa ruled over
Bactria when this change took place, or that Zarathrustra, a man of the race of Haechataçpa, gave the
impulse to the reform, and that the leading idea in it
belongs to him. If Vistaçpa ruled over Bactria about
the year 1000 B.C. the growth of the Bactrian monarchy
must be placed at least a century before this time, i. e.
about the year 1100 B.C.

CHAPTER V.

THE examination of the traditions of the East and West has simply led to the confirmation of the result, which we gain from the Avesta—that the name and the doctrine of Zarathrustra belong to Bactria. With regard to the antiquity of the doctrine, the inscriptions of Darius and the statements of the Greeks allowed us to draw the conclusion that it became current and dominant in Bactria about the year 800 B.C. ; and from the analogy of the development of the Arians on both sides of the Ganges we assumed that it was possible to place the date of Zarathrustra himself about two centuries earlier. That the Arians of Iran were not without gods and religious worship before Zarathrustra, if the fact needed proof, might be shown from the statements in the Avesta regarding the time previous to Zarathrustra. The examination of the legends of this time established kindred forms and traits in the Avesta and the Veda, and if, following this path further, we find in the Avesta views of the nature and character of the gods corresponding to those of the Veda, we might be confident in regarding them as the traditional possession of the Arians, and their earliest forms of religion. If, in fine, the coincidence of the Avesta with the Veda, on the one hand,

and with the accounts of the Greeks on the other, extended to all the essential points in the doctrine and the law, the question stated above—whether in the restoration of the canon of the sacred writings in the midst of the fourth century of our era, under king Shapur II., the Avesta underwent material alterations, would have to be answered in the negative.

The poems of the Veda showed us in what directions the religious feeling of the Indians in the Panjab moved. Drought, gloom, and night were numbered among the injurious forces; the clear sky, the light, and fertilising water were beneficent. The high spirits of light, which gave new courage to the heart each morning, and exhibited the world in fresh brilliance, were praised with thanksgivings; the spirits of the highest heaven, Mitra and Varuna, the guardians of the world, the protectors of purity and justice, were invoked earnestly, but less frequently than the warlike victorious god who gave water, the god of storm and tempest, who defeated the demons which obscured the sky and wished to carry away the water (IV. 48). His comrades in the fight were the morning wind which drove away the clouds of night, the winds which shattered the gloomy clouds, and swept them from the sky. The spirit of fire, who by his brilliant glow in the darkness of night kept off the beasts of prey and fiends, who gathered men round the hearth, and summoned the gods to the sacrifice, and carried up to them the food of the sacrifice, received zealous worship in the hymns of the Veda.

We can call to mind the invocations of the Rigveda to Ushas, the goddess of the dawn, who drives forth on the sky with red cows; to Surya and Savitar, the spirits of the sun (IV. 45, 46). In the Avesta, prayers are addressed to Ushahina and Hvare Kshaeta, the

bright sun-god. Ushahina is here the pure spirit of
the celestial dawn, "who is possessed of bright horses."
Of the sun-god we are told: "Mount, bright sun, with
thy swift horses, and shine for all creatures on the way
which Auramazda has created in the air, the way rich
in water which the gods have created;"[1] just as in the
Veda the sun is invoked to approach on his ancient
firm paths in the air, which are free from dust (IV. 46).
Sacrifice is offered to the sun, according to the Avesta,
when he rises above Hara berezaiti (the divine mountain).[2] The prayer to Mithra is as follows: "To the
mighty Yazata (i. e. the worthy of prayer), the strong
one, who brings good, will I offer sacrifice with libations; I will encompass him with songs of thanks-
giving. With libations we offer sacrifice to Mithra,
the lord of wide pastures, who speaketh true things, the
wise one, comely in shape, of a thousand ears and ten
thousand eyes, standing on a broad tower, strong, sleep-
less, and watchful, who mounts above Hara berezaiti
before the immortal sun, the guider of horses—he who
first in a form of gold ascends the beautiful summits.
For him the creator Auramazda has prepared a dwelling above Hara berezaiti, where is neither night, nor
darkness, nor winds chilling nor scorching, nor the corruption of the slain; no filth created of demons nor
vapours ascend Hara berezaiti. From thence the giver
of good beholds the abode of the Arians, whose horse-
guiding lords govern splendid hosts, whose high mountains, rich in water and in pastures, supply nourishment
for the ox, where are deep lakes with broad streams,
and wide navigable rivers burst forth in tumult, on
Iskata and Pourata,[3] on Mouru (Merv), Haraeva

---

[1] "Gah Ushahin," 5; "Mihr Yasht," 13, 143.

[2] "Mihr Yasht," 118.

[3] Pouruta may be referred to the Παρυηται of Ptolemy, whom he
places in the north of Arachosia.

(p. 11), and Gao, Çughdha (Sogdiana), and Hvairiza (Choaresm). Where first they sacrifice to him, there Mithra, the lord of wide pastures, descends with the victorious wind. From anguish and pain, O Mithra, carry us, undeceived. Come to us for our protection; come to us with joy; come to us with mercy; come to us with healing; come to us with purification, the mighty, the strong, the all-knowing, the tamer of dragons, the undeceived. Never lulled to sleep, Mithra protects with his weapon the creatures of Auramazda. On him the lord of the land, of the canton, the village, the house, calls for help with uplifted hands, whose voice of woe, whether his voice be loud or soft, reaches up to the stars and down to the earth. He to whom Mithra is favourable, to him he cometh with aid; but with whomsoever he is angry he destroys his house and village and canton and land, and the glory of the land. Mithra gives swift horses to those who do not deceive him; to the habitation in which he is satisfied he gives troops of cattle and men. The fire of Auramazda gives the straightest path to those who do not deceive Mithra. But if the lord of the house, the village, the canton, the land deceives him, then Mithra in anger destroys house and village, canton and land. Not all evil deeds, not all deception, are seen by Mithra, saith the wicked man. But Mithra sees all that is between heaven and earth. With ten thousand eyes he beholds the man who hates and deceives him. His long arms with the might of Mithra grasp what is in Eastern India (Hendu), and what is in Western, and what is in the midst of this earth. The swiftest deceivers of Mithra do not reach the goal; they do not escape on horseback, nor reach the goal in chariots.

" Mithra, the lord of lands, whose countenance beams like the star Tistrya, travels forth to the right end of

the earth from the brilliant Garonmana (the abode of
the gods), equipped with golden helmet, and silver
coat of mail, with sharp long-shafted lance and swing-
ing arrow, on a beautiful chariot with a golden wheel
and silver spokes, which four white horses draw, their
fore-hoofs shod with gold, their hinder hoofs with
silver, harnessed in the yoke which is bent over them.
In his hand is a club with a hundred studs, and a hundred blades, heavy at the end, making havoc of men;
bound with brass on the handle, mighty and golden,
the strongest and most victorious of weapons.   Before
him goes Verethraghna in the form of a boar, sharp of
tusk, fat, enraged, striking at once with feet, claws, tail,
and back of brass.[1] Next to him goes the kindled fire,
the strong, royal grace. As a protection of the chariot
are a thousand bows of bone, whose strings are made
of the sinews of oxen, a thousand arrows plumed with
feathers of the Kahrkaça, with golden points and
wooden shafts, and flakes of bone and iron, a thousand lances with sharp points, a thousand missiles of
copper, a thousand two-edged swords. Strong as spirits
they travel onward, strong as spirits they fall on the
skulls of the Daevas.

"Before him of a truth, Angromainyu (the evil
spirit) trembles, the deadly one; before him trembles
Aeshma, the wicked-minded, and body-destroying;
before him trembles Bushyançta, the long of hand,
and all invisible Daevas and the sinners from Varena.
When the evil one, who works wickedness, runs forth
with swift step, Mithra, the lord of wide pastures,
swiftly harnesses his chariot, and Çraosha, the pure
and strong, and Nairyoçangha, the herald, beats him
and his ranks. When Mithra comes where the lands

[1] Cf. "Mihr Yasht," 127, where the boar is not Verethraghna but
the "curse of the sage."

are against him (*i. e.* do not honour him) he brings down his club on horse and rider. Against them he brings mighty destruction and terror; he bears away the heads of the men who deceive Mithra. Their arrows, swift-feathered, sent swiftly forth by the string from the well-stretched bow, strike the air only; the lances, sharp and running out with long shafts from the arm, strike the air only; the missiles from the strings strike the air only; the well-directed swords and well-slung clubs beat the air only; meanwhile, angry, enraged, and not propitiated, Mithra approaches, the lord of wide pastures. Thou, O Mithra, angry and mighty, takest the force from their arms; thou takest the force from their arms, and the sight from their eyes, and the hearing from their ears. The wind carries away the lances which the opponents of Mithra throw; even though he throws well and hits the body he inflicts no wound. Standing on the field of battle Mithra annihilates the ranks; the wings quake, and he makes the centre to tremble. They say: Our war-horses were led away by Mithra; by him were our strong arms and swords annihilated. Mithra scares men before and behind; Çraosha, the pure, assists in slaying on all sides. Mithra sweeps them away, slaying them by fifties and by hundreds; by hundreds and by thousands; by thousands and tens of thousands, and without number. We cannot sustain the weight of the angry lord who with the force of a thousand meets the foe; who dashes on in his rage, and rests not from the slaughter; who destroys all at a blow. May not the mightiest, the swiftest, the most victorious of the Yazatas fall upon us. Come to our help, O Mithra, high lord, when the arrow hisses aloud and the horse neighs in his nostrils, and the missiles whizz, and the strings speed forth the sharp, bony arrows. Whomsoever

Mithra protects, him the well-sharpened lance cannot reach, nor the arrow flying past him.

"In his might Mithra approaches; in power he goes forth to dominion, and beholding from afar directs his glance with his eyes. Thou protectest the lands which seek after the beneficence of Mithra, lord of wide pastures; thou destroyest the lands which are wicked. O Mithra, lord of wide pastures, master of the house, of the villages, the land!—let us be protectors of thy fields, not the destroyers of them. As the sun arises above Hara berezaiti so may I obtain my desires over the evil Angromainyu. With uplifted arms, Mithra, the lord of wide pastures, conveys us to immortality. With sacrifice named by name, with becoming speech, O strong Mithra, will I make offerings to thee with libations. Listen, O Mithra, to our sacrifice. Come to our sacrifice; come to our libations. Carry them away to the place of meeting (*chinvat*); deposit them in Garonmana. Thou, O Mithra, art the saviour and helper of lands and men. Thou makest the dwellings, from which impurity is removed, famous for women and chariots. Thou hast power over the peace and the disquiet of lands; prosperous art thou in the battle, and strong. Give us the gifts for which we entreat thee; abundance and power, prosperity and purity, renown and bravery, and victory given by Ahura, the overwhelming power of the highest purity (*asha vahista*), and instruction in the sacred word, that so we may slay all enemies and haters, and annihilate the hate of men and Daevas, of magicians and Pairikas, of the violent, blind, and deaf. Stretch out thy widely grasping hand, O Mithra; thou art the protector of the dwelling, and of them that deceive not. Protect us in both worlds, the corporeal and incorporeal, from the evil death, the evil Aeshma, the evil hosts, who seek to raise their cruel banners, from the attacks which Aeshma may make with Vidhatu the Daeva-created."[1]

The modern traits which have been introduced into this poem are easily distinguished and removed. The relation in which Mithra is placed to Auramazda, the chief of the good spirits, to the corporeal and incorporeal world and the maintenance of the law, to Rashnu, the spirit of justice, and other spirits of an abstract nature, and to the instruction in the sacred word, are like the " Western and Eastern India," obviously of the later origin. Setting them aside, the old form of the god of light of the Arians in Iran meets us in vigorous and powerful outlines. Indeed we have here more original conceptions of Mithra than in the Veda, and find that idea of the god which formed part of the yet undivided stock of the Arians in Iran and on the Indus (IV. 51). In the Avesta Mithra is still in direct conflict with the evil spirits, from which in the Veda he is displaced by the storm-god, who first came into prominence in the Panjab. That Mithra was once the supreme deity of the Arians of Iran, is clear, not only from his position as the most victorious opponent of the demons, but also from the difficulty—which the Avesta betrays in more than one passage—of subordin- ating him to Auramazda, who subsequently became supreme, and establishing the precedence of the latter. In Mithra's habitation it is never night. Highest of the spirits of light, he goes before the sun, and first plants himself on the summits of the mountains. He is the mightiest warrior against night and the spirits of night who tremble before him. His light overpowers and destroys them. Thus he is able to give victory in the battle to the army which worships him in

[1] Windischmann, " Mithra ; Abhl. für Kunde des Morgenlandes," 1, 1 ff.

truth; the host with which he fights he fills with
courage and power; that with which he is angry he
fills with terror, and causes their arrows to fly forth
in vain. In brilliant armour he travels onward, his
club in his hand; before him is victory, and beside
him is fire. Mithra's club is called Vazra, Indra's club
is Vajra; the word is the same, the distinction is due to
the change of sound which separates the old Bactrian
from the language of the Veda and Sanskrit.[1] Lord
of the lands and nations, he looks down on the abode
of the Arians; most brilliant of deities, he sees all
that is between heaven and earth. He cannot be
deceived and beguiled; the most secret wickedness is
not hidden from him; the swiftest criminal does not
escape from him, and the strongest succumbs to his
anger. God of purity and truth, he watches over
purity and truth among men, punishes falsehood,
rewards justice and fidelity; he blesses the nations and
houses which worship him with goodly increase in
men and flocks.

We saw what importance the Veda ascribed to the
conquest over Vritra, the cloud serpent, the black
demon. The Arians in Iran also are acquainted with
the slaying of Vritra. The prayer to Mithra represents
Verethraghna as going before Mithra's victorious car
(p. 110). Verethraghna means slayer of Verethra, or
Vritra, and is the same word as Vritrahan. Hence
the attribute of Indra, which denotes the most important achievement among his actions, is among the
Iranians an independent spirit. As the club of Indra
belongs in the Avesta to Mithra, so is Verethraghna
his companion. No doubt at one time Mithra had himself the surname Verethraghna in Iran, the attribute

---

[1] Haug. "Essays," p. 185. The Sassanids also carry the club now
called *guzr*.

ignifying the conqueror of the worst and strongest of
the evil spirits. But just as in the Panjab, owing to
the tropical storms of that region, the form of Vritra
came into prominence, and with it the form of Indra,
so in the Avesta did Verethraghna fade away when
separated from Mithra. Here Verethraghna is only
the victorious strength, the conquest and slaughter
of the enemy,—victory itself. Verethraghna is the
best armed of the heavenly spirits, the strongest in
might, the most victorious. Yet even in the Avesta
the Soma is offered to Verethraghna before the battle,
as in the Veda it is offered to Indra. Auramazda
says to Zarathrustra : "When the armies meet in
battle, the orderly ranks are not defeated in which
sacrifice is liberally offered to Verethraghna, whom
Ahura created. The Arian lands should offer him
sacrifice, and strew sacrificial branches for him. They
should offer beasts to him, bright and gold-coloured."
"To him the pure Zarathrustra offered sacrifice, and
Verethraghna came to him in the form of a strong
wind, in the form of a beautiful bull with golden ears
and golden hoofs, in the form of a shining horse, of
a large, biting, and fierce camel, in the form of a boar
with strong tusks (as also in the prayer to Mithra), in
the form of a youth, in the form of a man carrying a
sword with a golden handle, in the form of the swiftest and largest of birds, in the form of a ram, and a
fighting goat. And Verethraghna gave Zarathrustra
strength of arms, health and vigour of body, and
power of vision, like that of the horse which sees
in the night, and the gold-coloured vulture." In the
battle Verethraghna hastens through the ranks and
inquires with Mithra and Rashnu : "Who lies against
Mithra ? to whom shall I give death and destruction,
for I have the power ?" "Verethraghna, the created of

Ahura, the bearer of splendour, I will praise"—such is a prayer in the Avesta—"with audible praise, with offering. To Verethraghna will I sacrifice. I will bring Haoma in order that I may conquer this army, which comes up behind me. Verethraghna holds back the hands of the ranks of the men who lie against Mithra; he veils their sight, and dulls their ears, and suffers not their feet to advance. Verethraghna brings the ranks together in battle; he destroys the ranks, and annihilates them."[1]

In the Veda, the winds, the swift and strong Maruts, aided Indra against the demons; Vayu, i.e. the blowing, the morning wind which chases away the dark clouds, was Indra's charioteer (IV. 49). In the Avesta also, Vayu, who blows before the morning light and the sun, and scares away the goblins of the night, who first drinks "the Soma draught at the morning sacrifice," takes a prominent position, and under his Vedic name. The heroes of ancient days cried aloud to Vayu for victory, and he brought help to them all. He is the strongest of the strong, the swiftest of the swift, girded up and active, higher in stature, broader in the hips and shoulders, than the rest of the gods. He sits on a golden throne (p. 35); wears a golden helmet, golden armour, a girdle and neckband of gold, and rides on a golden chariot. He says to Zarathrustra: "I am called the beneficent, because I do good for Auramazda. I am called the pure, the strong-winged, the mightiest, the swiftest, the powerful for defeat, the expeller of the Daevas. I am called the Hurling one, the Biting one, the sharp lance, the flashing lance. I am called the Conqueror. These names must thou invoke at the shock of the

---

[1] "Yasht Bahram," 57—62. Burnouf, "Commentaire sur le Yaçna," p. 285.

ranks in battle, in the stress of the conflict."[1]   In the
Avesta, as we saw, Verethragna also appears in the
form of the wind.   The "pure swift winds," the air,
"which works on high, which purifies the heaven
from the right·hand," are frequently invoked; the
"strong wind, created by Ahura," brings the rain-
clouds which Tistrya (p. 120) has liberated over the
earth; the wind carries away the lances, which those
hurl who are hostile to Mithra.   We saw above, how
the Bactrians were defeated by Artaxerxes I., "because
the wind blew in their faces" (p. 25).   If in the
Avesta, in accordance with the character of the
doctrine, the purifying force of the winds and fresh
air is made prominent, the other traits quoted are
sufficient to permit us to recognise the original conception formed by the Iranians of the spirits of the winds.

The pure waters, the well-flowing, the waters of the
springs, pools, and rivers are often mentioned in the
Avesta and highly extolled.   As with the Arians in
India, so in the Avesta, the great waters are placed high
up in the sky.   The stars contain the seed of water; just
as among the Arians in India certain constellations at the
appearance of which rain fell, were considered to be the
home of the waters.   In the Avesta also the water of
the sky is the source and origin of the waters on earth.
In that book a female deity is the guardian of these
waters, the goddess Ardviçura Anahita, i. e. the lofty,
stainless one, "to whom Auramazda gave the waters in
charge."   She is at one and the same time the source
of the heavenly water, which springs up on the golden
height of Hukairya, the summit of the divine mountain, and the spirit of this source and of the water
coming from it.   At the height of a thousand men,
the spring Ardviçura flows down from the golden

[1] "Ram Yasht," 43—57.

Hukairya ; it has a thousand basins, and a thousand
streams, each stream is forty days' journey in length
for an active traveller.[1] The goddess who pours out this
water is a strong, well-grown maiden of brilliant countenance, and beautiful arms, which are more brilliant
and larger than horses. On her brow she bears a
golden diadem, adorned with a hundred stars ; she has
golden ear-rings and neck-band, a flowing lower garment
with many folds of gold, and golden shoes on her feet.
Her breasts fall down over her girdle ; her upper robe
is of bright otter skins, *i. e.* of the smooth skins of the
animal of the water. She carries a golden Paitidana,
and holds the reins of her chariot which is drawn by
four white beasts of draught. The deity of the water
of the sky is in the Avesta the most beneficent of the
goddesses ; the source of water is also the source of
fruitfulness and life. She cleanses the seed of men,
and gives a happy delivery to women ; those who are
with child entreat her assistance. To men she gives
swift horses and strong comrades, if duly invoked and
worshipped. We have already seen how the heroes
of old days, Yima, Thraetaona, Kereçaçpa, Kava Uça,
Kava Huçrava, Vistaçpa, sacrificed horses, cows, and
smaller cattle to Ardviçura, in order to win victory
over the evil spirits, the dragons, the giants, and the
enemies of Iran (p. 32, 34 ff.). Zarathrustra asks the
stainless Ardviçura what sacrifice he must offer to her,
in order that Auramazda may not hold back his course
in the height above the sun, that serpents may not
injure the water by their sweat and poison. And
Ardviçura gave command that prayer and sacrifice
should be offered to her from the ascent of the sun till
daybreak ; the sacrifice was to be consumed by the
sacrificers and priests in honour of the goddess ; the

---

[1] "Aban Yasht," 64 ff. ; "Yaçna," 74.

impure, blind, dumb, and all afflicted with infirmities
were to be kept far from it. "Come to me, come down,
Ardviçura," is the invocation, "from the stars to the
earth which Auramazda made ; to thee, the excellent,
mighty lords of the lands, the sons of the lords of the
lands, will offer sacrifice." [1]

The divine mountain, on which the Ardviçura rises,
is in the Avesta "the mighty navel of water (*apam
napat*)," "in a course swift as the horse, Auramazda
causes the water to stream forth from it." On this
mountain is the deep lake Vourukasha, *i.e.* having
wide shores, in which the waters collect together. Out
of this lake the water-clouds rise, which are to bring
the fertilising rain to the earth. Though the tropic
storms are wanting in Iran, the fertilising of the land
by the water of the springs, rivers, and lakes, and by
rain was of no less importance there than in the Panjab.
Hence in the Avesta we again meet with the contest
of the good spirits against Vritra, and in Iran also
these spirits are opposed to the demons of blight. It
is demons of this kind, which, according to the Avesta,
keep back the rain-clouds above Vourukasha, and men

---

[1] Haug, "Essays," p. 179. The passages given in the text from the
Aban Yasht, notwithstanding the swelling breasts, shows how definitely
the form of Anahita belongs to the Iranian conception, how peculiarly
this goddess of fountains is represented in this form, and how intimately
connected she is with the whole Iranian system of the boon of water,
and the legends of the heroes. A brass tablet found at Grächwyl in
the canton of Berne, which exhibits the Persian Artemis with swelling
breasts, surrounded by four lions, with a bird of prey on her head and
serpents instead of ears, and wings on the shoulders, has decided J.
Stickel ("De monumento Graechwyliano") to regard the Persian
Artemis as identical with the Semitic goddess of birth. This tablet is
due to the syncretism of Roman times. Certain similarities between
the Syrian goddess of birth and fertility, Mylitta-Derceto, and the
Persian goddess of water, might lead to such a syncretism even under
the Achæmenids, and this coincidence might determine Artaxerxes
Mnemon to erect images of Anahita in Ecbatana and Susa after the
pattern of the Semites. Beros. fragm., 16 ed. Müller, and below.

say : " When will Tistrya (Sirius) rise, the bright, the
majestic, the lord of the stars ? When will the streams
of water flow which are stronger than horses ? " " And
Tistrya, whom Angromainyu slays not, nor the magicians and Pairikas, nor the magicians among men,
gleams forth from the navel of the waters ; he runs to
Lake Vourukasha like an arrow, in the form of a horse,
a beautiful brilliant horse, with yellow ears, and
golden horse-cloth. Auramazda and Mithra prepare
the way for him. Ashi vanguhi and Parendi follow in
his wake with swift chariots. There goes to meet him
the Daeva Apaosha, *i. e.* the witherer, in the form of a
black, bald horse, with bald ears, bald back and tail,
and ugly brand. For three days and three nights
they struggle ; and the Daeva Apaosha scares away
the brilliant Tistrya from Lake Vourukasha for the
distance of a *Hathra*. And Tistrya speaks and says :
" If men honour me with the sacrifice named by name,
with duly performed sacrifice, and prayer, then at the
appointed time I shall come to the pure men ; hostile
chariots and uplifted banners will not come nigh to the
Arian lands, and I shall have gained the strength of
ten horses, ten bulls, ten mountains, and ten flowing
waters." And Auramazda sacrificed to Tistrya and
brought him that strength, and Tistrya fought with
the Daeva Apaosha till midday, and conquered and
overpowered him, and scared him away from Vourukasha. And Tistrya announced blessing for the waters
and the trees ; the streams of the waters will come
to you without opposition, the cloud rises out of
Lake Vourukasha, and the vapours gather above on
Mount Hendava in the midst of Lake Vourukasha, and
Tistrya drives forth the vapours, the pure ones, whence
clouds are formed, and the strong wind drives clouds
and rain to the villages and hamlets, to the seven

Kareshvare (the seven parts of the earth). And Aura-mazda gave command to Zarathrustra that the Arian lands should offer sacrifice to Tistrya, should sprinkle sacrificial rice, and sacrifice a bright, light-hued, Haoma-coloured animal in order that he might withstand the Pairika Dushyairya (*i. e.* blight). "If I had not created Tistrya," Auramazda says, "this Pairika would have carried on war day and night, but Tistrya binds her with two and three fetters." "We praise Tistrya, the brilliant majestic star, which drives away the Pairika ; he blows her away from Lake Vourukasha ; then the clouds draw up, spreading themselves afar, which contain the fertilising water." [1]

Another spirit which fights against the demons in the Avesta is called Çraosha. On the divine moun-tain stands "his triumphant dwelling with a thousand pillars, on the topmost height of the great mountain, illumined within with a light of its own, decked with stars without;" his chariot is drawn by four spot-less horses, which are swifter than clouds, swifter than winds, swifter than storms, swifter than birds with strong wings. A strong, well-armed, victorious youth, the strongest and swiftest among young men, who fears not the Daevas, and before whom they fly in terror to the darkness, Çraosha is the companion of Mithra; with him he overthrows the ranks of the hosts with whom Mithra is angry (p. 111). Thrice in each day he comes to smite the Daevas, with the axe of a woodman in his hand. Thus he fights against the evil Angromainyu, against Aeshma, and the Daevas Kunda, Banga, and Vibanga; thus he forces the con-quered Daevi Druj to answer him. In the dark he is wakeful against the evil ones; he protects the world from them when the sun has set ; in each night he comes

---

[1] "Tistar Yasht," 24 ff., 40, 49—58.

thrice upon the earth with his weapons in his hand.
About the third watch of the night he arouses the
bird Parodarsh, *i. e.* the cock, that by his cry he may
scare away the goblins of the night, and may banish the
Daevi Bushyançta, which holds men imprisoned in
sleep.[1] Çraosha, moreover, protects the sacrifices which
are offered to the good gods, and which the evil one
would carry away or defile. One of the priests who
took part in the sacred ceremonies held a club, the
Çraosha-club, in his hand, in order to scare the demons
and keep them back. Of the two instruments which
in the book of the law are used for flagellation, and by
which the evil spirits are driven from the bodies of men,
one is called the Çraosha-whip (*Çraosha charana*).

We remember the numerous hymns of the Veda
which celebrate the benefits conferred upon men by
Agni, the spirit of fire, who is born from the double
wood, and descends to earth in the lightning from the
water-bed of the storm-cloud; the glow of this bright
youth preserves men from beasts of prey, from murderers and evil spirits, helps the gods to victory, and
contends in battle in the van; at the same time a
royal house-lord and priest, Agni is in the Veda the
upholder of the religious worship, the mediator between
heaven and earth (IV. 40). The Avesta is filled with
similar conceptions, though less poetical in form. Here
the power as victorious of fire against the demon takes
the first place. We saw that Mithra's chariot carried
the kindled fire. "The sacred, strong fire" is invoked
as a "warrior," as a "protector," as a slayer of the evil
spirits, as the giver of good. To whatever side, we
are told in the book of the law, the wind carries the
smoke of the fire, it comes back thence as a slayer of
thousands. "Happy is the man," we are told in an

[1] "Yaçna," 56; "Vend." 18, 39.

invocation, "to whom thou comest in strength, O Fire,
son of Auramazda, more friendly than the friendliest,
worthy beyond others of supplication. O Fire, we
approach thee with perfect purity, with a good spirit;
mayest thou come down to us bringing help."[1] He
who uses dry selected wood for the fire, him the fire
blesses, saying : "May herds of cattle gather round
thee, and abundance of men ; may all things succeed
according to the wish of thy soul. Live out thy life
happily to the full extent to which thou wilt live.
The fire speaks with all those for whom it shines the
whole night through, and cooks food ; from all it
demands good nourishment. The fire looks on the
hands of all who come ; what does the friend bring to
the friend, he who approaches to him who sits alone ?[2]"
The Gathas of the Avesta also speak of the pieces of
wood for friction, out of which springs the fire that
shows the way ;[3] and in another passage we hear of the
fire Urvazista which dwells in wood. The Avesta distinguishes between the fire Çpenista, i. e. the house-
lord, the hearth-fire (it is the same name that is given
to the hearth-fire in India), the most victorious fire
Verethraghna, which slays all the demons, and by
which, according to the custom of the Parsees, the fires
of the hearth must be renewed year by year, and the fire
of lightning, which is called Vazista. This last, which
comes down direct from heaven, is the "most sacred
of all fires, which slays the demon Çpenjaghra."[4] In
the Avesta the priests are called Athravas, a name
which, no doubt, goes back to the worship of fire
(athar) ; among the Indians Atharvan entices the fire

---

[1] "Vend." 8, 248—250 ; "Yaçna," 26, 61, 23 ; "Yasht Farvardin,"
77.   [2] "Vend." 18, 57—63, 19, 134.
[3] Roth, "Ueber Yaçna, 31," Tübingen, 1876, s. 6, 20.
[4] "Vend." 19, 135 ; "Yaçna," 17. 69.

from the wood, and together with Manu and Dadhyanch kindles the first sacrificial fire; the fourth Veda is called after him (IV. 280). In the Avesta also the red glowing fires, which gleamed on the earth in the days of King Yima, are repeatedly mentioned (p. 32); it extols "the brilliance of the Arian lands," denotes the fire-priests as possessors of the true faith, and assures us that what is right may be known from the clear, blazing flames.[1]

The sacrifice offered by the Arians beyond the Indus to Indra, the Maruts, and spirits of light, to strengthen them against the demons, the draught prepared from the Soma, is known to us; we have shown how this Soma which strengthens the gods became itself a god in the fancy of the Indians—a mighty nourisher and sustainer of the gods. The same custom and deity are found in the Avesta, only the name has become Haoma, according to the phonetic laws of the Bactrian language. The legend has already shown us what importance was ascribed in Iran to the worship of the god Haoma, and the sacrifice of this liquor. Yima was born to Vivanghana as a reward because he had first poured out the Haoma and worshipped the god. To Athwya, the second worshipper of Haoma, Thraetaona was born; and to Thrita, the third, Kereçaçpa, the hero (p. 27, 28). To Zarathrustra, who was born to Pourushaçpa for a similar service, when he is dressing the sacred fire at the break of dawn, and singing the sacred hymns, the god Haoma appears: "Who art thou," asks Zarathrustra, "who appearest to my sight as the most perfect in the corporeal world, with thy brilliant, immortal body?" Haoma answered him: "I am the pure Haoma, who protect men from evil. Call on me, press out my juice in order to enjoy me; praise

[1] "Yaçna," 31, 3, 19.

me as all other fire-priests praise me." Then said Zarathrustra : "Supplication to Haoma ! Haoma, the good,
is well-created ; duly-created is he, and gives health ;
he bestows kindness, is victorious, and of golden colour.
Thy wisdom, O golden one, I praise ; thy strength, thy
victory, thy healing power, thy greatness. I praise
the mountains, the high ones, where thou, Haoma,
growest ; I praise the earth, the wide and patient, thy
mother, O pure Haoma. Mayest thou grow on the
paths of the birds. To the horsemen, who spur their
horses, Haoma gives power and strength ; to the
maidens who have long remained unmarried, he gives
true and vigorous husbands, gifted with good understanding, and to wives beautiful children and a pure
posterity. To those who repeat the Naçkas (the
chapters of the Avesta) he gives sanctity and greatness. Praise to thee, Haoma ; thou knowest the words
which are spoken with truth. Praise to thee, Haoma,
who by thine own power art a mighty king. To thee
Auramazda first gave the girdle glittering with stars ;
girt with this thou lingerest on the summits of the
mountains in order to maintain in sincerity the commands of the sacred sayings. O Haoma, lord of the
house, of the village, of the land, lord of wisdom, I call
on thee for greatness and victory, for favour to my
body, and rich food. O thou who art of golden colour,
I entreat thee for skill and power, passing through the
whole body, for beauty and health, for prosperity and
increase, for greatness spreading over the whole form.
The first boon for which I entreat thee, O Haoma, who
removest death, is that I may attain to the excellent
habitation of the saints, the bright dwelling where there
is abundance of all good things ; the second boon is
that this body may endure ; the third, that my life may
be long ; the fourth, that I may go through the earth

powerful and glad, troubling the tormentors, and slaying the Druj; the fifth is that I may walk victorious on the earth and slay the evil. For this thing also, as a sixth boon, O Haoma, who removest death, I entreat thee: may I be the first to see the thief, the murderer, and the wolf: may none of these previously see me. Keep far from us the hatred of those who hate us; tear out the hearts of those who give poison. If in this house, this place, this village, this sacrifice, there is a man who does harm, take from him the power to go, obscure his reason, break asunder his heart with the commandment. Let him not be mighty in the feet, let him not be mighty in the hands. O Haoma, I make a prayer to thee, that thou mayest go a sovereign lord through the worlds, triumphing over hatred and the evil. Thou shouldest triumph over the hatred of all who hate thee, over the hatred of the Daevas and men, the evil spirits and magicians, the perverse, blind, and dumb, the two-footed murderers and insidious creatures, the four-footed wolves, and the numerous hosts which creep and fly."[1]

Further, we find in the Avesta that the "priest" offers Haoma to Mithra, Çraosha, and Drvaçpa on the divine mountain.[2] The plant of which this god is the genius, grows, according to the books of the Parsees, as white heavenly Haoma only on the tree Gaokerena, i. e. the heavenly tree which stands on the divine mountain or in the spring Ardviçura; the yellow Haoma which grows upon the earth is only a copy or descendant of the white Haoma. In Iran also the preparation and expression of the Haoma juice is accompanied by a long and minute ritual; and the offering of

[1] Yaçna," 9, 10, according to Burnouf, " Journ. Asiat." 1844—1846. Cf. Spiegel " Avesta," 2, 68 ff.
[2] " Gosh Yasht," 17 ; " Mihr Yasht," 88; " Yaçna," 56, 8.

the sacrifice, which is still performed among the Parsees of India, requires long invocations and responses
between the celebrant and the ministering priests. At
the present day the Parsees send from time to time
one of their priests to Kerman in order to bring from
their ancient home twigs of Haoma for the sacrifice.

The coincidence which we find above, in the forms
of the legend, between the Avesta and the Veda—
Vivanghana, Yima, Athwya, Thrita, Kereçaçpa, and
Uça are found in both—is not less marked in the
conceptions of the gods and their functions, and in
the character of the worship. There can be no doubt
that the Arians of Iran believed themselves to be protected and injured by the same spirits as the Arians
in the Panjab. If on the Indus invocations were addressed to Vritrahan, Vayu, the Maruts, and Mitra, in
Iran men prayed to Verethraghna, Vayu, and Mithra.
In both places Vritra and Ahi are the opponents of
the god of light; in both fire was worshipped; in both
the power of the sacrificial liquor was elevated into a
mighty life-giving god. Among the Indians, as we
saw, the priest who addresses the invocation to the
god at the sacrifice is called Hotar; in the Avesta
the Zaotar utters the prayers. Further coincidences
in the number and nature of the gods, in the worship,
in the laws and forms of purification, in the cere-
monial, and even in the shape of the universe, will
show themselves as we proceed. It is true that
differences may also be found. Many of the numerous
spirits of the Rigveda are wanting in the Avesta;
and again, some spirits in the Avesta, such as Anahita,
Çraosha, Tistrya, are unknown to the Indians. Variations such as these must occur where there has been
a separate development from a common root. But
the factors in the coincidence of the most important

forms of the gods and heroes, and the distinctive modes of worship, in the Avesta and the Rigveda, the very oldest monument of the Arians in India, are so great that any doubt whether the Avesta remained free from alterations and influences of an alien or later nature in the revision under Shapur II., is entirely removed, and we know that we possess in it the remains of an original document of Iran, going back beyond the time of Cyrus. In the Avesta we have before us the faithful expression of the ancient Iranian faith. Though not in its original form this result is the more certain, because on the one hand some deities, as for instance Mithra, and some myths like that of Yima, exhibit older forms in the Avesta than in the Rigveda, while in others we have almost an identity of language between the two. In the Avesta as in the Veda the Soma is praised as "gold-coloured;" in both fire is the "house-lord;" the sun goes on his "path free from dust;" the power of the gods is increased by the sacrifice (p. 120). In both one god offers sacrifice to another, in order to strengthen him; and the invocations of the Avesta, like those of the Rigveda, ask for health and long life for the suppliant; for possessions and wealth and favour, for the power to see the thief, the murderer, and the wolf before they are seen by him.

CHAPTER VI.

THE REFORM OF THE FAITH.

In the Gathas of the Avesta the spirit who keeps watch over the increase of the flocks speaks to the heavenly powers, saying: "All creatures are distressed; whom have ye for their assistance?" Auramazda makes answer: "I have one only who has received my commands, the holy Zarathrustra; he will proclaim my exhortations and those of Mazda and Asha, for I will make him practised in speech."[1] Then Auramazda sacrificed to Ardviçura that he might unite with Zarathrustra the son of Pourushaçpa, to the end that the latter might think, speak, and act according to the law.[2] Pourushaçpa, i. e. rich in horses, of the race of Haechataçpa,[3] was the fourth who offered the sacrifice of Haoma in Airyana Vaeja after Vivanghana, Athwya, and Thrita. For this Zarathrustra was born to him.[4] At his birth and his growth the grass and the trees increased, and all the creatures of Auramazda greeted each other because the priest had been created who would sacrifice for them and spread abroad the

---

[1] "Yaçna," 29; Roth; "Z. D. M. G." 25, 6 ff. *Geus urva* means soul of the bull; the priests identified the soul of the first created bull with the protectress of the flocks, the Drvaçpa, *i. e.* having mighty horses. Spiegel, "Avesta," 3, 74.

[2] "Aban Yasht," 17—19. [3] "Afrin Zartusht," 4.

[4] "Yaçna," 9, 42.

law of Auramazda, over the seven Kareshvare of the
earth.[1] Çraosha, accompanied by the sublime Asha,
appeared to Zarathrustra, and the latter declared himself ready to swear enmity against the liars, and to be
a mighty source of help to the truth. And the god
Haoma appeared to Zarathrustra and commanded him
to press out his juice and to praise him, as other fire-
priests praise him. And Zarathrustra praised Haoma
and his mother the earth, and addressed six prayers
to him (p. 125). Ashi vanguhi also came at Zarathrustra's command on her chariot, and inquired :
Who art thou who callest on me, whose speech is the
most beautiful which I have heard from all those who
invoke me ? Come nearer to me ; approach my chariot.
Then she surrounded him with her right arm and her
left and said : Beautiful art thou, Zarathrustra, well
grown, with strong legs and long arms. To thy body
has been given brilliance, and to thy soul long prosperity."[2] And when Zarathrustra sacrificed to Verethraghna, he granted him strength of arm, health, and
vigour of body, and power of vision, such as that of
the horse, which sees by night, and the gold-coloured
vulture.[3] But Auramazda taught Zarathrustra "the
best words," prayers, and invocations, and charms
against the evil spirits.[4] "How," Zarathrustra inquires of Auramazda, "how ought I to protect the
creatures from the evil spirits, from the wicked Angromainyu ?" Then Auramazda answers : " Praise
Auramazda, the creator of the pure creation ; praise
the victorious Mithra ; praise the Amesha Çpentas (the
immortal saints), which rule over the seven parts of
the earth ; praise the holy Çraosha, who holds the club
against the head of the Daevas ; praise Verethraghna,

---

[1] " Farvardin Yasht," 93, 94.   [2] " Ashi Yasht," 17 ff.
[3] " Bahram Yasht," 28—33.   [4] " Yaçna," 13, 18 ; 64, 38 ; 69, 65.

created by Ahura, the bearer of the splendour; praise
the shining heavens, and the glowing Tistrya; praise
Vayu, the swift; praise Çpenta Armaiti (the holy
earth), the beautiful daughter of Auramazda. Praise
the tree, the good, the pure, created by Ahura, the
well-grown and strong; praise the glittering Hae-
tumant (Etymandros); praise Yima Kshaeta, the
possessor of good herds. Praise the good laws, the
law against the Daevas, the law of the worshippers of
Auramazda; praise the splendour of the Arian land;
praise the abode of the pure. Praise the fire Vazista
(p. 123), which smites the Daeva Çpenjaghra. Bring
hard wood and perfumes, and water of purification to
the fire."[1]

Zarathrustra first proclaimed the words which
Auramazda had taught him to Maidhyomao,[2] the son
of Araçta, his father's brother, and spoke to the
members of his race, the Haechataçpas: "Ye holy
Haechataçpas, to you will I speak; ye distinguish the
right and the wrong." The announcement did not
remain confined to the circle of the family and the
race: "To you that come," we are told in another
passage, "I will announce the praises of the all-wise
lord, and the praises of Vohumano. Look on the
beams of fire with pious mind. The fair sayings of
the fire-priests are the way of Vohumano. Thou
gavest ancient sayings, O Ahura; by these will I
annihilate among you the sacrifices of the lying gods.
The worshipper of fire should accurately understand
the correct words which have come from Vohumano
(the good disposition and its spirit) in order that
truth may be his portion." In other poems Zarathrustra laments: "The liar possesses the fields of
the true man, who protects the earth; none of the

[1] "Vend." 19, 36—137.   [2] "Farvardin Yasht." 95.

K 2

servants worship me ; none of the lords of the land,
who are unbelievers. The dominion is in the hands of
the priests and prophets of the lying gods; whither
shall I go for refuge ?—to what land shall I turn ? I
cry for help for Frashaostra and myself. May the fire
grant this help to both of us."[1] Frashaostra of the
race of Hvova, is mentioned in the Avesta as the
closest adherent of Zarathrustra, and often in connection with Jamaçpa. The help for which Zarathrustra cried in this invocation was granted to him
by King Vistaçpa. Zarathrustra offered the Haoma
draught in Airyana Vaeja to Ardviçura, and prayed
to her : "Grant to me that I may combine with the
son of Aurvataçpa, the strong Kava Vistaçpa, to the
end that he may think, speak, and act according to
the law ;" and the goddess granted him this favour.[2]
And Zarathrustra sacrificed to the Drvaçpa (the goddess of flocks) in Airyana Vaeja, to the end that he
might unite with the good and noble Hutaoça (the
wife of Vistaçpa), that she might impress the good
law on her memory.[3] Finally, we read : "Who is
thy true friend on the great earth ; who will proclaim
it ? Kava Vistaçpa, the warlike, will do this."[4]

Of King Vistaçpa and Frashaostra the Avesta then
tells us, "that they prepared the right path for the
faith which Ahura gave to the fire-priests." In the
prayers Kava Vistaçpa is praised because as an arm,
an assister, and helper, he has subjected himself to
the law of Ahura, the law of Zarathrustra ; because he
has opened a wide path for purity, and has established
the law in the world. The mighty brilliance of the

[1] "Yaçna," 28, 9, 44, 45 ; 46, 1—4 ; 49, 8 ; 50, 16, 18, according
to Haug's translation, which however has been called in question.
[2] "Aban Yasht," 104—106.
[3] "Gosh Yasht ;" cf. "Ram Yasht," 36 ; "Farvardin Yasht," 142.
[4] "Yaçna," 45, 14 ff.

ruler supported Zarathrustra, "in establishing the law
and making it highly esteemed."[1] When Jamaçpa saw
the army of the Daeva-worshippers approach, he sacrificed to Ardviçura a hundred horses, a thousand
oxen, and ten thousand head of small cattle, and
Ardviçura granted to him to fight victoriously against
all the non-Arians. And Zairivairi, the brother of
Vistaçpa, besought Ardviçura that he might smite the
skilful Peshana, who worshipped the Daevas, and
Arejataçpa. Kava Vistaçpa himself offered sacrifice
in order to obtain the victory over Asta-aurva, over the
Daeva worshippers Çpinjauruska, and Darsinika, and
the murderous Arejataçpa.[2] And Vistaçpa smote
Peshana and Arejataçpa, and Zarathrustra blessed
him : " I praise thee, O ruler of the lands. May life
be given to thy wives and thy children, which shall
be born from thy body. Be thou possessed of swift
horses, like the sun, shining like the moon, glowing
as fire, sharp as Mithra, a conqueror of enemies like
Verethraghna, well grown and victorious as Çraosha.
Mayest thou be a ruler like Yima ; mayest thou be
victorious and rich in cattle like Thraetaona, bold and
strong as Kereçaçpa, wise as Urvakshaya, brilliant as
Kava Uça, without sickness and death, like Kava
Huçrava, stainless as Çyavarshana, rich in horses as
Pourushaçpa, a friend of the heavenly ones, and
conqueror of men."[3]

The Avesta gives Zarathrustra three sons : Urvatat-
nara, Hvareçithra, Daevotbi (Punisher of the Daevas) ;
and three daughters : Freni, Thriti, and Pourushiçta.[4]
His work is summed up in the fact that he compelled
the Daevas, who previously had been in human form

1 " Farvardin Yasht," 99 ; " Zamyad Yasht," 84 ff.
2 " Ashi Yasht," 49 ; " Aban Yasht," 112.
3 " Afrin Zartusht," 1—4.
4 " Yaçna," 52, 3 ; " Farvardin Yasht," 98.

upon the earth, to hide themselves in the earth.[1] His doctrine prevents the Daevas from injuring the creation, as before, and gives to all the creatures of the good god the means of protecting themselves more effectually against the evil. Hence Zarathrustra is the increaser of life; in this sense he is described, invoked, and worshipped as the lord and master of all created life. But in time Çaoshyant will be born, who will make the evil creatures wholly powerless, and bring on for man the time of undisturbed happiness, in which there will no more be any battle; the time of uninterrupted life, i. e. of immortality. In this period all who once had life will have life again; i. e. the life destroyed by Angromainyu and the evil spirits will be restored, and the dead will rise to a new life.

Zarathrustra's birth and growth struck terror into the evil spirit Angromainyu. " The Yazatas" (the gods), he exclaimed, " have not forced me from the earth, crossed with paths, round, and wide-reaching; but Zarathrustra will drive me from it."[2] And the Daevas took counsel on the summit of Arezura, whither they are wont to come together from their caves with the Druj: "Alas! in the dwelling of Pourushaçpa the pure Zarathrustra has been born. He is the weapon with which the Daevas are smitten; he takes away the power from the Daevi Druj, and the Daevi Naçu (νέκυς, i. e. the spirit of the dead), and the false lies; how shall we compass his death?" And from the region of the north Angromainyu dashed forward, who is full of death, the Daeva of Daevas, and said: " O Druj, go up and slay the pure Zarathrustra." And " Zarathrustra said in the spirit: The wicked, evil-minded Daevas are considering my death. And he

---

[1] "Yaçna," 9, 46.   [2] "Ashi Yasht," 19.

arose and went forth, bearing in his hand stones of
the size of a Kata, which he had received from the
creator Auramazda, and he praised the good waters of
the good creation, and the law of the worshippers of
Auramazda, and uttered the prayer: *Yatha ahu vairyo.*
The Druj ran round about him, and the Daeva Buiti,
the deceiver of mortals; and the Druj ran in alarm
from him and said to Angromainyu, the tormentor:
In him, in the holy Zarathrustra, I see no death.
And Zarathrustra said to Angromainyu: Evil-minded
Angromainyu, I will smite the creation which is created
by the Daevas; I will smite the spirit of the dead
which the Daevas have created, until Çaoshyant the
victorious shall be born from the water of Kançava,
in the region of the east. Angromainyu answered
him: Wherewith wilt thou smite my creatures? With
what weapons wilt thou destroy them? Then spake
Zarathrustra: The pestle, the bowl, the Haoma, these
are my best weapons, and the words which Auramazda
has spoken. By this sacred word will I annihilate thy
creatures, O evil Angromainyu. Slay not my creatures, O pure Zarathrustra, answered Angromainyu.
Thou art the son of Pourushaçpa, and hast life from a
mother. Curse the good law of the worshippers of
Auramazda, and attain the prosperity which Vad-
haghna has attained, the ruler of the lands. But
Zarathrustra spake: I will not curse the good law of
the worshippers of Auramazda; no, not though my
bones and soul and power of life were torn asunder.
Then the evil Daevas ran and took counsel on the
summit of Arezura, and Angromainyu spoke: What
will the Daevas bring thither? But they said: 'The
evil eye;' and hastened to the bottom of hell, the
dark, the evil, the wicked."[1]

[1] "Vend." 3, 23; 19, 1—32, 140—147.

With Zarathrustra, according to the Avesta, a new era begins. He is the proclaimer of a new law. But along with this we are told that even in Yima's time the earth glowed with red fires; the power of the old sayings of the fire-priests is extolled; the professors of the first, and those of the new law receive commendation. Zarathrustra is born to his father as a reward for offering an ancient sacrifice, the sacrifice of Haoma. He himself dresses the fire at daybreak before he comes forth to announce his new doctrine; and even while announcing it he sacrifices to the old gods Verethraghna and Ardviçura; the gods whom the heroes of the old days invoke appear to him also, the prophet of the new teaching; they demand that he shall offer sacrifice, and insist on their worship; they grant him favour and gifts. It is precisely the ancient sacrifice of Haoma, the common possession of the Arians in Iran and India, which is declared by Zarathrustra to be the best means of repelling the evil ones, and not Zarathrustra only, but also Auramazda sacrifices to an ancient divinity that the son of Pourushaçpa may be obedient to his commands, and then directs the latter to invoke the ancient gods, Mithra, Verethragna, Çraosha, Vayu, and Tistrya, and to worship fire. Hence it was no new religion which Zarathrustra taught; it was nothing more than a reform of the ancient faith, and traditional modes of worship.

We were able definitely to ascertain from the fragments of the Avesta that it arose in the east of Iran; the districts of the north-east are especially prominent in it. It denotes Bactra as the abode of dominion (p. 31). A doctrine which, as we shall see, lays the greatest stress on the cultivation of the land, could not have grown up in the deserts of the Gedrosians, or the steppes of the Sagartians. If, according to the

Avesta, " the evil custom of the burial of the dead
prevails " in Arachosia (Harahvaiti) ;[1] if Haetumat
(Drangiana) is reproved for the sins which are practised
there ;[2] if we are told of Haraeva (the land of the
Arians) that it is indeed rich in houses but full of
poverty and idleness,[3] and of Ragha that it is indeed
Zoroastian but full of utter unbelief[4]—if the sin of
burning corpses prevails in Chakhra (Chirhem ?),[5] it is
clear that these lands are distinct from the region in
which the pure doctrine of Zarathrustra, proclaimed in
the Avesta, arose, and became so firmly established as
to be universally current. Hence of all the lands in
Iran, mentioned in the Avesta, only Airyana Vaeja,
Margiana, Sogdiana, and Bactria remain. In the
Avesta Zarathrustra is famous in Airyana Vaeja; in
that land he sacrifices; and, as the Avesta allots but
two months of summer and ten months of cold winter
to this region, we must look for it on the high mountain
range of the North-east (p. 73). Zarathrustra stands
in a close relation to Queen Hutaoça and King Vistaçpa, who fights against the worshippers of the
Daevas and Arejataçpa, and prepares a way for the
new doctrine. Among the heroes of the ancient time
and the spirits of the pious who are invoked in the
prayers of the Avesta, the immortal part of King
Vistaçpa is repeatedly invoked besides Zarathrustra
and Frashaostra. We have already shown in what a
contrast the Bactrians and Sogdiani stood to the
nations of the steppes of the Oxus, and what a position is allotted to King Vistaçpa as repelling the
Iranians. In thus celebrating him as the protector
of Zarathrustra, the Avesta plainly puts Zarathrustra
himself in Bactria.

[1] "Vend." 1, 46—48.   [2] "Vend." 1, 50—52.
[3] "Vend." 1, 30—32.   [4] "Yaçna," 19, 51, 52; "Vend." 1, 60—62.
[5] "Vend." 1, 64—66.

If we may assume the fact that the reform of the
religion must have proceeded from Bactria and Sogdiana in the north-east of Iran, the next question to
be decided is, whether it is possible to determine the
meaning and import of this reform. The forms and
views, which are found to agree in the Avesta and
Rigveda, we have already established, with complete
certainty, to be the ancient possession of the Arians of
Iran. The elements of the religious conception, and
several very definite forms and traits in the belief and
worship, were the same in the Panjab and Iran. The
leading principle was the contrast of the bright beneficent powers who give life and increase and the evil
spirits of darkness, drought, and death. This possession was therefore in existence before the reform. This
principle must have become more prominent among
the Arians of Iran owing to the nature of their
country. The fertile land and the desert were in far
greater proximity there than in the Panjab. The
centre of Iran was filled with a vast desert; wide and
barren table-lands spread out on north and south; the
most favoured regions were almost like oases. Closely
adjacent to the most fruitful valleys and slopes lay
endless steppes; blooming plains, shaded by thick
groups of trees, were surrounded by hot deserts of
sand. If the alpine districts of the north possessed
the most splendid forests and luxuriant pastures, yet
the snow fell early, and the winter was severe; if
vegetation ran riot on the fringe of the Caspian, fever
and reptiles infested the marshy plains. Close beside
abundant productiveness lay drought and desert, bare
flats of rock, deserts of sand, and fields of snow. The
inhabitants of Iran had not only to suffer from the
heat of summer but also from the cold of winter, from
the scorching winds of the desert as well as from the

snow-storms which came from the table-lands of the north. On the one hand, pastures and fields were covered for many weeks with snow; on the other, sand-storms from the desert ruined the tillage; in one district camels succumbed to the cold of the lofty terraces, or slipped from the icy slopes down the precipices; in another, the desert wind dried up fountains and springs. Here the winter, " which flies past to slay the herds, and is full of snow," as the Avesta says, was " of endless duration ; " it was " on the water, the trees, and the field," and " its cold penetrated to the heart of the earth ; " there the herds were tormented by the fly in the heat, bears and wolves fell upon the folds, and it was necessary to find protection against serpents and ravenous beasts of prey.[1] In this land life was a conflict against the heat of summer and the south, against the chill of winter and the mountain heights, a struggle for the maintenance and protection of the herds; and as soon as these tribes had become settled in the more favoured regions and passed over to agriculture, there began on the edge of those oases the struggle against the desert and the steppe. Here water must be conveyed to the dry earth, there the tillage must be protected against the sand-storms of the desert. To these difficulties and contrasts in the nature of the land was added a contrast in the mode of life of the population. The majority of the tribes of the table-land of the interior, and a part of the inhabitants of the mountainous rim, could not, owing to the nature of the land, pass beyond a nomadic pastoral life, and even to this day the population of Iran is to a considerable extent nomadic ;[2] while other tribes

---

[1] " Vend." 1, 9—12, 24 ; 7, 69.

[2] " Herodotus states expressly that some tribes of the Persians were nomads (1, 125); beside the Sagartians nomadic tribes are also mentioned among the Carmanians, Areians, etc.

toiled laboriously in the sweat of their brows, these
wandered with their herds in idleness, ever ready for
battle ; and thus there could be no lack of ambuscades
and plunder, of attacks and raids on the cultivated
districts.

All these contrasts are most marked on the slopes
of the north-eastern edge, in Margiana, Bactria, and
Sogdiana, which lay open to the steppes of the Caspian
Sea. Here were fruitful, blooming valleys with luxuriant vegetation on the banks of the mountain streams,
yet, wherever the mountains receded, the endless desert
at once began. If the stars shone clear through the
night on mountains and table-lands, in the pure and
vapourless atmosphere of Iran, sand-storms and mist
lay on the northern desert. The winds blowing from
the north brought icy cold in the winter ; in the
summer they drove the sand of the deserts over the
fruitful fields, to which water has to be laboriously
conveyed in the time of the greatest heat, while
eternal winter reigned in the heights of Belurdagh
and Hindu Kush. There was also the continual fear
of the nomads who dwelt on the steppes to the north,
who made attacks on the fruitful slopes and valleys.
We have already shown that it was precisely on the
slopes of the Hindu Kush that the necessity of protection against the nations of the steppes led to a
combination of the forces of the tribes who were settled
there, and gave the impulse to the formation of a
larger polity.

In such a territory, when the tribes had once become
settled in the more favoured regions, amid such struggles against nature and the plundering neighbours,
it is clear that the conception of the contrast between
good and evil spirits must become more widely developed and sharply pointed—that it should indeed

form the hinge of all religious ideas. The good spirits had given fruit and increase to many excellent lands ; but the evil spirits destroyed these blessings with their storms of sand and snow, their cold and heat, their beasts of prey and serpents. Wherever the herds throve and the fields were fruitful, there the good spirits were gracious ; where the pastures withered, and the fields were covered with sand, the wicked spirits had maliciously rendered of no avail the labours of men. In the valleys of Bactria and Sogdiana there was labour, industry, increase and fruit ; beyond, in the steppe, all was barren ; the storms went whirling round, and wild hordes of robbers roamed to and fro. Thus in these regions the conception of the struggle of the good spirits, and the evil, which injure, torment, punish and murder men, was most lively, the religious feeling of these conceptions most completely penetrated and governed the minds of men.

All creatures were oppressed by the evil spirits, so the Avesta told us (p. 129) ; and therefore Auramazda determines to teach Zarathrustra "the wise sayings." No new belief or new forms of worship are to be introduced ; the means of protection against the evil ones were to be multiplied and strengthened. We know what importance the Arians in India ascribed to the correct prayer and invocation, what power over the spirits and indeed over the deities themselves they ascribed to the correct words, what a defensive power they attributed to the sayings of the Atharvan. The same ideas were current among the Arians of Iran. The heaven of the good god and holy spirits is, in the Avesta, the "dwelling of invocations" (Garonmana). Hence the first point in the reform was that new formulæ and prayers should be added to the old prayers and incantations. The fire that slays demons is to burn day and night on the hearth, and must always be tended with hard, dry, well-hewn wood; the spirits of light, the great Mithra, the sun, the stars, are to be earnestly invoked along with the victorious Verethraghna, and Çraosha the slayer of demons, the life-giving god, to whom Haoma is to be offered; and the libation of Haoma is to be frequently offered to the spirits of light. If men prayed constantly to the good spirits, and cursed the evil, if they made use of the holy sayings when they observed that the evil beings came, then wicked creatures would certainly remain far from house, and farm, and field. According to the Avesta, Zarathrustra first uttered the Ahuna vairya, and Angromainyu says that though the deities have not been able to drive him from the earth, Zarathrustra will smite him with the Ahuna vairya.[1] In the minds of the priests of the Avesta, this prayer is itself a mighty being to which worship is to be offered, just as in the Vedas the holy prayers and some parts of the ritual— nay even the verse-measure of the hymns—are treated as divine powers.

It was an old Arian conception, which we have observed widely spread on the Ganges, that filth and pollution and contact with what is impure and dead gave the evil spirit power over those who had contracted such defilement. This uncleanness must be removed, and its operation checked. The reform, which bears the name of Zarathrustra, must have extended and increased in Iran the rules for purification and the removal of uncleanness. These regulations, carried out in long and wearisome detail on the basis of this new movement, are before us in the Vendidad. The Avesta says: Zarathrustra was the first who praised the Asha Vahista (i. e. the best truth-

---

[1] "Yaçna," 9, 44; "Ashi Yasht," 20.

fulness which is at the same time the highest purity)
and represents Angromainyu as exclaiming ; " that
Zarathrustra made him as hot by the Ashi Vahista as
metal is made in the melting." [1]

Whatever gave increase and life, water and trees
and good soil, and the animals which were useful to
men, were the work of the good spirits, the good
creation ; the steppes, the desert, the heat, the fierce
cold, the beasts of prey, these were the work of the
evil ones, the bad creation. Did not a man increase
life and growth if he industriously cultivated his field,
watered it well, and extended it towards the desert, if
he destroyed the animals and insects which did harm
to the fields and trees, if he gave room to fruitfulness
against unfertility ? Did he not extend and sustain
the good creation, and lessen the evil, if he planted and
watered, and diminished the harmful animals, the
serpents, the worms, and beasts of prey ? By such
work a man took the side of the good spirits against
the evil, and fought with them. It was in the will
and power of man by the act of his hands, by labour
and effort, to strengthen the good creation. The
importance which the Avesta ascribes to the cultivation
of the land, we may regard as a prominent trait of the
reform, as an essential part of its ethical importance.
Beside warriors and priests the Avesta knows only
the agricultural class.

In the Veda the gods of the light and the highest
heaven, Mithra and Varuna, are the guardians of truth
and purity, the avengers and punishers of evil deeds.
The invocation of Mithra in the Avesta, given above,
showed us that the Arians of Iran recognised in this
deity the spirit of purity, the inevitable avenger of
injustice. With his all-penetrating eye he watches,

[1] " Ashi Yasht," 20.

not only over purity of body, but also over purity
of soul. We may regard it as certain that the reform carried a long step forward the ethical impulse
which lay in this conception of Mithra—a conception
current on both sides of the Indus. This view is
supported by the great importance which the Avesta
ascribes to truthfulness, in the decisive value given
to this virtue for the purity of the soul, and the
identification of purity with truthfulness. As filth
defiles the body, so, according to the Avesta, does a lie
defile the soul. Lying and deception are the worst
sins of which a man can be guilty. The ethical
advance is obvious when the evil spirits are not merely
regarded as doing harm to men, but it is emphatically
stated that they deceive men, and a lie is the essence
of the evil spirits. In the Avesta a part of them have
simply the name of the spirits of deception, of the
Druj. The suppliants of the true gods are called
Asharan, i.e. the true, the pure ; the worshippers of
the evil spirits are liars.

The ideas of the Veda about the hosts of the spirits
of ancestors, and the entrance of the good and pious
into the heaven of light, are also current among the
Arians of Iran. These the reform could not leave
untouched. From the ethical characteristic which
marks them, from the severe inculcation of a pure, true,
active life, it proceeded to the idea of a sort of judgment on the souls after death. The detailed form in
which this idea is presented to us in the Avesta will
be given below.

In all religions, when they have reached a certain
stage of development, the impulse arises to find the
unity of the divine being among the multifarious crowd
of deities. On the Ganges the Brahmans or priests
attained to this unity by elevating the power of the

holy acts which controlled the deities, and was mightier than they, into the lord of the gods, by uniting with this conception the great breath or world-soul, the source of life springing up in nature. In Iran the reform did not look on nature as one, like the Brahmans on the Ganges, and owing to the character of the land and the strong contrasts there met with it could not easily perceive in it any single whole ; on the contrary, it comprehended in unity, on the one hand, the good beneficent side of nature, which gives increase, light, and life to men ; and, on the other, ranged the harmful powers together in opposition to the good. Hence it came about that the spirits which worked on either side were, so to speak, combined, and the two totals came forward in opposition. To these totals the reform sought to give unity by placing a chieftain at the head of each, the good and the bad. The chief of the good was Ahura, *i. e.* the lord, who is also denoted by the name Mazda, *i. e.* the wise, but he is generally invoked by the united title Ahura Mazda (Auramazda in the dialect of Western Iran), the wise lord ; occasionally, in the Avesta, he is called Çpentomainyu, *i. e.* the spirit of holy mind, the holy spirit. In the Rigveda the name Ahura Mazda, in the form Asura Medha, is used for more than one god of light. The chief of the evil spirits was Angromainyu, *i. e.* he that thinks evil, the destroying spirit.

The good and the evil spirits are regarded as active, the one on the beneficent, the other on the injurious side of nature. It was a step in advance when the reform arrived at the conception, that as the good and evil spirits ruled the life of nature and man, so in the beginning of the world, at the time of its origin, the good and evil spirits must have been active ; the good was from the beginning the work

of the good; the evil the work of the evil. As
the heavenly and infernal spirits were regarded as
in perpetual activity, the reform could not here, as in
India, look on nature and men as emanations from a
being in repose—from the world-soul—the nature of
which became ever less pure and bright, less really
itself, as the emanations advanced. Instead of an
emanation, the active force and contrast of the spirits
gave rise to the idea that the world was brought into
being by the will and power of the two supreme spirits
to a creation of the world. The good side of the
world must have been the work of the chief of the good
spirits, the evil side the work of the evil. Auramazda created the good, but immediately he created
it, Angromainyu created the evil in order to destroy
the good. And as at the creation, so also in the
created world, the mutual opposition of the good and
evil god, the struggle of their hosts, goes on. There
is no direct contest between Auramazda and Angromainyu; they operate against each other for increase
and destruction, life and death, and for the souls of
men; the direct conflict against evil remains, even
after the reform, with the old spirits, with Mithra,
Verethragna, Çraosha, and Tistrya.

From this we may without hesitation draw the
inference that Auramazda and Angromainyu did not
belong to the original belief of the Arians of Iran.
From the absence of any myth about Auramazda, and
the character of the names, "the wise lord," "the
destroying spirit," it further follows that the gods
thus named could not be the creation of any primitive
religious feeling. These names belong to a period of
reflection, which strives to make a presentment of the
general operation of the good and evil powers, of
their intellectual and ethical characteristics, and at

the same time seeks to express their nature, as well
as their relation to the world. Finally, the wavering
position which Auramazda takes up in the Avesta
towards the old deities, shows that he is of later
origin. Though now the supreme deity, he sacrifices
to Tistrya, in order to give him strength for the victory over Apaosha (p. 120) ; to Ardviçura, that Zarathrustra may be obedient to him (p. 129) ; and to other
gods of the old period. Beside him Mithra is praised
in the old style as the highest power ; he instructs
Zarathrustra to invoke the old gods, who still continue
in their traditionary activity. But we have express
evidence that Auramazda belongs to the reform.
"The first man," so the Avesta says, "who sacrificed
to Auramazda was the sacred Zarathrustra."[1] In the
transformation, however loose, of the divine nature
into "the wise lord," with his change from a natural
force to an ethical and intellectual power, and elevation to be the creator "of the heaven and the earth"
(p. 87), lay the most decisive step taken by the
reform ; by these conceptions it had raised the ancient
possession of the Arians of Iran to a new stage.

It is a remarkable fact that the evil spirits in the
Avesta bear the name of Daevas. The Arians of India
called their good gods, the gods of light, Devas ; from
the same root has sprung the general name of the gods
among the Greeks, Italians, and the Celts. Hence
among the Arians of Iran also it must once have been
in use for the spirits of light. Why the names Bagha
and Yazata became used in the Avesta for the good
gods, while the evil spirits received the name of Daevas
we cannot discover ; nor can we decide whether this
change of name came in with the reform. We can
only discover that an analogous change has taken

[1] "Ashi Yasht," 18.

place in India also. In the Rigveda the good gods
are comprised under the name Asura (old Bactrian
Ahura), *i. e.* the lord ; at a later time the evil spirits
among the Indians were always called Asuras, while
in Iran the name is allotted to the highest among
the good spirits.

CHAPTER VII.

THE DOCTRINE OF THE AVESTA.

WHEN the tribes of the Aryas advanced from the Panjab towards the East, and established themselves on the Ganges, the gods to whom they had offered prayers on the Indus faded away amid the abundant fertility of the new land; and the lively perception of the struggle of the gods of light against the spirits of darkness made room for the conception of the world-soul, from which nature and all living creatures were thought to have emanated. Similar religious principles led the Arians in Iran to a religious reform of an opposite kind. The idea of an emanation of the world, proceeding without any opposition, could not maintain itself in a life occupied in labour for the means of sustenance, in toiling and struggling against nature. Luxuriant growth and dreary desolation, scorching heat and severe winter, such as were found alternating in Iran, could not flow from one and the same source. There man must be active and brave, and therefore the divine being could not be regarded as existing in repose. The nature of the table-land, divided between fertile tillage and desert, between heat and cold, not merely caused the old idea of the conflict between good and evil spirits to continue, but even increased and extended it. All nature was made subject to this

opposing action of the gods, and the old conception of
the conflict was developed into a complete system.
With the extension of the operation of the beneficent
and harmful power over the whole of nature, man was
drawn into the conflict as active force. He must not
only invoke the assistance of the good spirits; he
must himself take part in the struggle of the good
against the evil. In this way he provided for his soul
and salvation better than by prayer and sacrifice; he
strengthened so far as in him lay the life and increase
of the world, and lessened the sphere in which the
power of the evil spirits could operate. If the Indians
by the elevation of Brahman arrived only at the great
contrast between nature and spirit, between soul and
body; if all nature was regarded as something evil and
to be annihilated, so that the mortification and tortur-
ing of the body and annihilation of self became the
highest ethical aims—the Bactrians or Arians in Iran
were directed by their reform to more energetic work
and activity against the harmful side of nature, and
the evil part of the soul. With the free choice of this
or that side, with the duty of working on nature, and
educating self, the conditions of a more happy and
powerful development were given them.

It was the duty of any earnest and eminent adherents of the reform, and afterwards of the priestly
races who joined it, or grew up in it, to guide the
impulse it had given, and bring the new ideas and the
rules to be deduced from them into harmony with the
old conceptions. If the contrast between the beneficent
and harmful powers once took the shape of opposing
spirits, the next object was to represent more exactly
the character and nature of these spirits, and define
more closely the good and evil Deity. As the reform
tended to elevate the natural side in these shapes into

ethical qualities, it was inevitable that advance in this direction should lead at an early time to abstract views —that both spirits should be identified with the pure contrast of light and darkness, of truth and lying, of moral good and moral evil.

If the good spirit was supreme purity and truth, he must originally have created the world in accordance with his nature. Whence then came the injurious, the evil? Had the evil spirit also a creative power? Or was the evil first introduced after the creation of the world? If this was the case, and evil was not always in the world, then it must again disappear from it; if the pure god was the more powerful, he must again overcome the resistance of the evil. Moreover, with the subordination of the light and dark powers to Auramazda and Angromainyu, and their combination into these two forms, an impulse was given which gradually forced the ancient deities into the background. The first point was, to put the latter in the right relation to the new god, who had created heaven and earth, and even these ancient gods. In the same way the old Arian legend of the golden age of Yima must be harmonised with the new doctrine of the creation, and a relation must be established between the sacrificers of the old days, who were without the good law of Zarathrustra, and the latter. The sayings which held in check the evil spirits, and which the reform took from the body of ancient invocations or added to them in their spirit, must be accurately preserved if they were not to lose their force, especially the prayers and incantations which Zarathrustra himself had spoken or was thought to have spoken. Lastly, the mode of worship must be regulated in accordance with the tendencies of the reform. Which and what kind of sacrifices, which invocations and songs of praise

were the most efficacious, was a matter which required
settling. The old customs of purification so indispensable for keeping at a distance the evil spirits, which
the reform, as we ventured to assume, largely increased
by new prescripts, must be united with the increased
importance attached to truth and purity and combined
into a comprehensive rule for the life pleasing to
Auramazda. What means were there for wiping out
offences against this rule, and sins when committed,
for turning aside the anger of Mithra, for expiating
falsehood, lying, and deception? We have already
indicated (p. 101) how numerous and complicated
were the duties of the priesthood arising out of
pollution and its removal. The answers which the
priesthood of Iran gave to all the questions which
successively arose have been collected in the Avesta.

The Gathas of the Avesta, in which the metre has
been retained, and along with it the older forms of the
language—poems which, according to another part of
the Avesta (the Çrosh Yasht), Zarathrustra composed
and Çraosha first sang [1]—are the most speculative
part of the book. They tell of the existence of the
good and evil spirits, place both in the beginning of
things, identify Auramazda with the truth and Angromainyu with the lie, bring forward Auramazda as the
creator of the world and of living creatures, as the
source of what is good in man and nature, and describe the duties of the true worshippers and the rewards which they may expect, together with the punishments which will come upon the worshippers of the
Daevas. The ancient gods, Mithra, Haoma, Tistrya,
Anahita and Drvaçpa are not mentioned in the
Gathas; though emphasis is laid on the blessing of
the "imperishable red fire of Auramazda." In their

[1] "Yaçna," 56, 3, 1—3.

place we have Asha (Truthfulness), and Vohumano (Good disposition), Armaiti (Piety), and Kshathra (Dominion); these are at times merely ideas, at times they are personified beside Auramazda.

In these poems Zarathrustra addresses a number of questions to Auramazda : "This question I will ask of thee; answer it truly, O Ahura. Who is the first father and begetter of truth? Who created their paths for the sun and stars? Who causes the moon to wax and wane? Who sustains the earth and holds the clouds above it? Who created the water and the trees of the field? Who is in the wind and the storms that they move so swiftly? Who created the beneficent lights and the darkness? For whom didst thou create the imperishable cow Ranyoçkereti (the Earth)? Who formed the earth with its great blessings? Who are the Daevas, which fight against the good creation? Who slew the hostile demons? Who is the truthful one, who is the liar? How are we to chase away the lies, how shall I put the lies into the hand of Asha (Truthfulness)? How can I come to your dwelling (the dwelling of the gods), and to your song? Give me now the command, what ought to be and what ought not to be, in such a way that we attentive ones may understand it, O Mazda, with the tongue of thy mouth, how am I to convert all living creatures, and guide them to the right path, which leads to him who hears the praises of the truly pious in heaven (Garonmana). Tell me clearly, what ye command me as the best, that I may keep it in my heart, and remember what has been forgotten, Mazda Ahura, all that ought to be, and ought not to be. Teach us, O True one, the way of Vohumano created by thee. Let us, O Mazda, receive thy sayings which bring blessing."

" On thee have I looked as the source in the
creation of life, because thou, O rich in gifts, didst
establish the sacred customs and announce the words.
He who first willed that the spaces of the sky should
clothe themselves with lights, he in his wisdom establishes the law of duty for the pious. In the spirit a
man must think of thee that thou art ever the same,
Ahura. I regarded thee as the most excellent, O
Mazda, whom thy people have to worship in spirit, as
the father of the pious, since I saw thee with my eye,
as the eternal law-giver of the world, living in his
works. Since thou of old, O Mazda, didst create all
beings and spirits according to thy will, and gave
them reason and a material body, all men, the wise
and the unwise, cause their voices to sound, each
according to his heart and mind; he who strives after
wisdom proves in his spirit on which side is error.
All gleaming bodies with their manifestations, everything that by Vohumano has a bright eye, the stars
and the sun, the herald of the day, move for thy
praise, O Mazda. In thee the holy earth exists, and
the highly-intelligent framer of the body of the earth,
O living spirit Mazda. Thou didst create the world,
the earth with the fire that rests in its bosom. With
pleasant fields thou didst adorn it, after taking counsel
with Vohumano, O Mazda. Thou didst first create
the fields, and didst devise the sayings by thy spirit,
and the various kinds of knowledge ; thou didst then
create this world of existence, by holy acts and speeches.
To Mazda belongs this kingdom which he causes to
grow by his grace." [1]

"To you, all ye that come, I will announce the

---

[1] " Yaçna," 28, 29, 42, 43, 44, 46, according to Haug's translation,
which is not universally accepted; " Yaçna," 31 after Roth. " Z. D.
M. G." 25, 6 ff.

praises of Mazda the all-wise lord, and the hymns to
Vohumano. O wise Asha, I will entreat that friendship
may display itself through the stars. Hear with your
ears the glorious, see with your spirit the clear, that
every one for himself may choose his faith before the
great work begins. Those two primæval spirits, which
are twins, represent themselves in thought, words, and
works as this dualism, the good and the evil, and
between both the virtuous know how to decide, but
not the evil. When these two deities first came
together, they created the good creatures and the bad,
and (arranged) that at the last hell should be awarded
to the bad and blessedness to the good. Of these two
spirits the evil one chooses the worst way of action ;
but the increase-giving spirit chooses virtue, he whose
robe is the firm heaven,—and those who in faith make
Auramazda content by truthful acts. Between them
the worshippers of the Daevas, the deceived, cannot
rightly decide ; they chose the worst disposition, and
came to the evil ones when in council, and together
they hastened to Aeshma, that by him they might
bring plagues upon the life of men. But when the
punishment of their evil deeds shall be accomplished,
and thy kingdom as the reward of piety shall come
upon those who put the Druj (the lie) in the hands of
Asha (Truthfulness), then destruction overtake the
destroying Druj ; but those who possess high renown
will gather as immortal in the beautiful dwellings of
Vohumano, of Mazda, and Asha. Thus then let us
work to make this world eternal, O Auramazda, O
Asha that givest blessing ; may our thoughts be there,
where wisdom is enthroned."[1]

"Teach me to know both, that I may walk in the
way of Vohumano, the sacrifice, O Mazda, which is fit

[1] "Yaçna," 30, after Hübschmann's rendering.

for a god like thee, and the pure words of thanks-
giving; give me the duration over which Ameretat
presides, and the blessings of Haurvatat.[1] May he be
praised, who in complete truth, so far as he knows it,
will tell the charm of Asha, the utterance of prosperity
(Haurvatat, *i. e.* health—and afterwards the spirit
of prosperity and the waters) and of immortality
(Ameretat immortality, and afterwards the spirit of
long life and good plants)."[2] "The acts, words, and
sacrifices by which I, O Mazda, might attain immortality, purity, and power over Haurvatat, I will, so far
as I can, perform for thee.[3] Grant to me, O most
holy spirit, Mazda, thou who didst create the cow, the
waters, and the plants, grant me immortality and
health, power and duration, that I may follow the
doctrine of Vohumano."[4] "From thee comes the
nourishment of Haurvatat and Ameretat; may piety
(Armaiti) increase with truth under the dominion of
Vohumano, and power and continuance as a counter-
protection."[5] "Send us the blessing of a long life."[6]
"I ask thee, answer me truly, Ahura, When shall I
win this reward by truthfulness?—ten mares with their
stallions and a camel, that Haurvatat and Ameretat
may be in my possession, and I make an offering to
thee of their blessings."[7] "I will proclaim what the
most holy one says to me, the best word for mortals
to hear; those who for its sake lend ear to me, to
those will Haurvatat and Ameretat come." "To every
one who is a friend to him in thought and word,
Auramazda has given power over the rich Haurvatat
(health), over the rich Ameretat (freedom from death);
he has given him dominion and independence and the

---

[1] "Yaçna," 33, 8. [2] "Yaçna," 31, 6. [3] "Yaçna," 34, 1.
[4] "Yaçna," 50, 7. [5] "Yaçna," 34, 11.
[6] "Yaçna," 41, 10, 11, ; cf. 57, 20. [7] "Yaçna," 43, 18.

riches of Vohumano." [1] "Let none of you listen to the counsel and command of the evil one, for he brings farm and community, canton and land, into distress and ruin, but punish him with the weapon." [2] "On the day when Asha will slay the Druj, on the day of immortality, when that comes forth, that was denied, when the Daevas and men will receive their reward; then, O Ahura, a mighty song of praise will be raised to thee." [3]

"To thy kingdom and thy truth, I offer praise, Ahura, Asha. Listen to this with kindly spirit, Mazda; incline thine ear, Ahura. Let the worshippers of the liar be few; may all these turn themselves to the priests of the truthful fire! The good must rule over us, not the evil! Ahura, the all-knowing, cannot be deceived. I will think of thee, most glorious one, at the final departure of life. With prayers, O Mazda, Asha, will I come forward to praise thee, and with the works of Vohumano. In your dwelling, O wise one, sound the praises of them that give thanks. I will be called the singer of thy praises, and will continue to be so as long as I can, by advancing the laws of life, that the life of the world may continue of itself. With the verses which have been composed and handed down for your praise, I will approach both of you, and with uplifted hands. As a worshipper I will invoke you one and all, ye who give blessing, as well as all those who attain to the strong bridges of your blessedness, Auramazda, Asha, and Vohumano; those bridges which belong to you. Come ye to my aid." [4]

---

[1] "Yaçna," 44, 5. The passages in the text concerning Haurvatat and Ameretat are given after Darmesteter, "Haurvatat et Ameretat," p. 35 ff.

[2] "Yaçna," 31, 18. [3] "Yaçna," 47, 1.

[4] "Yaçna," 47—49, according to Haug's translation.

These are the essential traits of the doctrine of the
Gathas. Auramazda, himself a shining one (*hvathra*),
has created the shining bodies of the heaven, the earth,
the waters, the trees, and men ; he has appointed their
paths for the stars. He is the sustainer of the world,
inasmuch as he devises the good sayings (*daena*) for
the protection of the good creation. He is light and
truth, and therefore is not to be deceived ; he shows
the right way to Zarathrustra, and gives him the
proper charms against the evil spirits. That at this
stage of ideas there can be no myth attached to
Auramazda, *i. e.* to the concentrated essence of the
gods of light, is obvious. In the Gathas it is only the
quite abstract forces of Vohumano and Asha, of good
disposition and truthfulness, which stand beside him.
Auramazda is simply the creator and lord ; and the
same position is ascribed to him as we saw (p. 87) in
the inscriptions of the Achæmenids. In spite of the
strongly-marked trait of spiritualisation and abstraction which runs through the Gathas, there is no lack
in them of unreflecting and naïve conceptions, which
have come down to us from ancient days. It is true
that the contrasts in nature and men are elevated to
the opposition of truth and falsehood, and the service
of truth is proclaimed as the highest command ; but
on the other hand, it is the strong fire of Auramazda
which causes the right to be recognised, and gives
the decision in battle.[1] It is the good sayings which
sustain the world, *i. e.* the old magic of prayers and
invocations is to keep off the evil, and increase the
strength of the good, spirits. However high may be
the conception of Auramazda, he who walks in his
way, and performs the commands of purity, not only
expects his reward, but insists on it ; he desires to

[1] "Yaçna," 31, 3, 19 ; 33, 3 ; 46, 7.

obtain ten mares and stallions, and at least one camel; he wishes for the blessings of Haurvatat in order to sacrifice from them; he desires continuance and power, health and long life. In these traits the old contrast between powers that give increase, blessing, and life, and powers of destruction, is plainly retained.

From the beginning the evil one was ranged over against Auramazda as his twin brother. He has created all that is evil, but nevertheless he is without any independent power of creation. If the Gathas express this merely in such a manner that they give prominence to Auramazda as the creator, they were as far from setting up a dualism of equally-balanced forces, as any other religion has been from attempting such a task, and carrying it out. The other fragments of the Avesta leave no doubt of the fact, that Angromainyu was not in a position to create the world according to his own will; he can only implant the form of evil in the good creation of Auramazda; he puts desolation, destruction, and death in the place of increase. The Vendidad quotes a whole series of lands which Auramazda created good, and enumerates the evils which the deadly Angromainyu brought into each:—into one winter, into another excessive heat; in one case vermin, in another disease, in a third beasts of prey. In the same way, in opposition to moral good, the evil one creates idleness, lies, lust, doubt, disbelief. An equally poised power of the two deities would have led to a direct conflict between them, which occurs nowhere in the Avesta; God and the devil only contend for the increase and injury of the world, and for the souls of men. The relative inferiority of the evil deity has not escaped the Greeks. "Some are of opinion," Plutarch says, " that there are two opposite deities, one of which framed the good,

the other the evil. Others, however, name the better
power the god, the other the demon, as Zoroaster
the Magian. He calls one Oromazdes, the other Areimanius, and states that Oromazdes most resembles
light among perceptible things, and Areimanius gloom
and uncertainty."[1] It is a later speculation, diverging
from the Avesta, which formed the good and evil
spirits into simple forces, and ranged them against
each other with equal powers.[2]

---

[1] Plut. " De Isid." 46.

[2] From the invocation of the time without limit, *Zrvana akarana*, in
the Avesta (p. 79), some have sought to draw the conclusion, that
this is the supreme principle, and that Auramazda and Angromainyu
proceeded from it. This is no less incorrect than if it were maintained
that according to the Christian dogma God and the devil owed their
origin to eternity. In the Avesta Zrvana akarana does not assume an
important place either at the creation or in the worship. I have
already remarked above, that the spirits of light are called in the
Rigveda sons of Aditi, *i.e.* of the unlimited, the eternal. Parallel
similitudes which, however, mean no more than the eternity of the
gods, could be made even among the Arians of Iran. But there is a
difference between speaking in similes, and derivation from a principle.
The faith of Iran was not a philosophical system, but a religion; a
religion cannot combine the good and evil god into one unity. It is
only when speculation becomes master over religion, that conceptions
of this kind can find a place; and this speculation, which sought for
primeval cosmical unity, arrived as a fact at an identical origin for the
good and evil spirit; but this was not the case with the Avesta.
Centuries after the establishment of the canon we find the oldest form
of such teaching in a demand made to the Armenian Christians that
they should join the faith of Auramazda. In this we are told that the
great deity Zrovan had sacrificed for a thousand years, and had
received two sons, Ormuzd and Ahriman. The first had created heaven
and earth, the other had opposed him with evil works. About the same
time Theodorus of Mopsuestia in Cilicia (Phot. " Biblioth." p. 63, ed.
Bekker), tells us: " Zoroaster called the creator of all things Zaruam,
and described him as fate; " and in the sixth century Damascius (" De
prim. princip." p. 384) writes: "The Magi and the whole Arian nation
call the Whole and One in thought, space and time respectively ; from
this One arose the good and evil god, Oromasdes and Areimanius, or as
others say light and darkness were divided before these." The sect of
the Zarvanites, who deviated from the faith of Zoroaster, inasmuch as
they carried these principles still further, has been already mentioned
(p. 67).

In the Gathas we have the nucleus of the conceptions from which the reform of the ancient faith of Iran arose, but not in their original state. On the contrary, they have been systematised in the circles of the priests. Hence the contents and prescripts of other parts of the Avesta, which do not present a speculative tendency, are not on that account to be regarded as of later origin than the Gathas—least of all the invocations to the ancient deities. It was an essential object of priestly meditation to bring these old gods, which existed vividly before the soul of the nation, into harmony with the new faith. On every page of the Avesta it is clear that the priests of Eastern Iran did not attain to an accepted system in this direction ; that the old gods remained in existence beside Auramazda, and the direct contest against the evil spirits, after the reform as before it, was carried on by Mithra, Verethraghna, and Vayu, Tistrya and Çraosha, while Auramazda is in the background, and sits somewhat passively on his golden throne in the heaven of Garonmana. When the Avesta was written down and collected, the ideas of the priests were still so naïve, or still preserved such a respect for the traditional forms of the gods of light and water, as they obviously lived in the mind of the people, that they represent Auramazda himself as offering sacrifice to Mithra,[1] Anahita, Vayu, and Tistrya, with Haoma and the sacred bundle of twigs, in order to strengthen their power or carry out his own wishes, just as the gods of the Aryas in India offer sacrifices to one another. In India the old gods received a subordinate position as protectors of the world after the rise of Brahman, but in Iran this was not the case ; nor were they brought into any genealogical connection with

[1] "Mihr Yasht," 123.

their new head Auramazda, though fire is occasionally
spoken of in a figure as the son of Auramazda, and the
earth (Armaiti) is once or twice called his daughter.[1]
The only bond of union between the new god and the
old gods in the Avesta is the fact that Auramazda is
made the creator of the old gods, and even of Mithra.
Yet the old position of Mithra appears, when Auramazda says to Zarathrustra: "When I created Mithra,
the lord of wide pastures, I created him as mighty to
pray to, mighty to worship as myself." Tistrya also
was created by Auramazda as worthy of adoration and
praise as himself.[2] We are already acquainted with
Auramazda's command to Zarathrustra to invoke and
worship Mithra, Vayu, the other ancient gods, and
fire (p. 131). The existence and extent of this worship
is proved not only by the prayers of the Yaçna, but
also by the accounts of western writers which we have
already examined.

As a compensation for the independent life of the
ancient gods by the side of Auramazda, the priests
surrounded his throne with six spirits, who were his
associates and helpers. These are called Amesha
Çpentas, i. e. the holy immortals; as good and wise
kings they rule with Auramazda over the seven girdles
of the earth,[3] as in India the eight protectors of the
world rule over the eight zones. The views out of
which these spirits arose are found in the Gathas, but
they did not receive their complete form till the
Gathas had been composed and generally received.
Plutarch tells us that, according to the faith of the Persians, Oromazdes had created six gods: the first, the
god of good disposition (εὔνοια); the second, the god

---

[1] Ashi vanguhi is in one passage called the daughter of Auramazda
and Armaiti: "Yaçna," 44, 4; "Vend." 19, 45; "Ashi Yasht," 16.
[2] "Tistar Yasht," 50.   [3] "Vend." 19 40; "Yaçna," 56, 10, 2.

of truth (ἀλήθεια) ; the third, the god of order and law
(εὐνομία) ; the three remaining deities were the gods of
wisdom (σοφία), of wealth (πλοῦτος), and of delight
in the beautiful (ἐπὶ τοῖς καλοῖς ἡδέων). The two first,
good disposition (Vohumano), and truth or truthfulness,
we already found frequently mentioned in the Gathas,
but chiefly as ideas rather than persons. With the
priests Vohumano and Asha vahista (the most excellent truthfulness) became the Amesha Çpentas, who
stand next to Auramazda. The Avesta speaks not
only of the good way of Vohumano, but also of
his acts, his dwelling, and his kingdom. According
to the books of the Parsees it is his duty to protect
the flocks. Asha vahista, as the truthful one, is the
protector of fire, which points the right path, and,
according to the Gathas, gives the decision in the
contest against the liars. According to the books of
the Parsees, Asha builds the bridge of Chinvat, to
which the souls come after death, making it wide
when the pious souls step upon it. Not less correctly
does Plutarch describe the third Amesha Çpenta as
the spirit of order and law. Kshathra, *i. e.* the kingdom, the dominion, is mentioned impersonally in the
Gathas; and this idea the priests have elevated into
Kshathra vairya, *i. e.* the good spirit of the desired
dominion, of good order and law, which is the third
Amesha Çpenta. Metals were allotted to him as the
king of the Ameshas.[1] The fourth figure in this circle,
which Plutarch correctly describes as the spirit of
wisdom, though he is wrong in calling it a god, is the
earth spirit Armaiti. In the Rigveda Aramati (the
earth) is a maiden worthy of praise, who, morning
and evening, brings butter to Agni. In the Avesta
Armaiti is " the beautiful daughter of Auramazda, the

---

[1] " Vispered," 23, 1.

bearer (*barethri*) of cattle, of beasts of draught, and men;" with "her hands Auramazda performs pure actions," while the Gathas also ascribe to her special relations to the corporeal world.[1] Among the priests the spirit of the "patient humble earth" has become the spirit of humility and piety. According to the books of the Parsees Armaiti gives patience and firmness.[2] The fifth and sixth spirits also, whom Plutarch calls the gods of wealth and delight in the beautiful, were found in existence by the priests, and merely ranged by them in the circle of the Amesha Çpentas. These are Haurvatat and Ameretat. We saw how earnestly the Arians of India besought the gods for wealth and length of life; and in this matter the Arians of Iran were not behind them. Here, as there, the powers which could grant such gifts were elevated into special spirits, to whom, naturally, all that gave wealth and long life, good and healing plants and refreshing water, belonged. The good plants were the kingdom of Ameretat, refreshing water the domain of Haurvatat. In the fancy of the Arians of Iran good plants sprang from the tree of heaven, the Gaokerena, which grew in Ardviçura (p. 126); the water flowed down from this source in heaven, or came from Vourukasha, the lake on the divine mountain. Those two spirits, who ruled over plants and water, were brought by the system of the priests into the circle of the Amesha Çpentas; the province over which they ruled had long been apportioned to them. They were distinguished from the first four by the fact that those were personifications of moral ideas, these two were personifications of real goods.[3] With wealth,

---

[1] "Yaçna," 44, 4; 46, 2; 13, 6; "Vend." 19, 45; Haug, "Essays," p. 231.　　　　　[2] Spiegel, "Eran," 1, 435.

[3] Darmesteter, "Haurvatat et Ameretat," p. 68, 81 ff.

prosperity and happy life is given, with length of
life the complete enjoyment of its blessings, and so
the Greeks could arrive at the conclusion that these
two spirits were gods of wealth and delight in
beauty. Thus Auramazda now ruled surrounded by
six sacred forms. The semblance of this circle on
earth was the throne of Cyrus and his successors,
which was surrounded by the six tribal princes of
the Persians.

The personification of ideas—the process of trans-
forming old figures, and changing them into abstractions
—did not come to an end with the Amesha Çpentas.
We are acquainted with Çraosha, the warrior against
the Daevas, his habitation on the divine mountain, his
horses, his club, and how he fights at the side of
Mithra, and keeps watch in the dark of the night
against the demons (p. 121). Now it is he who first
sang the sacred four Gathas of Zarathrustra, who first
bound the sacred withes, "three twigs, five twigs,
seven twigs;" he not only knows the sacred word;
the sacred word is the body of Çraosha. Instead of
the club which he held raised against the head of the
Daevas, the invocations of the Avesta and the prayer
Ahuna vairya are now the weapons with which he,
"the pure lord of the pure," "advances the world."
We remember the process by which the Arians in
India came to represent Indra as smiting Vritra, and
shattering his cave, not as formerly with the lightning,
but with Brahman, the power of the prayer and the
sacred acts. Obviously we have some influence of
these old Arian conceptions of the mysterious power
of prayer, and the control of the spirits possessed by
the correct invocations and sayings against gods and
spectres, when we find Çraosha fighting with the
prayers of the Avesta, and in the Avesta the sacred

word is praised as a Divine power—[1] when Zarathrustra
offers sacrifice to the good law.[2]　More liberal creations
on the part of the system of the priests are the
elevation of " excellent thought, knowledge, and conception," of " the long study," " and the thought of
the pure man," which are invoked and praised in the
Avesta, into Divine powers.　Of not less abstract
nature are other forms, like Rashnu razista, *i. e.* the
most straight-forward justice,[3] which, according to the
Dinkart, tests the souls on the bridge of Chinvat ; time,
which is invoked as unlimited, as the ruler of the long
periods, and like the genius of the five portions into
which the priests divided the day.　Of older origin,
though also modified by the reform, is the invocation
of the heights, which Mithra first illuminated with his
light.　In the Avesta this invocation is mainly addressed to the high " navel of the waters," the Divine
mountain, which reaches to the sky, " on which were
asked the holy questions," *i. e.* on which Zarathrustra
has received the revelation ; " by reason of the revelation of the sacred word we invoke the height, which
preserved the knowledge."[4]　Many of the traditional
forms of ancient times were partly modified by the
priests and partly allowed to fade away.　The goddess
Drvaçpa, to whom the ancient heroes had sacrificed,
they changed into the soul of the primeval bull, which
Angromainyu had slain.[5]　Nairyoçangha, the Nara-
çansa of the Veda, an ancient name of the spirit of
fire, which we learned to know in the Veda as the
messenger of men to the heavenly beings, as priest
and mediator between heaven and earth (IV. 39), appears in the Avesta merely as the messenger of the

---

[1] " Vend." 19, 30—34, 54.　　　　[2] " Din Yasht," 2.
[3] " Rashnu Yasht," 8.　　　　[4] Burnouf, *l. c.* p. 417, 468.
[5] " Gosh Yasht ;" Yaçna, 29 ; 39, 1.

gods.[1] The form of Vayu, the more ancient conception
of which still plainly breaks through (p. 116), becomes
merely the air "whose operation is on high;" and
Ashi vanguhi, whom the ancient sacrificers and heroes
invoked, together with Ardviçura, for victory, bears
traces which can hardly any longer be recognised.
We merely perceive that she could once confer
power, fertility, beauty, and wealth. We saw above
how she called Zarathrustra to her chariot, and promised splendour to his body, and long prosperity
to his soul (p. 130). If the luminaries of heaven,
in spite of the creation described to Auramazda, are
extolled as "having no beginning," we have in this
fact a glimpse of the old position of the spirits of light.
The struggles of Tistrya against the demons of
drought were allowed to remain (p. 120). Plutarch
observes that, according to the doctrine of the Magians,
Oromazdes had placed Sirius (Tistrya) as a watchman
and advanced guard. On the other hand, the worship
of the sun-god appears but faintly in the Avesta—in
our fragments at any rate. Yet Herodotus informs us
that with the Persians the neighing of horses at sunrise was regarded as a favourable sign from the gods,
and Xenophon states that the Magians offered bulls
to Zeus, but horses to the sun-god, and that on the
journeys of the Achæmenids the chariot of Zeus went
first, then that of the sun-god; both were white and
crowned; and these were followed by a third chariot
covered with purple, which as it seems was the chariot
of fire. In the march of Xerxes to Hellas, according
to the account of Herodotus, a sacred car, yoked with
eight white horses, went before him; and ten sacred
horses were led, clothed in the most beautiful trappings.
Curtius represents the emblem of the sun as glowing

[1] "Vend." 19, 111, 112; 22, 22.

over the tent of the last Darius, who invokes " the sun,
Mithra, and the sacred eternal fire ; " and he tells us
of the chariot of Zeus in the army, yoked with white
horses, behind which was led a horse of remarkable
size, the horse of the sun, with golden bridle and
white covering, like those before the chariot.   Dio
Chrysostom tells us that the Magians reared a yoke
of Nisaean horses for Zeus, *i. e.* for Mithra, which were
the largest and most beautiful in all Asia, and a horse
for Helius.[1]   We can call to mind the battle-chariot
of Mithra, " with golden wheels and silver spokes"
(p. 110).   These were imitations of the divine chariots
of which the Greeks tell us, and if they were not in
a position to distinguish accurately what belonged to
Mithra (Auramazda does not come into the question),
and what to Hvare Kshaeta (the sun-god)—Strabo is
of opinion that the Persians called the sun Mithras[2]—
we may still conclude with certainty from these
statements, that the worship of Mithra and the sun-
god remained more vigorous and effectual among the
princes and nations of Iran than our fragments of the
Avesta would allow us to assume, if the old invocations
to Mithra, Tistrya, Haoma, Vayu, and Verethraghna
had not been preserved in them.   Yet the fragments
do present us with an invocation to the sun-god,
though weakened, it is true, and adapted to the new
faith.   " We celebrate the brilliant, immortal sun,
whose horses are unwearied.   When the sun gleams
in heaven, the heavenly spirits come by hundreds and
thousands, and spread the light over the earth for the
salvation of the pure world, for the salvation of the
pure bodies.   As the sun rises, the earth purifies
herself, and the fructifying waters of the springs,

[1] Herod. 7, 40, 55 ; Xenoph. " Cyr. inst." 8, 3, 12 ; Curtius, 3, 3, 8 ;
4, 48, 12.   Dio Chrysost. 2, 60, ed. Dindorf.   [2] p. 732.

pools and lakes; the sun-god purifies all creatures that belong to Çpentomainyu. If the sun came not, the Daevas would slay all that inhabits the seven girdles of the earth, and the heavenly beings would not be able to withstand them; they could not drive them away. He who sacrifices to the sun in order to withstand the dark Daevas, the thieves and robbers, he sacrifices to Auramazda, to the Amesha Çpentas and to his own soul." [1] In the time of the Sassanids, the worship of the sun comes definitely forward.

Plutarch states that the demon Areimanius had created an equal number of evil spirits to match the six good gods of Oromazdes, *i. e.* the Amesha Çpentas. The Vendidad mentions five of them : Andra, Çaurva, Naonghaithya, Tauru, and Zairicha,[2] to which we have only to add Akomano, which has been mentioned already in the Gathas, in order to make up the number. They are all of them creations of the priests, partly invented to match the Amesha Çpentas, partly borrowed from older forms, which had lost their brightness among the Arians of Iran. Akomano, *i. e.* Bad disposition, is naturally the counterpart of Vohumano, or Good disposition: opposite Asha vahista, *i. e.* the most excellent truthfulness, the priests placed the demon Andra (Indra), *i. e.* an old Arian name which the Arians beyond the Indus had elevated to be the best warrior against the demons, the god of the storm. No special qualities of Andra are known or mentioned in the Avesta ; the books of the Parsees can only say that he brings care and sorrow of heart to men, and makes narrow the bridge of Chinvat. The demon Çaurva is the opponent of Kshathra vairya, of order and law, of good dominion; hence, according to the

[1] "Khorshed Yasht," in De Harlez, "Avesta," p. 34.
[2] 10, 17, 18.

Sad-der-Bundehesh, he leads kings astray into despot-
ism, and nations into lawlessness and robbery. Naonghaithya is the opponent of Armaiti, the spirit of
humility and piety; this spirit therefore, as the Bundehesh maintains, makes men impatient and proud;
the science of languages claims to find in this name
a Vedic name for the two Açvins,—Nasatya (IV. 42).
Only the last two opposing spirits of the Amesha
Çpentas, the opponents of Haurvatat and Ameretat,
display, like these beings, real characteristics. If they
are the spirits of water and plants, of prosperity and
long life or immortality, then Tauru is the spirit
of thirst and sickness, and Zairicha of hunger and
death.[1]

If the ancient gods have preserved more lively traits
than the Amesha Çpentas, the old demons have also
more definite outlines than the opposing spirits. Such
are the Daeva Apaosha, who parches up the land and
keeps back the water from the earth; Çpenjaghra, the
comrade of him who was struck by lightning; Zemaka,
the spirit of the cold winter; and finally Azhi, who
seeks to steal away the fire from men in the night.
Among these evil spirits may further be reckoned a
female demon Bushyançta, with long hands and of a
yellow hue, who leads men astray into much sleep and
idleness, who does not allow them to see the rise of
the sun, and shortens the joy of existence;[2] the three
Daevas of drunkenness, Kunda, Banga, and Vibanga;
the Daeva Buiti, the spirit of lies and falsehood, who
deceives men;[3] the spirit of flattery, Ashemaogha;[4] and
the very wicked Ashma "of evil glance," who attempts

[1] "Zamyad Yasht," 96; Darmesteter, *l. c.* p. 10.
[2] "Vend." 18, 38.   [3] "Vend." 19, 6, 146.
[4] Burnouf, "Journ. Asiatic," 1845, p. 433.

to slay the sleeping, and withstands Çraosha by night with terrible weapons.[1] Very evil also is Açtovidhotu, *i. e.* the destroyer of bodies, and a female goblin, the spirit of the Daevas, the Druj Naçu. This spirit enters the body immediately after death, and exercises power over all who come in contact with it.

Under Auramazda are united the gods, the Amesha Çpentas, the rest of the Yazatas (those worthy of adoration), in opposition to the troops of hell, the Daevas, Druj, Pairikas and Jainis, which are led by Angromainyu. The first are found in the light of sunrise, in the clear gleam of the pure sky; the latter in the gloom of sunset, or in the distant clouds of the north; in burial-places, and where the dead are placed; in all corners into which the light of heaven does not pierce; in the dark abyss under earth; in " the worst place."[2] On the summit of the mountain Arezura (Demavend, apparently), they take counsel how they are to turn the evil eye on men; how they can injure and slay them.[3] To them belong gloom, cold, drought, the barren land and the wilderness, thorns and poisonous herbs, hunger and thirst, sickness, death, dirt, laziness, lying, sin. Theirs are the harmful beasts, the Khrafçtras; beasts of prey, wolves, serpents; all animals which live in holes and corners, lizards, scorpions, toads, frogs, rats, mice, gnats, and lastly mosquitoes, lice, and fleas.[4] To the good spirits belong light, water, springs, rivers, the fruitful earth, good plants,[5] trees, fields, pastures, good food, purity, truth, life in this world and the next; and theirs are the good animals, the animals of the flocks, the birds

---

[1] "Vend." 10, 23. Windischmann, " Zoroastrische Studien," s. 138.
[2] "Vend." 19, 147.   [3] "Vend." 4, 139.
[4] "Vend." 12, 65, 71 ; 14, 9 ff. ; Plut. " De Isid." c. 46; Agath. 2, 24.
[5] Plut. " De Isid." c. 46.

which nestle on the heights, and live in the clear air.
The dog and the cock are worshipped in the Avesta
as fighting with men against the Daevas. The first
protects the flocks against the beasts of prey of
Angromainyu. Of the cock the Avesta says: "The
bird Parodarsh, which evil-speaking men call Kahzkataç
(*i. e.* Kikeriki or the like), lifts up his voice in the
last third of the night, roused by the holy Çraosha
at every divine dawn. He cries: 'Rise up, ye men;
praise the most excellent truth; drive away the Daevas.'
Who gives a pair of these birds to a pure man, in
purity and kindness, gives as much as if he had given
a palace with a thousand pillars and a thousand
beams, ten thousand windows, and a hundred thousand
turrets." "And whoever gives to a pure man as
much meat as makes the size of a Parodarsh"—the
book of Auramazda tells us in another place—"I
who am Auramazda will ask him no other question
on his way to Paradise."[1] According to the Avesta
the dog and cock unite their powers against the
Druj.[2] The bird Asho-zusta fights against the
Daevas, and the bird Karshipta (the sacred hawk)
announces the good law in the garden of Yima.
Two other mythical birds, the two eagles (çaena) of
the sky, Amru and Chamru, are invoked as helpful
powers.[3] They nestle on the tree of life in the
heaven. Besides the tree Gaokerena, which grows
in Ardviçura and bears the heavenly Haoma, the
Avesta has also the tree Viçpataokhma, which grows
in the Lake Vourukasha, and bears all seeds. When
Amru sits on this tree, the seeds fall down, and Chamru
carries them away where Tistrya collects the water,
who then rains down the seed with the water to the

---

[1] "Vend" 18, 34—37: 64—69.　　　　[2] Cf. "Bundehesh," c. 19.
[3] "Yasht Farvardin," 109; "Yasht Bahram," 19—21.

earth. In the book of kings of Firdusi, Simurgh (Çin-murv), the king of the birds, carries Rustem on his pinions over the broad earth as far as the sea of Chin (China) to the tree of life.[1] A prophet of the Hebrews represents Jehovah as saying of Cyrus: " I summoned from the East the eagle, the man of my counsel." [2] Xenophon tells us that Cyrus, and the Achæmenids who succeeded him, carried as a standard a golden eagle on a tall lance ; [3] and Curtius says, that a golden eagle with outspread wings was attached to the chariots of the Persian king.[4]

The fragments of the Avesta which have been pre-served do not give us very full information on the sacrifices. The essential matters are hymns of praise and prayers. The chief sacrifice is offered to one of the old deities, Haoma, the supporter and protector of life. When Plutarch represents the Magi as pounding a certain herb of the name of Omomi in a mortar, with invocations to avert Hades, he gives a correct account of the supposed tendency of this sacrifice. According to the Avesta the utensils for this sacrifice—the mortar, cup and bundle of twigs—were found in every house. The sacrifice consisted in the offering, *i. e.* the elevation of the cup filled with the juice of the Haoma, during the recitation of the proper prayers. Beside this offering, which even now is offered twice each day by the priests of the Parsees, the fire is to be kept up perpetually, and fed with good dry wood and perfumes. The flesh of the sacrifice (*myazda*) is

[1] Kuhn, " Herabkunft des Feuers," s. 125; Darmesteter, *loc. cit.* p. 55. Çinmurv has arisen out of *Çaena* (*Çin*), *i. e.* eagle, and *mereghu,* "bird;" Middle Pers. *murv ;* New Pers. *murgh.* In New Pers. Çin-murv becomes Simurgh.

[2] Isaiah xlvi. 11. In Aeschylus also an eagle represents the Persians and a falcon the Hellenes; " Pers." 205—210.

[3] " Cyri instit." 7, 1, 4.   [4] 3, 7.

not often mentioned; yet the book of the law provides
that a thousand head of small cattle must be offered
in expiation of certain offences,[1] and we are told in
the invocations that the heroes of old time, from
Thraetaona down to King Vistaçpa, had offered great
sacrifices of animals to Ardviçura and Drvaçpa, in
order to gain the victory, viz. 100 horses, 1000
cattle, and 10,000 head of small cattle. Herodotus
tells us that the Magians, when Xerxes marched
into Hellas, sacrificed 1000 oxen on the summit of
Pergamus to Athene of Ilium, and at a later time
white horses in Thrace; Xenophon maintains that the
Persians sacrificed beautiful bulls to Zeus, i.e. to
Auramazda, and horses to the sun, and burnt them
whole; Athenæus tells that with the king of the
Persians a thousand animals were daily slaughtered
as sacrifices; camels, horses, oxen, apes, deer, and
especially sheep. According to Arrian, the Magians
who kept guard over the burial-place of Cyrus received
a horse every month, and a sheep every day, for sacrifice.[2] Herodotus has already told us, that the animals
were led to a pure place, and when the sacrificer had
invoked the god were killed, cut up, cooked, and then
laid out on delicate grass. The Magian then sang the
theogony, and after some time, the person who offered
the sacrifice " carried away the flesh, and used it at his
pleasure " (p. 85). Herodotus is better informed than
Xenophon; according to the Avesta only the head of
the animal belongs to the gods.[3] Obviously, as the
nature of the gods became more spiritualised—and the
reform prepared the way for this—the sacrifice of

[1] "Vend." 18, 137, 138, 149.
[2] Xenophon, "Cyri instit." 8, 3, 11, 24; Athen. p. 145; Arrian,
"Anab." 6, 29.
[3] "Yaçna," 10. 38, 11, 16. Strabo, p. 732, tells us that the deity of
the Persians received nothing from the sacrifice.

animals was restricted in this manner, so that it consisted essentially in the offering of the animals, *i. e.* in the consecration of the flesh. We may conclude from the statement in Athenæus, that only consecrated flesh could be eaten at the court of the kings. Xerxes certainly would not have sacrificed to Athene, "a lying deity" of the Greeks, on the summit of Ilium; but he might very well have selected the last eminence in Asia Minor, "the many-fountained Ida," in order to offer there a sacrifice of 1000 oxen to Ardviçura for his victory beyond the sea—a sacrifice which corresponds exactly to the first offering made by Kava Huçrava and Kava Vistaçpa to the same goddess for victory over the Turanians.[1]

Temples and images are unknown to the Avesta. The reform preserved for the nations of Iran the traditional form of worship without images, on which it was founded. The accounts of western writers, from Herodotus and Xenophon downwards, establish the fact that there were only sacrificial places on the heights and consecrated fire-altars in Iran.[2] But this must not be taken to mean that the forms of worship and the images of the nations with which the Persians became acquainted after the foundation of their supremacy, especially of their nearest neighbours, the Semites on the Tigris and Euphrates, remained

---

[1] What Herodotus tells us of the sacrifice of girls and boys by the Magi in Thrace contradicts his own statement that the Magi did not venture to kill any one, and the whole conception of the Avesta. If Cambyses is said to have caused twelve Persians to be buried alive, this is not to be regarded as a sacrifice, but as a barbarous form of execution, which occurs also under the Sassanids. What Herodotus says of the fourteen boys offered by Amestris as a sacrifice, if true, must have its origin in some other superstition, not in the Avesta; and the actions of Amestris and Parysatis in this direction, as recorded by Ctesias, were in any cases crimes, not sacrifices.

[2] Strabo, p. 732.

without influence on them. On the monuments of
Darius we see the picture of Auramazda, cut exactly
after the pattern which the Assyrian monuments
exhibit in the portraiture of their god Asshur. We
are also told of images of Anahita. Berosus maintains
that Artaxerxes Mnemon erected statues to Aphrodite
Anaitis at Babylon, Ecbatana, and Susa, and taught
this form of worship to the Damascenes and Lydians.[1]
From this statement, taken in connection with the
account of Herodotus that the Persians had learnt to
sacrifice to Mylitta,[2] the conclusion has been drawn
that Artaxerxes II. introduced the worship of Bilit
among the Persians. But it was not necessary to
teach this worship to the Damascenes and Lydians
(I. 358, 563), and even in the Avesta, Anahita as the
goddess of the heavenly water is the goddess of fertility.
Hence the statues made by Artaxerxes were, no doubt,
images of Anahita the goddess, whom he invokes along
with Auramazda and Mithra in his inscription at
Susa. Strabo describes the worship of the Magians at
the fire-altars of Cappadocia in a manner which completely agrees with the accounts given in the Avesta,
and then adds that these functions were also per-
formed in the enclosures ($\sigma\eta\kappa o\acute{\iota}$) which were consecrated there to Anaitis, Amardatus, and Omanus, and
the image of Omanus was carried round in processions.
He concludes with the words: " this (*i. e.* the form of
worship described) I have myself seen."[3] According
to this account, then, Amardate,[4] *i. e.* the Amesha
Çpenta Ameretat, who averts death, was worshipped
there beside Anahita, and Omanus, *i. e.* the Amesha
Çpenta Vohumano, the protector of the flocks, had

---

[1] Fragm. 16, ed. Müller. [2] 1, 131. [3] Strabo, p. 733.
[4] Windischmann has shown, " Abh. Bair. Akad. phil. philol. Kl." 8,
90, 120, that Ἀμαρδατός must be read for Ἀναυδατός.

an image. As this is all that we can discover about the image-worship of the Persians, it is clear that the influence of the picture-worship of Hither Asia and Egypt had no great influence even on the western nations of Iran. It is limited to the facts that Darius added the symbolical picture of Auramazda to his inscriptions without, however, building him a temple; that a century after him Artaxerxes II. erected statues and a temple to Anahita at Ecbatana; and that at a later time a portable image of Vohumano was in existence in Cappadocia.

The nucleus of the old religious conceptions of the Arians—the desire to obtain increase and life from the gods—has been sufficiently disclosed; and that which could not be obtained in this world, the continuance of the individual life, heaven was to bestow upon them. This line was followed up by the reform; the spirits of health and long life were added by the priests to the circle of the Amesha Çpentas. When Zarathrustra had increased the means for the protection and support of life; when it became a fixed maxim that purity preserved life in this world and ensured it after death; the sharp insistence on the command of the pure and active and truthful life which men ought to lead in this world, became developed into the conception of a judgment on the souls after death. He who had lived purely, and given the Daevas no room to exercise their power on his body, became himself pure and bright, and could therefore enter after death as a pure spirit among the spirits of light. Thus the Avesta announces that "when body and soul have separated," the soul on the third night after death, as soon as the brilliant sun arises, and the victorious Mithra seats himself with "pure brilliance" on the mountains, comes over the

Hara berezaiti to the bridge of Chinvat, *i. e.* the bridge
of assembly or of assembling, which leads to Garonmana, *i. e.* to the dwelling of hymns, the abode of the
good gods. Here the Daevas and the gods contend for
the soul;[1] the judgment of the souls takes place;[2]
here Auramazda asks the souls about their conduct.[3]
The pure soul, whose odour the Daevas dread,[4] which
approaches with virtue and sanctity, is joined by the
other pure souls and by the souls of the dogs which
keep watch over the bridge of Chinvat,[5] and the host
of the heavenly Yazatas brings the soul of the good
over the bridge into heaven. In contentment the
pure soul goes to the golden throne of Auramazda, to
the thrones of the Amesha Çpentas, to the dwelling of
the pure. And Vohumano rises from his golden
throne and inquires of the pure one: " How hast
thou, O pure one, come hither out of the perishable to
the imperishable world?"[6] But the souls which come
to the bridge full of terror and sick, find no friend
there; the evil spirits, Vizaresha by name, lead them
bound down into the place of the bad, into the darkness, the dwelling of the Druj.[7]

In the Veda the spirits of the fathers are invited to
the sacrificial meal; they are to enjoy the gifts which
are laid for them on the grass, to support the prayers
of their descendants, to keep away the evil spirits, and
to increase wealth. Each day water was poured there
for the forefathers, and corns of rice were scattered for
them; on the new moon the clans held the funeral
feast for the dead; and we are acquainted with the
consequences which attended expulsion from this

1 " Vend." 7, 132—136; 19, 90—100.   2 " Vend." 19, 89.
3 " Vend." 18, 68, 69.   4 " Vend." 19, 108.
5 " Vend." 13, 22, 25.   6 " Vend." 19, 100—108.
7 " Vend." 8, 252, 310; 19, 94; cf. 3, 118—121. In the Dinkart the
proceedings on the bridge are related at greater length.

banquet.[1] The belief in the spirits of the ancestors, and their continued relation to their descendants, existed also among the Arians of Iran, and the Avesta alters it only so far as to limit consistently the assistance given by the spirits of the fathers to the souls of those who have lived in truth and purity, and have thus found entrance into heaven. According to the Avesta the Fravashis of the pure—this is the name given to the Pitaras, or fathers of the Indians—protect their descendants against the Daevas, help them in distress and danger, and fight for their families on the day of battle, if they are honoured and satisfied by their descendants. It is only an old conception, repeated in the Avesta, when we are told: "We invoke the good, strong, holy Fravashis. Where strong men fight in severe conflict, there come the Fravashis with strong shield, iron helmet, and iron weapons; with Mithra and the victorious wind they go forward; strong warriors against the enemies, they are mighty saviours; strong conquerors, they destroy the victory of the enemy—the Turas (Turanians)."[2] It is due to the additions and modifications introduced by the priests that we hear that the hosts of the Fravashis watch the body of Kereçaçpa till the resurrection, and the seed of Zarathrustra, and protect the sleepers from the rising of the stars till midnight.[3] As among the Arians of India the ancient belief in the fathers was retained in spite of all changes of the religious system, so also in Iran. At the close of the year, on the intercalary days which were added to it, the Fravashis come to their families, abide among them for ten nights, and ask: "Who will receive us, and sacrifice to us, and praise us?" and "if any one

[1] Vol. IV., 61, 163, 230. [2] "Farvardin Yasht," 35—48, 70, 71.
[3] "Farvardin Yasht," 61, 62.

offers to them prayers and flesh and clothes, him they
bless, and in his dwelling there will be abundance of
oxen and men, swift horses and a strong car." [1]   The
Greeks had therefore reason to say that according to
the doctrine of the Magians the air was full of spirits. [2]

In another direction the system of the priests
deviated far more widely from the ancient conception
of the spirits of the ancestors. They held that only
the pure and bright part of the soul could live on
after death.   Hence, even in the living they distinguished this part from the polluted part, and in
the pure immortal half they saw the side created by
the good gods, its true being, the Fravashi or protecting spirit allotted to each man. In the Avesta therefore rules can be given for the invocation of this pure
part and nature of the individual soul, of the separate
Fravashis. The priests then transferred this notion to
the heavenly spirits, and even to Auramazda himself.
His purest nature, his best self, must be praised and
invoked for aid.   Auramazda says to Zarathrustra in
the book of the law : " O Zarathrustra, praise thou my
Fravashi, the Fravashi of Auramazda, the greatest,
best, most intelligent, best-formed, highest in holiness,
whose soul is the holy word." [3]   And in the prayers
we are told : " We praise the Fravashis of the Amesha
Çpentas, of the holy Çraosha, of Mithra, together with
all the Fravashis of the heavenly Yazatas. I invoke the
Fravashi of the holy Zarathrustra, the Fravashis of the
men of the ancient law, and the Fravashis of the men
of the new law, the good mighty Fravashis of the
pure, of the nearest relations, and of my own soul." [4]
The Persians at the king's gate, according to the

---

[1] "Farvardin Yasht," 50—52.   [2] "Diogen. Laert. "Prooem." 6.
[3] "Vend." 19, 46, 48.
[4] "Yaçna," 1, 47 ; 23, 6 ; Burnouf, "Commentaire," p. 571.

Greeks, set apart a separate table at each meal with bread and food for the " demon " of the king, and at a Persian banquet the host, according to Plutarch, calls on his guests, "to honour the demon of king Arta-xerxes." Hence it clearly follows that the priestly doctrine of the Fravashis of the living was current even in Western Iran under the Achæmenids.[1]

Zarathrustra had increased the means for keeping off the evil ones, and had made the struggle against the wicked spirits easier for men. But the time will come when the struggle will be no longer necessary, and the bright spirits alone will rule. This doctrine is indicated even in the Gathas.[2] In the book of the law Zarathrustra says to Angromainyu: he will smite the Daevas till Çaoshyant is born from the water of Kançava in the eastern region.[3] Çaoshyant, i.e. the useful, the saviour, is called in the Avesta, "the sublime, the victorious;" he will smite the Druj, and Aeshma will bow before him. He will make the world to live for ever, without age and death; the dead will rise again, and the living will be immortal. Vohumano will smite Akomano, Asha will kill the lies. Haurvatat and Ameretat will destroy thirst and hunger: " The evil-doer Angromainyu, robbed of his dominion, bows himself."[4] This doctrine of the Avesta also was well known to the western world. In Hero-dotus Prexaspes tells Cambyses that when the dead rise again he will see Smerdis and Astyages.[5] Theo-pompus of Chios tells us: Zoroaster had proclaimed that there would be a time in which the dead will arise, and men will be immortal, and everything will

---

[1] Plut. "Artax." 15; Theopomp. Fragm. 135, ed. Müller.
[2] "Yaçna," 45, 3; 47, 1; above, p. 156.
[3] " Vend." 19, 17—19; above, p. 135.
[4] "Zamyad Yasht," 89, 95, 96.   [5] 3, 62.

be done by their invocations. Last of all, Hades will
pass away ; men will then be happy ; they will need no
nourishment, and throw no shadows, and the god who
will accomplish this rests for a time, but not a long
time for a god.[1] It is true that men required no
nourishment when Çaoshyant had appeared, in the
meaning of the Avesta, for Haurvatat and Ameretat
had overcome hunger and thirst as well as sickness
and death ; and as the dark side of man was taken
away, and only the bright side remained, they could
not cast any shadows.

As already remarked, it was part of the duty of the
priests to bring the ancient legends of the old time into
harmony with the new doctrine. We saw that the
legends of Iran began with the happy age of Yima,
and his reign of a thousand years full of increase and
blessing. This conception of a perfect age for the
creatures of earth at the very beginning of things did
not suit with the struggle, which, according to the new
doctrine, Angromainyu commenced immediately after
the creation. The priests, therefore, conceived the
beginning of things in a different manner. In their
system Auramazda first created the heaven, then the
water, then the earth and the trees, and after these
the four-footed bull, and the two-legged pure man
Gayo maretan.[2] In the Avesta the primeval bull and
man are at the head, and time extends from Gayo
maretan to Çaoshyant.[3] The books of the Parsees
then tell us that Angromainyu killed the primeval
man and bull, but from the seed of the bull proceeded
a pair of oxen, and then all kinds of good animals ;
and out of the seed of Gayo maretan grew up the first

---

[1] Theopomp. Fragm. 71, 72, ed. Müller.
[2] "Yaçna," 19, 16—18.
[3] "Yaçna," 26, 32 ; "Farvardin Yasht," 135.

man and the first woman. As we have already remarked, our fragments of the Avesta identify the soul
of the first created bull with the Drvaçpa, the ancient
guardian spirit of the flocks; next to Gayo maretan
they place Haoshyangha, the Paradhata (p. 36), and
represent him as sacrificing to Ardviçura, Vayu, and
Ashi vanguhi, in order to obtain the dominion over
the evil spirits.[1] After him Takhmo urupa rules the
earth of seven parts; he sacrifices to Vayu in order to
obtain grace to restrain Angromainyu for thirty years.[2]
Then, according to the system of the priests, follows
the dominion of Yima the son of Vivanghana, during
which there was no cold and no heat, no age and no
death, as was represented in the old views. Yima
kindles the red-glowing fire. Flocks and men, i. e.
life, increase; and the earth must be made larger. The
end of this happy period, and the death of Yima, is
brought about, according to the priests, by the fact that
Yima refused to be the preacher of the doctrine of
Auramazda, that he was unable to maintain purity
and truth, and began to "love lying speech" (p. 41).
As Yima was born to Vivanghana as a reward for his
Haoma sacrifice, there follows a series of those who
have offered the sacrifice: Athwya, Thrita, Pourushaçpa, and their sons. To the first Thraetaona was
born, who smites the serpent Dahaka; to Thrita Kereçaçpa, who smites the serpent Çruvara; and to Pourushaçpa was born Zarathrustra, who receives the law
of Auramazda and proclaims it; by this law the
Daevas will be warded off till Çaoshyant appears,
when everything which has once had life will come
to life again.

---

[1] "Aban Yasht," 21—23; "Farvardin Yasht," 157; "Ashi Yasht,"
24; "Zamyad Yasht," 26.
[2] "Ram Yasht," 11; "Zamyad Yasht," 28.

CHAPTER VIII.

In the form in which we have them the books of the Avesta are the work of the priests of Eastern Iran. According to the evidence repeatedly furnished by them, there were three orders in Sogdiana and Bactria : priests, warriors, and husbandmen. This sequence, which is uniformly preserved both in the invocations and in the book of the law, shows that the priests had risen above the warriors, and claimed to be the first of the three orders.[1]

In considering the civilisation of the Bactrian kingdom we found ourselves compelled by the proximity of the nations of the steppes to assume, that when the Arians had become established there, the tribes which had a capacity or love for battle, undertook the protection of the land, the flocks and fields, against the incursions of the nomads of the north, and made battle and strife their special vocation. Such attacks increased with the increasing culture of Bactria, and led to a consolidation of powers; these clans raised one of their number distinguished in battle to be their

[1] "Vend." 2, 87—89 ; "Yaçna," 14, 4—6. If in "Yaçna," 19, 46 four occupations are mentioned instead of the four orders, and artisans are added to the husbandmen, this is only another theory, which does not, however, alter the series and system ; in India the order of Vaiçyas comprises husbandmen, merchants, and artisans.

leader, or followed him, and thus was laid the basis for the foundation of a great state. The importance ascribed in the Avesta to the splendour of majesty—we find the personification of good government in the Avesta among the Amesha Çpentas—in combination with the battles which, as we learn from the book, the princes of Bactria carried on against the Turanians, and with the statements in the West Iranian Epos about the kingdom of the Bactrians, together with the later condition of the country, allowed us to draw the conclusion that at one time the kings of Bactria were not without power and importance. They reigned, surrounded by the families of the warriors, who were enabled by their possessions in lands and flocks, to devote themselves to the practice of arms and to battle. The invocations to Mithra, Verethraghna, and Vayu, bear upon them very evident traces of a war-like spirit (p. 110, 114). That the spirits of the sky, which once fought with the cloud-dragons, have become mortal heroes in the Avesta, also proves—since even among other nations the Epic poetry which follows periods of warlike excitement transforms shapes of the sky into heroes of old time—that once on a time Bactria had experienced a period of warfare, when difficulties arose which it was mainly the business of the monarchy and the nobles to settle. The Avesta can tell us of arms and robes as well as of palaces with pillars and turrets; of earthen, iron, silver and golden vessels; of mats, carpets, and adornments of gold,[1] such as are found among noble families; and those hecatombs of horses, cattle, and sheep which the heroes in the Avesta sacrifice to Anahita and Drvaçpa, in order to obtain their favour by victory, are no doubt borrowed from the sacrifices

[1] "Vend." 8, 254.

which princes and nobles were wont to offer in cases
where the numbers must be enlarged in honour of the
heroes. Yet we see that Xerxes orders a thousand
oxen to be sacrificed at one time. We have already
shown (IV. 390), how important and pre-eminent
was the position which the races of the warriors, " the
princes," occupied on the Indus and the Ganges, and
what respect they commanded among " the free Indians" in the Panjab, even in the fourth century B.C.
That a warlike nobility of a similar character, attitude,
and position, existed in Eastern Iran, is the less to be
doubted, as the order of warriors in the Avesta is
denoted by a name (*rathaestar*) which goes back to the
chariots of war. The husbandmen, who were settled
beside and among them, bear in the Avesta the name
of Vaçtrya,[1] but the word Vaeçu is also used for them,
which simply repeats the name of the Indian Vaiçyas.

Like the Arians of India, the Arians of Iran believed
in the power of the correct invocations, prayers, and
sacrifice; among them also the sacrifice strengthens
the gods and increases their power. In India too,
the priests, and minstrels, and sacrificers handed down
in their families the knowledge of the effective invocations and ceremonies which exercised compulsion on
the gods, and the same was the case in Eastern Iran;
priestly families arose at a very early period. They
did not here retain the name of supplicators, as in
India; but are called Athravas in the Avesta. In the
Veda Atharvan kindles the sacrificial fire, and among
the Arians of India the incantations of the race of
Atharvan passed from the most powerful. In a similar
way powerful invocations and sentences were handed
down in Iran from father to son in the race of the

---

[1] Under the Sassanids we find a chief of the husbandmen (*vaçtriosan*),
and a chief of the warriors (*arthestaran*); Nöldeke, " Tabari," s. 110.

Athravas. These families preserved the ancient invocations to Mithra, Verethraghna, Anahita, Tistrya, which are preserved to us in the Avesta, though in a modified form. The god Haoma instructs Zarathrustra to praise him, as the other fire-priests had done (p. 124). The reform which bears the name of Zarathrustra cannot have left the condition of the priests unchanged. The doctrine may, as invocations in the Avesta would seem to show, have first found adherents in the race of Hacchataçpa, to which Zarathrustra belonged, and to which he first proclaimed his law (131), and next in the race of Jamaçpa and Frashaostra, who are spoken of as Zarathrustra's most zealous followers. According to the creed of the Parsees the good law also came to Aderbat Mahresfant by family descent (p. 62). These new races of priests, who knew the sayings, invocations, and prayers of Zarathrustra, would then be joined by those among the races of the old fire-priests who approved of the reform, and the priesthood thus formed would be further strengthened by those who, deeply impressed by the new doctrine, sought and found reception as pupils into a family of the priests, thus entering into their circle, and becoming members of their families. United by a new doctrine and settled tenets, the priests who represented the reform would become united together more firmly than the priestly families of the old time.

The priesthood could very well claim precedence of the warriors; on their prayers and sayings, their knowledge of the custom of sacrifice, depended the favour of the gods, the power of averting evil spirits, the removal of pollution, salvation in this world and the next. Yet they could not obtain such a position as the Brahmans held on the Ganges after the reform of

the ancient faith, and the victory of Brahman over
Indra. For in Iran there was no order of Çudras, no
vanquished remnant of an old population, which
created a sharp line of division even among the orders
of the Aryas; and moreover the Brahmans were the
first-born of Brahman, a purer incarnation of the divine
nature than any other order. The world had not
emanated from Auramazda; there were in Iran no
gradations of beings in which the divine essence
existed in a more or less pure condition. All had to
fight against evil deities and against evil; the priests
were the leaders in this struggle—this leadership and
nothing more could they claim. In their lives they
studied especial purity of body and mind; and they
were pre-eminently "the pure men." Only by their
means, at any rate with their assistance, could sacrifice
be offered; from their mouths alone could the correct
invocations be uttered to the gods, and the evil ones
be driven away. Men were compelled to submit to
the rules of the life acceptable to the gods of light, of
pure conversation, which were accurately known to the
priests only; they had to take upon themselves the
expiations which the priests prescribed, in order to
wipe out offences and sins and their consequences—
but they had not to reverence in them, as was the case
beyond the Indus, a class of creatures raised by birth
to a higher level. Hence the sharp separation of the
priesthood from the rest of the orders, in the Brahmanic fashion, was at once placed out of the question.
The priesthood of Iran perpetuated their knowledge
and wisdom in their families; but they had not the
right to bar all entrance into their families or their
order on the score of higher birth, or to prohibit the
marriage of priests with women of other orders, on
the ground of their superior nature.

From our fragments of the Avesta we may assume that although, as is obvious, the precedence of the priests above the remaining orders was strongly marked, and they were especially denoted as "pure men," the limits of their political and social position were far more modest than those of the Brahmans. So far as we can see, the Avesta allots no special income to the priests beyond the camels, horses, or small cattle given to them by warriors and husbandmen in quittance for the purifications they have performed. The penalties also which have to be paid in expiation of certain offences are to be given to " the pure men," and the Avesta repeatedly recommends the presentation of gifts to them. On the other hand, the priests do not possess the exclusive right to perform purifications. The Vendidad merely says that any one who wishes to perform purifications must have learned the law from one of the purifiers, i. e. it is only the instruction of the priest which is indispensable in this matter. Any one who performs purification without such instruction (except in the case of necessary purifications, p. 230), will take away from the places where it is performed, " food and fatness, health and all remedies, prosperity, luxuriance and growth, and increase of corn and fodder; and corn and fodder will not return to such places until for three days and nights the holy Çraosha has been praised at the burning fire with bound withes and uplifted Haoma." The uncertified purifier is to be put in chains, his clothes taken from him, and his head cut off.[1] If it was permitted to learn the purifications, it follows that men not of priestly descent could enter the order of the Athravas, and the boundary line between this order and the rest was not impassable. Among the Parsees of India any one can become a

---

[1] "Vend." 9, 172—180, 187—196.

priest. The duties of the priest, according to the book of the law, consist in watching and tending the sacred fire, in praising the good spirits, in offering sacrifice, and performing purifications, and in the ceaseless study of the holy scriptures. The priest is to be provided with a mortar made according to certain rules, a cup (for the Haoma sacrifice), the snake-switch (a stick for killing impure animals), and the Paitidana, *i. e.* a piece of cloth for veiling the mouth, in order that he may not approach the sacred fire with breath that is possibly impure. For the rest, the Vendidad lays down the rule that the priests are to be patient and content, and satisfied with a little bread, and they ought to eat what is offered to them.[1] Auramazda says ; " Many men, O Zarathrustra, carry the Paitidana, the serpent-switch, the sacred bundle of twigs, without being guided according to the law. These are wrongly called priests ; do not thou call them priests, O Zarathrustra. He who lies the whole night without praising or hearing, or reciting, or learning, or teaching—call not such an one a priest. Call him a priest, O pure Zarathrustra, who inquires of the pure intelligence the whole night, of the wisdom which purifies from sins and makes the heart wide, which has merits in store on the bridge of Chinvat, and causes us to attain the purity and bliss of Paradise."[2] The Avesta distinguishes different classes of priests, but the distinction only rests on the various acts which they perform in the sacred rites. The first rank is taken by the Zaotar, who utters the prayers and invocations (the Hotar, *i. e.* the Repeater of the Veda) ; next to him apparently is the Çraoshavareza, " who speaks very wise and truthful things;"[3] he bears the club of Çraosha,

---

[1] " Vend." 13, 126—129.   [2] " Vend." 18, 1—17.
[3] " Vispered," 3, 13, 14.   Above, p. 165.

in order to keep the evil spirits at a distance from the sacred acts; then comes the Atarevaksha, *i. e.* the priest who causes the fire to increase, and attends to the worship of it; then the Açnatar (the Washer), who has to cleanse the instruments of sacrifice to keep them from pollution; the Frabaretar, *i. e.* the Carrier, etc. In the modern ritual of the Parsees all the duties of the sacred service have been transferred to the Zaotar and the Raçpi, which latter discharges the functions of ministering priest.

If we were only approximately correct in placing the date of Zarathrustra and the reform of the ancient faith at 1000 B.C., the formation of this priestly order, which took place on the basis of the new doctrine, may have come to an end about the year 800 B.C. We saw that from this date onwards the spread of the new doctrine must have begun in the west of Iran towards the Medes and Persians, since there existed among the Medes from 700 B.C. an hereditary priesthood, charged with the worship of the gods according to the regulations of Zarathrustra, and in this century it was already sufficiently numerous to be placed as an equal division beside the tribes of the Medes.

We have no better information about the priests of the West than we have on the political and social position of the priests of Eastern Iran. They are not called Athravas but Magush. This name is first found in the inscription which Darius caused to be cut on the rock-wall of Behistun; afterwards it was consistently used by Western writers, from Herodotus to Agathias, for the priests of Iran. The Avesta has the words *magha* and *maghavan*, i. e. the powerful, the great,[1] but

---

[1] The Mobedh of Middle Persian is *magupat*, i.e. lord of the Magians (p. 60). The derivation of the name Magus from the Turanian *imga* (apparently = honourable) can only be adopted by those who regard

does not use it of the priests, which are always called
Athravas. If the last title is taken from the fire-
worship, the first allows us to see the importance of the
priests. He who can use incantations to the gods and
spirits—can summon or remove them—is the mighty
one, the powerful. If in this name we have evidence
of the respect with which the laity of Western Iran
looked up to the priests, the difference between the
names in the East and West shows that there were
priestly races among the Medes and Persians before
the religion of Zarathrustra reached them. Had not
such existed before the reform, and had they not
possessed a definite name in the West—had priestly
families become known there for the first time at the
rise of the reform—they would never have had any
other name than that of Athravas. Even without this
positive proof we might assume that from all antiquity
there had been priests among the Medes and Persians
who understood how to invoke the gods of light in the
old Arian faith—Mithra and Verethraghna, Vayu and
Tistrya—and tend the fire which destroyed demons.
When the new doctrine reached from the East to
Ragha and then to Media (p. 96), the old races who
passed over to the new faith united with the families
the members of which were the prophets of the new
doctrine. The teachers of the Medes in old times,
which Pliny called successors of Zarathrustra, might
have stood at the head of this transformation of the

the Magians as descendants of the Turanians, or at any rate as con-
taining a strong admixture of Turanians ; a view which rests on the
theory that the second series in the inscriptions of the Achæmenids is
the Median translation of the Persian inscriptions. With this view
I cannot agree; all that we learn from the Greeks of the customs,
manners, and names of the Medes bears the mark of an Arian origin,
and is in harmony with what is attributed to the Persians. In the inscription of the second class at Behistun, Gaumata is not called *imga*
but *magush*.

ancient priestly families, of the creation of the Median
priesthood on the basis of the new religion (p. 92).
However this may have been, the priestly families
among the Medes were so numerous, their connection
and union so close and firmly fixed, that they could be
counted as a sixth tribe beside the other five Median
tribes.

Among the tribes of the Persians Herodotus mentions no tribe of Magi. It would be a mistake to
conclude from this that there were originally no
priests among the Persians, and to put faith in Xenophon's statement that Cyrus was the first to give the
Magians the care of the sacred fire, "because he
preferred to go on board with the pious rather than
the impious."[1] No one will maintain that the Persians in ancient times were without worship and
religious rites, or that when they accepted the doctrine
of Zarathrustra, which did not permit sacrifice without
Magians, they used the services of none but alien
priests. Such a proceeding would be absurd. The
proper conclusion from the fact that Herodotus does
not mention a tribe of Magians among the Persians
is that the priestly families there were less numerous ;
they had not broken away from the tribal connections
to which they originally belonged, and formed themselves into a separate community. Further, from the
fact that the priestly families of the Persians in old
times had not formed themselves into a separate community, we may conclude—and indeed the conclusion
follows from the position of Media and the notice in
the Avesta about Ragha, and the observation about
the ancient teachers of the Medes, who are said to
have been followers of Zarathrustra—that the reform
of the faith first came from Bactria to the Medes,

[1] "Cyri instit." 8, 1, 23.

that it was adopted and more strongly represented
among them, and so passed on to the Persians. We
cannot doubt that there were Persians belonging to
the order of Magians. If Plato and his pupils call
Zoroaster the "teacher of the Magians," and at the
same time "a Persian," they must assume that there
were Magians among the Persians; if, according to
Plato's statement, the four teachers of the heirs to the
Persian throne, of which one had to teach the Magism
of Zoroaster, were selected out of "all the Persians;"
—if at the time of Xerxes there were Persians who
wrote on the doctrine of Zoroaster, they must have
been initiated in the wisdom and knowledge of the
Magians, and have known their invocations and customs; the contents of the holy scriptures and the
scriptures themselves can hardly have been hidden
from them. In order to prove that the Magians, i. e.
the priests, belonged exclusively to the Medes, the
fact has been brought forward that the Persians, after
Darius had dethroned the Pseudo-Smerdis, celebrated
each year the feast of the slaughter of the Magians,
at which no Magian allowed himself to be seen, but
all were obliged to remain at home.[1] The Mago-
phonia was not the celebration of a victory over the
Magi generally, but over the removal of a usurper, and
the restoration of the dominion to the Achæmenids,
which had been taken from them by one who happened to be a Magian. Herodotus at any rate calls
this Magian a Mede.[2] Darius contents himself with
calling him the "Magian." Hence there is no ground
to doubt that both before and after the reform, families of the Persians were charged with the worship
of the gods; the less so because Plato, as already

[1] Herod. 3, 79.   [2] Herod. 3, 73.

remarked, represents the heirs to the throne in Persia as being instructed in the doctrine of Zoroaster, while Strabo and Pausanias speak expressly of "Persian Magi," and the chief Magian is enumerated among the tribes "which dwell in the districts of Persis."[1]

When the dominion of the Achæmenids had been established over Iran, the priestly families of all the West must have been united into one community. There is no doubt that this remained an order in which the priestly wisdom and knowledge were traditional. Strabo, like Herodotus, calls the Magians a tribe; he adds that the members of it sought after a holy life. The tribe was large, he tells us in another place; Magians could be found even in Cappadocia. Ammianus also informs us that the Magians handed down their doctrines to later times, each by his descendants. Growing up through centuries from a small number, the Magians became a nation, and being regarded as dedicated to the service of the gods, they had acquired respect through their religion. They inhabited open villages, lived according to a law of their own, and possessed fruitful fields in the district called Nisæa. Agathias also calls the Magians a tribe.[2] But the separation of the priestly order in the West cannot have been more strict than that of the Athravas in the East. Marriage with the women of other orders was not forbidden, nor transition from other orders into that of the Medes. The Avesta speaks of the teacher and the pupil (p. 203); and it is expressly said—though the statement comes from the beginning of the third century of our era— that the Magians among the Persians, i. e. the Magians

[1] Strabo, p. 727; Pausanias, 5, 27, 3.
[2] Ammian. 23, 6, 32—35; Agathias, 2, 26.

under the Arsacids, instructed even those who were
not Persians in their doctrine, but only at the special
command of the king.[1]

We find the Magians in close proximity to the rulers
of the Medes and Persians ; they were not without
importance and influence. In Herodotus they tell
Astyages that they had and would have great honours
from him.[2] Xenophon speaks of them as determining,
at the time of Cyrus, which god is to be honoured on
each day.[3] Cambyses charges Magians with the duty
of watching the grave of Cyrus, and this office became
hereditary in their families ;[4] he also entrusts a
Magian with the care of the royal household, while he
marches with the army into the remote parts of Egypt
and Nubia. The inscriptions of Darius showed us
how much in earnest he was with the doctrines and
regulations of the religion—how lively was his faith.
On his march to Hellas, Xerxes was accompanied by
Osthanes, a man skilled in the priestly dogmas, and by
Magians ; they offer sacrifice, and charm the storms.[5]
The sacred fire which was carried before the kings[6]
was conducted by Magians, and so also were the sacred
chariot, the sacred horses of Mithra and the sun-god,
in the campaigns of the Achæmenids (p. 167). Of
greater importance was it that the heirs to the throne
in Persia were instructed, as Plato tells us, in the
Magism of Zoroaster,[7] which could only be done by
Magians. Nicolaus of Damascus relates that the
Persian princes were instructed by the Magians in
truthfulness, justice, and the laws of their country ;[8]
and, according to Plutarch, Magians were the educators

[1] Philostratus in Rapp, " Z. D. M. G." 20, 71.
[2] Herod. 1, 120.   [3] " Cyri instit." 7, 5, 20 ; 8, 1, 8.
[4] Arrian, " Anab." 6, 29.   [5] Herod. 7, 191.
[6] Curtius, 3, 7 ; Ammian. 23, 6, 34.   [7] " Alcibiad. I." p. 122.
[8] Nic. Dam. fragm. 67, ed. Müller.

of the Persian princes; Magians also under the Achæmenids performed the consecration at the accession of
a new king.[1]   We are also told that this king of the
Medes and that of the Persians, took the advice of the
Magians on important occasions.   Under the Arsacids
they formed, along with the members of the race of
the kings, the supreme council of the kingdom; in
the time when this dynasty was at its height they
ruled, as Pliny told us, "over the king of kings;"
and we have seen (p. 60) that their influence under
the Sassanids, at court, in the administration of law,
and in politics, was even more powerful.

Herodotus maintains that the Magians also occupied themselves with soothsaying and prophecy; like
Ctesias, he ascribes to the Medes the interpretation of
certain dreams and other miraculous acts.   Of such
interpretations and prophesying on the part of the
priests the Avesta knows nothing, and those Greeks
who were better informed, warmly contested the assertion that the Magians were occupied with such
things.   Plato tells us: "The Magism of Zoroaster is
the worship of the gods;" and Aristotle assures us that
the Magians knew nothing of soothsaying.[2]   What
Herodotus tells us, on the other side, he certainly did
not invent, but repeats after his informants.   The
Medo-Persian Epos, which, though indirectly, forms
the basis of Herodotus' account of the rise of Cyrus
and the death of Cambyses, allowed a wide field, even
in the account of the fall of the Assyrian empire
(III. 264), to the astrological and prophetic wisdom of
the Chaldæans.   From this we may conclude that
prophecies of the Chaldæans were not left out of
sight at the overthrow of Astyages.   In Nicolaus of
Damascus it is a Chaldæan of Babylon who expounds

[1] Plut. "Artaxerxes," c. 3.   [2] Diog. Laert. prooem. 6.

her dream to the mother of Cyrus,[1] and possibly
the kings of the Medes followed the example of the
Assyrian and Babylonian courts in having astro-
logers and interpreters of dreams from Babylon about
them.

Whatever was the influence employed by the Magians
at the court of the Achæmenids, the Arsacids and
Sassanids, their influence was of a moral nature; it
was only through the effect of religion on the heart
and conscience of the king, that they could work;
their position did not rest on any hierarchical insti-
tutions. In Iran the priesthood had no real means
of power which permitted it to come forward in opposition to the power of the State. The priest was a
subject of the king like any one else. It was within
the king's power to proceed at his pleasure with the
severest corporal punishment against the Magi, and
it is abundantly clear that the kings did not shrink
from inflicting such punishments, even if we do not
regard as established facts the stories that Astyages
impaled the Magians who had given him a false report,
and that Darius caused forty Magians to be executed
at once.[2]

Diogenes Laertius relates that the Magians lived on
lentils, bread and cheese, which agrees with the Avesta
to the extent that the priests are there commanded to
be content with a little food.[3] What Herodotus tells
us of the duties and occupation of the Magians agrees
entirely with the rules given in the Avesta for the

[1] Fragm. 66, ed. Müller; cf. infra Bk. 8, c. 4.
[2] Herod. 1, 128; Ctes. "Pers." 15. The excerpt says 40 Chaldæans,
but obviously Magi are here meant.
[3] Prooem. 7. Above, p. 190. The further statements of Diogenes
about the white robes of the Magians, their avoidance of all ornament
and gold, of their lying on the ground, and staff of reed, deserve little
notice, inasmuch as the source whence they are derived is unknown.

Athravas. No one could sacrifice without a Magian; the sacrifices were offered on high places (in this Xenophon agrees[1]) or in "pure places;" the most delicate grass was spread—we remember the importance of the Kuça-grass in the Veda and the Brahmanas—on this grass the flesh of the sacrifice was laid; the Magians sang the theogony, *i. e.* long sacrificial prayers, and the sacred rite is fulfilled. Herodotus also asserts that the Magians took great pride in killing serpents, ants, and other winged and creeping things with their own hands; that human life was greatly respected by them; that the dog was held in high honour (p. 86); and the corpses of the Magians were exposed to dogs or birds of prey. This he declares that he knows to be the truth; Xenophon represents the Magians as beginning their songs of praise with the break of day, and as offering their sacrifices at certain places, which were selected for the gods. Curtius relates that they sang native songs.[2] Strabo told us above that the Magians sought after a holy life; he observes also that whatever was the god to which they sacrificed they first prayed to fire. At every sacrifice the Magians conducted the sacred rite; the victims were not slain with the knife but struck down with a club. No part of the flesh of the victim was set apart for the deity, for they declared that the god required only the soul of the animal; yet according to some they placed a small portion of the fat in the fire. "In Cappadocia there were enclosed places," Strabo continues, "in the midst of which was an altar, heaped up with ashes. On this the Magians kept up the unquenchable fire. Each day they went and sang for an hour before the fire, holding in their hands a bundle of twigs. On their

[1] " Cyri instit." 8, 7, 3.
[2] " Cyri instit." 8, 7, 3; 7, 5, 20; 8, 1, 8; Curtius, 3, 3, 8.

heads they wore tiaras of felt, which fell down on
both sides so far that the side-pieces covered the lips."[1]
Pausanias, who observed the worship of the Magians
in the cities of Lydia, says: "At both places there
was a shrine with a cell, and in the cell is an altar;
on this are ashes the colour of which is not the
ordinary colour of ashes. When the Magian comes
into the cell, he lays the dry wood on the altar, puts
the tiara on his head, and sings the invocation to some
god or another, in a barbarian manner, quite unintelligible to the Hellenes; but he sings from a book.
Then the pieces of wood, without being kindled, ought
to become lighted, and a flame from them should flash
all round the cell."[2]

---

[1] Strabo, p. 733.   [2] Pausan. 5, 27, 5, 6.

CHAPTER IX.

THE rules concerning purity and purification, the expiations and penances necessary to avert the Daevas, which we possess in the Vendidad of the Avesta, are only the remnant of a far more comprehensive law. From the list of books and chapters traditional among the Parsees, we can see that it was intended to include not only all the invocations and prayers which the worship required, the rules of sacrifice, and the entire ritual, together with the Calendar of the year of the Church, but also the arrangement of the process of law, the civil and criminal code, and, moreover, rules for agriculture and medicine. If to this we add the statements and quotations of the Greeks (p. 53), we may assume that the scriptures of Eastern Iran comprised the whole sum of the knowledge of the priests. In the Avesta the Athravas had sketched the ideal picture of the correct conduct pleasing to Auramazda in every department of life. How far the princes of Bactria and the viceroys of Cyaxares and the Achæmenids, or even these princes themselves, and the judges, wished or allowed themselves to be bound in their decisions by these regulations of the priests, may be left out of the question. The priests here, like the Brahmans in India, could only influence the action of

the State and those charged with it, so far as the
reverence for the principles of religion and the force of
their own authority extended.

The existing part of the law has obviously arisen
out of the questions and considerations sketched
above, which in consequence of the reform must have
forced themselves into the circles of the priests. The
reform also required above all things purity from men,
but no supernatural purity, such as the Brahmans
demanded. The body is not in the Avesta, as it was
to the Brahmans and after them to the Buddhists, the
impure prison of the soul which must be abandoned;
on the contrary the Avesta rejoices in its health and
vigour. It requires that the body should be kept
pure from filth, from contamination by the impure,
which gives the Daevas power over mankind, *i. e.* it
demands the exclusion of the harmful side of nature;
it desires that the soul should be pure from pollution,
freed from untruthfulness, lying, and deceit, which are
contradictory to the nature of the clear bright gods,
and Auramazda, and make men companions of the
Daevas, and sharers in their nature. In other words,
it demands the invigoration of the light and wholesome
side of man. The kingdom of the good spirits is
truth, increase, and life; the kingdom of the evil is
deception and falsehood, lying, destruction, and death.
The Avesta praises Auramazda as purity itself; and
next to him Asha vahista, *i. e.* the best purity; the
gods are chiefly extolled as "the pure," and Zarathrustra as the master and teacher of purity. The
Avesta repeatedly declares "that purity after birth is
the best thing for men." Hence it is the foremost of
all duties to keep the soul and body pure. The
worshipper of Auramazda must preserve his purity by
good thoughts, words, and works; truth is required

in thinking, speaking, and acting; uprightness and honesty in all the relations of life; the sacredness of promises and pledges, and solemn assurances, at which Mithra is summoned to bear witness It is an old function of the god which appears here. He is the guardian of the word, and the compact. "Mithra is twenty-fold between friends and kinsmen, thirty-fold between tradespeople, forty-fold between companions who live together, fifty-fold between man and wife, sixty-fold between associates in sacrifice, seventy-fold between scholar and teacher, eighty-fold between step-son and step-parents, ninety-fold between brothers, a hundred-fold between son and father." "Miserable are the houses, without descendants the dwellings, in-habited by those who deceive Mithra. Miserably does the cloven-footed cow go on the wrong path, which is oppressed by the burden of Mithra-deceiving men." [1] In accordance with this view deception is in the eyes of the law the worst offence; worse than robbery or theft. Evil-speaking and calumny also are, according to the Vendidad, "lies and sins" against Mithra. The gravest offence of this kind is the calumny by which "a pure man" is disparaged "with a man of another religion," for this sin is committed with full knowledge, and by a man's own intelligence; and the worst of all lies is teaching a false law. "One who teaches such a law," says the Vendidad, "does no better than if he killed a thousand horses, slew the men in a village inhabited by worshippers of Auramazda, or carried off the cows on the wrong way." [2]

It is not the least proof of the currency of the doctrines of the Avesta in the West of Iran that their ethical side, which gathers round the command of truthfulness, was there most distinctly recognised.

[1] "Mihr Yasht," 38, 116, 117.   [2] "Vend." 1, 18, 20; 18, 22—32.

King Darius has already told us that "the lie" had
brought his kingdom into rebellion ; the leaders of the
rebellious lands, who gave themselves out to be descendants of the ancient royal families, he calls "liars
against the kingdom." From their youth up, Herodotus tells us, the children of the Persians were
instructed in truthfulness. He adds : Among the
Persians it was forbidden to speak of that which it
was forbidden to do ; the Avesta requires truth "in
thought, speech, and action." Lying and borrowing,
Herodotus says, passed with the Persians for the most
disgraceful acts, for they were of opinion that any
one who contracted debts was generally compelled to
tell lies. The Avesta says : "He who does not restore
that which has been borrowed, seeks day and night to
deceive the creditor." Plato states that the heirs to
the Persian throne had, besides three others, a teacher
whose special business it was to instruct them in truth.
Xenophon assures us that pledges and oaths were
religiously kept among the Persians ; and Diodorus,
that the pledge of hands was the strongest security
among them.[1] Practice in Persia was, it is true, not
equal to these injunctions, however sharply expressed ;
on the contrary, we often find the two in the most
glaring contradiction.

Not falsehood and lies only, but also laziness and
sloth pollute the soul of man. The pious man must
rise early. Çraosha awakes the bird Parodarsh, we
are told in the book of the law. At the return of the
divine Ushahina, i. e. of the morning (p. 108), this
bird speaks to those who are in their beds : "Friend,
up, arise. Praise purity, and the Daevas will fly away.
Long sleep, O man, is not good for thee. The Bush-

[1] Herod. 1, 136 ; Plato, "Alcib. I." p. 122 ; Xen. "Cyri instit." 8,
8, 2 ; Diod. 16, 43.

yançta runs up to thee, who lays again in sleep the whole corporeal world. Turn yourselves not away from the three best things: good thinking, speaking, and acting. He who rises first will come into Paradise; he who first brings pure, dry, old, well-hewn wood to the fire of Auramazda, him will the fire bless (p. 122)." [1] The pious man should be industrious and work; the best work is that which increases nourishment and fruit for men and animals, which furthers the increase and life of the world, and thus diminishes the kingdom of the evil, the power of the dark spirits. For this reason running water and growing fruits should be spread over the earth; " the field should be tilled, and trees planted which produce food." "When there are shoots," the law-book says, " the Daevas are in alarm; when there are stalks, the Daevas weep; when there are ears, the Daevas hiss; when there are grains, the Daevas fly." [2] "In the house where there are most ears, the Daevas are smitten most heavily." "The earth is not glad which lies untilled. The greatest pleasure is given to the earth where a pure man builds his house, provided with fire and cattle, and good flocks, with wife and child, where most corn, fodder, and grain is produced by husbandry, where the dry land is most watered, where fruit-bearing trees are planted, where cattle and beasts of draught leave the most urine." [3] "He who plants fruits and trees, who gives water to the earth where it is needed, and takes it away where too abundant, he worships the earth." When a man tills the earth she bestows life upon him; " as a friend to a beloved friend, she gives him descendants and wealth." To him who tills her, the earth says: " O man, who

[1] " Vend." 18, 35—42; 53—57.   [2] " Vend." 3, 105 ff.
[3] Loc. cit. 3, 1—20.

tillest me with the left arm and the right, with the
right arm and the left, in love will I bear thee all
kinds of fruit." But to him who tills her not the
earth says : "Thou wilt go to the doors of others and
there stand, in order to beg for food ; in idleness thou
wilt ask for it and get but little." He who sows corn,
sows purity ; the law of Auramazda increases with the
fruits of the field ; they extend the law of Auramazda
by 100, 1000, and 10,000 meritorious works.

These regulations of the Avesta were fully accepted
in the West. The great reverence paid to splendid
trees by the Achæmenids is shown by Herodotus'
story of Xerxes, that he furnished a beautiful plane
tree, which he saw in Lydia, with golden ornaments,
and appointed a perpetual guardian for it.[1] Ameretat,
as already observed, was the special protecting spirit
of trees (p. 164). Xenophon tells us that the Persian
kings gave special attention to agriculture; on their
journeys they inquired into the tillage of the land,
and demanded similar attention from their satraps.
Round their palaces and wherever they came they
caused the most beautiful gardens to be laid out,
planted with trees and all the most excellent shrubs in
the world.[2] The satraps also had gardens of this kind
(*pairidaeza*) round their residences, and the younger
Cyrus assures Lysander, "in the name of Mithra,"
that he never took food before he had induced perspir-
ation by work in the garden or exercise in arms.[3]
The satraps, says Xenophon, whose provinces were
found deficient in population and poorly cultivated,
were punished and removed from their office, while
those whose provinces were in good order, were rewarded by presents. When the king of the Persians

[1] Herod. 7, 31. [2] "Œconom." 4, 13 ff.
[3] Ibid. 4, 20—24.

conferred distinctions, those were summoned first who had distinguished themselves in war, and next came those whose districts were best cultivated.[1] Respect and reverence for trees was so deeply rooted in Iran, that even Islam did not extirpate the feeling. To this day in Shiraz old trees are presented with dedicatory offerings, and hung with amulets; and the pious prefer to pray under tall trees rather than in the neighbouring mosques; while in the barren regions of Iran even groups of bushes receive offerings.[2]

Besides the care of trees, plants, and the soil, the labour of mankind must be directed to the care of the flocks, to the increase of the animals of the good god, and the destruction of the Khrafçtras, or animals belonging to the evil spirit (p. 171). Cows are not held in such veneration in Iran as beyond the Indus, yet even here the "cow is not to be driven on the wrong way," and gomez (the urine of oxen) is the most effectual means of purification; in the theory of the priests Auramazda began the creation of living things with the bull. We have already mentioned the rank taken among the animals of Auramazda by the cock and dog. In the Vendidad Auramazda says: "I have created the dog with clothes and shoes of his own, with keen scent and sharp teeth, attached to men, savage against the enemy, for the protection of the flocks. No thief or wolf comes to the village or the fold and carries away anything unobserved, if the dog is healthy, in good voice, and among the flocks. The houses would not stand firm upon the earth if there were not dogs in the villages and flocks. The dog is patient, contented, and satisfied with little food, like a priest; he goes forward, and is before and

[1] Ibid. 4, 8—12; "Cyri instit." 8, 6, 16.
[2] Darmesteter, "Haurvatat et Ameretat," p. 64 ff.

behind the house, like a warrior; he sleeps less than
the husbandmen, is talkative like a child, and friendly
as a mistress."[1] The dogs are to receive good food,
"for of all the creatures of Auramazda old age comes
upon them the most quickly;" especially must the
watch-dog be provided with milk, fat, and flesh,
"the proper food" for a dog; and a dog must never
be among those who are eating without receiving
something to eat. Any one who gives unbroken
bones or hot food to a sheep-dog or house-dog, and
the bones injure him, and the hot food burns his
mouth and tongue, so that he dies—is worthy of
death.[2] Dogs with young are treated with the same
care as pregnant women. It is a sin to chase or beat
a dog which has brought forth; if she is injured or
dies in running the sinner is worthy of death; and
any one who beats a pregnant dog is to receive twice
seven hundred stripes. It is the duty of every
man to bring up for six months the dogs born on
his ground, until they are able to run round in a
circuit of twice seven houses.[3] Sick dogs are treated
with the same remedies as rich men; and to the
question of Zarathrustra—"If the dog will not take
the remedies?" Auramazda answers that in this case
"the dog can be tied, and its mouth opened with a
flat piece of wood."[4] Wounds inflicted on dogs are to
be punished with stripes to the number of twice eight
hundred;[5] and besides this, compensation is to be given
for the damage which thieves or wolves do to the
village so long as the dog is prevented by his injuries
from keeping watch. The book of the law everywhere threatens all those men who beat dogs that

[1] "Vend." 13, 125—162.   [2] "Vend." 15, 2, 3, 4.
[3] "Vend." 15, 5, 20, 21, according to Goldner's translation. [Cf.
Darmesteter.]
[4] "Vend." 13, 97—105.   [5] "Vend." 13, 26—47.

their souls will go from this world full of terror, and sick. To kill a water-dog is the greatest crime;[1] and is menaced with the worst penalties and expiations known to the Vendidad. As a general rule punishments do not go beyond 2000 stripes, or the necessity of killing 2000 noxious animals; but the slayer of the water-dog is to receive 10,000 stripes. Besides this, if he would save his soul, he must give 10,000 parcels of hard wood, well hewn and dried, for the fire of Auramazda, and also 10,000 parcels of soft, fragrant wood; he must kill 10,000 snakes, and an equal number of tortoises, lizards, and water-lizards, ants, flies, and rats. He must fill up 10,000 impure holes in the earth; give to the priests all the utensils required for the holy rites; to a warrior a complete set of armour; to a husbandman he must give all that is needed for agriculture: a house, provided with a beautiful mat, and arable land for tillage. In addition, he must give, as an expiation for his soul, fourteen head of small cattle to the " pure men," and bring up fourteen young dogs, and build fourteen bridges over running water. He must cleanse eighteen dogs from fleas, and make eighteen bones into edible food; and satisfy eighteen "pure men" with wine and flesh. If he does not perform these expiations he will go into the dwelling of the Druj, and " the heat which is injurious to the pasture will not depart from his dwelling until he has offered sacrifice for three days and nights for the pure soul of the water-dog, on the burning fire, with bound rods and uplifted Haoma."[2]

In order to extirpate the animals of Angromainyu,

---

[1] It is not certain whether the *udra* of the Vendidad is the water-dog (spaniel?) or the otter.

[2] "Vend." 13, 169—174; 14, 4—75.

the priest is to be provided with a stick, the Khrafçtra-killer. Herodotus has already told us, that the Magians held it a duty to kill serpents, ants, and other creeping and winged insects. For the expiation of sins the Avesta universally requires the killing of serpents, lizards, and ants; rats and mice, which do harm to the crops; flies, midges, fleas, lice, and other vermin. Plutarch tells us that the Persians count him a happy man who slays most water-mice; Agathias observes that in honour of the chief festival in Persia every one killed as many snakes, and beasts of prey, and animals living in the desert, as possible, and then brought them to the Magians as a proof of his piety. In this way they believed that they did what was pleasing to the good god, while they injured and distressed Arimanes.[1]

According to the Avesta, the soul of man is kept pure by truthfulness, industry, and diligence, by good thoughts, good words and acts, which advance the kingdom of life; the body is to be kept free from dirt and the house from filth and dead creatures; from all that belongs to the evil spirits and is in their power. The soul of man is created pure; but from the first the body has certain impure parts, and the defilement which Angromainyu brought into the bodies of men. This defilement consists in the spittle, the excrements, dead skin, sores, etc; in everything that has an unpleasant smell, or is removed from the living body, like the hair and nails. These when cut are dead, and therefore belong to the kingdom of darkness; hence in Iran as in India they are impure things. "Wherever cut hair and nails lie," says the book of the law, "there the Daevas gather to these unholy places; there the impure animals come, which men call

[1] Agath. 2, 24.

lice. Therefore carry away—so saith Auramazda—cut
hair and nails, ten paces from the pure men, twenty
from the fire, thirty from the water, fifty from the
sacred bundle of rods. Dig a hole below the house in
the earth, pronounce the prayer Ahunavairya thrice,
six times, nine times, and then say : To thee, O bird,
Asho-zusta, I show these nails. These nails I dedicate
to thee ; may they be thy lances, thy swords, thy bow,
thy swift-flying arrows, thy sling-stones against the
Mazanian Daevas. If these nails are not announced to
the bird Asho-zusta, they are weapons for, not against,
the Daevas." [1] Spittle is among the worst impurities.
The priests could only approach the fire with veiled
mouth, and even now the Parsees invariably cover the
mouth in praying. They eat in silence, and two
never use the same spoon, because the food would
then be polluted by spittle. The removal of the excrements requires as much care in the Avesta as it did
in the Brahmanic law, and the Vendidad gives minute
regulations in regard to these matters. [2] A man is
rendered impure by excess and debauchery ; a woman
by her courses, "by marks and blood," and by the
birth of a child. She must be carried to an elevated
place in the dwelling, which is strewn with dry sand,
fifteen paces from the fire, from water, and the sacred
bundle of rods, "at a distance also from the trees," and
so placed that she cannot see the fire on the hearth.
No one may touch her. Only a definite amount
of certain kinds of food can be given to her, and that
in metal jars, because these contract the least amount
of impurity, and are most easily cleansed ; the person
who brings the food must remain three paces distant

---

[1] " Vend." Farg. 17.

[2] "Wer den Urin mit vorgestrecktem Fusse lässt macht die Drudsch
schwanger," so dass sie neue Unholde gebären.

from her bed.   After childbirth a woman is unclean
for three days; then she must wash her body with
water and gomez.   If she has had a miscarriage her
body is also polluted by the dead child: she must be
placed thirty paces away from the fire and the sacred
objects of the house, and must pass a longer period on
her dust-bed—at the present time forty-one days are
required.   The first thing she is allowed to taste is
ashes mixed with gomez—three, six, and then nine
drops.   The nine apertures of her body—that number
is common to the Indians and Iranians—must be
washed with ashes and gomez.   She may not drink
any water out of her impure hand; if she does so, she
must receive two hundred blows with the rod, and
two hundred with the whip.[1]   Fire and water, springs,
streams and rivers, the best gifts of the good gods,
must, like the human body, be carefully preserved
from all filth and defilement.   The accounts of Western
writers prove that the Persians and Medes observed
the rules of purification given in the Book of the Law;
it was not the custom among the Persians to spit in
the presence of another, still less to sneeze, etc.   They
avoided the defilement of a river, or of the shadow of
a man; and it was forbidden to uncover in the sight
of the sun or moon.[2]

"The sun, the moon, the stars shine unwillingly,"
we are told in the Vendidad, "on the polluted man."[3]
"The impure takes away prosperity and increase; he
brings sickness and death; after death he will not go
into heaven."[4]   But whatever pollution a man has
contracted, and whatever sin he has committed, the
good law quenches all impurity and sin, if the purifi-

[1] "Vend." 5, 45—55, 136—157; 7, 158—182.
[2] Herod. 1, 133; Xen. "Cyri instit." 1, 2, 16; 8, 9, 11; Plin. "H.
N." 28, 19.
[3] "Vend." 9, 161.   [4] "Vend." 9, 187.

cations, expiations, and penalties which it prescribes are
performed and paid; for the good law of Auramazda
surpasses all others in greatness, goodness, and salvation, as far as the heaven rises above the earth, and
as the sea of Vourukasha includes all other waters."[1]
"The good law of Auramazda takes from the man who
praises it and commits no evil actions afterwards, his
deception; it takes away the murder of the pure man,
and the burial of the dead; it takes away inexpiable
actions, and accumulated guilt; it takes away all evil
words, thoughts, and actions, even as the strong swift
wind purifies heaven from the right side."[2]

Slight pollution is removed by washing with pure
water accompanied by certain prayers and impre-
cations on the Daevas, such as: "I contend with thee,
O evil Angromainyu; away from this dwelling, away
from the fire, the water, from this place, from all the
blessings which Auramazda has created. I contend
against pollution, direct and indirect; against the
unclean spirits; I contend against the Daeva Andra,
Çaurva, Zairicha (p. 169); against the Pairika, who
goes to the water, the earth, cattle, and trees," etc.[3]
More serious impurities require ablutions with gomez,
which in certain cases have to be repeated thirty
times, with various prayers.[4] The most efficacious
purification, which removes even the worst taint, is
that of the nine nights. This can only be performed
by a priest, who knows the law accurately, can repeat
the sacred word by heart, and speaks the truth. A
special place must be constructed for it; thirty paces
(which are equal to ninety times the length of the
foot) from the fire, the water, and the sacred bundle
of rods. In the middle of this space nine pits are

[1] "Vend." 5, 23—25.   [2] "Vend." 3, 140—147; 8, 87.
[3] "Vend." 10, 11, 12, 17, 18, 26—28.   [4] "Vend." 8, 275, 276.

dug in the earth, and round them twelve furrows are
drawn with a metal instrument. The purifier sprinkles
the person who requires cleansing (who is entirely
naked) with gomez, from a leaden vessel, with many
prayers. He is then rubbed fifteen times with earth;
he must then wash himself at each of the nine pits
once, twice, thrice with water, after which he is fumi-
gated with fragrant wood. Then follow washings with
water and gomez in the third, sixth, and ninth night.
" After this," says the book, " the purified person shall
bring water of purification to the fire, hard wood, and
perfumes; he is to utter praises to Auramazda, to the
Amesha Çpentas, and to the rest of the pure ones—
so will the man be purified." The purifier must be
rewarded for this purification; according to the measure of the man's property the payment rises from
small cattle and cows to camels; " in order that the
purifier may go away contented and without hatred."
Instead of cattle, goods of another description can be
given. But if the purifier goes away discontented,
the wicked spirit of impurity comes again into the
purified persons, and they are impure for evermore."[1]

In the view of the Avesta impurity consists essentially in that which is opposed to life; hence there is
no worse form of uncleanness than that caused by the
corpse. The body, as soon as the soul has left it,
belongs to Angromainyu. The fiend of death, the
Druj Naçu, obtains possession of it, and from it she
springs on all who touch it, or come near it. If a
man dies, or a dog—and in this matter dogs are put
quite on a level with men—and other men and women
are in the same house—two, five, fifty, or a hundred
—the Druj Naçu comes immediately from the north
in the form of a fly, and settles on all the inhabitants

[1] " Vend." 9, 119–158; 19, 69–80.

of the house and makes them impure with infection, pollution, and uncleanness.[1] In the first instance she is to be met by incantations—the Gathas, Bisamruta, Thrisamruta, Chathrasamruta, must be repeated ; then the fiend falls to pieces like grass that has been dead a year.[2] After this the hearth-fire must be removed from the house of the dead, and the sacred utensils—the mortar, the cup, the sacred bundle of rods, and the Haoma. In winter the fire can be kindled again upon the hearth after nine nights ; in summer, when the need for warmth and cooked food is less pressing, after a month ; any one who does not observe these periods is to be punished with twice two hundred stripes.[3] After purification the kinsmen are to utter prayers for the departed, and the number of these is fixed, in the Vendidad, in the same fanciful manner which is so often met with in the book of Manu. The number decreases according to the degree of relationship ; for the nearest kinsmen thirty prayers are spoken ; for the most remote, five ; if the dead man has led an impure life the number of prayers is doubled in order to give efficacy to the petition.[4]

The preservation and increase of life is the foundation of the teaching of the Avesta. The good life of nature is promoted by planting and agriculture, by tending the useful and destroying the pernicious animals ; and by posterity provision is to be made for the life of men. From this point of view the Vendidad lays especial weight on marriage. " I declare," Auramazda says, " that the married is before the unmarried, and he that has a house before him that has none, and the father of children before the childless."[5]

1 "Vend." 5, 83—108 ; 7, 4 ff.   2 "Vend." 9, 168—171 ; Farg. 10.
3 "Vend." 5, 124—135.   4 "Vend." 12, 1—59.
5 "Vend." 4, 130—133.

We can only ascertain very incompletely from the
remaining fragments of the Avesta the rules which
it prescribed for family life. We see that bringing
about a marriage was regarded as a meritorious work,
and marriage between close relations was considered
happy. Yet maidens are not to be given in marriage
before their fifteenth year.[1] To those who have long
remained unmarried the god Haoma, the special protector of life, sends truthful, active husbands, gifted
with good understanding (p. 125). We never hear of
any difference of the orders in contracting marriage;
nor is there the least hint that the priest can only
marry a wife of priestly blood, or the husbandman
a wife of his own class. On the other hand, the strict-
est directions are given that the worshippers of
Auramazda are only to marry among themselves;
marriage with those of an alien religion is severely
reprobated. "A man who mingles the seed of the
faithful and the unbelievers, the seed of the worshippers of the Daevas with the worshippers of Mazda,
keeps back a third part of the flowing water, a third
part of the increase of the blooming plants, and their
golden fruits; he annihilates a third part of the
clothing of Çpenta Armaiti (the Earth); he robs the
just men of a third part of their power, their merits,
their purity. They who do this are more destructive
than forked serpents, than howling wolves, than the
she-wolf which rushes on the flocks, than the thousand-fold brood of the lizard, which pollutes the
water."[2] The Vendidad gives the house-father a
similar power over his wife and children to that given
in Manu's law—so far as we can conclude from
certain indications. He is to be spoken of with the

[1] "Vend." 14, 64—66.
[2] "Vend." 18, 123—133, after Harlez' translation. [Cf. Darmesteter.]

same reverence as the house-father on the Ganges; the wife is to be honoured, but is to "be watched perpetually, like the fire of Auramazda."[1]   With regard to the education of children, we can only gather from the Vendidad they were to be tended for seven years; "protect dogs for six months, children for seven years;"[2] and boys are to be invested in their fifteenth year with the sacred girdle.[3]   We remember the sacred girdle which the three upper castes wore and still wear beyond the Ganges; the investiture with this, and adoption into the family and caste— "the second birth" takes place, according to Manu's law, among the Brahman boys in the eighth year, among the Kshatryas, in the eleventh, and the Vaiçyas in the twelfth.   The habit of wearing the girdle, which prevails on both sides of the Indus, proves that this custom was in use before the two branches of the Arians separated.   Originally the girdle was intended to be a protection or amulet against the evil spirits.[4] In the girdle which the priests prepare with traditional ceremonies, and put on boys in their seventh or tenth year, the modern Parsees see the bond which encloses and unites the worshippers of Auramazda.

If I attempt to supplement the scanty hints of the Avesta on family life from the accounts preserved to us on this subject by Western writers, it must be remembered that the more ancient of these statements hold good only of the West of Iran.   But as we have hitherto found the worship and manners of the Persians and Medes, as described by the Greeks, agreeing with the rules of the Avesta, we may suppose that in this province also East and West were in agreement. Herodotus states that the Persians married many

---

[1] "Vend." 15, 126.   [2] "Vend." 15, 125.
[3] "Vend." 18, 115.   [4] "Vend." 18, 23.

wives, and had concubines in addition. They considered it honourable and right to have as many
children as possible ; next to bravery in war it was the
greatest merit to have many children, and the king
sent presents every year to the man who had most.[1]
Of all days the Persians celebrated most the day
on which they were born. A more abundant meal
was served on this day : among the wealthy an ox,
a horse, or a camel was roasted whole ; and smaller
animals among those who were poorer. Plato adds :
" When the first son, the heir of the kingdom, was
born to the king of Persia, all the subjects of the king
celebrated the day, and on the birthday of the king
there were festivals and sacrifices throughout all
Asia."[2] Herodotus observes, that the respect of children for their parents was great. The Persians
regarded the murder of parents by a son as impossible ; if such a thing happened they believed that the
child was supposititious.[3] Aristotle tells us that the
power of the father over the sons among the Persians
was tyrannical, *i. e.* unlimited ; he treated them as
slaves.[4] That the mother was also treated with
respect follows from the statement that the son
might not remain seated when the mother entered,
and could only resume his seat at her permission.
At the court of the Achæmenids the mother of the
king had the first place, the king the second.[5] That
the queen-mother often exercised great influence is
shown by the history of this ruling family. Of the
careful education of the heir to the throne, the other
princes, and the sons of the wealthy Persians, both
in the exercise and strengthening of their bodies and

---

[1] Herod. 1, 135, 136.   [2] Plato, "Alcib. I." ; p. 121.
[3] Herod. 1, 137.   [4] "Ethic. Nicom." 8, 10, ed. Zell.
[5] Curt. 5, 9 ; Plut. " Artax." c. 5.

in moral training, the Western writers had much
to tell.

What the Greeks narrate respecting the celebration
of the birthday among the Persians, the distinction of
the satraps whose provinces were best cultivated and
populated, and the rewards given to those who had
most children, agrees entirely with the delight in life
which runs through the Avesta, and the exhortations
to increase life everywhere present in that book.
The Avesta always speaks of one wife only. The
polygamy noticed by the Greeks was limited to the
rich (the number of wives among the Persians, says
Ammian, was regulated by property[1]) ; in consequence
of the religious feeling just noticed, it prevailed, no
doubt, far more extensively among the Arians of Iran
than among the Indians. Yet the harems of the
Indian princes were large. However numerous the
harems of the Achæmenids, only one wife was the
lawful wife ; and she alone, as in India, bore the name
of queen : only her sons could be considered heirs to
the throne. The other wives greeted the queen on
their knees : the queen must belong to the race of the
Achæmenids, or at any rate to one of the six tribal
princes.[2] The same was the case among the rest of
the Persians who had several wives ; one only was the
house-wife. The Avesta told us above that the wife
must be watched. According to Plutarch the Persians
were more strict in this matter than the rest of the
barbarians ; they kept not only the wife but the concubines shut up, and they left the houses in covered
cars only.[3] Manu's law also requires that women
should be watched (IV. 263). The power of the father,

---

[1] Ammian, 23, 6.

[2] Herod. 3, 70, 88 ; Dinon. fragm. 17, ed. Müller ; Ctes. " Pers.
Ecl." 44.　　　　　　　　　　　　[3] Plut. " Themist." c. 26.

and the respectful attitude of the children to the mother, correspond to the principles of family life which we have seen beyond the Indus. Yet, so far as we can see, marriage was not in Iran so close and firmly established a relation as among the Arians of India, where the wife belonged absolutely to the man, and surrendered herself in complete devotion to him ; nor did the relation of children to parents in Iran experience that excellent and happy development which on the whole attended it in India, and of which we can still perceive the results. If Western writers maintain that it was the custom among the Persians to take the nearest relations in marriage, so that even the brother married the sister (of which Herodotus gives an example in Cambyses) and the son the mother after the father's death (the latter is said to have prevailed especially among the Magi)[1]—the Avesta, as we have seen, declared marriages between near relations to be good, and the history of the Achæmenids mentions marriage with sisters more than once. The more extreme assertions, especially in regard to the Magi, are to be regarded as exaggerations of the Greeks, and owed their origin to their astonishment at a custom which was more than revolting. On the relation of the sexes both before and after marriage, and other matters connected with procreation, the Vendidad supplies a number of minute regulations.[2]

The preservation of life also receives great attention in the Avesta. We remember the incantations of the

---

[1] Herod. 3, 31 ; Diogen. Laert. Prooem. 6 ; Plut. "Artax." c. 26 ; Ctes. "Pers. Ecl." 44 ; Agathias, 2, 23 ; Heracl. Cum. fragm. 7 ed. Müller.

[2] The regulations respecting sexual intercourse, abortion, etc., which here follow in the German text will be found in "Vend." 16, 33—40 ; 18, 100—122, 136, 152 ; ib. 15, 9—17, 60 ; 18, 115 ; ib. 18, 115—119 ; ib. 8, 74—82 ; ib. 8, 96—106.

Rigveda which banish sickness into thrushes and wood-peckers, and the sentences of the Atharvaveda against sickness and death (IV. 281). The remedies of the Veda are water and plants. All remedies are in water; the waters of the springs and the waters of the rivers drive away sickness. The plants said, when they came from heaven, that they descended from the water of the sky. "The mortal whom we touch will suffer no harm." "May Agni protect me with the waters, and Soma with the plants," we are told in the Veda; and again: "The plants whose king is Soma, have rescued me from death."[1] The priest who knows the sentences is at the same time the physician, though the Rigveda has a separate name for the latter (IV. 35). How highly the Indians respected doctors and physicians at a later time, in spite of the theory of the Brahmans of the unworthiness of the body, and how it was the custom there in the sixth century B.C. to send for the physician in every sickness, has been mentioned in its place (IV. 323). Proceeding from precisely the same conceptions, the Avesta went on to fill several books with medical remedies. The best mode of healing is that by charms, and the sacred word. In such incantations of the Avesta we are told: "I contend against sickness, I contend against death, I contend against pain, I contend against fever, I contend against the corruption and pollution which Angromainyu has created in the body of men. Sickness, I curse thee; fever, I curse thee; death, I curse thee."[2] The sacred word is invoked to heal by its power. "Mayst thou heal me, O Manthra Çpenta. As a recompense I will give to thee a thousand stall-fed oxen, a thousand spotless cattle, a thousand swiftly-running horses, a

---

[1] "Rigveda," 10, 97, 17; "Atharvaveda," 2, 10, 2; 8, 1, 18 in Darmesteter *loc. cit.* 73, 76.　　　　[2] "Vend." 20, 19, 25.

thousand camels, swift and with strong backs.   I will
bless thee with beautiful, pious blessings ; with dear,
pious blessings, which make the deficient full, and the
full to overflow, which bind the friend and make the
bond firm."[1]   As in the Veda, the remedies are water
and plants, " Draw up, ye clouds, draw up," we are
told in the Vendidad ; " Let the water fall as thousand-
fold, ten thousand-fold rain, to drive away sickness, to
drive away corruption, to drive away death.   May it
rain for the renewal of the waters, the earth, the plants,
the means of healing."[2]   As in the Veda Soma is the
king of plants, so in Iran Haoma, the god of life, is
the lord of plants.[3]   The white heavenly Haoma grows,
as we have seen, on the Gaokerena, the tree of heaven ;
from it springs the earthly Haoma and all plants of
which the seed falls from the tree Viçpotaokhma in
Vourukasha, which the bird Chamru carries where
Tistrya collects the clouds, in order to let the seed fall
down from them to the earth.[4]   " I, who am the giver
of all blessings," says Auramazda, " created this dwelling (the earth), the beautiful, brilliant, and note-
worthy; then Angromainyu, who is full of death,
created nine diseases, ninety diseases, nine hundred
diseases, nine thousand diseases, nine and ninety thousand diseases.   Thrita desired as a favour a means to
withstand death, to withstand pain, to withstand the
heat of fever, and the evil corruptions and filth which
Angromainyu has brought into the body of men.
Then I, who am Auramazda, brought forth the healing
plants, many hundreds, many thousands, many tens of
thousands, around the one Gaokerena."   The invocation
then follows :   " We bless thee, we invoke thee, we

[1] "Vend." 22, 7—38.   [2] "Vend." 21, 3—19.
[3] Justi, " Bundehesh," c. 24.
[4] West, " Mainyo-i-Khard," c. 62.   Above, p. 172.

worship thee for the healing of the body of men, in order to drive away sickness, in order to drive away death, the hot fever and the cold fever." [1]

Thrita, a spirit of heaven, who has a place among the sages and sacrificers of old time (p. 42) was, in the Avesta, the first physician who kept back disease and death; and every one who follows in his course, every physician, must appear as a willing combatant, an active co-operator against the evil spirits, from whom death and disease proceed. According to the Vendidad, those have the first place among the physicians who heal by charms, i. e. by the sacred word, the words of the law; these are the "physicians of physicians;" next come the physicians who heal by remedies; and last of all, those who heal by the knife. [2] These latter must first use the knife on the worshippers of the Daevas; when they have done so three times, and the patient has died each time, they are incapable for ever of practising the art of healing. But if they have healed three worshippers of the Daevas, they are capable of "healing the worshippers of Auramazda, and they can try their skill upon them as they please." The physician is not only to heal sick men, but sick animals also, and above all the sick dog. The Vendidad fixes the sum which the physician is to receive for his services. He is to heal a priest, and ask for no more than his blessing. For healing the overseer of a district he is to receive a yoke of four oxen, and for his wife a she-camel; the overseer of a canton is to pay a large beast of draught, and his wife a mare; the head of a village pays a smaller beast, and his wife a cow; the head of a house a small beast, and his wife a she-ass. For healing a large beast of draught the price is a beast of moderate size; and for one of

[1] "Vend." 20, 11—20.　　　　[2] "Vend." 7, 118, 121.

moderate size, a head of small cattle, etc.[1] Pliny quotes
a number of remedies and means of cure used by the
Magi, some of them of an extraordinary character;
indeed, the impression made on Pliny by the importance ascribed to medicine in the doctrine of Zarathrustra was so great, that he maintained that the
Magism of Zoroaster had arisen out of the art of
healing, and had introduced, as it were, a higher and
sacred medicine. To this was subsequently added the
power of religion, and the mathematical arts of in-
vestigating the future by the heavens, so that Zoroaster's doctrine had taken possession of the mind of
men by a three-fold bond.[2] How greatly he is mistaken in ascribing to the Magians the astrology of the
Chaldæans, has been remarked above; the mistake
is explained by the fact, that the Avesta includes the
astronomical knowledge of the priests of Iran in the
books which treated of medicine (p. 52).

The astronomical chapters are lost as well as those
on medicine. From our fragments we cannot so
much as fix the year by which the Avesta reckons.
We merely perceive that it counted by nights, not by
days. It is from the Bundehesh that we first learn
that the year of Eastern Iran is made up of 360 days
in twelve months of thirty days, with five additional
days. This year is said to have begun with the
vernal equinox, i. e. the period when the vigour of
nature again shows itself. In the last five nights of
the old year, and the first five nights of the new one,
the spirits of the forefathers, the Fravashis, come to
their descendants in the houses; they awake with
nature to new life (p. 179). The first month is called
Farvardin after these spirits; of the remaining eleven,
six are called after the Amesha Çpentas, and the

[1] "Vend." 7, 105, 117.   [2] "H. N." 30, 1.

remaining five, which are inserted between the six, after Mithra, Tistrya, the spirits of fire and water, and lastly after the law (Din). The inscriptions of the Achæmenids give us nine names of months entirely different from these. Hence the West had its own calendar, as well as its own alphabet, and made use of it as early as the year 500 B.C. In the East the calendar of the Avesta was in use; and this seems to have been current in the West also in the first half of the fourth century B.C. There is no doubt whatever that it was the standard for all Iran at the time of the Sassanids.[1]

We have already set forth in detail what weight the Avesta lays on purity, and the avoidance of contact with dead matter, which has fallen into the power of the Daevas. From these points of view, in consequence of the reform, the priests in Iran came to adopt a peculiar mode of burial. Among the Arians of the Panjab the oldest form of burial was interment, and in time cremation came into use (IV. 62). But could

[1] Von Gutschmid ("Das iranische Wandeljahr, Berichte der K. Sächsischen Gesellschaft der Wiss." 1862) places the establishment of the cycle, by which, in order to bring the year of 365 days into agreement with the natural time, a month was inserted every 120 years, and consequently the introduction of the East Iranian calendar into the whole kingdom, in the year 411, or between 428 and 381 B.C. That the beginning of the year was universally placed in the spring after the introduction of this calendar, and fixed between March and the middle of June, would follow from the importance of the Farvardin festival, even if it were not sufficiently vouched for by other evidence. The Bundehesh (c. 25) speaks of the year as fixed, inasmuch as it reckons the shortening of the days from a certain day in the month of Tir, and puts the shortest day on the 20th of the month of Din, yet it adds that the priests reckoned on this basis, and that the lunar year did not correspond to the year thus calculated. The Cappadocian names for the months are those of the East Iranian calendar; and the Cappadocians cannot have obtained these till the calendar was current throughout the whole kingdom of the Achæmenids. On this ground also Von Gutschmid's dates do not seem to be too high.

the Athravas allow anything so unclean as a corpse to
be laid on fire, the pure "son of Auramazda"? If the
corpse was thrown into water the pure water was
defiled; if buried in the earth pollution was cast
on the beautiful, submissive daughter of Auramazda.
Nothing therefore remained for the priests but to leave
the corpse above the earth; in this case it served the
pure animals, the birds and dogs, for nourishment,
and was thus destroyed in the best manner. To
throw a corpse into water, to bury or burn it, are
great sins, actions which do not admit of expiation,[1]
and those who do such things "help the drought
which destroys the pasture, and the evil onsweeping
winter, which kills the flock, and is full of snow; such
men are impure for ever."[2] Any one who buries a
dead dog or a dead man in the earth, and does not
dig the body up again within half a year, is to receive
twice five hundred stripes; any one who allows it to
remain in the earth for a year, is to receive twice a
thousand stripes; but if a man leaves a corpse in the
earth for more than two years, there is for him neither
penalty, nor expiation, nor purification.[3]

The dead are to be carried away on peculiarly dry
paths, little trodden by cattle, beasts of draught, and
pure men, and laid on the driest and barest places in
the earth, on the highest eminences where carnivorous
birds and dogs may most easily see them.[4] The soil
is to be dug out, waist deep, if the earth is soft; if
hard, to the depth of half a foot, and this depression
is to be filled with tiles, stones, and dust; for damp
earth contracts pollution most readily, whereas stones,
tiles, and dust contract it very slowly. To this place
(Dakhma) the naked corpse is to be taken on a bier,

[1] "Vend." 1, 48; 6, 6 and loc. cit. [2] "Vend." 7, 65—71.
[3] "Vend." 3, 122—136. [4] "Vend." 6, 93—95; 8, 13; 3, 50—54.

which has a foundation of stones or tiles, by two strong
men—never by one : one bearer would pollute himself
for ever, and the Druj Naçu would never leave him.
Any one who throws a cloth on the dead must be
punished with twice four hundred, or twice a thousand
stripes, according to the size of the cloth. The corpse
is to be placed on the Dakhma, with the face turned
to the sun (any one who does not place the body with
its face to the sun, is to pay the same penalty as is
prescribed for the murder of a pure man[1]): the corpse
is then to be secured in its place by iron, stones, or
lead, attached to the feet or hair, in order that the
birds and dogs may not carry away the bones and
remains to water and trees : the neglect of these
fastenings is to be punished with twice two hundred
stripes.[2] If it rains or snows, or the wind is strong, so
that the necessary preparations cannot be made on
the day of death, the corpse can be carried on its own
bed and mat to the Dakhma.[3]

At these burial-places the Daevas hold their meet-
ings ; there they propagate and assemble, "in order
to bring to death, fifty, a hundred, a thousand, ten
thousand, an innumerable host of men ;" there the
Daevas are most dangerous and deadly to men : for
in the places of burial are "infection, disease, fever,
impurity, ague, trembling, and old hair." A Dakhma
is not pure till the body has been eaten by dogs and
birds, till the remains have entirely changed into dust,
and become utterly mixed up with the foundation of
mortar, tiles, and stones. When this point has been
reached, the Dakhma should be levelled. Such destruction of the place of burial is regarded by the law-
book as the annihilation of death itself; as one of the
highest virtues of the faithful. " He who levels only

[1] "Vend." 5, 13, 14, 17, 48.　　[2] "Vend." 6, 98 ff.　　[3] "Vend." 6, 106.

so much as the size of his own body of a burial-place,"
says the book of the law, "has repented of all his
sins which he has committed in thought, speech, and
action ; he has not only repented of them, but he has
expiated them, and the two heavenly powers will not
begin a contest about his entrance into paradise." [1]

The prescriptions of the law for the purification of
the vessels and clothes which have touched the corpse,
are given from regard to utility, and from the point of
view of a certain simple rationalism, which forms an
advantageous contrast between Iran and India. Vessels
of lead, wood, and earth, are impure for ever; vessels
of gold and silver can be taken into use again after a
number of washings with gomez. Garments on which
spittle, moisture, or dung have fallen are to be cut in
pieces and buried ; in other cases they can be purified
with gomez, water, and earth, and aired, and then
again taken into use for women at the time of impurity. The house of the dead is pure when the
period for the extinction of the fire is over, when
the prayers appointed for the dead have been said,
and the inhabitants of the house have had their
bodies and clothes washed three times, and the sacred
hymns have been sung (p. 215).

For the bearers, who have carried a corpse to the
Dakhma, and those who in any way have come into
contact with a corpse, special forms of purification are
necessary. The washing of the bearers must be begun
immediately after the corpse has been deposited. For
this purpose the gomez of the nearest male and female
relation of the dead is required as well as that of
"cattle and beasts of draught." At the last washing
the Druj Naçu springs out of the forehead between
the eyebrows, from thence to the shoulders and under

[1] "Vend." 7, 126—147.

the arms, until at length by continued ablutions she
is driven into the left toes, and is compelled to pass
away from there to the north in the form of a fly.[1]
In order to purify the way on which the dead has
been carried to the Dakhma, a dog must be led along
it, three times, six times, and nine times. Then a
priest must walk along it, who pronounces the " victorious words," *i. e.* certain exorcisms. " I drive
back the Daevi Druj, so that she flies to the North.
Avaunt! She must not slay the corporeal world of
the pure. May Auramazda and Çpenta Armaiti protect
us from our enemies ; may Çraosha come, and Vohumano."[2] The worst of all forms of pollution is that
contracted by touching a corpse in a distant place in
solitude, for here the power of the demon was greatest.
Any one to whom this has happened, is to wash himself fifteen times with water, and rub himself an equal
number of times with earth, to hurry away from the
spot, and call out to every one whom he meets : " I
have touched a dead body, without wishing it in
thought, word, or deed ; my desire is purification."
Every one is to avoid him unless he wishes to bring
on himself the guilt of the impure man.[3]

Pools and streams are polluted by corpses till the
corpses have been removed and rain has thrice fallen
upon the water ; after this cattle and men can again
drink of the water. So long as the corpse lies in a
river, the fiend of death extends over nine paces
above and three paces below it, and six paces on
either side ; in a pool the domain of the fiend is six
paces in every direction ; in snow and ice-water it is
three paces. When Zarathrustra asks, whether the
water which falls from heaven on the corpse is impure,

[1] " Vend." 8, 34—36 ; 130—228.   [2] " Vend." 8, 38—64.
[3] " Vend." 8, 271—310 ; 9, 164—166.

the god answers, " I, Auramazda, allow the water to
go forth from Lake Vourukasha, with storms and
clouds, and to fall on a corpse ; I, Auramazda, and to
flow upon a burial-place, and upon a dung-heap, and
carry away a bone, and wash all into Lake Puitika (the
pool of purification in heaven). When purified the
waters flow from Lake Puitika into Lake Vourukasha.
I, Auramazda, rain down herbs of all kinds, to be
food for the pious men, food for the useful cattle.
With such speeches Auramazda appeased the just
Zarathrustra."[1] Zarathrustra further inquires, whether
corpses which have been carried by dogs, wolves, and
panthers to a field make the field and men impure?
Auramazda, as frequently happens in such cases,
argues from the point of view of the possible and
attainable. "If such corpses," says the god, "rendered
men impure, all mankind would quickly be rendered
impure owing to the multitude of the corpses which
are upon the earth." But Zarathrustra is not satisfied ;
he says : " A man dies in the hollow of a valley ; from
the heights of the mountains a bird flies down to the
valley, and then back to the summit of a mountain,
and alights on a tree of hard or soft wood. There he
is sick and voids excrements. Then a man goes up
from the valley to the summit of the mountain, and
comes to the tree, on which the bird has sat, and seeks
fuel for his fire. He cuts the tree down, splits it up,
and kindles a fire with it. What is his penalty?"
Auramazda again replies that nothing carried away
by wolves, dogs, birds, flies, or winds pollutes men.
But now it occurs to Zarathrustra, or rather to the
priests who have written these things down, whether
the animals which have eaten the corpses are not
impure. This difficulty Auramazda solves by declar-

---

[1] "Vend." 5, 15—21, according to Geldner's rendering.

ing the animals pure; but no flesh of such animals is
to be eaten within a year, or offered for sacrifice.[1]

With the exception of Herodotus, Strabo, and
Agathias, the Western writers give us only very exaggerated accounts of the peculiar mode of burial in use
among the Persians. Herodotus has already told us
that the corpses of the Magians were exposed to dogs
and birds; with regard to the corpses of the rest he
had no accurate knowledge, for a mystery was made of
the matter.[2] Onesicritus relates that those Bactrians,
who were weakened by disease and age, were thrown to
dogs brought up for the purpose and called buriers of
the dead; and Strabo says that among the Caspians,
parents, when they had reached seventy years of age,
were shut up by their children, and so killed by starvation;[3] though he also observes that the Magians
gave over the corpses to birds.[4] Cicero narrates that
it was not the custom of the Magians to bury the
corpses of their dead before they had been torn by
wild animals: in Hyrcania a peculiar kind of dog
was reared—by the lower classes in common; of the
wealthier men each had his own—by which they
might be torn after death, and this was considered
the best kind of burial.[5] From Eusebius we hear
that the Medes gave the dying to carefully-reared
dogs; the Hyrcanians and Caspians those who were
still alive; the Bactrians the old; others the dead.[6]
Agathias, on the other hand, tells us, that the dead
among the Persians were carried out before the
gates of the cities naked and without a coffin, and
eaten by dogs, so that the bones lay about in the
fields. If any man's corpse was not at once eaten, the

---

[1] "Vend." 5, 1—22; 7, 189—191. [2] Herod. 1, 140; 3, 16.
[3] Strabo, p. 517. [4] Strabo, p. 735. Cf. p. 520.
[5] "Quaest. Tuscul." 1, 45. [6] Euseb. "Praep. Evang." p. 277.

Persians believed that he had been of an unholy mind, that his soul was unjust and wicked, and so had come into the power of the evil spirits, and would be carried into hell. Such men were lamented by their friends, because they had no part in the better lot. Those who were most quickly eaten up, the Persians praised as fortunate; they called their souls the best, and like the gods, and said of them that they had gone into the good land.[1]

The Greeks maintained that the Achæmenids were buried at Pasargadae and Persepolis, and that the corpse of Cyrus rested at Pasargadae.[2] Of Darius we are told that even in his lifetime he caused his tomb to be prepared on the summit of a mountain. The corpses of Artaxerxes I. of Damaspia, and of his son Xerxes, were buried, according to Ctesias, in Persia.[3] The last Darius was buried by Alexander in the royal sepulchre, when he had already given the honours of burial to the Persian queen Statera.[4] Diodorus tells us that these tombs were on the eastern side of the citadel of Persepolis, at a distance of four hundred feet, in the "royal mountain." The rock was hewn out, and contained several chambers. But these tombs had no entrance; the corpses were drawn up by machines to the summit, and so laid in them.[5]

The burial-places of the rulers of ancient Persia can still be recognised. Some hundred paces to the east of the remains of the royal palace at Persepolis, towards the rising of the sun, precisely as Diodorus describes the place, are three stone pictures in Mount Rachmed. Sculptures which begin three hundred feet

[1] Agath. 2, 23. [2] Diod. 17, 71; Arrian, "Anab." 3, 22; 6, 29.
[3] Ctes. "Pers. Ecl." 44, 46; Strabo, p. 730.
[4] Arrian, l. c.; Justin, 11, 15; Aelian, "Var. Hist." 6, 8; Plut. "Alex." c. 30.
[5] Diod. 17, 71; cf. Ctes. "Pers. Ecl." 15.

above the ground on the perpendicular front of the mountain form three high façades, with pillars, which present a gateway with woodwork, supporting a large canopy, on which are seen several rows of dogs; the same animals are to be seen on the lower lines of ornamentation. Within this framework are the pictures of the buried sovereigns. In the left hand is the bow without a string; the right is raised in an attitude of prayer, and the figures are standing before an altar of burning fire. The king is supported on a foundation upheld by the arms of several rows of men, who represent the conquered lands. Two leagues to the north of Persepolis are four great sculptures, now called Naksh-i-Rustem, *i. e.* pictures of Rustem, of a similar kind, but beginning only sixty or seventy feet from the ground, deeply cut in the perpendicular wall of two hundred feet in length. Three of these pictures are close together; the fourth is on a spur of the rock, at right angles to the other three. The centre of the three marks the tomb of Darius, the son of Hystaspes. It is the only one among the seven monuments which has inscriptions.

The corpses of the princes might have been exposed to the sun, the dogs, and birds on the summit above these pictures. In that case they would merely mark the place of exposure, and these rocks would be burial-places like those of the modern Parsees in Bombay. But behind the sculptures, though not accessible from them, sepulchral chambers have been discovered. From this, and from the description which the Greeks give us of the tomb of Cyrus, we must draw the conclusion that the Persian custom of burial did not agree with the rule of the Avesta—with the exception of the priests, whose corpses, as Herodotus expressly states,

[1] K. Niebuhr, "Reise," 2, 150 ff.

were exposed. The Vendidad laments that in certain
districts of the East, Arachosia and Chakhra, the dead
were burned, or buried.[1] Under the Sassanids exposure was strictly observed both in the East and
West, as is clear from the account of Agathias already
quoted, and all the statements which relate to this
later period.

The regulations of the book of the law with regard
to the burial of corpses and the places of exposure are
still strictly observed by the Parsees. Great care is
taken at the erection of a Dakhma that the rain-water
can run off from the bier of the corpse. At the last
moment a dog is brought into the presence of the
dying person, so that its eye may be directed on him;
and when a woman with child dies two dogs are
brought, because two lives are in question. The eye
of the dog has the power to keep the evil spirits at a
distance. But every one must remain at nine paces
distance from the dying person. After death the two
corpse-bearers at once strip the body—their hands are
protected from immediate contact by napkins made of
old clothes—and carry it on a bier of iron—for metal
contracts less pollution than wood—accompanied by
the prayers of the priests, to the place of burial. The
kinspeople follow the corpse in silence to within ninety
paces of the Dakhma. For the first three nights the
priests and kinsmen repeat continually the prescribed
prayers for the soul of the dead; in the third night
the decision is made at the bridge of Chinvat (p. 178).
The burial-places of the Parsees at Bombay are
situated on a mountain on the coast, on the summit of
which several hollows have been cut. From a distance
the relatives look eagerly to this summit, to see
whether the vultures are already attacking the corpse,

[1] "Vend." 1, 46, 48, 60, 64; cf. above, p. 137, 138.

and which part of it they first consume. For the first year after death a prayer is said daily before meals for the soul of the dead to the Fravashis of the pure,[1] and a service is held on the day of the month on which the death took place. In the years that follow, on the fourth, tenth, and thirtieth day of each month, as the book prescribes, but above all on the festival of all souls—*i. e.* on the feast of the ten nights during which the Fravashis come down (p. 224)—prayers are said for the dead.

It is hardly possible to ascertain the arrangement and life of the state from the very scanty and obscure traits in the existing fragments of the law. We have no rules on the rights and duties of the monarchy, though these were included in the Avesta, if we may trust the list of contents.[2] But the splendour of majesty as it dwelt with the rulers of old time, with Yima, Thraetaona, and Kereçaçpa, and was imparted to Çyavarshana and Vistaçpa, is brought strongly into prominence; and among the Amesha Çpentas we found the spirit of good order, of good government. Of the position of the orders so much only is clear—that the priests claimed precedence over the warriors and husbandmen; that the Avesta allows them certain privileges of moderate extent (p. 187); and that the priestly families did not form exclusive castes, though the priestly functions were hereditary in them. Still less can we learn of the families of the warriors. We do not hear that they enjoyed a favoured position; they

---

[1] "Yaçna," 26.

[2] Above, p. 52. The Mainyo-i-Khard contains some rules on the duties of the king. The prince is to defend the city and land against enemies and risings, to respect water and fire, to keep at a distance bad laws and customs, and promote the worship of Auramazda, and good works, and to bring back to the right way those who have left it. A king of this kind is like the Yazatas and Amesha Çpentas: c. 15, 20, 33, 68, ed. West.

are merely mentioned before the husbandmen; and the Vendidad also gives us some information about their armour. It should consist of a coat of mail and helmet, a girdle and greaves, a bow with thirty arrows, a sling with thirty stones, a sword, a club, and a lance.[1] Under the Achæmenids there were rich families in Bactria and Sogdiana, in which we may no doubt venture to find descendants of the old military families, enjoying an influential position in politics; under the Sassanids the knightly nobility of Iran comes plainly to the front. The Avesta speaks of great and intermediate houses, of important and unimportant inhabitants of the villages. We also read of rich and poor, men who have property and beggars; and mention is made of tradespeople and slaves. The Avesta rises from the lord of the house to the lord of the village or community (viç), then to the lord of the tribe or canton (zantu) and to the lord of the province (danhu); an arrangement which corresponds to the Indian government as fixed by Manu's regulations. When Alexander of Macedon forced his way to Bactria and Sogdiana, he met with resistance from the native overseers of cantons or chieftains, whom he had summoned to Zariaspa, "the largest city" in Bactria (p. 12).[2] When the castles of the most powerful had been taken, and their lords had submitted, he sought to gain them by marrying their daughters to the captains of his army, while he himself took to wife the daughter of the Bactrian Oxyartes.

The protection of property is obviously a matter of great importance in the Avesta. The utility of dogs is frequently mentioned, which protect flocks and villages from thieves and wolves. Theft is looked on

---

[1] "Vend." 14, 32—40.   [2] Arrian, "Anab." 4, 1, 5.

as especially wicked, because the thief leads a roving
life, eats raw and unprepared food, and carries on his
evil work in the darkness.[1] In regard to contracts the
Vendidad distinguishes six kinds, according as they
are concluded by word, by the pledge of hands, and
are concerned with the value of a head of small cattle,
a beast of draught, a man (*i. e.* a slave), and a piece of
land. Anyone who violates the first kind is to receive
300 blows with the rod, and 300 with the whip, and
the punishment increases in the violation of the other
kinds up to 1000 stripes with both instruments.[2] To
check injury of the person the Vendidad lays down
the rule, that anyone who lifts up his weapon against
a man without beating him, is to receive twice five
stripes the first time, and twice two hundred on the
seventh occasion of committing the offence, if he has
not expiated the preceding six offences ; if he has expiated them, the measure of the first offence is dealt
out on each occasion. Anyone who attacks another
not in anger but with malice, is to be punished with
twice fifteen, and on the sixth occasion with 200
stripes, in case he has not expiated the former offences.
Anyone who inflicts a wound on another, is punished
the first time with twice thirty, the fifth time with
twice two hundred stripes. The same punishment is
inflicted on a man who breaks the bones of another, if
he does not expiate the offence. If the wound proves
fatal, he is to be punished with twice ninety stripes,
and on a second offence with twice two hundred.[3]

[1] "Vend." 13, 143—145.

[2] "Vend." 4, 4—53 according to Harlez.

[3] "Vend." 4, 54—113. Even after all that has been advanced by De
Harlez, "Avesta," p. 101, I cannot convince myself that the stripes
appointed here and elsewhere in the Vendidad are to fall, not on the
guilty, but on animals of Angromainyu. If animals are to be killed,
we are told so expressly in the Vendidad, and this duty is often mentioned along with the stripes (p. 209). To kill twice 90 or 200 flies or

We have but few indications in the Avesta from
which to draw conclusions as to the state of civilisation. The amounts to be paid to the purifier and the
physician are given in animals; the series of contracts is determined according to the value of small
cattle, beasts of draught, slaves, and landed property.
But other property may be given in place of the
animals; we find mention of money (*shaeta*),[1] and, as
has been observed, of tradespeople; of mats and
carpets, vessels of earth, silver, and gold, rich garments,
palaces with pillars and turrets, ovens for smelting and
for glass. The art of the physician cannot have been
in a primitive stage, when so much space is devoted to
remedies (p. 223), and the physicians who heal with
the knife are designated as a separate class. So far as
I can see, the Avesta betrays a state of civilisation,
which, beginning from the pastoral condition, has
remained in close connection with cattle-breeding and
agriculture, but has also reached a more advanced
stage. The unions of the tribes seem dissolved, and
neither the previous importance of the warlike families
nor their present position is brought prominently
forward. This, no less than the liberal imposition
of bodily punishment, shows that long before the
dominion of the Achæmenids, the East of Iran must
have been in the hands of princes who ruled with
despotic power.

lizards is no equivalent for murdering a man. I allow that no one
could endure blows by thousands, if they were given in earnest, yet in
running a " muck " five and six hundred very severe blows have been
endured. In my opinion the punishments of the Avesta are not intended for legal penalties : they mark what was needed, in the opinion
of the priests, to expel the evil disposition, which could recur again
and again.

[1] " Vend." 4, 120 ; " Astad Yasht," 1 ; Justi, "Handbuch," *sub. voc.*

CHAPTER X.

OF the tribes of the Arians occupying the table-land
called by their name, those which had their habita-
tions on the northern slope of the Hindu Kush, in the
valleys of the Murghab and Zarefshan, outstripped the
rest in combining their forces, and uniting into a larger
community. In these regions they held advanced
posts over against the steppes and the migratory
nations of the low plains stretching before them without limit towards the north. We had good reason to
suppose that it was the repulsion of the attacks of the
nomads from the steppes of the Oxus and Jaxartes,
which brought these tribes, whose possessions consisted
of flocks and pastures, into the habit of living in
arms, and of undertaking the protection of the country.
From their midst arose the monarchy intended to lead
and combine the defence, the formation of which we
placed about the year 1100 B.C., and having its centre
at Bactria and Zariaspa. The tribes of the West, on
the other hand, for four centuries after this time lived
in isolation under their chieftains. The continuance
of the struggles which Bactria had to undergo, even
after the formation of the monarchy, is proved, not
only by the proximity of the nomads of the steppes,
but also by the traits of warlike feeling preserved

in the Avesta; by the order of warriors which existed
beside the orders of priests and husbandmen; by the
chieftains and their citadels, which we found here in
the fourth century B.C.; and lastly, by the circumstance, that the old shapes of the myth of the Arians,
the spirits of the sky which smite the demons, are
changed in the Avesta not merely into ideal patterns,
but even into ancestors of the Bactrian kings, and
connected with the genealogical tree of the nation.
Yima, Thraetaona, Manuschithra, Airyu, Uça, and
Huçrava, are changed into ancestors of the kings
and the people.

Like the Aryas in the Panjab, the tribes of the
Airyas in Iran prayed to Mithra, to the spirits of light,
the clear air, the wind, and fire, which protected them
against the demons of the night and gloom, and
gave increase to their pastures and flocks, and recovered the water of the sky which the demons
sought to carry away. As in India, the juice of the
Soma plant was the principal offering presented to
the gods; as Soma was not only the king of plants,
the lord of nourishment and life — so the liquor
which gave strength to the gods was here also a god,
Haoma. The belief in the opposition of the spirits of
light and the spirits of destruction, in the power of
the correct sacrifice, in the influence of the good
sayings, the sacred words, was on both sides of the
Indus, the starting-point of religious ideas, and in
Iran it became the hinge on which they turned.

Iran was divided into fertile land and deserts;
next to the most luxuriant growth lay wide tracts, in
which heat or cold, morass or drought, storms of sand
or of snow, made life and agriculture impossible.
These contrasts were most striking on the upper Oxus,
in Sogdiana and Margiana. Hence it came to pass

that in Bactria the ancient belief in the struggle of
the good and evil spirits made an essential advance.
The old gods and spirits, the ancient worship of fire,
were not indeed overthrown by the doctrine of Zarathrustra; on the contrary, the struggle between the
good and evil powers was spread over the whole of
nature, and the means of repelling the evil ones were
increased. The good and evil spirits were respectively
ranged under chiefs, on the counter-operation of whom
and their spirit-armies rests the life of nature; and
on this life depends the life of man. Henceforth
man must not merely keep the evil ones from himself,
he must take part in the struggle of the good against
the evil powers, increase so far as he can the good
creation which now belongs to Auramazda and has
proceeded from him; and thus restrict the sphere in
which the evil spirit exercises his power. After death
he will receive the reward of his conflict; and if in
and through this struggle he has been made a partici-
pator in the nature of the pure and bright deities, he
will continue to live in their heaven of light.

This development of the old Arian views and
reform of the religion received the impulse which
eventually called it into life at the time when Vistaçpa
was king of Bactria. It must have taken place about
the year 1000 B.C., *i. e.* about the time when the
Brahmans on the Ganges came to reform their ancient
faith, and exalted Brahman above Indra and the
ancient deities. From the idea of this new god, in
which the power of the Holy and the world-soul were
equal factors, the Brahmans arrived at a sharp distinction between spirit and matter. Their ethics, beginning with the rejection of nature, could not but
require the annihilation of the body as their final
goal, and this led to the vain pursuit of impossibilities,

to the ascetic suicide of body and soul. The doctrine
of Zarathrustra does not recognise the contradiction
of spirit and matter. The good God has not created
the world in order to entangle men in evil and
wickedness, but in order to give to it and to mankind
life and increase. It is only one side of nature, not
the whole of it, and that side harmful to men, which
has proceeded from evil, and this evil does not come
from the good, but from the wicked spirit. Evil is
here limited to gloom, desolation, drought and death.
As it is this part, and this only in nature, which has
to be removed, man is not called upon to lay aside his
whole nature, but on the contrary to rejoice in the
beneficial side of it. This he must tend and strengthen
in himself, while he keeps the harmful side at a distance, struggles against and annihilates it so far as
possible both in himself and all around him. He
must strengthen the light side of his soul against the
dark, and make it the master of the dark; he must
banish from his soul lying and deceit, idleness and
filthiness; purity of soul consists in truthfulness.
Thus must a man watch and work with the good
gods and under their eyes. It is not contemplation,
meditation, or asceticism, as in the doctrine of the
Brahmans; it is practical activity and inward effort
that the teaching of Zarathrustra requires from men;
the object it placed before men was not self-annihila-
tion, but the purification of soul and body, and true
assertion of self. If a man kept his body and soul
pure; if he was truthful in word and work, and increased the good creation in meadow, field, and forest;
if he slew the animals of the evil spirits, then all
would be well with him; he would have abundance
of cattle and descendants, long life in this world, and
eternal life in the heaven of the spirits of light.

This reform had been accomplished in its fundamental principles in Bactria, and Auramazda had been
elevated above Mithra as the creator of heaven, of
the gods, and the earth, when about the middle of the
ninth century B.C. the armies of Shalmanesar II. of
Asshur invaded the East of Iran.   About this time,
or soon after, the order of Athravas was formed.   It
rose, on the one hand, out of the ancient families of the
fire-priests, who understood the custom of sacrifice,
and had preserved the efficacious prayers to Mithra,
Verethraghna, Haoma, and Tistrya, to Ardviçura and
Drvaçpa down to the period of the reform, so far as
they came over to the new doctrine ; and on the other
hand, out of the race of Zarathrustra, and the families
of the zealous adherents of the new doctrine, who
devoted themselves to the service of religion.   This
order of priests, which handed down in its families
the sayings of Zarathrustra and those of old days, the
ancient invocations as well as those of the new teaching, took precedence of the families of the nobles,
warriors, and husbandmen, though they were not
separated from them by any rights of connubium or
other privileges.   From the whole tendency of the
reform there could not be any thought of acquiring
such a position as that which the Brahmans—the first
created of Brahman—attained among the orders of
India.   When the army of Tiglath-Pilesar II. entered
Arachosia about the middle of the eighth century B.C.
the new doctrine had already advanced to the West.
It was represented among the Medes by eminent
teachers.   In this region, at the time when the Medes
were under the supremacy of Assyria, a priestly order
grew up out of the old families of the priests or
Magians, i. e. the powerful, and adherents of the new
doctrine ; the families of this order abandoned their

R 2

tribal connection among the Medes, and thus formed
an hereditary caste, which preserved the name already
in use in the West for the priests, and became so
numerous that it could be ranked as a tribe among
the other tribes of the Medes. The formation of this
order was already complete when, after the middle of
the seventh century B.C., the Medes rebelled against
the kings of Asshur.

Meanwhile the Athravas of the East were busily
occupied in developing and fixing the contents and
meaning of the new idea of God, and of the ethics
resulting from it. They ranged the old gods under
the new doctrine, and determined their relation to the
new supreme deity; they peopled heaven with shapes
corresponding to the reformed teaching, and brought
mythology into harmony with it; from the commands
of purity they developed in the spirit of the reformed religion the rules of purification and the
removal of impurities as required in every occurrence
of life. Thus, beside the old invocations of the
gods, arose theories of a speculative cast which sought
to regard the gods as ethical forces, and prayers of a
formal character; from the dialectic of the priestly
schools was developed a very complicated system of
purity of life, of rubrics for expiation and purification, in which formalism and casuistry were not
wanting. Enquiries arose how law and justice should
be shaped so as to conform to the rules of religion;
while, on the other hand, the old sacrificial songs were
collected, the liturgy was fixed, as well as the order
of the festivals and sacrifices for the new moon and
full moon, and the course of the year; the prescriptions of medicine were written down, and those cycles
formed which comprised the battle between Auramazda and Angromainyu down to the last and eternal

victory of light and life.   After various attempts at
compilation, the priests of the East finally succeeded in
uniting the sum of these labours into one great whole,
which was the canon of the sacred scriptures.   We
may assume that the labours of the priesthood of Bactria, which came to an end with this result, may have
occupied the same space of time as the growth and
writing down of the Brahmanas on the Ganges.   There
are good reasons for supposing that the canon was
finally established about the year 600 B.C., and therefore, on the calculation given, the labours of the priests
upon it must have commenced about the year 800 B.C.

Like the kindred tribes in India, the Arians in
Iran were not destitute of imagination and a tendency to abstraction.   But from the first these qualities were restrained within narrower limits owing
to the nature of the land,—while the scenery and
phenomena of the Ganges tended to develop them,—
and the teaching of Zarathrustra provided a counter-
poise in the practical requirements which it set up.
Labour took the place of idle dreaming, conflict and
energetic activity the place of asceticism, and the
imagination received impulses to simple and great
conceptions.   The ethics of this religion guaranteed
the conditions of a healthy human existence; man's
effort was essentially directed to this present world,
and the duties imposed upon him were such as he could
fulfil.   Thus they led to results different from the in-
trospection, quietism, and asceticism of the Indians,
and the relapse into sensuality which was the inse-
parable concomitant of the latter.   The doctrine of
Zarathrustra contributed essentially to educate the
tribes which followed it in truthfulness and manli-
ness, and to qualify them for energy and action.
In their sensible, intelligent view of the world,

in putting theory below practice, and aiming at an active life, the Iranians are as far before the Indians as the Romans are before the Greeks.

If Eastern Iran, in the first instance, discharged a religious mission, the duty of politics was undertaken by the West. The empire of the Medes and of the Persians rose and fell, but the religion of Auramazda survived the fall of the Achæmenids. It rose to renewed life with the empire of the Arsacids and Sassanids. The national reaction against the dominion of the Seleucids began with the Parthians; the empire of the Sassanids, which subsequently took the place of that of the Arsacids, was supported in the first place by the tribes of the Persians, and was connected with the remembrance of the Achæmenids. Yet from the first the Sassanids were prepared to deal equal measure to the East and West of Iran; in opposition to any attempt at religious innovation they held firmly to the tradition of the East. When after a rule of more than four centuries the Sassanids succumbed to the invasion of the Arabs, Yezdegerd III. attempted to maintain himself in Merv, as Darius III. had attempted to maintain himself in Bactria. The attempt failed. Iran succumbed to Islam. Yet it was the East from which, not quite two centuries after the fall of the Sassanids, a reaction commenced against the Arabs, and this gradually increased till it rescued the nationality and the language of Iran. It was the viceroys in the districts of the East who rebelled against the Chalifate, and they found support in the population of their provinces. A process similar to that which had previously broken down the dominion of the Seleucids over Iran shattered the empire of the Abbasids. The impulse to this movement rose in Taberistan, where the Taherids appeared as independent princes soon after

the death of Harun-al-Rashid; some decads later the
Soffarids rebelled in Sejestan, and towards the end of
the ninth century the power of the Samanids sprang
up in Sogdiana, Balkh, and Merv, and founded seats
in Samarcand and Bokhara.   Not long after the Ziads
obtained an independent position in Dilem and Jorjan
(the ancient Hyrcania).   Towards the end of the tenth
century the Ghasnavids, who had hitherto been the
servants and captains of the Samanids, threw off
their allegiance; and united under their dominion all
the lands which had been subject to the Soffarids,
the Samanids, and Ziads.   Soon after the year 1000
B.C. they ruled from their abode in Ghasna over
Cabul, Balkh, Merv, and Chovaresm to the north, and
over Sejestan and Afghanistan to the south, and to
the west over the lands of Elburz, while their armies
crossed the Indus to the east, and advanced beyond
the Panjab to the valley of the Ganges.   The ancient
religion of Iran was not wholly lost even in the time
of Harun-al-Rashid; Magians were tolerated at the
court of the Chalifs for the sake of their skill in
medicine.   The Barmecides, who came from Balkh,
displayed, even under the Chalifate, a partiality for
the legends and the religion of Iran.   The Samanids
boasted to be sprung from the Sassanids, the Ziads
were reproached with being idolaters in heart and
Moslem in tongue.   They called themselves once more
by the names celebrated in the legends of Eastern
Iran: Minocher after Manuschithra, Kai Kobad after
Kava Kavata, Kai Kaus after Kava Uça, Isfendyar
after Çpentodata; and in the list of the Ghasnavids,
the Afghan princes in India, we meet at a later time
with the name of Kava Huçrava (Chosru).

The regeneration of Old Iran, in opposition to
the Arabs, found its firmest stronghold in Ghasna.

The deeds of the Achæmenids were completely forgotten in the East which had no part in them; but
the legends of Yima, Thraetaona, Kava Huçrava, and
Kava Vistaçpa, had lived on under the dominion of
the Achæmenids, the Seleucids, the Greek princes of
Balkh and Cabul, and under the Arsacids. Then
came the revival of the Avesta under Shapur II.
about the middle of the fourth century A.D. (p. 61).
The first Chosru (531—578 A.D.) caused the legends
and traditions of the nation and the priests to be
collected and copied; a comprehensive exposition of
the whole was made under the last Yezdegerd. Thus
as early as the last days of the Sassanids the tradition
of Iran was collected and fixed, and this, transcribed
in Pehlevi, outlived the fall of the kingdom, and descended as a legacy of ancient glory to the Soffarids,
Samanids, and Ghasnavids.[1] On the basis of this
"book of kings," which he possessed in an Arabic
translation, Firdusi of Tus on the Tejend, a city of
which at the present day some scanty ruins remain
not far from Meshhed, undertook to restore to life the
remembrance of the past of Eastern Iran and the
fame of her ancient heroes in a great Epic poem. He
gathered together the entire existing tradition, and
under the dominion of Islam cast a new glory on
the ancient belief in Auramazda, who was now known
as Yazdan. This poem, the book of kings (Shahnameh)
exhibits at the same time the New Persian language
in its pure form, developed out of the Eastern dialects,
and not yet contaminated with Aramæan and Arabic
elements.

The first king in Firdusi is Gayumart. He assembles men and animals, and teaches the first to hide

---

[1] Flügel, "Mani," s. 407; Mohl, "Livre des Rois," Intro. Mordtmann, "Z. D. M. G." 19, 485 ff; Nöldeke, "Tabari," s. xv.

their nakedness with the skins of leopards. His son Siyamek is torn in pieces by a demon. We are acquainted with the primeval man Gayo maretan ; whom the priests placed at the beginning of things (p. 183). Then king Hoshang taught men to harness the bull, to tame the horse, to forge iron, to till the field, and introduced the worship of fire. After Hoshang king Tahmurath reigned, who overcame the Divs (Daevas), and compelled them to teach him the art of writing. He taught his people the art of weaving, and rode round the world on Angromainyu (now Ahriman) till the latter threw him off on Elburz, and so killed him. In the Avesta Haoshyangha sacrifices in order to obtain power over the evil spirits, and Takhmo urupa also sacrifices in order to curb Angromainyu for the space of thirty years (p. 183). After Tahmurath, Jemshid (Yima) is king. He teaches the art of forging weapons and weaving precious stuffs, divides men into priests, warriors, husbandmen, and artisans ; discovers the art of healing, and compels the demons to build houses, and erect for him a splendid palace and a gorgeous throne adorned with gold and precious stones. Three hundred years passed away while he was king, in which the Divs were bound, and death could not approach mankind. Then Jemshid boasted that he had saved the world by his remedies from sickness and death, and demanded divine honours. This sin alienated from him the princes of his kingdom. Jemshid was compelled to fly before Zohak, the king of Babylon. Zohak pursued him. In the remote East, on the sea of China, Jemshid was overtaken and slain.

The old Arian legend of the happy age of Yima show sitself even yet through Firdusi's version. Death could not approach men under his dominion ; there

was no sickness, and therefore Jemshid is said to have
discovered the art of healing. The Avesta had already
found a motive for the fall of Yima in the fact that
he had refused to announce the law, and at length
had begun to love lies (p. 41). The Zohak of Firdusi
is no other than the ancient cloud dragon, Azhi
dahaka, which attempts to carry away the waters of
the sky, and swallows up men and horses. He is
now a foreign, hostile, bloodthirsty king, who puts an
end to the blessings of Yima's reign in order to bring
the reverse of blessing upon Iran. Azhi dahaka had
three heads and three throats; Zohak has two serpents
growing from his shoulders, to which by degrees
thousands fall as sacrifices, for they are fed with the
brains of men, and for this purpose two youths are
slaughtered every day. That Zohak is called king of
Babylon is due to a reminiscence of the fact that the
Assyrians ruled over Western Iran, and the Seleucids
and Chalifs over the whole country. Zohak perse-
cutes severely the descendants of Jemshid. Abtin, the
last of these, finally falls into his power; he causes
him to be slain for his serpents; but Abtin's wife
carries off his young son Feridun in safety to Elburz.
When the latter is sixteen years of age his mother
discloses to him the fate of his father; the discontented gather round him, and the angel Serosh
teaches him how to overcome the magician Zohak.
In the citadel at Babylon Feridun strikes Zohak to
the ground with a blow of the club which Kave, the
smith, has forged for him. But Serosh bids him
not to kill Zohak, who is now chained in a deep
cave in Elburz, under Demavend, the highest summit
on the chain. Abtin, the descendant of Jemshid, is
the Athwya of the Avesta; Feridun is Thraetaona,
the son of Athwya, the slayer of Dahaka; the angel

Serosh is the well-known god Çraosha. Feridun is not permitted to slay Zohak, because Azhi dahaka is also a demon.

Feridun has three sons—Salm (Çairima), Tur (Tuirya), and Yrej (Airyu) ; to the last, who was the youngest, Feridun gives Iran, the best part of his dominions, while Salm receives the West and Tur the North. Filled with envy at the favour shown to their youngest brother, Salm and Tur slay the pious Yrej. Feridun is deeply moved ; but he gives the daughter whom Yrej has left in marriage to Pesheng. The son of Pesheng is Minocher, who grows up to avenge his grandfather's death. In order to prevent this, Salm and Tur invade Iran. The battle continues for three days, till Minocher has slain Tur with his own hand. He also overtakes Salm in flight, and slays him. Feridun can now die in peace, as he has seen the kingdom handed over to Minocher. After the death of the latter the kingdom descended to his son Naudar.[1] Then Afrasiab of Turan, the great-grandson of Tur, whom Minocher had slain, invaded Iran to avenge the death of his ancestor on the descendant of Minocher. Naudar's army was defeated ; he was taken captive with many princes of Iran, and be-headed by the order of Afrasiab.

Besides the race of Abtin, Jemshid had left other descendants. In union with the daughter of the king of Cabul, whose kingdom extends from Bost on the Hilmend to Ghasna (and consequently includes the region of Sejestan, the ancient Haetumat),[2] he had begotten Gershasp, a mighty hero who stood by the side of Minocher in the struggle against Salm and Tur ; the sons of Gershasp are Neriman and Sam, and

---

[1] Nohodares in Ammian, 1, 14, 3 ; 1, 25, 3.
[2] Spiegel, "Eran," 1, 557.

his grandson is Zal. The Gershasp of Firdusi is the
Kereçaçpa of the Avesta, the son of Thrita, of the race
of Çama (p. 35), who slays the serpent Çruvara and
the giant Gandarewa. The Avesta gives him the
epithet Nairimanao, *i. e.* the man-hearted, heroic, and
represents him as seizing the brilliance of majesty,
when it departed for the third time from Yima (p.
36). This hint was enough to give the royal power
to Kereçaçpa; his epithet and his tribal name are
personified, and become his descendants Neriman and
Sam. In accordance with their origin these princes
from Zabul are in Firdusi the most faithful adherents
of the race of Feridun, which has rewarded them with
the dominion over the South. In this way the legend
of Sejestan is woven into the closest connection with the
legend of the Avesta. The power of the descendants of
Feridun is extinguished with Naudar, from whose sons
" the splendour of the royal majesty shines no longer ; "
thus does Firdusi repeat the metaphor current in the
Avesta. The princes of Zabul now take their place
as the protectors and guardians of Iran. The son of
king Sam of Zabul is Zal. After Naudar's melancholy
fall he makes peace between Iran and Turan; the
Oxus is fixed as the boundary, Afrasiab returns to his
own country, and in the place of the sons of Naudar
Zal allows Zav to be chosen king of Iran. Zav is
already aged and soon dies ; Afrasiab invades Iran
again. Then Zal deliberates with the Mobedhs (*i. e.*
with the chiefs of the Magians, p. 60), who is to be
king of Iran. It is resolved to raise Kai Kobad to the
throne, who like Feridun before him dwells on Elburz.
Zal sends his son Rustem (Moses of Khorene is the
first who mentions the Persian legend of Rustem), a
youth of great strength, who as a boy had slain an
infuriated elephant, to fetch Kai Kobad from Elburz.

Rustem finds him prepared, for he has seen in a dream
two white falcons who place a golden crown upon
his head. Afrasiab's army, which opposes him, is
defeated ; Kai Kobad ascends the throne of Iran,
the Turanians are defeated in a great battle, Rustem
seizes Afrasiab by his girdle and drags him from his
horse ; but the girdle breaks, Afrasiab falls to the
ground, and is saved by his own people. In the peace
the Oxus is once more fixed as the boundary between
Iran and Turan. Kai Kobad is followed by his son
Kai Kaus. Against the advice of his vassals and of
Zal he leads his army against Mazanderan, a land
inhabited by demons, which take the king captive
with his whole army. A single warrior escapes to bring
the terrible news to Zal. As Zal is now 200 years old,
Rustem undertakes to liberate the king. He has to
overcome seven terrible monsters before he can arrive
at the demons. At last he makes his way to them,
and on his horse Reksh, he destroys the army of the
demons. Then he slays their chief, the white demon,
in the dark cave, and liberates Kai Kaus and the army
of Iran. Kai Kaus now causes the conquered demons
to build him splendid palaces on Elburz, and resolves
to fly up to heaven, in order to see the course of the
sun. Four eagles bound to his throne carry him
upwards, but then allow him to fall to earth. Ashamed
at his pride he humbles himself, and his penance
appeases the wrath of heaven. When Afrasiab breaks
the peace and again invades Iran, Kai Kaus sends his
son Siavaksh, under the guidance of Rustem, against
the Turanians. For three days the battle rages at the
gates of Balkh, and at length Siavaksh is victorious.
Afrasiab sues for peace, Siavaksh concludes a treaty ;
but Kai Kaus will not confirm it. That he may not
break his word, Siavaksh gives himself up to the

Turanians. Afrasiab receives him with honour, and
gives him his daughter Feringis to wife. Subsequently
he harbours suspicion against him, causes him to be
executed, and the son, whom Feringis bears after the
execution of her husband, to be brought up among
the shepherds without any knowledge of his birth.
To this son an abode is then allotted in a remote
region of Turan.

To avenge the execution of Siavaksh Rustem invades Turan. Victorious in the battle he causes
Surkha, the son of Afrasiab, whom he captures in the
battle, to be put to death in the same way as Siavaksh,
pursues Afrasiab to the extreme border of his kingdom,
and does not return till the whole of Turan has been
laid waste : the booty is immense. Many years afterwards it was revealed in a dream to Guderz (Gotarzes),
a descendant of that Kave, who had once forged for
Feridun the club used against Zohak, that a son of
Siavaksh survived. Gev, the son of Guderz, arose to
seek in Turan the right heir to the throne of Iran.
For seven years he seeks in vain. At length he
discovers Kai Chosru, to whom his mother Feringis has
already revealed the secret of his birth. In spite of
the most severe persecution on the part of Afrasiab,
Gev succeeds in carrying away mother and son to
Iran ; they swim through the swollen Oxus on horseback. But when Kai Kaus wishes to make the grandson so happily discovered his successor, Tur, the son of
king Naudar, opposes the elevation of a king who has
Turanian blood in his veins. Kai Chosru proves his
higher claim by capturing a citadel of the demons,
and erecting a fire-altar in its place. Then he sets
himself to avenge the death of his father on Afrasiab.
But the first army of the Iranians under Tur is
defeated ; and when Feriborz receives the command

the warriors of Iran are again severely beaten in the
valley of Peshen ; a third army is shut up on Mount
Hamaven.   To liberate this Rustem sets forth, and
conquers in the most terrible battle which he has ever
fought.   At length Afrasiab and Kai Chosru take the
lead of their armies.   After a bloody struggle the
Turanians are compelled to retire, first beyond the
Oxus, and then beyond the Jaxartes.   Afrasiab flies
for refuge to his fortified city Kang Bihist ; the city
is taken, but he escapes into a cave.   Kai Kaus and
Kai Chosru entreat the fire Adar guçasp, that Afrasiab
may not escape them.   A pious penitent, Hom, who
hears the lament of Afrasiab in his cave, recognises
him, overpowers and binds him, and leads him forth.
Afrasiab entreats the penitent to loose his bonds, and
then escapes once more, into a lake.   The pious Hom
obtains possession of him again, and hands him over
to Kai Chosru, who has his head cut off in revenge for
his father Siavaksh.   Kai Kaus has now seen the
fulfilment of vengeance on Afrasiab for the death of
Siavaksh ; his days draw to a close.   For sixty years
after him, Kai Chosru rules over Iran in peace, and
then resolves to enter on a pilgrimage to heaven.
When the angel Serosh has bidden him nominate
Lohrasp as his successor, he fulfils this injunction,
establishes Rustem as general-in-chief of the kingdom
and successor of his father Zal in the kingdom of the
South, and after long meditation, accompanied by the
sons of Naudar, Tus and Gustehem, and the heroes
Gev and Feriborz, he begins the pilgrimage to the
East.   When high up in the mountains he advises
his companions to return ; soon they will see him no
more.   He disappears after bathing in a spring ; his
heroes, in spite of the command to return, seek for
him, and are buried in a storm of snow.

We saw above that in the Avesta, Manuschithra and Airyu are connected with Thraetaona, and that the group of the Paradhatas comes to an end with these names. Hence Firdusi also represents the crown as being brought to the first ruler of the new group, Kai Kobad, *i. e.* the Kava Kavata of the Avesta, from the sky by two falcons; he also represents him as being fetched from Elburz, *i. e.* from the holy mountain of the old legend, in order to overcome Zohak, just as Thraetaona descended from the same mountain. Kai Kaus, the Kava Uça of the Avesta, who succeeded Kai Kobad, betrays his divine nature in Firdusi by his march against the demons, by the castles which these demons build for him on Elburz, and by his attempt to fly into heaven. In the Avesta Kava Uça offers sacrifice, in order to obtain the dominion over men and Daevas, and this favour is granted to him. That the march against the demons is made in the direction of Mazanderan is due no doubt to the frequent mention of the Mazanian Devs in the Avesta. Siavaksh, the son of Kai Kaus, who honourably gives himself up to the Turanians, is the Çyavarshana of the Avesta—from which we merely learn that he was spotless, and that after Kava Uça the royal majesty united with the beautiful body of Çyavarshana, and that he died by a violent death (p. 37). The destructive Turanian Franghraçyana, who is now called Afrasiab, is known to the Avesta. "Thrice," we are told, "he sought after the royal majesty which belongs to the Arian lands, but he found it not." [1] Kai Chosru, *i. e.* Kava Huçrava, is in the Avesta also the son of Çyavarshana; he offers sacrifice, in order that it may be granted to him " to put an end to the long period of dimness," " to bind the Franghraçyana filled with abundance ; "

---

[1] "Zamyad Yasht," 56 ff. Above, p. 37.

he is said to be " without sickness and death." Firdusi's poem neglects none of these traits. After the
triple war which, kindled by Afrasiab, has lasted for a
long time, Firdusi represents Chosru as invoking the
fire Guçasp, that Afrasiab may not escape him. In
the Avesta the god Haoma is said himself to bind
Franghraçyana, and to carry him away as a captive of
king Huçrava, in order that the latter may slay him
beyond the lake Chaechaçta (p. 37). In Firdusi the
pious Hom discovers the hiding-place of Afrasiab ; he
binds him and carries him away a prisoner. Afrasiab
escapes; but Hom captures him once more in lake
Kanyesht. As Huçrava is "without sickness and
death," Firdusi represents him as vanishing on a
pilgrimage to heaven.

In Firdusi, Lohrasp, whom Chosru has made his
successor, erects a fire-temple at Balkh, his royal
abode, and after reigning 120 years, abdicates in
favour of Gushtasp, his elder son, in order to devote
his life to pious exercises at his temple. When Zartusht proclaims the Avesta, Gushtasp and his wife
receive the new doctrine. But Arjasp, the king of
Turan, sent Gushtasp a command not to listen to the
words of Zartusht. To this request Gushtasp did not
accede ; a battle took place on the banks of the Oxus,
which turned in favour of Iran, owing to the bravery
of Zarir, the brother of Gushtasp. An arrow from an
ambush lays the hero low at the moment of victory.
His death terrifies the Iranians ; not one of them
ventures to avenge it till Gushtasp promises Isfendyar,
the strongest and bravest of his sons, that he will
give him the crown if he succeeds in avenging the
death of Zarir. Isfendyar overthrows the warriors
of Iran, brings the arms and horse of Zarir into the
camp of Iran, and Arjasp retires into his land. In

the place of the promised crown, Isfendyar receives from his father the high mission of spreading abroad the new faith. By means of a chain which he places on his neck, Zartusht makes Isfendyar invulnerable, and surrounds him with a charm so that anyone who slays him will himself quickly die. When Isfendyar returns home after a long time, his mission fully accomplished, as all have received the law of Zartusht, accusations are made against him that he is collecting an army to dethrone his father. On this unfounded charge Gushtasp causes Isfendyar to be cast into prison. But while he remains in Zabul, the Turanians attack Balkh. The aged Lohrasp takes up arms; he cannot check the Turanians; he falls; the city is taken: Zartusht with the fire-priests is slain in the fire-temple, the sacred fire is quenched in their blood, and two daughters of Gushtasp are carried away to Turan. In vain does Gushtasp hasten up, when he has collected his army; thirty-eight of his sons are slain in the battle against the Turanians. Gushtasp takes to flight, and with his warriors finds refuge in a mountain which is quickly invested by Arjasp. Then Jamasp, the faithful adviser of Gushtasp, passes in disguise through the camp of the Turanians, to fetch Isfendyar out of prison, and urge him to save his father and Iran. Forgetting his deep injury and wrong, Isfendyar forces a way through the camp of Arjasp, and in the subsequent battle slaughters so many of the enemy's men that he takes to flight. But the task is not yet accomplished; it still remains to set at liberty the two sisters whom the Turanians had carried away from Balkh, and whom Arjasp keeps imprisoned in "the brazen fortress." After seven conflicts, corresponding to those which Rustem had to undergo, when he liberated Kai Kaus from the power of the demons,

Isfendyar reaches the fortress. He sends his army back, and in the guise of a merchant obtains entrance into the citadel. Here he asks Arjasp, to whom he is unknown, for permission to give a feast to the principal men on the turrets of the citadel. When the wine has done its work, Isfendyar gives the signal of fire already agreed upon to his followers; the garrison is overpowered; Arjasp is slain by Isfendyar in single combat, and Isfendyar returns victorious with his sisters to Balkh.

Here a new and yet more dangerous task awaits him. Rustem, who made Kai Kobad ruler of Iran, and has since done such good service, and achieved such noble acts for Kai Kaus and Kai Chosru, remains at a distance from the court and army of king Gushtasp. He despises the doctrine of Zartusht. At Gushtasp's bidding Isfendyar must break down this opposition, and bring him to the king. Isfendyar marches out and commands Rustem to follow him in chains to the court. With a heavy heart Rustem seeks to withdraw from the contest; he treats with Isfendyar; but the latter obstinately insists on his terms. Nothing remains for the aged hero but to give battle against his will. Isfendyar's invulnerable body resists his blows, and Reksh, the horse of Rustem, is wounded; Rustem is himself wounded and compelled to retire. He has no hope of conquering in the battle which is to begin again on the next day. In his deep distress he calls to the bird Simurgh, who comes, sucks the blood from his wound, and heals the horse. Simurgh is acquainted with the future, and advises a compromise: there is indeed a way of overcoming Isfendyar, but anyone who takes his life "must not expect salvation in this world or the next." Rustem cannot bring himself to suffer defeat in the

battle, and therefore in the night Simurgh carries him
away to the tree of life, on the sea of China, and bids
him break off the branch to which Isfendyar's life is
bound. Out of this branch is cut the death-arrow for
the conflict of the morrow. With it Rustem hits
the place in the eye in which alone Isfendyar is
vulnerable. But for Rustem also the lot of death is
cast. He is invited by the king of Cabul, a tributary
prince, to hunt; and the king's son-in-law, Sheghad,
prepares a pit filled with swords and lances, for the
destruction of the aged hero. Into this Rustem falls
with his horse, but even in the moment of death his
arrow hits Sheghad, who had concealed himself in a
hollow tree, in order to watch the success of his
scheme. Rustem's son Feramorz avenges the murder
of his father on the king of Cabul; but Gushtasp
renounces the world, and transfers the government
to his grandson Bahman, the son of Isfendyar.

Here also we find traces of the Avesta underlying
the poem. In the Avesta Aurvataçpa, now Lohrasp,
and Vistaçpa, now Gushtasp, form a group distinct
from the most ancient princes. Firdusi represents
Kai Chosru as making Lohrasp his successor in spite
of the murmurs of the nobles. Arejataçpa, now Arjasp,
the Turanian, sacrifices in the Avesta in order to
obtain victory over Vistaçpa, and the great equestrian,
Zairivairi, the brother of Vistaçpa. In Firdusi this
brother, the bravest warrior of Iran against Turan, is
Zarir. In the Avesta Vistaçpa conquers Arejataçpa; in
Firdusi Arjasp finally succumbs in the conflict. In the
Avesta Jamaçpa is a prince of great influence with Vis-
taçpa; in Firdusi he is his faithful counsellor. In the
Avesta Zarathrustra offers sacrifice that he may unite
with the warlike Vistaçpa, and that the king's consort
Hutaoça may impress the law on her memory (p. 37);

in Firdusi Gushtasp and his wife receive the new law.
According to the Avesta Vistaçpa has given his support and protection to the law, has set up the law in
the world, and given it a high position, and made the
path broad for purity. In Firdusi Isfendyar is sent
to spread abroad the new law over the earth. The
Avesta mentions twenty-nine sons of Vistaçpa, Firdusi
even more; in both Çpentodata (Isfendyar) has the
first place. In the Avesta Zarathrustra pronounces a
blessing on Vistaçpa, in Firdusi he pronounces it on
Isfendyar. That the latter was extolled, even in the
Avesta, as supporting the faith and spreading it abroad
—though our fragments do not allow us to draw any
further conclusions—is nevertheless clear from the
creed of the Parsees : " I abide in the law which the
lord Ormuzd taught to Zartusht, and Zartusht to
king Gushtasp, and Gushtasp to Frashaostra (p. 62),
Jamasp, and Isfendyar, and these to all the faithful
in the world." Firdusi has made use of the spread of
the new law by Isfendyar, in order to bring to a conclusion the legend of Sejestan which he connects with
the tradition of the Avesta, and to provide an adequate
motive for the fall of the mighty Rustem of Ghasna,
the descendant of the mighty Kereçaçpa. In his zeal
for the faith, Isfendyar demands more than Rustem
can grant; the champion of the faith is stronger in
the conflict than Rustem ; and the latter, in order
to keep his honour, avails himself of wicked magical
arts. We have seen what was the occupation of the
two eagles of the sky, Amru and Chamru, at the tree
in Lake Vourukasha, which bears the seeds of all life
(p. 172). To these arts the champion of the faith
succumbs, but by his success the victor has pronounced judgment on himself.

In the form which Firdusi has given them, the

legends of Ancient Iran have to some extent continued to live among the people, and to some extent
they have failed. The Shahnameh celebrates Jemshid's
(Yima's) glittering palace and splendid throne ; hence
the ruins of the great palace of the Achæmenids at
Persepolis have gained the name of the throne of
Jemshid ; ruins near Bamiyan in the Hindu-Kush, on
the road from Balkh to Cabul, are still called Zohak's
castle. The smoke rising out of the crater of Demavend is the breath of Zohak chained in the depths of
the mountain. Each year, on the last day of August,
the inhabitants of Elburz celebrate the festival of the
overthrow of Zohak with bonfires on every height,
and demonstrations of joy. The ruins of Takt-i-Bostan
are called the garden of Kai Chosru, and in Iran
Balkh is still the mother of cities.[1] A lofty and steep
rock in Lake Zirreh in Sejestan is said to have been
crowned with the castle of Rustem, and the site of a
second castle is pointed out at Aivan. Aqueducts
and dams pass for works of Rustem. In the desert
of Beluchistan, the ancient Gedrosia, the tracks of the
camels of Rustem are still shown by large stones in
the sand. In Mazanderan is the battle-field where
Rustem defeated the Divs in order to liberate Kai
Kaus (p. 253). The sculptures of the Achæmenids on
the tombs at Persepolis are called pictures of Rustem
(Naksh-i-Rustem), and in the bed of the Hilmend his
grave is shown. When Timour's Mongols devastated
Sejestan in the fourteenth century, the people called
on Rustem to raise his head from the grave, and
behold Iran in the hand of his enemy, the warrior of
Turan. By a strange misconception the nobles in
Mazanderan assume the name Div as a title of honour.
A large family of nobles in Sejestan call themselves
Kaïanids, and boast of their descent from Jemshid

[1] Ritter, " Erdkunde," 8, 153, 183, 491, 561.

and the ancient kings, and to this family, down to the most recent times, the viceroyalty of Sejestan belonged as an hereditary office. When the holder of it died, the eldest of the family went to court in order to apply for the office, and was duly installed by investment with the robe of honour and armour.[1]

While the ancient legends have lived on in Iran, the religion of Zoroaster has passed beyond Iran, and survives on the Malabar coast. Every day the Parsees utter their invocations before the sacred fire, and present bowls filled with the juice of the Haoma. Each month, as we have seen, belongs to one of the heavenly deities, who is then specially invoked; each of the thirty days of the month has its own protecting spirit, who is especially honoured on his own day. Six yearly festivals, each of five days, celebrate the creation of the heaven, water, the earth, the trees, animals, and men (p. 182); on each of which special prayers are said. At the close of the year the Parsees purify and adorn their houses, in order to receive worthily the souls of their ancestors: sacrificial bread, fruits, milk, wine, and meat are put ready for them. The Fravashis, now called Farvars, are invoked "to receive the sacrifice, to lift up their hands to it, and depart in peace from the dwelling."[2] On these days the priests read the liturgies appointed as prayers for the souls of the damned, and for ten days the laity have to repeat many thousands of times the prayers "Ahuna-vairya" and "Ashem Vohu." Each morning, on waking, the Parsee prays: "The best purity is to the just, who is pure. He is pure who does pure works. I pray with purity of thought, of word, and act." When removing, and again when putting on, his girdle (p. 217), he says, with face turned to the East: "May Ormuzd be king; may

<hr/>

[1] Chanikof, in Spiegel, "Eran," 1, 556.   [2] "Farvardin Yasht," 147.

Ahriman be defeated and destroyed; may the enemies be confounded, and remain far off; of all my sins I repent." Then he takes gomez for ablutions, washes his face and hands with it, rubs himself with earth, and with gomez in his hand says: " May Ahriman be destroyed; may the thirty-three Amshaspands and Ormuzd be victorious and pure." After a prayer to Çrosh (Çraosha)—"the pure and strong, may he increase to greater majesty, whose body is the word, and whose club is victorious"—follows ablution with water, dressing of the fire with wood and perfumes, and the proper morning prayer to Ushahin, the spirit of the morning : " Praise to thee, high Dawn." When it is light, a prayer is offered to Mithra, and two others at midday and sunset. In the morning a prayer to Ormuzd is recited, in which all his names and qualities are enumerated. Before eating, the Parsee must wash himself and pronounce the prayer "Ahuna-vairya," and after eating, the prayer "King Ormuzd." When the Parsee goes to rest he must arrange his bed in such a way that he lies towards the fire, or the moon, or the East. Before sleeping, a prayer is offered to Ormuzd. On turning over in bed, sneezing, the discharge of natural or sexual functions, kindling a light, approaching water or fire, special prayers are uttered, and the sum of daily duties is increased on many occasions in family life—at the time of a birth, or death, or festivals, and when impurities have been incurred. However external and formal these numerous prayers and rituals may appear, the Parsee forms of confession are nevertheless evidence of the depth of their religious feeling, and their retention in the family and social life proves that the ancient religion still possesses a powerful influence.

BOOK VIII.

THE EMPIRE OF THE MEDES AND PERSIANS.

THE EMPIRE OF THE MEDES AND PERSIANS.

CHAPTER I.

THE FOUNDATION OF THE MEDIAN KINGDOM.

On the northern edge of the table-land of Iran, where the mountains descend to the Caspian Sea, we found dwelling towards the east the Hyrcanians (*Vehrkana* in the Avesta, *Varkana* in the inscriptions of Darius).[1] Their territory may have corresponded to the modern district of Jorjan, which has preserved their name (p. 9). To the west of the Hyrcanians, between Elburz and the Caspian, lay the Tapurians, whose name has survived in the modern Taberistan, and further yet, on the sea-coast, and at the mouth of the Mardus (now Safidrud), were the Mardians. Adjacent to these, on the shores of the Caspian Sea as far as the mouth of the Cyrus, lay the nation whom the Greeks called Cadusians, but whose native name was Gaels[2]—a name still preserved in the name of the district of Ghilan.[3] To the south of these tribes—the

---

[1] "Vend." 1, 42 ; Behist. 2, 92.   [2] Plin. "H. N." 6, 18, (48).

[3] Alexander came from Hyrcania and Parthia to the land of the Tapurians. According to Arrian's statements, the Hyrcanians, Parthians and Tapurians were all under one leader in the army of Darius III. "Anab." 3, 8, 4 ; 3, 11, 4 ; Strabo, p. 507, 508, 514, 524 ; Justin, 12, 3 ; 41, 5.

Tapurians, Mardians, and Cadusians—the north-west of the table-land was entirely occupied by the Medes.

The country of the Medes, Herodotus tells us, is very high and mountainous in the north towards the Euxine, and covered with forests, but the remainder of it is flat.[1] Polybius gives a more minute description of the nature of Media. "It is difficult to speak adequately of the natural strength and of the extent of the country of the Medes. It lies in the centre of Asia, and in the size and elevation of the land surpasses all other parts, while the situation enables it to govern the strongest and most populous nations. Towards the east it is protected by the desert which lies between Persia and Parthia, it has control of the Caspian gates, and abuts on the mountains of the Tapurians, which are not far distant from the Hyrcanian Sea. Towards the north it is bounded by the Matieni and Cadusians, on the west it extends to the Saspeires, who dwell close to the tribes which lie on the Euxine. Towards the south it extends to Mesopotamia and abuts on Persia; on this side it is protected by the range of the Zagrus, which reaches an elevation of one hundred stadia, and is broken into various ranges and groups, separated by deep valleys and open plains, in which dwell the Carchi, Cossaei, and other warlike tribes. Media itself is traversed by several ranges in the direction from east to west, but between them are plains filled with cities and villages. The Medes possess corn and cattle in untold abundance, and in horses their country is superior to the whole of Asia, so that it takes the first place, not only in virtue of its extent, but also owing to the number and excellence of the men and horses."[2] Strabo allows Media an extent of 4000 stades (500

[1] Herod. 1, 110.   [2] Polyb. 5, 44; 10, 27. Cf. Curt. 3, 2 ff.

miles) in length and breadth. It reached from the
Zagrus to the Caspian gates. The greater part of the
land was high and cold, but the district below the
Caspian gates on the lower ground was very fertile.
Even in the rest of the land, with the exception of
some mountain districts, there was no lack of the
means of subsistence, and everywhere on the high
ground there was excellent pasture for horses.[1]

The nation of the Medes belongs to the group of
the Arian tribes, which occupied the table-land of
Iran. This has been already proved by the statement
of Herodotus that in ancient time the Medians were
called Areans by all men (p. 14), by the religion of
the Medes, and by all the Median words and names
that have come down to us.[2] According to Herodotus
the nation consisted of six tribes: the Arizanti, Busae,
Struchates, Budii, Paraetaceni, and Magi. Whether
certain parts of the land belonged to these tribes as
their habitation, is not clear from this statement.
The Magians we have already found to be a hereditary
order of priests (p. 191), and therefore we can hardly
assume a separate part of the country as their habitation. The question thus becomes limited to the
remaining five tribes. The name of the Paraetaceni
occurs in the mountain district, which the later Greeks
call Paraetacene. This district separated Media from

---

[1] Strabo, p. 523—525.

[2] In the most recent times it has been maintained that the Medes
were of Turkish-Tatar (Altaic) family, but this view rests simply on
the assumption that the inscriptions of the second class in the inscriptions of the Achæmenids must have been written in the language of
the Medes. This hypothesis contradicts everything that has come
down to us of Median names and works, and the close relationship
between the Medes and Persians. Whether the Arians, on immigrat-
ing into Media, found there Turkish-Tatar tribes, overpowered, expelled or subjugated them, is another question. If this were the
case, the fragments of the population could hardly have exercised any
influence worth mentioning on the Arian Medes.

Persia, and there is therefore nothing remarkable in
the fact that the Paraetaceni are counted among the
Persians or spoken of as an independent tribe.[1] If
the Paraetaceni had a special province, we shall be all
the more justified in allotting the same to the Arizanti,
the Budii, Struchates, and Busae, as the tribe of the
Matieni, which Strabo reckons among the Medes,[2]
had a special habitation and territory in the district of
Matiene, i. e. in the region which after the time of the
Seleucids was known as Atropatene; and the tribes
of the Persians, who were closely akin to the Medes,
were also settled in special regions, or marched through
them with their flocks. The name Arizanti (Arizantu)
might signify the noble families, i. e. an eminent tribe,
which tribe might nevertheless possess a separate
habitation. Among the Persians there was a privileged tribe, to which the royal family belonged, which
ruled over all the tribes, and this tribe like the rest
had a special territory.

The districts of Media, as we know them from
the accounts of later writers, are beside Atropatene:
Choromithrene, Nisaea, Rhagiana, Cambadene, and
Bagistana.[3] Atropatene is the elevated plain which
spreads round the lake which Ptolemy calls the
Matienian lake (now Urumiah). The inscriptions of the
kings of Asshur call the inhabitants of this land Mati
and Mala.[4] Shut in by mighty summits which reach

[1] Paraetacene is derived no doubt from parvata, mountain, or par-
vataka, mountainous. Strabo remarks that when the Persians had
conquered the Medes, they took some land from them. The distance
between Persepolis and Ecbatana was twenty marches; Alexander
reached the borders of Media on the twelfth day after leaving Persepolis. Arrian, "Anab." 3, 19.

[2] Strabo, p. 73; 509.

[3] Under the Sassanids Media (Mah) consisted of four regions:
Aderbeijan, Rai (Rhagiana), Hamadan (Ecbatana), Isfahan.

[4] Herodotus allows the Matieni a considerable extent, for he

a height of more than 12,000 feet, naked ridges, fields
of snow, mountain pastures, green forests and meadows
here make up the wildest, but at the same time most
beautiful, Alpine landscape in the west of Iran.   The
snow lies on the backs of the heights for about nine
months, but in the valleys there reigns for the most
part uninterrupted spring; in the deeper clefts the
summer is hot, and the naphtha springs must have
caused this region to appear as one highly favoured
by the gods in the eyes of such zealous worshippers
of fire as the Arians of Iran.   We have already seen
(p. 74) that the name Atropatene, which in middle
Persian is Aturpatkan, and modern Persian Aderbeijan,
means " protected by fire."

In the ranges of the Zagrus, which, running from
the Alps of Atropatene to the south-east, separate
the table-land of Iran from the valley of the Tigris—
these summits rise above the hilly land of Assyria to
a height of 15,000 feet—we must seek the territory
which Ptolemy calls Choromithrene, *i. e.* by a name
which beyond doubt goes back to the worship of
Mithra.   Further to the east, beyond the isolated
mountain-group of Elvend, on the eastern foot of the
mountains, lay the territory where Ecbatana was subsequently built.   To the south-east were the "Nisæan
plains" of Herodotus, on which, as he tells us, were
kept the most beautiful and largest horses, superior
to those of the Indians.[1]   Polybius has already
stated, that in regard to horses Media surpassed
the rest of Asia; the mares of the Parthian kings
were kept in Media owing to the excellent pastures.

includes under the name the Armenians and the inhabitants of Atropatene.   Later authors confine the Matieni to the region round the
lake of Urumiah; in this sense, Polybius, quoted above in the text,
limits Media in the North by the Cadusians and Matieni.

[1] Herod. 3, 106; 7, 40.

According to Strabo, there were 50,000 mares on the "horse pastures" in the time of the Achæmenids; these pastures any one going from Babylonia and Persia to the Caspian gates, i. e. to the Sirdarra-pass in Elburz, would cross. Diodorus places them seven days' march to the east of Behistun, and tells us that at one time there were 160,000 wild horses here, though Alexander found only 60,000. Arrian puts the previous number at 150,000, and the number found by Alexander at 50,000, as the greater part had been carried off by robbers.[1] That Herodotus has given the name of this region correctly is shown by the inscriptions of Darius, which speak of a province of Niçaya in Media.[2] To the north-east of the region of Ecbatana, on an elevated plateau, lay the district of Raghiana. It takes its name from the metropolis Ragha, a city on the southern foot of Elburz, mentioned both in the Avesta and the inscriptions. Under the Arsacids Ragha was the largest city of Media. Its later name was Rai; the ruins (near the modern Teheran) are said to cover the land for leagues. Besides Ragha there were at one time numerous flourishing cities in Raghiana.[3] Campadene,[4] the Campada of the inscriptions of Darius, we must look for in the south of Media, to the east of the Zagrus; it is no doubt the district now called Chamabatan.[5] According to the statement of the Greeks, the district of Bagistana extended to a mountain which was sacred

[1] Strabo, p. 525; Diod. 17, 110; Arrian, "Anab." 7, 13.

[2] Behist. 1, 13. Strabo's Νησαία (p. 509, 511), the Nisiaea of Pliny (6, 29), the Parthaunisa of Isidore of Charax, must be sought in the neighbourhood of Nishapur, which was built by Shapur II. The Avesta puts Niça between Merv and Balkh.

[3] Diod. 19, 44. Alexander in eleven forced marches advanced from Ecbatana to Ragha.

[4] Isid. Ch. "M. P." c. 5.

[5] Mordtmann, "B. d. Bair. Akademie," 1876, s. 364.

to Zeus. As Diodorus says, it was a region fit for
the gods, filled with fruit-trees and every other
kind that ministers to delight and enjoyment.[1] The
name of the mountain consecrated to Zeus, Bagistana,
and the similar name of the district, go back to the
title under which the gods are comprised in the Avesta
and the inscriptions of Darius (Old Bactr. *bagha*,
Old Pers. *baga*, New Pers. *bag*) ; and if Diodorus tells
us that the region was a land fit for the gods, the
name Bagistana means the abode of the gods. The
district may have been held peculiarly sacred by the
Medes, or the name may have been intended to express
their gratitude for its fertility and beauty. We can
fix precisely the position of this district by the hill
consecrated to Zeus near the modern Behistun. It
lies south-west of Elvend, between that mountain and
the Zagrus in the valley of the Choaspes, and is the
district now known as Kirmenshah.

According to the statements of Berosus, the historian of Babylon, the Medes in the most ancient
period had already reigned over Babylonia for more
than two centuries. They had suddenly collected an
army, reduced Babylonia, and there set up tyrants of
their own people. According to the succession of the
dynasties which Berosus represents as ruling over
Babylonia, the beginning of this supremacy of the
Medes fell, as has been shown (I. 241, 247), in the
year 2458 B.C. The first of the Medes who thus ruled
in Babylon is called Zoroaster by Syncellus, after
Polyhistor ; according to this writer the seven Medes
reign till the year 2224 B.C. Whether Berosus
called the first Median king who reigned in Babylon

---

[1] Diod. 2, 13; 17, 110. The city of Baptana, which Isidore (c. 5)
mentions "as situated on a mountain in Cambadene," is in any case
Bagistana (Behistun).

Zoroaster, or Polyhistor has ascribed that position to him as the most famous name in Iran, or the only name known in antiquity, must be left undecided, no less than the actual fact of the Median supremacy.

The Medo-Persian epos told us that Ninus of Asshur, after subjugating Babylonia and Armenia, attacked the Medes. Pharnus, their king, met him with a mighty army, but was nevertheless beaten. He was crucified with his wife and seven children by Ninus; one of his retinue was made viceroy of Media; and for many years the Medes were subject to the successors of Ninus on the throne of Assyria (II. 3 ff). Herodotus' account is as follows: "When the Assyrians had reigned over upper Asia for 520 years, the Medes were the first to revolt, and as they fought bravely for their freedom against the Assyrians, they succeeded in escaping slavery and liberating themselves. Afterwards the rest of the nations did what the Medes had done. And as all the nations of the mainland lived according to laws of their own, they again fell under a tyranny in the following manner:—Among the Medes was a man of ability, called Deioces, the son of Phraortes. He desired the tyranny, and did as follows: The Medes dwelt in villages, and Deioces, who was previously a man of importance, set himself more and more zealously to the task of doing justice, since lawlessness reigned throughout the whole of Media. When the Medes of his village discovered these qualities in him, they chose him for their judge. And as his heart was already set on the empire, he acted justly and rightly, and thus got no small credit among his fellow-citizens, so that the men from other villages, when they found that Deioces alone judged rightly, gladly resorted to him, since hitherto they had had to endure unjust sentences, and at last they would not go to any one else.   As the number of the applicants became greater, and Deioces found that everything depended upon him, he refused to sit any longer in court and pronounce sentence, saying, that it was of no advantage to himself to neglect his own business and spend the day in settling the disputes of others.   Then robbery and lawlessness became more rife than ever in the villages, and the Medes gathered together and consulted on the position of affairs.   In my belief the friends of Deioces were the first to speak : ' As things are, it is impossible to live in the land ; let us choose some one to be king, and thus the land will obtain good government.   We can occupy ourselves with our own business, and shall not be compelled to wander from home.'   With these words they persuaded the Medes to set up a monarchy.   And when they at once began the discussion who should be king, Deioces was highly commended and put forward by every one, so that at last he was chosen by all to be king.   Then Deioces commanded the Medes to build him a palace suitable for a king, and strengthen his power by a body-guard.   This they .did, and built a great and strong palace, on the place which Deioces pointed out to them, and allowed him to choose his lance-bearers out of all the nation.   When he had obtained the sovereign power he at once compelled the Medes to build him a large city, in order that, being thus occupied, they might trouble him less about other things ; and when the Medes obeyed him in this matter also, he erected the great and strong citadel now known as Ecbatana.   The walls formed seven circles, in such a manner that the inner was always higher by the turrets than the next outer circle, an arrangement assisted by the locality, for the town was situated on a hill.   In the seventh wall was the palace and the

T 2

treasure-house of Deioces. After erecting this fortification for himself, and his palace, the king commanded the people to settle round the citadel. When the building was completed Deioces first made the arrangement that no one should enter in to the king, but every thing was done by messengers, in order that those who had grown up with him, and were of similar age, equal in descent and bravery, might not envy him, and set conspiracies on foot, but that by being invisible he might appear a different being ; it was also disgraceful to laugh or spit, or do anything of that kind in his presence. When he had made these arrangements, and thus strengthened his tyranny, he adhered strictly to justice. Plaints had to be sent in to him in writing, and he sent back the sentence. Thus he managed this and all other matters, and if he found that any one was guilty of insolence, and did violence to others, he punished him according to the measure of his offence, and his spies and emissaries were everywhere in the land.[1] In this manner Deioces united the Medes, and governed them for 53 years. After his death, his son Phraortes succeeded to the throne. Not content with ruling over the Medes only, he marched against the Persians, and first made them subject to the Medes. When he had become master of these two powerful nations, he subjugated all Asia, attacking one nation after another. Finally, he marched against the Assyrians, who had previously ruled over all men, but, though otherwise in excellent condition, were then abandoned by their allies, who had revolted. In the war against these Phraortes fell, after a reign of 22 years, and with him the greatest part of his army."[2]

The account of the history of the Medes given by

[1] Herodotus, 1, 95—101.   [2] Herod. 1, 102.

Ctesias is wholly different. As their subjugation to Assyria is coeval with the founding of that kingdom, so is their liberation coeval with the fall of it. When the Medes, after their conquest by Ninus, had been subject to the rulers of Asshur, down to his thirty-sixth successor, Arbaces, the viceroy of Media, with Belesys, the viceroy of Babylonia, revolted from the Assyrian king. The kingdom of Assyria still remains unbroken; it is only after severe struggles, and in consequence of the desertion of the Bactrians and other nations during the conflict, that it is overthrown. After the capture of Nineveh, Arbaces, as supreme lord, takes the place of the king of Asshur.

According to the dates of Herodotus Deioces ascended the throne of Media in the year 714 or 708 B.C.[1] The time which elapsed between the liberation of the Medes and Deioces' elevation is not given by him. According to Ctesias Arbaces established the dominion of the Medes at least 170 years before the date given by Herodotus for Deioces. In Herodotus Phraortes, Cyaxares, and Astyages follow Deioces in the dominion over the Medes, with a total of 97 years. In Ctesias the successors of Arbaces, who reigns 28 years, are Mandaces with a reign of 50 years, Sosarmus with 30, Artycas with 50, Arbianes with 22, Artaeus with 40, Artynes with 22, Astibaras with 40, and finally Aspadas with 38 years. On this calculation the dominion of the Median kings lasted 320 years, and consequently Arbaces must have overthrown the Assyrian and established the Median Empire in the year 878 B.C.; or as Ctesias puts the fall of the last Median king in 564, and not in 550 B.C.—in the year 884 B.C.

[1] Vol. III. 257 ff. According to the reigns which Herodotus allows to Deioces and his successors, 150 years before the overthrow of Astyages, which took place 558 B.C., i. e. 708, but, according to the total given by Herodotus—156 years, 714 B.C.

—*i. e.* precisely at the time when Assyria began to rise into the position of a widely dominant power (III. 269, 270). In the list of kings given by Ctesias Mandaces and Artycas each rule fifty years, Arbianes and Artynes 22 years, Artaeus and Astibaras 40 years. This uniformity points to an artificial extension of the series by duplicates.[1] If it is reduced by striking out the three seconds in these pairs, and Arbaces is followed by Mandaces with 50 years, Sosarmus with 30 years, Arbianes with 22 years, Artaeus with 40 years, and Aspadas with 38 years, we obtain a period of 178 years for the kings of the Medes, and so arrive at a point nearer that given by Herodotus for the commencement of the Median kingdom, the year 736 B.C. (558 + 178), as the first year of Arbaces. Yet even so we do not find any coincidence whatever between the two narratives.

In the narrative of Herodotus we find with surprise that the Medes attained their liberation without any combination in the people ; without the leadership of a single head. Yet soon after the time at which he describes the Medes as revolting from the Assyrians, Herodotus tells us that Sennacherib marched against Egypt, and asserts that for 75 years after the accession of Deioces, "the Assyrians were indeed without allies, since they had revolted, but were otherwise in a good condition," so that Phraortes and the greatest part of his army fell in battle against them. If after acquiring their freedom the Medes lived isolated in villages, as Herodotus states, would not the Assyrians have made use of this anarchy close upon their borders in order to reduce the Medes again to subjection, rather than engage in campaigns against Syria and Egypt? According to the account of Herodotus,

---

[1] Volney, "Recherches," 1, 144 ff.

it was the justice of Deioces which won for him
ever-increasing importance, and finally helped him
to the throne. But had Deioces, who sits on the
throne for 53 years afterwards, sufficient time before
his elevation to make himself known for his love of
justice throughout all Media, unless we are willing to
assign him a very unusual age?[1] And if such dire
anarchy did indeed prevail among the Medes, what
man in such times submits to even the most righteous
sentence? Least of all are the mighty and powerful
willing to do so. How did Deioces obtain the means of
compelling the insubordinate to obey his sentence?—
how could he give protection to the accused, oppressed,
and weak against their opponents? And supposing
that he was able to do this, would he have been
unanimously elected king? Herodotus himself remarks that Deioces knew that "the unjust are the
enemies of the just."[2] Moreover, if the Medes at that
time lived in the simplest manner, how could a
sovereign elected from their midst change these conditions at a single stroke, or at any rate in the course of
a single reign, though a long one, so entirely as Herodotus supposes? Village life is changed into city life,
the Medes are settled in one city round the royal
fortress, and in the place of a patriarchal government
over a simple people, Deioces, "as the first," establishes
the whole apparatus of Oriental tyranny. Immense
palaces, citadels, and walls are built; the wide outer
walls are adorned with gold and silver; the secluded
life of the sovereign in the palace becomes the established law; the legal process is carried on by writing;

[1] In order to remove this objection, the dates of Deioces and
Phraortes must be transposed, and the 22 years of Phraortes given to
the former, the 53 years of Deioces to the latter. Phraortes would
then have marched out against the Assyrians in extreme old age, and
fallen in the battle.   [2] Herod. 1, 96.

and a system of espionage is introduced over the whole
country. It is obvious that in this narrative elements,
belonging to the tradition of the Medes, have been
taken by Herodotus and mingled with the views of the
Greeks, who were familiar with the combination of
villages into one canton, and the union of hamlets
into a city, and had experience of the establishment of
a monarchy by setting up a tyranny in consequence of
the services rendered by the aspirant to the multitude.
Herodotus expressly calls the dominion of Deioces
a tyranny. It is a fact beyond dispute that Herodotus was influenced by such conceptions in shaping
and forming the material which came to him from
tradition.

Apart from the motives which influenced him in
describing the elevation of Deioces, Herodotus wishes
to show how the nations of Asia obtained their freedom,
and subsequently lost it. He begins with the statement, that the Medes revolted from Assyria, and all
the nations of Asia followed their example. According
to his dates, which have been already mentioned, the
Medes must have revolted precisely at the time when
Tiglath Pilesar II. and Sargon reigned over Assyria,
i. e. in the period between 745 and 705 B.C. The
liberation of the remaining nations must therefore have
taken place under Sargon or his successors, Sennacherib and Esarhaddon, *i. e.* between the year 705
and 668 B.C. That this general liberation from the
sovereignty of the Assyrians did not take place at
this period is abundantly clear from the inscriptions
of the kings and the Hebrew Scriptures. We have seen
above to what an extent Tiglath Pilesar caused the
whole of Syria to feel the weight of the Assyrian
arms ; he reduced Babylonia to dependence as far as
the Persian Gulf; Sargon was sovereign of Babylonia,

maintained Syria, and received the homage of the
island of Cyprus, and the islands of the Persian Gulf.
His successor, Sennacherib, though unable to protect
Syria against Egypt, yet retained Babylonia and the
eastern half of Asia Minor under his dominion.   Esarhaddon united the crowns of Asshur and Babel,
restored the supremacy of Assyria over Syria, subjugated a part of Arabia and the whole of Egypt.[1]
Hence it is clear, that precisely at the time when,
according to Herodotus, the rest of the nations following the example of the Medes threw off the Assyrian
yoke, that kingdom reached a wider extent than at any
previous time.   If, nevertheless, we wish to maintain
the statement that the rest of the nations followed the
example which the Medes are supposed to have set
about the year 736 B.C.,[2] we must place these events
in the last decade of the reign of Assurbanipal, i. e. in
the period between 636 and 626 B.C.   We must therefore bring them down a full century, and this was a
very late result of the action of the Medes.

Let us attempt, by a comparison of the statements
of the Assyrian inscriptions on the events which
took place on the table-land of Iran and the narrative of Herodotus, to ascertain the real facts of the
liberation of the Medes.   We saw above (p. 19) that
Shalmanesar II. of Asshur (859—823 B.C.) carried his
campaigns as far as the East of Iran.   In the year
835 B.C. he imposed tribute on twenty-seven princes
of the land of Parsua, and " turned against the plains
of the land of Amadai ; " in 830 B.C. his general-in-
chief, Dayan Asshur, went down into the land of
Parsua, and laid tribute on the land of Parsua, " which
did not worship Asshur," obtained possession of the

---

[1] Vol. III. Bk. 4 ; Chaps. 1, 4, 5—8.
[2] According to Von Gutschmid.   Cf. supr. p. 278.

cities, and sent their people and treasures into the
land of Assyria.[1] Tiglath Pilesar II. (745—727 B.C.),
in the campaign which carried him to Arachosia, subjugated "the land of Nisaa" and "the cities of the
land of Media (Madai)." In the following year he
occupied "the land of Parsua;" "Zikruti in rugged
Media, I added to the land of Assyria; I received the
tribute of Media;" and on his ninth campaign he
again marched into "the land of Media." In an
inscription which sums up all his achievements, he
declares that he has imposed tribute "on the land of
Parsua," the city of Zikruti, "which depends on the
land of the Medes," and on the chieftains of "the land
of Media."[2] The books of the Hebrews tell us that
after the fall of Samaria in 721 B.C. "the king of
Assyria carried Israel away, and gave them habita-
tions in Chalah, and in the cities of the Medes." It
was Sargon (722—705 B.C.) to whom Samaria yielded.[3]
His inscriptions also tell us that he carried away the
inhabitants of Samaria, and they make mention of the
cities of the Medes. According to them, he received
heavy tribute from twenty-five chiefs of the Medes in
the year 716 B.C., and set up his royal image in the
midst of their cities. In the next year he carried
away captive "Dayauku with his people and his
family, and caused him to dwell in the land of Amat,"
"built fortresses in order to control Media, received
tribute from twenty-two chiefs of the Medes, conquered
thirty-four cities in Media, and united them with

---

[1] Vol. II. p. 319. I cannot accept the theory which Lenormant has
attempted to establish on the geographical differences in the inscriptions of Shalmanesar II. and Tiglath Pilesar II.—that the Medes and
Persians obtained possession of Western Iran shortly before the middle
of the eighth century. "Lettres Assyriolog." and "Z. Aegypt. Spr."
1870, s. 48 ff.

[2] Vol. III. 3—5.   [3] Vol. III. 85.

Assyria. In the year 713 B.C. he marched against
Bit Dayauku, reduced the chief districts of Media,
which had cast off the yoke of Assyria, and received
tribute from forty-five Median chiefs; 4609 horses,
asses, and sheep in great abundance. Sargon repeatedly
boasts that "he has reduced the distant land of Media,
all the places of distant Media, as far as the borders
of the land of Bikni; that he brought them under the
dominion of Asshur; and that his power extended as
far as the city of Simaspati, which belonged to distant
Media in the East."[1] The inscriptions of his successor
Sennacherib (705—681 B.C.) tell us that on his return
from his second campaign (against the land of Ellip),
he received the heavy tribute of the distant land of
Media, and subjugated the land to his dominion.[2]
Esarhaddon (681—668 B.C.), the successor of Sennacherib, according to the Hebrew Scriptures, deported
people from Persia to Samaria. He tells us himself:
"The land of Patusarra, a district in the region of
——, in the midst of distant Media, on the border of
the land of Bikni, the copper mountains. None of
the kings my forefathers had subjugated this land.
Sitirparna and Iparna, the chiefs of the fortified
places, had not bowed before me. I carried them
away with their subjects, horses, chariots, oxen, sheep,
asses, as rich booty to Assyria." "The chiefs of the
cities of Partakka, Partukka, and Uraka-zabarna, in
the land of Media, who lay far off, and in the days
of the kings my forefathers had not trodden the soil
of Assyria—them the fear of Asshur, my lord, threw
to the ground; they brought for me, to my city
Nineveh, their great animals, copper, the product of
their mines, bowed themselves with folded hands
before me, and besought my favour. I put my viceroys

[1] Vol. III. 101.   [2] Vol. III. 113.

over them, who united the inhabitants of these regions with my kingdom; I imposed services upon them, and a fixed tribute."[1] The period at which this tribute was imposed on the most distant part of Media can only be so far fixed that it must lie between 681 and 673 B.C. Assurbanipal, who succeeded Esarhaddon (668—626 B.C.), tells us: "I captured Birizchadri, the warden of the city of Madai (?); Sariti and Pariza, the sons of Gagi, the warden of the cities of the land of Sakhi, and 75 citadels had cast off the yoke of my dominion; I took the cities; the chiefs fell alive into my hands; I sent them to Nineveh my metropolis." These events belong to the period between the years 660 and 650 B.C.[2]

To weaken the contradiction between this series of statements and the narrative of Herodotus, we may call to mind the gross exaggerations in which the kings of Assyria indulge in describing their acts and successes, and the grandiloquence which we have already noticed more than once in the statements of Assyrian history (III. 139, 200). But however great or however small may have been the success of the campaigns of Tiglath Pilesar II., Sargon, Sennacherib, Esarhaddon and Assurbanipal against the chiefs of the Medes, it cannot be denied that these campaigns took place. And if from the very frequency of such campaigns, after the reign of Tiglath Pilesar, we are inclined to draw the conclusion that they are a proof of the lax and nominal character of the dominion of Assyria over Media, this conclusion proves too much. The same repetition of warlike enterprises on the part of the kings of Asshur takes place, as we saw, in every direction. We shall have as much right to conclude

[1] Vol. III. 150.　　[2] Vol. III. 167.

that there was no such thing as an Assyrian empire, either before the year 736 or after it, over the Medes or any other nation. As I have shown (III. 185), the Assyrian kingdom never acquired a firm dominion over the subjugated nations, still less an organisation of the empire, like the subsequent kingdom of the Achæmenids. Their sovereignty consisted almost exclusively in the collection of tribute by force of arms, in the subjugation or removal of the princes who refused it, and setting up of others, who in turn soon withheld it. At the most, Assyrian fortresses were planted here and there; and no doubt Assyrian viceroys were placed over smaller regions. The same procedure is seen in the inscriptions as in use towards the Medes; and if this is not regarded as the sovereignty of Assyria, no such sovereignty existed before Tiglath Pilesar. If, to meet this objection, the existence of an Assyrian dominion is allowed, in the very lax form which is everywhere characteristic of it, we may, from the same frequency of the campaigns against Media, draw the opposite conclusion, that the Medes had struggled very vigorously for freedom, that in the first place the most remote tribes acquired it, and for them the liberation gradually spread, and the tradition of the Medes has accepted the beginning of the movement as the completion of it.

Setting aside any conclusions of this kind, even tradition can only have regarded the beginning of the struggle for freedom as the beginning of liberation, if it covered the nucleus of a firm resistance, either in some definite district, or in a dynasty which took the lead in the struggle and carried it on. Herodotus is not acquainted with any leader in the struggle and does not mention any, while the campaigns of the Assyrians are always directed against a greater or

less number of princes and cities; sometimes they
fall on this chieftain and sometimes on that.[1] If,
moreover, the fact that Sargon receives tribute from
twenty-five, then from twenty-two, and then from
forty-five chieftains, is brought forward to confirm
the narratives of Herodotus about the anarchy which
prevailed among the Medes, it is not the separation of the Medes under different chiefs which con-
stitutes the anarchy as described by Herodotus, but
actual lawlessness. His description gives us no chieftains in Media, ruling their lands as captains in war
and judges in peace. The Medes dwell in villages,
and the inhabitants choose the village judge, though it
is in their power to go for decision to another village.
Chieftains, even if they had not forbidden their tribes
to seek for justice out of the tribe, would in any case
have left the decision of Deioces unnoticed.

However this may be, one harsh contradiction between the narrative of Herodotus and the inscriptions
cannot be removed by any exposition or any de-
ductions. According to Herodotus Deioces reigned
from the year 708 to 655 B.C., Phraortes from 655
to 633 B.C., over the whole of Media. The inscriptions
of Sennacherib mention the great payment of tribute
by the distant land of Media, and its subjugation
under Sennacherib (p. 282) ; Esarhaddon removes two
chieftains with their flocks and subjects out of Media
from the border of the land of Bikni to Asshur, and
three chiefs from the same district bring their tribute
to Nineveh ; he places his viceroys over them, and
they unite this district with Assyria. After the year

---

[1] That is the reason why I cannot regard the parallels which Von
Gutschmid suggests ("Neue Beiträge," s. 90 ff.) of the struggle
between the Arsacids and Seleucids, and the relations between the
Great Mogul and the Mahrattas, as pertinent.

660 B.C. Assurbanipal is said to have taken a chieftain of Media captive; and in the inscriptions there is nowhere any mention of Deioces, Phraortes, and the Median kingdom.

The inscriptions extend the land of the Medes to the East as far as the copper mountains, or borders of the land of Bikni.[1] The people lived separately under a considerable number of chieftains. The five tribes of the Median nation, enumerated by Herodotus, if they also possessed separate territory, were not isolated groups, but on the contrary broken up into yet smaller divisions. The booty taken by the Assyrians from the Medes, the tribute imposed upon them, consists chiefly in oxen, asses, sheep, and horses. The number of horses given by the chieftains to Sargon allows on an average a hundred for each, and we also hear of other property, treasures, and the product of copper mines. We have repeated mention of the cities of Media and their governors; Sargon conquers thirty-four cities. Though we ought to regard these mainly as citadels, yet civic life cannot have been so unknown to the Medes as the narrative of Herodotus would compel us to suppose. Other elements of civilisation also are known to the Medes at this time, i.e. in the second half of the eighth and first half of the seventh century B.C. It has been proved above that at the beginning of this period the doctrine of Zoroaster must have reached them, and the names could be given of the men in Media who published it; and the priests of the new religion became formed during this century into an order which perpetuated in their families the

[1] The Patusarra of Esarhaddon might be the Patisuvari of Darius; the Pateischoreans, whom Strabo quotes among the tribes of the Persians; Von Gutschmid, loc. cit. s. 93, but in the Babylonian version of the inscription of Behistun the Pateischoreans are called Pidishuris.

knowledge of the good sayings and the customs of sacrifice. To this order we may also attribute what the Medes acquired of the superior civilisation and skill of Assyria, especially the knowledge of the Assyrian cuneiform writing, which underwent a change in the hands of the Magians, and assumed the form known to us from the Achæmenid inscriptions of the first class. When Herodotus ascribes the introduction of written process at law to Deioces, the tradition presupposes an established and extensive use of writing.

The dominion of the princes under which the Medes stood is followed by the dominion of the monarchy, which must have arisen out of it. One of the families of these princes must have succeeded in obtaining influence and power over the others. The position of Deioces and Phraortes must have arisen and developed itself in this manner. Whether the Dayauku, whom Sargon carried off in the year 715 B.C. with his followers to Amat, is one and the same person with the prince of Bit Dayauku, against whom the Assyrian king marched in the year 713 B.C. (p. 282), would be difficult to decide; and even if the matter could be determined with certainty, it would not be of great importance. We often find the kings of Asshur replacing conquered and captive princes in their dominions. On the other hand, it is of importance that there was a region of Media, which could be called Bit Dayauku, i. e. the land of Dayauku, by the Assyrians in the year 713 B.C. There must have existed at this time a principality of Deioces among other principalities, and the beginning of this must be put earlier than the date allowed by Herodotus for the election, i. e. at the latest at 720 B.C. In course of time the land of Deioces may have increased in extent, and the importance of the ruler may have grown—though

he may not, after the conflict of 713 B.C., have taken
any leading part in the resistance to the payment of
tribute, the conflicts and successes of other chieftains
against the Assyrians; at any rate, there is no subsequent mention of the land in the inscriptions. Neither
Deioces nor his land is mentioned when Sennacherib
speaks of the tribute of the whole of Media, and the
subjugation of the country under his dominion; nor
even when Esarhaddon speaks of the conquest of the
most distant princes. Hence we can only grant to
the narrative of Herodotus that, in the times of Sennacherib and Esarhaddon, Deioces, the son of Phraortes, had a considerable territory among the chiefs of
the Medes, and greater importance than others, and
we have no reason to look for his dominion elsewhere
than at Ecbatana. His son Phraortes (Fravartis), who
according to Herodotus came to the throne in the year
655 B.C., must have succeeded in uniting the chiefs of
the Medes under his sway, and combining with the
tribes of the Persians, among whom at that time the
race of the Achæmenids had acquired a prominent
position,[1] in order to maintain their independence
against Assyria.

From this point downwards we can date the union
and independence of Media. Had the country been
free and united at the time of Sargon, Sennacherib,
and Esarhaddon, the rulers of Assyria would not have
marched against Syria and Cilicia, or undertaken
the conquest of Egypt. Assurbanipal could not have
employed the forces of the kingdom to maintain
Egypt, or reduce Babylon, or annihilate Edom, or
make campaigns to the distant parts of Arabia, if the
united power of Media had existed behind the Zagrus,
close on the borders of his native land, the very centre

[1] Von Gutschmid, *loc. cit.* s. 88; below, c. 3.

of the Assyrian power. Still less could he have looked on in inaction, while Phraortes, as Herodotus tells us, conquered the Persians, and attacked one nation after another till he had subjugated Asia. On the other hand, the annihilation of Elam by Assurbanipal, and consequent strengthening of the Assyrian power on the borders of Persia, may well have determined the Persians to unite with the Medes, and accept a position under Phraortes.

In considering the situation and importance of the powers, we may assume that Phraortes, in the first instance, thought rather of defence than of any attack on Assyria, and for this object undertook the fortification of Ecbatana on a large scale. What could have induced him to abandon the protecting line of the Zagrus, in order to attack under the massive walls of its metropolis the power which had just dealt such heavy and destructive blows on ancient states like Babylonia and Elam, unless we attribute to him the most reckless audacity? Nor, on the other hand, can we suppose that an ancient ruler like Assurbanipal, who had held his own successfully against the searching attack of his brother, and finally gained important conquests, would have allowed the formation of the Median power in the closest proximity, and its combination with the Persians, without the least attempt to prevent it. It was in repulsing this attack that Phraortes fell.[1]

If this inquiry leads us to attribute to Phraortes the foundation of a consolidated government, the establish-

[1] Vol. III. 280. The Assyrian inscriptions are silent from 644 B.C. downwards. Von Gutschmid, "Neue Beitr." s. 89. From this silence I have concluded, and still conclude, that the liberation of the Medes took place towards 640 B.C., and moreover that the victory of the Assyrians over Phraortes and his death in battle did not bring about a decisive change in favour of the Assyrians.

ment of monarchy in Media, the union of the Persians
and Medes, and the subordination of the former to
Phraortes, we can yet understand that the traditions of
the Medes, anxious to increase the glory of the country,
threw the monarchy further back, ascribed to Deioces,
the father of Phraortes, the consolidation of Media,
and represented the liberation from the sway of
Assyria as prior to the foundation of the monarchy.
What Median poems can do for the glorification of
their country, even in the teeth of the established
facts of history, will soon become even more clear.
How this tradition explained the elevation of Deioces
we cannot now discover; it is clear that Herodotus
gives a Greek turn to this part of the story (p. 280).
And if tradition ascribes to Deioces the extensive and
strong fortifications of Ecbatana, which more correctly
belong to Phraortes and his successors, it is Herodotus
who credits him with the discovery of the mode of life
usual among Oriental monarchs.   The Medo-Persian
Epos shows us the successors of Semiramis in the
seclusion of the palace.   On the other hand, the
Median tradition must have ascribed the reduction of
Asia to Phraortes.   We have already remarked (III.
280), that towards the close of the sixth century B.C.
Cyaxares and not Phraortes was regarded by the nation
as the founder of the power and greatness of Media.
Herodotus himself tells us " that Cyaxares was far
more powerful than his predecessors."   Hence the
later legend, which Herodotus reproduces, ascribed the
foundation to Phraortes, and the extension of the
Median power to Cyaxares.   But if Phraortes was to
be the conqueror of Asia, he must " when he had
attacked and conquered the other nations one after
the other," have finally marched against the Assyrians,
against whom he did in fact contend.

CHAPTER II.

THE EMPIRE OF THE MEDES.

" WHEN Phraortes had fallen, he was succeeded by his son Cyaxares. This prince collected all his subjects and marched against Nineveh, in order to avenge the death of his father and destroy the city. He defeated the Assyrians, and while encamped before Nineveh, there came upon him the vast army of the Scythians, led by their king Madyas, the son of Protothyas, who invaded Asia in pursuit of the Cimmerians, and as they did not come through the land of the Saspeires, but kept the Caucasus to the right, they reached the Median country. Here they attacked the Medes, and the latter being conquered in the battle lost their empire; the Scythians became masters of the whole of Asia, and ruled over it for 28 years. With reckless cruelty they laid everything waste; they not only imposed tribute on all the nations, but went round and took from every one all that he possessed. But Cyaxares and the Medes massacred the greater part of them after making them intoxicated at a banquet, and in this way the Medes recovered their empire, and again governed those who had previously been subject to them. Then a horde of Scythians, which had separated from the rest and put themselves under the protection of Cyaxares, were guilty of a crime against a Median boy who had been

entrusted to them, and fled for refuge to Alyattes, king
of Lydia, who refused to give them up. This led to
a war between Media and Lydia which continued for
five years, and was brought to an end by a treaty in
which Alyattes gave his daughter Aryanis to wife
to the son of Cyaxares. Cyaxares was master of all
Asia beyond the Halys, took Nineveh, and subjugated
the Assyrians, with the exception of the Babylonian
portion." Such is the history, given by Herodotus,
of Cyaxares, who, on his reckoning, ascended the
throne of Media in the year 633 B.C.

If Phraortes had fallen in battle against the
Assyrians with the greater part of his army, Cyaxares
(Uvakshathra) could hardly have at once undertaken
an attack on Nineveh, with a view of avenging his
father's death by the destruction of that city; his
first care, on the contrary, would have been to prevent
the Assyrians from making use of their great victory,
to guard against further advances on their part, and
to maintain the freedom of Media. This struggle
Cyaxares passed through with success; that his good
fortune carried him as far as the walls of Nineveh,
is indeed possible, but not probable; according to
Herodotus the collision of the Scythians and Medes
did not take place in the land of Asshur, but further
to the East, in Media.

The facts about the pursuit of the Cimmerians and
the invasion of the Scythians have been already examined, and it has been shown that Herodotus has
connected the immigration of the Cimmerians into
Asia Minor, which took place in the eighth century
B.C., with the incursion of Sacian tribes from the Oxus
into Media, about the year 630 B.C. He was deceived
by the circumstance that the Cimmerians from their
abode on the lower Halys penetrated to Sardis and

the cities of the Western coast, about the time when the Sacæ invaded Media and inundated Hither Asia (III. 276). The truth is that the hordes of the Sacæ not only overthrew Media, but passed through Mesopotamia into Syria as far as the borders of Egypt. Their attack shattered and destroyed the cohesion of the Assyrian empire.

About the year 620 Cyaxares succeeded in overpowering the section of the Scythians which remained in Media (these hordes were no doubt widely dispersed), and again became master in his own dominions. He made use of his advantageous position as the first who could again direct the forces of his people. He showed himself to the Armenians and Cappadocians as a champion to defend them from the plundering Scythians, and at the same time aided in liberating them from the dominion of the Assyrians. The incursion of the Scythians had prepared the way for him; in a few years he was able to extend his power to the West as far as the Halys.[1] Nabopolassar, the viceroy of Assyria in Babylon, who had determined to turn to account the severe blow which the incursion of the Scyths had given to the Assyrian kingdom, had already offered him his hand in alliance. Amyite, the daughter of Cyaxares, had become the wife of Nebuchadnezzar, the son of Nabopolassar. But in Asia Minor, far to the West, the princes of the Lydians had taken advantage of the disturbance and confusion which the advance of the Cimmerians had carried to the Western coast, to extend their power over Phrygia as far as the Halys (III. 435). Here the two rapidly-developing powers met. Though inferior in numbers the Lydians

---

[1] Herod. 1, 72. In Xenophon, who represents Astyages as reigning before Cyaxares, Astyages had subjugated the king of Armenia; the rebellion of this king was afterwards repressed by Cyaxares. "Cyri instit." 3, 1, 6 ff.

showed themselves a match for the Medes. After a war of five years, peace was established between them by Nabopolassar of Babylon and Syennesis of Cilicia, in order to set the power of Media free to act against Nineveh. The Halys became the boundary of the two kingdoms, and the peace was confirmed by an alliance. Alyattes of Lydia gave his daughter Aryanis to wife to Astyages the son of Cyaxares (610 B.C.[1]). Media and Babylonia now thought themselves strong enough to undertake the contest against the remains

[1] Vol. III. 287, 438. Even after the discussions of Gelzer (" Rhein- isches Museum," 1875, s. 264 ff.) on the date of the eclipse, I believe that Oltmann and Bailly's calculation may hold good for it, until it is proved astronomically that in the year 610 B.C. an eclipse of the sun would not have been visible in Asia Minor. If this were proved, Herodotus' dates for Cyaxares, who not only in his work but on the evidence of the inscription of Behistun, was the founder of the Median empire, would have to be thrown back more than half a century, which the date of Cyrus does not allow. To assume a confusion of Cyaxares with Astyages in Herodotus, is impossible, for Cyaxares is twice expressly mentioned (1, 74, and 103), and moreover Astyages is spoken of as the son of Cyaxares to whom Aryanis was married. Nor can I regard it as finally proved that the double capture of Sardis rests simply on Callisthenes, and a deduction from Strabo. Gelzer agrees that the incursions of the Cimmerians into Asia Minor and their establishment in Cappadocia must be placed at the least before the year 705 B.C. (" Z. Aegypt. Sprache," 1875, s. 18); the devastation of Phrygia by the Cimmerians he puts in the year 696 or 676 B.C. According to the dates of Eusebius Midas (the husband of Damodike) began to reign in Olymp. 10, 3 = 738, and took his own life in Ol. 21, 2 = 695 (Euseb. ed. Schöne, 2, 82, 85) ; his reign extended therefore from 738 to 695 B.C. Hence the devastation of Phrygia by the Cimmerians must have taken place in the year 695. If they were masters of Phrygia at this date, it is not easy to see why these successes did not carry them on into Lydia. As a fact, this is far from improbable ; and if the image at Nymsi is their work, they would not have had any time for it in 630 B.C., for that incursion was merely a "plundering raid," and the change in the dynasty of Lydia, the accession of Gyges in the year 689 B.C. (Vol. III. 416), seems to me to point to some previous violent change. Besides, Strabo's words, p. 61, and p. 647, are plain and conclusive enough, so that I see no reason to attach much weight to the interpretation of the passage, p. 627. Cf. Caesar, " Ind. lect. Marb. Sem. aestivum," 1876.

of the Assyrian kingdom. Cyaxares led out the Medes, Nabopolassar the Babylonians against king Assur-idil-ili. The latter offered a long and stubborn defence, and when at length the walls of Nineveh were broken through, he burnt himself in the citadel. The Assyrian country as far as the Tigris fell to the share of Media; Mesopotamia was united with the new kingdom of Babylon (607 B.C.[1]). Thus Media and Babylonia took the place of Assyria; and Babylon, as Herodotus says, was now the chief city of the Assyrians.

When the kingdom had fallen which for three centuries had ruled in the East and West, Cyaxares might indulge the thought of making his empire more complete on the table-land of Iran. According to the story which Ctesias has preserved for us from the Medo-Persian Epos of the fall of Assyria (III. 249), the Bactrians had been prevailed upon to join the Medes and Babylonians in the course of the war against Assyria, and the Persian songs which describe the contest of Cyrus and Astyages, represent the Hyrcanians, Parthians, Bactrians, and other nations of the East, as ruled by viceroys of the Median king.[2] We may regard it as certain that Cyaxares succeeded in subjugating the table-land of Iran to a considerable extent. No slight proof is afforded of the increase and greatness of the Median kingdom in his reign by the unusual care and extraordinary efforts of the successor of Nabopolassar to protect Babylonia and Babylon by fortifications against the event of a struggle between the two powers, whose united exertions had destroyed Assyria (III. 366).

The position which the Medo-Persian poems assign to the chief of the Babylonians beside the chief of

---

[1] Vol. III. 284 ff., 291.   [2] Diod. 2, 34; Nicol. Damasc. fragm. 66.

the Medes, during and after the common struggle, has been already explained. The Babylonian is the astrologer, the adviser, the helper; the Mede is the man of action. In the event of success against Assyria he promises the Babylonian the viceroyalty of Babylon, and has already given it to him, free of tribute, when the fraud is discovered by which the cunning Babylonian has acquired the most valuable part of the spoil of Nineveh. For this offence the chief is condemned to death; but the Mede pardons him, and in consideration of his former services and the promise made, leaves him the viceroyalty. So eager were the Median minstrels to conceal the independence of Babylonia beside Media, and represent a power as great as Babylon was under Nebuchadnezzar as a satrapy of their kings. This fiction is maintained in other episodes of the Medo-Persian Epos which have come down to us. We are told of the stubborn resistance which the Cadusians made to the Medes; and an explanation is given how this unimportant nation on the shore of the Caspian (p. 268) could withstand the mighty kingdom of the Medes. This episode has come to us in the Persian form. It is the fault of the Median king that the Cadusians have become stubborn and successful enemies. He failed to help to his rights a brave warrior in his service; this warrior betook himself to the Cadusians, and became their chief, led them well, and bequeathed his thirst for vengeance to his descendants. From such a point of view even a Median minstrel could lament the perversity of the Median king, and the power of Babylonian gold, the abundance of which is strongly marked in the narrative, could praise the ancient simplicity of the Medes: " who took no heed of silver, and did not regard gold," as we are told in the Hebrew Scriptures, and reprobate the victory of gold over strict justice. But it is a Persian to whom the wrong is done, who summons the Cadusians to freedom; and the resistance of the Cadusians to the Median kingdom, thus brought about by a Persian, subsequently furnishes Cyrus with a pretext for arming the Persians, and also provides him with allies in the Cadusians. It was the merit of a brave Persian to have provided this assistance for his people long before. The king of the Medes who was guilty of this mistake is called in Ctesias Artaeus; we have seen (p. 277) that Artaeus and Astibaras, who reigned 40 years each, are but one and the same person; and as the reign of Cyaxares occupies 40 years in Herodotus, we may conjecture that he is the king hidden behind the Artaeus-Astibaras of Ctesias. The king of Babylon, the satrap of the episode, is brought in as a descendant of Belesys (Nabopolassar), and described as an effeminate man. His name, in the form given by Ctesias, is Annarus. Evilmerodach or Neriglissar of Babylon must be meant; but, without doubt, we are dealing with mere fiction.

The episode is as follows: There was a Persian of the name of Parsondes, in the service of the king of the Medes, an eager huntsman, and active warrior on foot and in the chariot, distinguished in council and in the field, and of influence with the king. Parsondes often urged the king to make him satrap of Babylon in the place of Annarus, who wore women's clothes and ornaments, but the king always put the petition aside, for it could not be granted without breaking the promise which his ancestor had made to Belesys (p. 297). Annarus discovered the intentions of Parsondes, and sought to secure himself against him, and to take vengeance. He promised great rewards to the

cooks who were in the train of the king, if they succeeded in seizing Parsondes and giving him up. One
day Parsondes in the heat of the chase strayed far
from the king. He had already killed many boars
and deer, when the pursuit of a wild ass (the Sassanids also hunt this animal) carried him to a great
distance. At last he came upon the cooks, who were
occupied in preparations for the king's table. Being
thirsty, Parsondes asked for wine; they gave it, took
care of his horse, and invited him to take food—an
invitation agreeable to Parsondes, who had been hunting the whole day. He bade them send the ass
which he had captured to the king, and tell his own
servants where he was. Then he ate of the various
kinds of food set before him, and drank abundantly of
the excellent wine, and at last asked for his horse in
order to return to the king. But they brought beautiful women to him, and urged him to remain for
the night. He agreed, and as soon as, overcome by
hunting, wine, and love he had fallen into a deep sleep,
the cooks bound him, and brought him to Annarus.
Annarus reproached him with calling him an effeminate man, and seeking to obtain his satrapy; he had
the king to thank that the satrapy granted to his
ancestors had not been taken from him. Parsondes
replied that he considered himself more worthy of the
office, because he was more manly and more useful
to the king. But Annarus swore by Bel and Mylitta
that Parsondes should be softer and whiter than
a woman, called for the eunuch who was over the
female players, and bade him shave the body of
Parsondes and bathe and anoint him every day,
put women's clothes on him, plait his hair after
the manner of women, paint his face, and place
him among the women, who played the guitar and

sang, and to teach him their arts. This was done, and soon Parsondes played and sang better at the table of Annarus than any of the women. Meanwhile the king of the Medes had caused search to be made everywhere for Parsondes, and since he could nowhere be found, and nothing could be heard of him, he believed that a lion or some other wild animal had torn him when out hunting, and lamented for his loss. Parsondes had lived for seven years as a woman in Babylon, when Annarus caused an eunuch to be scourged and grievously maltreated. This eunuch Parsondes induced by large presents to retire to Media and tell the king the misfortune which had come upon him. Then the king sent a message commanding Annarus to give up Parsondes. Annarus declared that he had never seen him. But the king sent a second messenger charging him to bring Annarus to be put to death if he did not surrender Parsondes. Annarus entertained the messenger of the king, and when the meal was brought, 150 women entered, of whom some played the guitar while others blew the flute. At the end of the meal Annarus asked the king's envoy which of all the women was the most beautiful and had played best. The envoy pointed to Parsondes. Annarus laughed long and said, "That is the person whom you seek," and released Parsondes, who on the next day returned home with the envoy to the king in a chariot. The king was astonished at the sight of him, and asked why he had not avoided such disgrace by death? Parsondes answered: "In order that I might see you again, and by you execute vengeance on Annarus, which could never have been mine had I taken my life." The king promised him that his hope should not be deceived, as soon as he came to Babylon.

But when he came there, Annarus defended himself on the ground that Parsondes, though in no way injured by him, had maligned him, and sought to obtain the satrapy over Babylonia. The king pointed out that he had made himself judge in his own cause, and had imposed a punishment of a degrading character; in ten days he would pronounce sentence upon him for his conduct. In terror Annarus hastened to Mitraphernes, the eunuch of greatest influence with the king, and promised him the most liberal rewards (10 talents of gold and 100 talents of silver, 10 golden and 200 silver bowls) if he could induce the king to spare his life and retain him in the satrapy of Babylonia. He was prepared to give the king 100 talents of gold, 1000 talents of silver, 100 golden and 300 silver bowls, and costly robes with other gifts; Parsondes also should receive 100 talents of silver and costly robes. After many entreaties Mitraphernes persuaded the king not to command the execution of Annarus, as he had not killed Parsondes, but to condemn him in the penalty which he was prepared to pay Parsondes and the king. Annarus in gratitude threw himself at the feet of the king, but Parsondes said: "Cursed be the man who first brought gold among men; for the sake of gold I have been made a mockery to the Babylonians." The eunuch advised him to lay aside his anger, and be reconciled with Annarus, for that was what the king desired; but Parsondes determined to take vengeance for the sentence of the king, and waited for a favourable opportunity in order to fly with a thousand horse and three thousand infantry to the Cadusians, whose most distinguished chief had married his sister. Then he persuaded the Cadusians to revolt from the Medes, and was elected to be

their general. When the king of the Medes armed
against them, Parsondes armed in return, and occupied
the passes into the country with 200,000 warriors.
Though the Median king brought up 800,000 men,
Parsondes nevertheless put him to flight, and slew
50,000 Medes. In admiration of such noble deeds,
the Cadusians made Parsondes king, and they often
invaded Media and laid it waste. At the end of his
days, Parsondes commanded his successor to remain
an enemy of the Medes, and pronounced a curse: "If
ever peace should be concluded between the Medes
and the Cadusians, might his race and the whole
nation of the Cadusians perish." This is the reason
why the Cadusians remained the enemies of the
Medes, and were never subject to them.[1]

Another episode tells us of the contests which the
Medes had to sustain under the dominion of Asti-
baras-Artaeus, i. e. of Cyaxares, against the Parthians
and the Sacae. The Parthians, whose chief was
Marmares, revolted from the Medes, but handed over
their land and city to the king of the Sacae, Cydraeus,
that he might protect them against the Medes; and
the sister of Cydraeus, Zarinaea (Zaranya, i. e. the
golden), who was distinguished for her beauty and
wisdom, her boldness and bravery (for the women of
the Sacae took the field with the men), became the wife
of Marmares. As the Medians intended to reduce the
Parthians again to subjection, a war broke out between
them and the Parthians and Sacae, which lasted for
several years, and led to battles in which many fell
on one side and the other. In one of these battles
Zarinaea was wounded. Stryangaeus, the Mede, to
whom Cyaxares had given his daughter Rhoetaea

---

[1] Nicol. Damasc. fragm. 9, 10, ed. Müller; Diod. 2, 33; Ctes. Fragm.
52, ed. Müller.

to wife, pursued, overtook, and threw her from her
horse. But the sight of her beauty and youth, and
her entreaties, moved him ; he allowed her to escape.
Not long afterwards Stryangaeus with other Medes
was taken captive by the Parthians. Marmares wished
to put him to death, and though Zarinaea entreated
for his life, insisted on his execution. Then Zarinaea
loosed the bonds of the captive Medes, caused Marmares to be put to death by them, and allowed
Stryangaeus to escape. When, after the death of her
brother Cydraeus, she ascended the throne of the Sacæ,
she sent messengers to the king of the Medes to
conclude peace and friendship. The Parthians were
to return under the sovereignty of the Medes, the
Sacæ and Medes were to keep what previously belonged to them, and to be friends and allies for ever.
This was done. Stryangaeus, the real author of this
treaty, ever since the battle in which he had first seen
Zarinaea, had been possessed with violent love for
her, and went to Roxanace (*i. e.* the brilliant),[1] where
was the royal citadel of the Sacæ, in order to see the
beloved princess once more. Zarinaea, who returned
his affection, came to see him full of joy, received him
and his attendants in the most splendid manner,
kissed him in the sight of all, and ascended his chariot,
and thus, while conversing with each other they
arrived in the palace. Here Stryangaeus sighed in
the chambers assigned to him, and could not resist the
violence of his passion. At length he took counsel
with the most faithful of his eunuchs, who encouraged
him to discover his passion to Zarinaea. Easily persuaded, Stryangaeus hastened to the queen, and after
much delay and many sighs, sometimes blushing and

---

[1] Roxane and Roxanace are both formed from the old Bactrian
raokshna. Müllenhoff, " Monatsberichte Berl. Akadem." 1866, s. 562.

again turning pale, he ventured to declare that he
was consumed with love for her. Zarinaea answered
quietly and gently that it would be shameful and
fatal for her to surrender herself to him, and far more
shameful and dangerous for Stryangaeus, as his wife
was the daughter of the king of the Medes, and, as
she heard, more beautiful than herself and many other
women. He must be brave, not only against his
enemies, but against himself, and not bring about a
long calamity for the sake of a brief enjoyment. No
other wish of his but this should remain unsatisfied.
Stryangaeus was silent for a long time, then embraced
and kissed the queen, and departed. He was far more
dejected than before, and determined to take his life.
"Thou hast been saved by me," he wrote to Zarinaea,
"but through thee I am destroyed. If in this thou
hast done justly, then may all good things be thine,
and mayest thou be happy; if thou hast done evil,
may a passion like mine overtake thee." When he
had bound the eunuch by an oath to give this letter
to Zarinaea immediately after his death, he lay back
on his cushions and demanded his sword. As the
eunuch refused to give it, he ended his days by
starvation. Zarinaea ruled over the Sacæ with
wisdom and power. She conquered the neighbouring nations who sought to subjugate her people,
caused a great part of the land to be cultivated, and
built a considerable number of cities, and brought
the Sacæ into greater prosperity. In gratitude for
the benefits received from her, and in remembrance
of her virtues, the Sacæ erected on her grave a three-
sided pyramid, three stades in length on each side,
and ending in a point a stadium in height, on which
was placed a colossal golden statue of the queen.
Worship was also offered to her as to a hero, so

that she received greater honours than any of her predecessors.[1]

We have already acquainted ourselves with the land of the Parthians (p. 10). The Sacæ were neighbours of the Hyrcanians, the Parthians, and the Bactrians in the steppes of the Oxus. Herodotus tells us that the Sacæ were a nation of the tribe of the Scyths, and that their proper name was Amyrgians; the Persians called all the Scythians Sacæ. The inscriptions of Darius speak of Çaka Humavarka; in the second version the name is Omuvargap, and in the Babylonian-Assyrian version Umurga. According to the account of Herodotus the Sacæ wore trousers, and upright, pointed caps, and carried bows of a peculiar character, battle-axes and daggers. They fought as mounted bowmen. On the monument of Darius at Behistun Çakuka,[2] the leader of the Sacæ, wears a tall pointed cap. In the army of Xerxes the Sacæ were ranged with the Bactrians. What our episode tells us of the royal citadel and the cities built by Zarinæa does not harmonise with the nature of the steppe-country of the Sacæ, and the statement of the Greeks, that the Sacæ lived in variegated tents, and that their wealth consisted in flocks of sheep, but it does agree with the fact that the women went to battle on horseback with the men. The companions of Alexander describe the Sacæ as strong, warlike, well-grown men, with flowing hair; the Macedonians only came up to their shoulders. Later accounts speak of heavy-armed horse among them; both horse and rider were covered with armour, and the weapons of attack were long lances.[3] From the narratives given

[1] Ctes. Fragm. 25—28, ed. Müller; Nic. Damasc. fragm. 12 ed. Müller.
[2] Oppert gives the form of the second version as Çakuka Iskunka.
[3] Choerilus in Strabo, p. 303; Herod. 3, 93; 7, 64; 9, 71; Ptolem. 6, 13; Curtius, 7, 4, 6; Arrian, "Anab." 3, 13; Cf. Plut. "Crassus," 24.

in the episodes we may retain the fact that although the Persians followed the lead of the Medes from the time of Phraortes, Cyaxares, even after the fall of Nineveh, did not succeed in subjugating the remaining nations of Iran without severe struggles. There is no reason to doubt that the Cadusians made an obstinate resistance, and maintained their independence : The Parthians were able to combine with the Sacæ in order to preserve their freedom, and did not become subject to Cyaxares without severe contests. That the Sagartians on the edge of the great desert (p. 6) were subject to Cyaxares, is clear from the inscription of Darius at Behistun. If the Medes had to fight with the Sacæ, who were settled on the Oxus, Bactria must have been reduced to form a part of their kingdom. Beside the Hyrcanians, Parthians, and "other nations," the Bactrians and Sacæ are specially mentioned as subjects of the Median kings,[1] and Arrian assures us that the Açvakas, whom we found north of the Cabul on the right bank of the Indus (IV. 393), were subjects of the Medes.[2]

Herodotus tells us that Cyaxares was the first to separate the lance-bearers, archers, and horsemen, and combine them into divisions ; that is, he introduced a better and more manageable arrangement of the army. To the same prince, no doubt, is due the completion of the fortifications of Ecbatana, which we found had been strengthened by his predecessor Phraortes. When the fortifications were first begun, the place was merely intended as a point of defence against Assyria ; but as soon as it became destined to aid in the maintenance of independence, it was necessary that it should be capable of offering refuge and support to the Median army, if hard pressed. The mountains of the

[1] Nicol. Damasc. fragm. 66, ed. Müller.   [2] "Ind." 1, 1.

Zagrus form the boundary wall, and at the same time
the line of division between the Medes and Assyrians.
As Polybius told us (p. 268), it was an ascent of
twelve miles—*i. e.* four leagues—to the top of the
pass. If the Medes failed to hold these passes, and
were then defeated in their own table-land, the mountains of the Orontes formed a new point of protection
to their retreat. The Orontes (Old Persian, *Urvanda;*
now Elvend) is a steep range of mountains, traversing
Media from north-west to south-east; the heights
of the passes are given by travellers at 7000 or
10,000 feet; Ctesias puts the ascent at twenty-five
stades;[1] recent explorers fix the time at four hours.
On the eastern spur of this mountain wall, in a
fertile plain, six leagues long and four leagues broad,
lay Ecbatana, Old Persian *Hangmatana, i. e.* place of
assembly, the Achmeta of the Hebrews. If the
Orontes could not be held, the fortifications of Ecbatana
formed a last point of protection for the Median army.
From the Assyrians there was nothing more to be
feared after the fall of Nineveh, but Cyaxares had
no doubt felt, in the inundation of Media by the
nomadic tribes of the Sacæ, and then in the final
battles against Asshur, what a support was given
by a strong metropolis; what good service the walls
of Nineveh had rendered to the enemy, even in his
decline. He saw what measures were being taken
by Nebuchadnezzar, his step-son, to make his metropolis secure, and determined that the kingdom, which
he had so rapidly and brilliantly erected and developed, should not be without the nucleus of an
impregnable fortress and royal citadel. The booty in
silver and gold, which the Medes gained in Nineveh,
and of which we hear not in the Median poems only,

----

[1] Diod. 2, 13; 17, 110; Strabo, p. 127.

but also from the Hebrew prophets who lived at the
time of the fall of the city, provided no doubt ample
means both for the erection of the strongest works,
and for the adornment of these as well as the citadel.

Ctesias tells us that Semiramis built a splendid
palace at Ecbatana, a city lying in a plain, and as
there were no springs near, she cut through the roots
of the range of mountains, twelve stades distant from
the city (the Orontes), on the farther side of which
was a lake flowing into a river, in order to convey the
water of the river into the city. For this object a
tunnel was cut through the mountain, fifteen feet in
breadth and forty feet in depth, and through it the
river was carried into Ecbatana.[1] If Ctesias ascribes
the palace of Ecbatana and the tunnel, like other
monuments of Media, to Semiramis, we have already
seen that the queen is no more than a poetical fiction;
nor could any of the sovereigns who ruled over Assyria
entertain the project of building citadels and conduits
for the Median kings. These could only be the work
of Median princes, who resided in Ecbatana; and as
Phraortes could hardly have had the means and the
time for such important structures, we must ascribe
both the completion and adornment of the royal
citadel, as well as the tunnel, to Cyaxares, unless we
are to reject the latter as a pure invention, for which
there seems to me no sufficient proof.

" When the palace had been built at Ecbatana, it
was surrounded with large and strong walls," Herodotus tells us, " of which one encircled another, in
such a manner that the inner overtopped the outer by
the height of the turret. The situation, which was
on a hill, contributed to this result, and the natural
elevation was artificially increased. In all there were

[1] Diod. 2, 13.

seven circles; the innermost contained the king's
dwelling and treasure-house; the outermost wall was
of about the extent of the wall of Athens. The towers
of the first circle were white, of the second black, of the
third red-purple, of the fourth blue-purple, of the fifth
red; the towers of the sixth are covered with silver;
and those of the seventh, which surrounds the buildings
of the palace, with gold. The city was built round
the outermost wall." [1] Polybius describes the situation
of Ecbatana and the palace as they were under the
Achæmenids, who were wont to pass some of the hot
summer months in the cool and fresh air of Ecbatana.
" Ecbatana lies in the northern regions of Media, and
commands the parts of Asia which look towards the
Maeotis and the Euxine. The city was in old days
the royal abode of the Median kings, and it appears
to have far surpassed all other cities in wealth and
in the splendour of its buildings. It is built under
the spurs of the Orontes. Though without walls, it
possesses a citadel built by the hand of man, of surprising strength. Below the citadel is the palace,
which it is as difficult to speak of in detail as to pass
over in silence. Ecbatana is an excellent theme for
those who love to tell of marvellous things with adornment and exaggeration; but those who enter with
caution on anything which goes beyond the ordinary intelligence find themselves in difficulties. The circuit
of the palace is about seven stades, and the rich ornamentation of the various parts proves how flourishing
was the condition of those who founded it. Though
the entire wood-work consists of cedar and cypress,
this is never allowed to appear; on the contrary, the
beams of the roof and the panelling, the pillars in the
chambers and halls, are covered with gold or silver

[1] Herod. 1, 98, 99.

plates, and the roof consists wholly of silver tiles. Most of these were carried off at the time of the expedition of Alexander, and the remainder in the reign of Antigonus and Seleucus-Nicanor. Nevertheless the temple of Aine (*i. e.* of Anahita) at the time when Antiochus Theos (261—245 B.C.) came to Ecbatana, had gilded pillars round it; and some of the gold plates in the side-walls were still remaining, and the greater part of the silver plates, while the silver tiles of the roof were still there in considerable quantities."[1] At the time of Alexander, Diodorus allows the city of Ecbatana a circuit of 250 stades, *i. e.* of more than 30 miles.[2] Isidore of Charax mentions the treasure-house at Ecbatana, the metropolis of Media and the shrine of Anaitis, in which sacrifice was constantly offered.[3]

It is not clear from these descriptions whether the fortifications at that time included the whole city or not. Herodotus only speaks of the fortifications of the citadel, and represents the city as built at the foot of its walls. Yet we may assume that Phraortes and Cyaxares followed the pattern of the chief cities of Assyria and Babylonia in placing a strong wall round their city. A late and very uncertain authority, the book of Judith, states that the walls of Ecbatana consisted of splendid masonry, and reached a height of seventy cubits (about 110 feet) ; the towers of these walls were a hundred cubits in height, and there were gates in them.[4] When the Medes lost their empire and became subject to the Achæmenids, it was to their interest that the metropolis of the Medes should not be fortified, but that the citadel should be in the hands

[1] Polyb. 10, 27.   [2] 17, 110.   [3] "Mans. Parth." c. 6.
[4] Judith, i. 2—4. On the date of the composition of this book, cf. Volkmar, "Rheinisches Museum," 12, 481. In any case it dates from the end of the first or the second century of our reckoning.

of a Persian garrison. Cyrus himself, therefore, after
the conquest of Astyages, or Darius, after suppressing
the rebellion of the Medes, may have thrown down
the walls which surrounded Ecbatana. The silence of
Herodotus respecting them would then be explained
by the fact that they were no longer in existence
in his time. The circuit of the external wall Herodotus compares with the circuit of the city of Athens,
which, exclusive of the harbour cities but including the space between the Phaleric and the long
walls, reached 60 stades, or $7\frac{1}{2}$ miles.[1] If we chose
to assume that Herodotus included the Phaleric and
long walls in the circuit, the total extent would be
$22\frac{1}{2}$ miles, an incredible length for the wall of a
citadel. Of the outer walls of the royal citadels at
Babylon, Diodorus puts those on the one bank of the
Euphrates at 30 stades, and those on the other at 60,
and of the two inner walls of the latter the first was
40 stades in length and the second 20.[2] The circuit
of $22\frac{1}{2}$ miles may, therefore, refer only to the whole
extent of the citadel and city of Ecbatana, and it
would then come near the statement of Diodorus, who
puts the circuit of Ecbatana at 250 stades.

The royal citadel of the Achæmenids at Persepolis
was surrounded, according to Diodorus, with a triple
wall; the first wall was 16, the second 32, the third
60 cubits in height. These walls were decorated with
great expense, and adorned with towers. The citadel
of Ecbatana is said to have had seven walls, and,
however strange this may appear, religious no less
than military motives might have led to that number.
We know the importance ascribed in the Avesta to
the number seven—the seven supreme deities, and the
seven girdles of the earth. On the other hand, if we

---

[1] Thuc. 2, 13, and the Scholia.   [2] Diod. 2, 8.

leave out of sight the hill on which the citadel was
built, the elevated plateau of Ecbatana did not present
the natural difficulties such as rivers and heights,
which strengthened the fortification of the Assyrian
metropolis and the walls of Babylon; hence it was
more important to meet this deficiency by the number
of towers and walls. The successive walls would have
been of little service had not each inner one been higher
than the outer, and they would have been the reverse
of serviceable, had not the distance between them been
so great that the arrows and missiles of the enemy,
when they had gained the outer walls, failed to reach
from it to the next, so that the assault of the next
wall had to be begun afresh after the capture of the
adjacent outer wall, without any cover. If we might
assume that the words of Polybius: "The palaces, of
which the extent reaches to about seven stades, lie
below the citadel," are to be interpreted as meaning
that these buildings lay under the protection of the
walls of the citadel, i. e. behind them—and it is
scarcely conceivable that the Achæmenids should have
chosen an unprotected palace in Media for a constant
residence, and deposited there large treasures, and the
archives of the kingdom—the circuit of the buildings
of the palace and that of the external wall of 60
stadia would give a space between the walls of each
of about 2000 feet; a distance not much in excess of
that absolutely required. Hence the circuit of 60
stadia from the outer wall does not appear too large.

More astonishing still is the account given by
Herodotus of the ornamentation of the turrets of these
walls—the colours of the turrets of the first five, the
silver and gold of the two last. The attempt has
been made to explain these statements as a legendary
echo of the fame of the splendour of Ecbatana in

the time of Cyaxares and his successor Astyages.
But Polybius tells us very distinctly that the roof of
the palace and that of the temple of Anahita consisted
of silver tiles at the time of the Achæmenids, that
the beams and panels of the roofs as well as the
pillars were entirely covered with gold and silver
plates, and that these decorations remained in the
temple of Anahita at the time of Antiochus Theos.
This ornamentation might be extended to the turrets
of the inner walls. Considering the amount of the
spoil of Nineveh, it cannot be regarded as an impossi-
bility that the ramparts of the interior walls, the
length of which, according to the statement of Polybius, did not reach more than 4200 feet, were covered
with plates of gold, and of the next with plates of
silver, when the roof of the palace could consist of
silver tiles. That the overthrow of the Assyrian kingdom and the spoil of the cities brought considerable
possessions to the Median nation may be concluded
from the remark of Herodotus that the Persians had
adopted better clothing and more luxurious habits
from the Medes. The kings would without doubt
receive the richest part of the spoil. The decoration
of the turrets was possibly rude, but it exhibited in a
striking manner the splendour and exaltation of the
kingdom, which was thus encased in gold and silver,
while the sovereign dwelt in gold and silver chambers.
Such a parade of royal magnificence is not out of
harmony with the character of the ancient East. To
those who were not allowed to enter the wide and
high gates of the palace, these turrets showed far
and wide, through city and country, the splendour
of the citadel. The colours of the five outer walls
would be given by glazed tiles, such as those found in

the ruins of Nineveh and Chalah, of Babylon and
Mugheir. We may assume with certainty that Cyaxares desired to give to his palace and citadel a
splendour no less than that displayed by the palaces
of Nineveh, or the royal citadel of Nebuchadnezzar
in Babylon, or the golden citadel in Sardis. Religious
conceptions may also have determined the colours of
the decoration as well as the number of the walls.
As Auramazda sat in pure light, on a golden throne
on the golden Hukairya, so was the ruler on earth to
dwell in his palace of Ecbatana in golden chambers
surrounded by golden walls. The Avesta exhibits
Mithra with a golden helmet and silver coat of mail,
the wheels of his chariots are of gold, his horses are
greys,[1] shod on the fore hoofs with gold, and on
the hinder hoofs with silver; in like manner the
upper turrets of the citadel must shine with silver
and the highest with gold. We have seen that the
metals, owing to the brilliance inherent in them, belonged in the ideas of the Iranians to the good spirits.
And as the splendour of gold and silver belonged to
the highest gods, so must the colours of the other
turrets have been assigned to the good spirits, to
whose protection each separate wall was entrusted.[2]

[1] Diod. 17, 71.

[2] Hence I see no reason for connecting the colours of the turrets
with the Babylonian star-worship. The only fact in favour of this is
the black of the second wall; but as the highest turrets exhibited the
two most precious metals, the others may have received the colours of
the remaining five, over all of which Kshathra vairya presided, and in
the order of the Avesta in which silver and copper follow gold, while
iron and steel end the list. It can hardly be proved that Babylonian
star-worship had a decisive influence among the Medes at the time of
Cyaxares. Isaiah xiii. 17 might be quoted against the wealth of
Ecbatana, but this passage only gives the idea of the writer that the
Medes would not be bought off by Babylonian money, and abandons the
destruction of Babylon for the sake of gold. Setting this aside, the
episodes quoted above show that at the time of Astyages men could

The account which Polybius gives of the structure
of the palace, the cedar and cypress wood of which
the door-posts, pillars, roofs, and panels in the walls
were made, shows that wood was employed in building in Media, which agrees with the habits of mountaineers. In Teheran and Ispahan buildings of wood
of this kind are still in use, and no doubt the
mountain forests of northern Media provided better
materials in ancient times than now. The noblest
trunks and best kinds of wood were sought out for
the royal house. The kings of Asshur, and Nebuchadnezzar tell us in their inscriptions that they have
caused trees to be cut down on this or that mountain
for their buildings. The wooden palace, which Deioces,
and perhaps Phraortes, first erected, must have been
extended by Cyaxares, and may have been furnished
by him or his successor with the brilliant ornamentation. The inner walls of the palace of the Achæmenids
at Persepolis, if we may draw this conclusion from
the metal supports which are found in the remains of
the stone walls, were decorated in a similar manner.
When the palace of the Median kings at Ecbatana
had become the summer residence and treasure-house
of the Persian monarchs, it would, no doubt, be
enriched and adorned yet more. The temple of
Anahita, connected with the palace, which Polybius
has described above, is the work of Artaxerxes II.
Alexander caused the spoil he had taken in Babylon,
Susa, Persepolis, and Pasargadæ, to be brought to
Ecbatana, where he is said to have collected 180,000

regret the loss of ancient simplicity in Media, and extol it against the
gold which had come from Nineveh to Ecbatana, and against the gold
of Babylon (p. 301). The nation may also have remained in simple
habits of life however brilliant the royal citadel may have been. Yet
it has already been observed in the text that at the time of Cyaxares
and Astyages the upper classes lived in wealth and comfort.

talents in gold and silver.[1] At a later time, the
Arsacids are said to have resided at Ecbatana during
the summer like the Achæmenids.[2] At the present
day, Hamadan, which is built high up on a slope of
Elvend, marks the site of the ancient Ecbatana. It
contains about 40,000 inhabitants; the ruins of the
ancient city have not yet been satisfactorily explored.
The slender pillars with lotus-like capitals, discovered
here, are like the pillars of Persepolis, and therefore
might be the work of the Achæmenids; what has
been discovered in engraved stones and coins comes
from the time of the Arsacids and Sassanids. Some
cylinders covered with cuneiform inscriptions have
not yet been examined.

Cyaxares had rescued Media from the most extreme
peril. The consequences of the defeat, in which his
father, with the greatest part of his army, fell before
the Assyrians, had been averted. Though subsequently overpowered by the Scythians, he yet became
once more sovereign in his own country. This rise
of Media, and the weakening of the Assyrian kingdom
by the inundation of the Scythians, he used in order
to subjugate Armenia and Cappadocia. And though
he was not able to achieve anything decisive against
the Lydians, he attained a greater success; in combination with Babylonia he avenged on the Assyrians
the supremacy they had exercised over Media; he
overthrew the remnant of that kingdom, whose tough
vigour showed itself even at the final hour in an
obstinate resistance. It was a great achievement and
at the same time an important extension of the
Median dominions, not merely by the whole extent
of the Assyrian country on the left bank of the Tigris,

[1] Diod. 17, 66, 71; 19, 48; Strabo, p. 731; Plut. "Alex." 72.
[2] Strabo, p. 523.

which fell to Media, but also by the closer connection which Cyaxares thus obtained with Armenia and Cappadocia, the subject lands to the west. Then followed the spread of the Median power over the kindred nations in the north and east of Iran. The Persians were already subjected to Phraortes, and Cyaxares brought under his sovereignty the Sagartians, Hyrcanians, Parthians, and Bactrians; he made the Sacæ dependant on him, and in the east perhaps extended his power as far as the Indus. From his proud citadel at Ecbatana he ruled from the Halys to the Oxus. It was a powerful empire. Herodotus depicts the reign of Cyaxares when he says: " He was far more powerful than his predecessors." With the Medes he passes as the founder of their sovereignty; and his reign must have been held in grateful remembrance, not by the Medes only, but also by the subject nations. Those who afterwards attempted to bring the Medes and Sagartians under arms against the dominion of the Persians, called themselves the descendants of Cyaxares—and one even laid aside his own name, Phraortes, to do so.

After the fall of Assyria the leading portion passed to Media, Babylonia, and Lydia. As the two first had united for the overthrow of Assyria, and had come to terms with Lydia for this object, so in other respects they displayed a friendly feeling towards each other. The daughter of Cyaxares became the consort of Nebuchadnezzar of Babylon, and the daughter of Alyattes, king of Lydia, was married to his son Astyages. Afterwards, Babylon prevented the attempt of Egypt to unite Syria with the land of the Nile; it was eagerly occupied with subjugating Mesopotamia and Syria, while Lydia established its power over the tribes and cities of Asia Minor as far as the

Halys. Neither Media nor Lydia thought of putting any hindrances in the way of the extension of the Babylonian dominion over Syria and Phœnicia. Of these three kingdoms, thus connected by mutual alliances, Media was the strongest. Babylonia and Lydia were not equal either in extent of country or amount of population; Lydia was perhaps inferior in the vigour of the ruling tribe, and Babylonia certainly inferior in the military strength of the population. Even when united they did not reach the size or strength of the Median power, whose army Cyaxares had arranged, and for which he had provided at Ecbatana a strongly fortified centre, equidistant from the Halys and the Oxus. When Astyages ascended the throne, on the death of his father in 593 B.C., he entered upon the inheritance of a secure dominion in peaceful and friendly relations to all the neighbouring powers. While his father-in-law, Alyattes of Lydia, and his son Croesus were occupied in subjugating the Carians and the Greek cities on the west coast of Anatolia (III. 439), and Nebuchadnezzar carried on one campaign after another in order to incorporate in his kingdom the great trading marts of the Syrian coasts, Astyages could enjoy, for more than thirty years, the fruits of the efforts by which his father had founded and established the Median empire.

CHAPTER III.

THE TRIBES OF THE PERSIANS.

THE oldest subjects in the Median kingdom were the
Persians. Their country lay in the south-west corner
of the table-land of Iran. The heights of the Zagrus,
which run down to the sea in a south-easterly direction, divide it from the ancient kingdom of Elam,
and the land of the Tigris, just as in the north they
divide the land of the Medes from the valley of the
two rivers. The Eastern border of the Persian
territory was formed, almost down to the coast, by
the great desert, which fills the centre of Iran; the
northern boundary towards the land of the Medes
is marked by the range which the Greeks call Para-
choatras; the name would be *Kuruhvathra, i. e.* very
brilliant, in Old Persian. The southern boundary of
Persia was the sea. Nearchus, who sailed along the
coast of Persia, gives it an extent of 4400 stades, *i. e*
550 miles; their land began at the mouth of the
Oroatis (Old Persian, *Aurvaiti, i. e.* the swift),[1] the
Tsab, which falls into the Persian Gulf below the
modern Hindian, and reached to the east almost as
far as the entrance into this gulf, where it ended
opposite the island of Coloë (Kishm).[2] Euripides

---

[1] Burnouf, "Commentaire sur le Yaçna," p. 251.

[2] Arrian, "Ind." 38—40; Strabo, p. 727, 728, 738; Plin. "H.
N." 6, 26; cf. Ptol. 6, 4, 1.

contrasts the sun-lit mountain flats of Persia with the wintry land of Media and the citadels of Bactria.[1] According to Strabo the coast of Persia was hot and sandy, and, with the exception of some palms, produced no fruit. But beyond the coast was a land of very great fertility, abounding in lakes and rivers, and providing the most excellent pasture. Further to the north, the Persian land became cold and mountainous, and supported nothing but droves of camels and their keepers. Arrian tells us that to the north of the coast of Persia the air was temperate, and the land traversed by the clearest streams, in addition to which there were also lakes; the meadows were grassy and well watered, and provided excellent pastures for horses and other beasts of draught. The soil produced all kinds of fruits and even wine, but not olives. The forests were extensive and rich in game, and all kinds of water-fowl were to be found there. But further to the north the land of the Persians was wintry and full of snow.[2] What the Greeks relate of the desolation of the Persian coast is still applicable; it consists of naked sand-flats, broken only by scanty groves of palms. Above this coast the soil rises in terraces, which are separated from each other by yet higher ranges. Further to the north the slopes of the mountains provide excellent pastures, till the ground becomes more bare as we approach Media, while on the east it gradually passes into the great desert of the centre. On the mountain terraces and in the depressions between them are some favoured lands and valleys. The warmth of the southern situation is tempered by the elevation of the soil and the winds blowing from the sea. This happy climate allows a perpetual spring to reign, and increases the fertility which the

1 "Bacch." 14—16.   2 Arrian, "Ind." 40.

abundant mountain springs produce in such a degree
that groves of orchard trees, cypresses, and myrtles
alternate with vineyards and carpets of flowers. The
beauty of Persia and the fertility of the vegetation is
concentrated in the valleys of Kazerun, Shiras, and
Merdasht, which lie in stages one above the other,
between mountain walls which rise to a height of
8000 feet. The most extensive and at the same time
the highest valley is that of Merdasht. It is traversed
by the Murghab, which brings an abundant supply
of water from the snow-covered heights in the north-
west. The upper course is surrounded by steep cones,
and jagged walls of rock ; in the lower part it takes
another name, and is called the Pulwar. Further
down, it unites with the Kum-i-Firuz (the Araxes
of the Greeks), and from this confluence down to the
mouth in the great lake of Bakhtegan it is known
as the Bendemir. The Greeks called the Pulwar the
Medus, and the Bendemir, which is also known as
the Kur in modern times, they named the Cyrus.[1]

According to Herodotus the Persians regarded their
land as of moderate extent, poorly equipped, and
filled with rocks. In the Books of the Laws which
are ascribed to Plato, we are told that the Persian
land is naturally adapted to produce strong shepherds,
and as they had to watch their flocks night and day,
they were thus in a position to do good service in war.
As a fact Persia is a mountainous country ; the slopes
are admirably fitted for cattle breeding, but there is
little room or encouragement for agriculture. According to Xenophon's description, the Persians in ancient
times were much occupied in the chase, and in riding ;
they only ate once in the day, and at their banquets
goblets might indeed be seen, but no pitchers of wine.

[1] Spiegel, " Eran," 2, 260.

Strabo remarks, with reference to a later period, that the Persian youth remained long in the open air with their flocks, and were eager hunters; when thus engaged, their only drink was water, their food bread, flesh, and salt. The Greeks with one consent describe the Persians of ancient times as simple, hardy, self-controlled men, of great endurance and martial vigour, with few requirements. They were also called "Eaters of Terebinths," in order to mark the scantiness of their food : their drink was water; and their clothing, coats as well as trousers, were of leather.[1]

The nation of the Persians consisted of various tribes. Herodotus gives a special prominence to three, on which the rest were dependent. These were the Pasargadae, the Maraphians, and the Maspians. "Other tribes are the Panthialaei, the Derrusiaei, the Germanii, all of which are agricultural; while the remainder, the Dai, Mardi, Dropici, and Sagartii are Nomads,"[2] According to this statement six of the Persian tribes carried on agriculture, and four were pastoral. But the Germanians and Sagartians were distinguished from the tribes of the Persians in the narrower sense. The Sagartians (Açagarta) are spoken of in the inscriptions of Darius, and by Herodotus himself in other passages, as a separate nation; we have already found their country on the western edge of the great desert, and observed its character (p. 6). The Germanians of Herodotus are the Carmanians of the later Greeks, who also passed with them as a separate nation, though closely allied to the Persians and Medes.[3] They wandered to and fro to the east of Persia in

---

[1] Herod. 9, 122, 1, 171 ; Nicol. Damasc. fragm. 66, ed. Müller; Xenophon, " Cyri instit." 6, 2, 22 ; 8, 8, 5—12 ; Plato, " Legg." p. 695 ; Strabo, p. 734.

[2] Herod. 1, 125.   [3] Strabo, p. 727.

the district now called Kirman. The number of the tribes mentioned by Herodotus would therefore have to be reduced to the Pasargadae, Maraphians, Maspians, Panthialaeans, Derusiaeans, Dai, Mardi, and Dropici, if we did not hear of two others in the inscriptions of Darius, the Yutiyas and the Patisuvaris, whose names were known to the later Greeks in the form Utei and Pateischorei. These later authorities tell us also of other Persian tribes : Kyrtians, Rhapaesans, Stobaeans, Suzaeans, etc. They also reckon the Paraetaci, or Paraetaceni, among the Persians.[1] The Mardians of Herodotus are also called Amardians by later writers, who place them in the West, among the mountains which divide Persia from Elam.[2] With regard to the position of the rest of the tribes, we can only ascertain that the Pasargadae occupied the best part of the Persian land—the valley of the Pulwar ; that the Maraphians[3] and the Maspians were their neighbours, and the land of the Pateischorei followed next after that of the Pasargadae on the eastern side, towards Carmania. Besides these three chief tribes, the Pasargadae, Maraphians, and Maspians, the Persian nation, according to these statements, was made up of a considerable number of more or less powerful tribes, of whom each one, like the chief tribes themselves, must have had a separate territory, or, at any rate, a pasture for its flocks.

If the name Parsua could signify Persians, the inscriptions of the kings of Asshur would confirm the division of the Persians into several tribes. Shalmanesar II. tells us, that in the year 833 B.C. he received tribute from the heads of the Parsuas, as the

---

[1] Above, p. 270. Strabo, p. 728, 730 ; Ptol. 6, 4.

[2] Arrian, "Ind." 40 ; Strabo, p. 727.

[3] Aeschylus speaks of a Maraphis among the kings of the Persians, "Pers." 778.

inscription says : from twenty-seven princes of the
Parsuas.   Afterwards Tiglath Pilesar II. traversed the
land of the Parsuas and imposed tribute upon them
(744 B.C.).[1]   The books of the Hebrews confirm
Esarhaddon's dominion over Persia, inasmuch as they
tell us that he settled Persians and Dai (Dahas) in
Samaria (III. 154).

It must have been in the period of the supremacy
of Assyria, at the latest in the first half of the seventh
century B.C., that the worship of the gods, which the
Persians shared from all antiquity with their fellow-
tribesmen on the table-land of Iran, the worship of
Mithra, Vayu, Anahita, and fire, underwent the change
which bears the name of Zarathrustra.   As we saw
good reason to assume, the new doctrine first came to
the Medes from the North-East; from the Medes it
passed, without doubt, to the Persians.   If Herodotus
places the Magians, or special priestly order, among
the tribes of the Medes and not among those of the
Persians, among whom Strabo is the first to mention
them, the conclusion is, as has been sufficiently
proved, not that the Persians were without priests
before and after the reform, but rather that even after
the reform the priestly families remained in their
natural unions, and did not form themselves into a
special tribe (p. 192).

The supremacy of Assyria over the West of Iran
came to an end when Phraortes united the tribes of
the Medes under his leadership, and, towards the year
640 B.C., undertook to maintain the independence of
Media against Assurbanipal, the successor of Esarhaddon.   In this struggle the Persians joined the
Medes and ranged themselves under them.   Herodotus,
who obviously follows the tradition of the Medes, re-

[1] Above, p. 282.

presents Phraortes as marching against the Persians, conquering and subjugating them; according to the Persian account, which is preserved in Ctesias, the chief of the Medes induced the Persians to revolt against the Assyrians, and to join him, by the promise that they should remain free under his leadership (III. 250). The situation of affairs agrees better with the second version than with the first. Considering the enormous power which Assyria under Assurbanipal possessed down to the middle of the seventh century, it is hardly probable that Phraortes would have inaugurated the recent independence of Media by an attack on the Persians, which might, and indeed must, drive them into the arms of the Assyrians. It is far more probable that the two nations formed a league against Assyria. As already observed, the annihilation of the kingdom of Elam, which Assurbanipal accomplished in the year 645 B.C., would supply the Persians with a strong incentive to unite themselves with the kindred and more powerful nation of the Medes.

Of the three tribes of the Pasargadae, Maraphians, and Maspians, the most prominent—so Herodotus tells us—are the Pasargadae.[1] To them belongs the race of the Achæmenids, from which sprang the Persian kings. In the inscription of Behistun, King Darius says: "From old time we were kings; eight of my family have been kings (Kshayathiya), I am the ninth; from very ancient times we have been kings."[2]

---

[1] The place has the same name as the tribe; Pasargadae cannot in any case mean "Persian camp," as Anaximenes maintains in Stephanus. Oppert believes that he has discovered in the Pisiyauvada of the inscription of Behistun the original form of the name Pasargadae, which is the Greek form of the Persian word. Pisiyauvada (*paisi gauvada*) means "valley of springs;" "Peuple des Medes," p. 110.

[2] So Rawlinson and Spiegel. E. Schrader translates III. of the Babylonian version: "From old from the fathers we were kings."

He enumerates his ancestors: "My father was Vistaçpa, the father of Vistaçpa was Arsama, the father
of Arsama was Ariyaramna, the father of Ariyaramna
was Khaispis, the father of Khaispis was Hakhamanis;
hence we are called Hakhamanisiya (Achæmenids)."
In these words Darius gives the tree of his own family
up to Khaispis; this was the younger branch of the
Achæmenids. Teispes, the son of Achæmenes, had
two sons; the elder was Cambyses (Kambujiya), the
younger Ariamnes; the son of Cambyses was Cyrus
(Kurus), the son of Cyrus was Cambyses II.[1] Hence
Darius could indeed maintain, that eight princes of
his family had preceded him; but it was not correct
to maintain that they had been kings before him,
and that he was the ninth king.[2]

Abntav appears as a fact to leave no doubt about this sense. Oppert
now translates *duvitataranam* (IV. of the Persian text) by twice,
i. e. in two epochs we were kings: "Rec. of the Past," 7, 88; but his
previous translation, "in two tribes" (*i. e.* in the older and younger
line), we were kings, exactly corresponds to the facts.

[1] The list of the Achæmenids, which we obtain from a comparison
of Herodotus (6, 11), and the inscription of Behistun 1, 3—8, is as
follows:

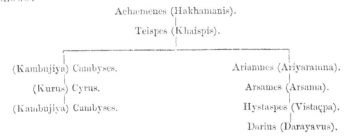

Achæmenes (Hakhamanis).

Teispes (Khaispis).

(Kambujiya) Cambyses.   Ariamnes (Ariyaramna).

(Kurus) Cyrus.   Arsames (Arsama).

(Kambujiya) Cambyses.   Hystaspes (Vistaçpa).

Darius (Darayavus).

[2] If Darius calls himself the ninth Achæmenid, Xerxes also in
Herodotus enumerates nine Achæmenids as his predecessors, in which
enumeration, it is true, Cambyses occurs but once, while Teispes is
twice mentioned, once as the ancestor of the older line, and then as
the ancestor of the younger. On a broken cylinder which has just
been brought from Babylon by Rassam, the genealogy of Cyrus is said
to be given thus: Achæmenes, Teispes, Cyrus, Cambyses, Cyrus,— so
the journals tell us. In this the older line has one member more as

In this series of the ancestors of Darius we find names belonging not only to the East of Iran, but also to the Arians of India. The name Cambyses (Kambujiya) points to the Cambojas, a nation which we found in the north-west of India (IV. 249); the name Cyrus (Kurus) to the ancestors of the ancient princely race who founded the first great empire in the land of the Ganges on the upper course of the river, whose contest with and overthrow by the Pandus is celebrated by the Indian epic, while the name Vistaçpa repeats the name of the King of Bactria, whom the prayers of the Avesta extol as the protector of Zarathrustra (p. 132). Of Achæmenes we are told that an eagle nourished him;[1] a prophet of the Hebrews calls Cyrus "the eagle;" we know the importance which the Avesta ascribes to the two eagles of the sky, and the modern Persian epic to Simurgh; and we have seen that the standard of the Achæmenids was an eagle (p. 173). Hence from this notice we may with certainty conclude that the tradition of the Persians ascribed to this ancestor of their kings a youth distinguished by the favour of heaven.

As Cambyses the father of Cyrus is a contemporary of Astyages of Media, Teispes the father of Cambyses must be reckoned a contemporary of Cyaxares, and Achæmenes, the father of Teispes, as a contemporary of Phraortes.[2] We must therefore assume either that Achæmenes was at the head of the Persians, at the time when they joined Media, or that he was

against the younger. Till the cylinder is published we must keep to the inscription of Behistun and Herodotus.

[1] Aelian, "Hist. Anim." 12, 21.

[2] Cyrus is said to have been forty years old in 558 B.C., so that he must have been born in 598 B.C., from which it follows that his father Cambyses was born in 620 at the latest. Astyages was married in 610, and must therefore have been born about 630 B.C.

established by Phraortes as the chief of Persia and
his vassal-king, and that his throne passed with the
duties of vassalage to his descendants Teispes and
Cambyses. It is not very probable that the traditions
of the Persians should have accorded signs of divine
favour to the youth of a man, who had been placed
over them after their subjugation as viceroy of Media.
Moreover, we find among the Persians, according to
this tradition, a form of constitution, such as a Median
viceroy would hardly have established, even for
the object of overthrowing the Median power. The
race of the Achæmenids belonged to the tribe of
the Pasargadae; we may therefore assume that
Achæmenes was the first to become chief of this tribe.

Aeschylus enumerates the seven men who stand at
the side of the king of the Persians.[1] Josephus says
that the "seven houses" of the Persians had named
Darius as king. As a fact we see that when Darius,
after the extinction of the older line of the descendants of Achæmenes, sets himself to ascend the throne,
six men stand at his side, whom Herodotus distinguishes as the "first of the Persians." The Laws
ascribed to Plato say that the empire was then
divided into seven parts between Darius and the Six,
and that a relic of this division was still in existence.[2]
In regard to the privileges of the Six and their
descendants we find that they consisted in the right
of free access to the king, and that the king could
choose his chief wife only from their families;[3] the
descendants of the Six had also the right to wear the
head-dress of the king, the upright *kidaris*, which was
the symbol of royal dignity. In the kingdom of the

---

[1] "Persae," 956—960.

[2] Joseph. "Antiq." 11, 2; Herod. 3, 77; Plat. "Legg." p. 695.

[3] Herod. 3, 84.

Sassanids, we find seven hereditary princes under the king; these princes, like the king, wear crowns, but their crowns are lower than that of the king; the "sons of the houses," *i. e.* the members of these seven families, form the highest rank of the nobility. Hence in these six chieftains of the Persians standing at the side of and beneath the seventh, who is the prince of the Pasargadae, we may suppose that we have the princes of the remaining tribes.[1] And in respect of the privileges

[1] This highest rank of nobility is called *waspur* in Pehlevi, and *bar bithan* is Aramaic. The book of Esther mentions the seven princes of the Persians and Medes, "who may behold the countenance of the king and have the first place in the kingdom," i. 14. The names of the six who aided Darius in slaying Gaumata, as given in Herodotus, agree with the inscription of Behistun, with the exception of one name. Herodotus gives Aspathines for the Ardumanis of Darius. The list of Ctesias is wholly different. If we examine them more closely we find that Ctesias has given the names of the sons of the comrades of Darius for the comrades themselves. Instead of Gobryas he puts Mardonius the son of Gobryas, instead of Otanes Anaphes (so we must read the name Onophes); Anaphes, according to Herod. 7, 62, is the son of Otanes. The name Hydarnes agrees with the inscription and with Herodotus, but the son of Hydarnes had the same name as his father (Herod. 7, 83, 211). The Barisses of Ctesias must be the eldest son of Intaphernes whom Darius allowed to live; he was called after his grandfather, Vayaçpara, as was often the case with the Persians. The Ariarathes, who afterwards governed Cappadocia, claimed to have sprung from Anaphes, whom Darius made satrap or king of Cappadocia. Anaphes was succeeded by a son of the same name; after him came Datames, Ariamnes, Ariarathes I., who governed Cappadocia at the time of Artaxerxes Ochus; his son Ariathes II. crucified Perdiccas in the year 322 B.C. when he had conquered him, though an old man of 82 years; Droysen, "Hellenismus," 2², 95. The Norondobates in Ctesias I cannot explain, unless we ought to read Rhodobates. Mithridates, who in Xenophon's time had been governor of Lycaonia from about 420 B.C., is called a son of Rhodobates (Diog. Laert. 3, 25), and his father and grandfather are said to have been viceroys of Pontus. The ancestor would be one of the seven, to whom the kingdom of Pontus was given for his services; Polyb. 5, 43. Mithridates Eupator calls himself the sixteenth after Darius; Appian, "Bell. Mith." c. 112; cf. Justin, 38, 7. These quotations will be sufficient to show that the rank of the six tribal princes of the Persians, like that of the chief princes, was originally hereditary, as the governorships left to their descendants outside Persia must have remained in their families.

of the six co-chieftains in the kingdom of the Achæmenids we may assume that they originally occupied
a position close to the king, and formed the council
and court of the chief tribal prince. These privileges
the Greeks ascribe to the services which the Six
rendered at the time when Darius ascended the
throne. But as the seven houses existed before, and
the Six had previously been "the first of the Persians,"
their privileged position must have been of an older
date ; it must have been introduced by Cyrus or be
of even more remote origin. It is not probable that
such a mighty warrior prince as Cyrus would, after
the reduction of the Medes, impose limitations on his
power by sharing the symbols of royalty and hereditary privileges. According to the narrative of Herodotus, Cyrus does not simply command the Persians
to take up arms against the Medes, but he assembles
the tribes, and ascertains their feeling. In considering the peculiar position of these six families we may
certainly assume, that under the ancestors of Cyrus
there were chiefs among the Persians with whom
the Achæmenids had to deal. If the Achæmenids
were the heads of the tribe of the Pasargadae, the
other tribes would have chiefs also. Yet we only
hear of "six princes" besides the Achæmenids,
though we have seen that the number of the Persian
tribes was considerably more than seven.

Following the indications thus given, we may
sketch the course of events as follows. When
Achæmenes had acquired the headship of the tribe
of the Pasargadae, he must have combined the two
neighbouring tribes, the Maraphians and Maspians,
whom Herodotus classes with the Pasargadae as the
most important among the Persians, into closer
union, perhaps by some understanding with the

chiefs. Supported by these three tribes, who possessed
the favoured regions of Kazerun, Shiras, and Merdasht, Achæmenes must then have subjugated the
remainder to his power. Herodotus told us above
that the remaining tribes depended on the three
mentioned. They must, therefore, have been combined into larger groups, and in fact into four
communities. To the chiefs who became the heads
of these new combinations, a position must have been
accorded similar to that enjoyed by the Maraphians
and Maspians beside Achæmenes—above all, the right
to bequeath the chieftainship to their descendants.
When the chiefs of the Persians, now seven in number,
mutually guaranteed to each other their position,
the foundation was laid of a community of interests,
and thus of a community of the Persian nation.
That the princes of the four new combinations of
tribes belonged to those tribes, and not to the three
first, is proved by the inscription of Darius at Naksh-
i-Rustem, where one of the princes of the date of
Darius is called a Pateischorean. In some such way
as this Achæmenes may have brought about the
union of the Persian tribes, and at the same time
have obtained the leadership of them. His position
thus rested essentially on the relation of the prince
of the Pasargadae to the other six tribal princes, a
relation of which we find no trace in the Medes.
That the number seven was normal for the combinations of the tribes we may ascribe to the influence
of the recently-introduced doctrine of Zarathrustra,
of which we found echoes in the legend of Achæmenes.

Achæmenes and his race after him must have had
their dwelling in the canton of the tribe to which
they belonged, at the place of assembly of the Pasargadae, the chief town, which bore the name of the

tribe. Supported by this tribe, Achæmenes succeeded
in uniting the people; on it and the neighbouring
Marapheans and Maspians depended the importance
of the Achæmenids. Strabo calls Pasargadae the
ancient seat, and with Persepolis the patriarchal
abode of the Persian kings,[1] and here, on ascending
the throne, they were consecrated. Here Cyrus deposited his treasures; here he found his last resting-
place. We must look for this place in "Hollow
Persia," as the Greeks call it, on the plain of Merdasht,
to the east of the later Istakhr, the city of the Sassanids, below the confluence of the Medus and Cyrus
(*i. e.* the Pulwar and Kum-i-Firuz) in the land of
the Bendemir.[2]

When Achæmenes had united the tribes of the
Persians by means of the new hereditary chieftain-
ships, and got into his hands the supreme power with

---

[1] p. 728, 729.

[2] Strabo, p. 729, puts Pasargadae on the Cyrus. Stephanus (Πασσαργάδαι) following Anaximenes of Lampsacus, represents Pasargadae as
first built by Cyrus; so Curt. 5, 11: Cyrus Pasargadum urbem con-
diderat. It cannot be doubted that Cyrus built there, and Alexander,
according to Arrian (3, 18), found there the treasures of Cyrus. Strabo
also tells us that Cyrus built the city and citadel, p. 730. From the
accounts of the march of Alexander from Persepolis to Pasargadae,
and from his return from the Indus to Pasargadae and Persepolis, it
is clear that Pasargadae lay to the east or south-east of Persepolis. If
Pasargadae is placed at Murghab, the only reason is the statement
that the grave of Cyrus was at Pasargadae, and this grave has been
identified with the pyramid of Murghab, in the immediate proximity
of which a relief exhibits the picture of Cyrus. But the portrait of
Cyrus there is very different from the portrait of Darius and his
successors on the tombs at Rachmed, and Naksh-i-Rustem; and the
building at Murghab may have served another purpose. According to
Pliny ("H. N." 6, 26, 29) we ought to look for Pasargadae to the
south of Lake Bakhtegan, near Fasa, or Darabgerd; flumen Sitioganus, quo Pasargadas septimo die navigatur. Sitioganus is the
modern Sitaragan. Ptolemy puts Pasargadae in the neighbourhood of
Caramania, and Oppert therefore identifies it with the ruins of Tell-i-
Zohak near Fasa, and looks for the mountain Paraga of the inscriptions in the modern Forg: "Journal Asiat." 1872, p. 549.

the co-operation of the six princes in council and jurisdiction, he joined the king of the Medes, who had also united the tribes of his people, soon after the year 645 B.C., as we were compelled to assume, for common defence against Assyria. Being weaker than the Median king, he ranged himself under his leadership and power, agreed to follow him in war, and accepted the position of his general and vassal. The relation must have been similar to that which Firdusi represents as existing between his kings and the princes of Sejestan (p. 252). In this combination the Persians shared the dangers of the war against king Assurbanipal, and the defeat of Phraortes, no less than the defeat of Cyaxares by the Scythians; on the other hand, they were the comrades of Cyaxares in his struggles against the Lydians, and in his victory over Assyria, while they took an active part in the annihilation of Nineveh. At the same time we may assume that this dependent position became more strongly marked as the power of Media increased, and we may believe Herodotus that their soldiers joined in subjugating the other tribes of the table-land of Iran, and marched with the armies of the Medes to the wars which Cyaxares carried on in the East. The episode of Parsondes exhibits a Persian at the court, in the council, and in the army of the Median king; and the position of the Persians under the successors of Achæmenes, Teispes, and Cambyses, must have closely resembled the position of the other nations subject to the Median power. Cyaxares and his successor Astyages would have regarded Teispes and Cambyses merely as their viceroys over Persia, though they did not disturb the succession in the tribe of Achæmenes. If Darius still calls all his ancestors kings, and extends this title to his father, grandfather, and great-grand-

father, who were not viceroys, that is merely the
custom and view of the East; even under the great
king, the King of kings, a vassal is still a king.   The
hereditary viceroys of Persia under the Arsacids, one
and all, put the title "king" on their coins.   When
Papek, and Ardeshir after him, had taken their place,
they call themselves kings; Ardeshir, the founder of
the dominion of the Sassanids, designates himself as
"king," "king of the divine stock," even before he
has overthrown his own king, Artabanus, the Arsacid.
As the youth of Achæmenes is ennobled in the
older tradition, so later legends surrounded the life of
the progenitor of the Sassanids with premonitory
indications.

CHAPTER IV.

THE FALL OF THE MEDIAN KINGDOM.

" CYAXARES was succeeded by his son Astyages on
the throne of the Medes "—such is the narrative of
Herodotus—" and the latter had a daughter named
Mandane. Once he saw his daughter in a dream, and
water came from her in such quantities that all Asia
was inundated. This vision Astyages laid before the
interpreters of dreams, among the Magians, and their
interpretation alarmed him. To guard against the
event portended, he gave his daughter, who was
already of marriageable age, to none of the Medes
of suitable rank, but to a Persian of the name of
Cambyses, the son of Cyrus, who was of a good
family, but quiet in disposition ; he regarded him as
of less account than a Mede of the middle class.
Mandane had not been married a year when Astyages
had a second vision ; from his daughter's womb there
grew up a vine-tree which overshadowed all Asia.
This dream also he laid before the interpreters, and
caused his daughter, who was with child, to be brought
from the land of the Persians and be kept under
watch ; his intention was to kill the child, which, as
the Magians said, was destined to reign in his place.
When Mandane bore a son, Astyages sent for Harpagus,
a man akin to the royal household,[1] the most faithful

[1] Herod. 1, 98, 99.

of his servants, in whose care he trusted on all occasions, and bade him take Mandane's child to his house
and there kill it, and bury it, in whatever way he
chose. When the boy was given to him, dressed as if
for a funeral, Harpagus went in tears to his house,
told his wife the orders of Astyages, and declared that
he would not be the perpetrator of this murder even
though Astyages should lose his reason more utterly
than at present, and fall into worse madness : ' the
child is akin to me ; Astyages is old and without male
heirs, if the throne passes to the daughter, whose
child he is now putting to death by my hands,
I shall find myself in the greatest danger. Inasmuch as my present safety demands it the child must
die. But the murder must be done by one of the
people of Astyages, not by any one of mine.' Without delay he sent a messenger to one of the cowherds
of the king, Mithradates by name, whose pastures
lay on mountains to the north of Ecbatana, where
wild beasts are numerous. When the herdman came
he found the whole house of Harpagus filled with
lamentation, and saw a struggling and screaming
child adorned with gold and variegated robes, and
Harpagus said to him : ' Astyages commands you
to expose this child on the most desolate mountains, in order that it may die as quickly as possible.' The herdman believed that the child belonged
to one of the household of Harpagus, and took it, but
from the servant who accompanied him out of the
city he ascertained that it was the child of Mandane
and Cambyses. Returning to his hut, he found that
his wife Spako (the Medes call a dog Spako) had just
brought forth a dead child, and when she saw the well-
grown and beautiful child which her husband showed
her, she clasped his knees in tears, and entreated him

not to expose it, but to take away her dead child in
its place, and bring it up as her own son :[1] Thus doing
you will not be guilty of wrong towards your master ;
the dead child will receive a splendid funeral, and the
other will not lose his life. The herdman took his
wife's advice, and did as she bade him. He placed his
own dead child in the basket, put on him all the
ornaments of the other, and placed him on the wildest
mountain. Three days after he told Harpagus that
he was ready to show him the corpse of the child.
Harpagus sent the most trustworthy of his bodyguard,
and buried the herdman's child. But the herdman's
wife brought up the other child, and gave him some
other name than Cyrus, by which he was afterwards
called. When he was ten years old an incident
happened which caused him to be known. He was
playing with his comrades, in the village in which the
herdman lived, in the street, and his playfellows had
chosen him whom they considered the herdman's son
to be king. He assigned to every one his work, and
bade one build houses, and another to be a lance-
bearer ; one he made 'the king's eye,' and another
'the bearer of his messages.' Among the boys who
were playing with him was the son of Artembares, a
man of high rank in Media. This boy failed to do
what Cyrus ordered ; and Cyrus bade the others take
him, and whipped him severely. The boy hastened to
the city and complained to his father of the treatment
he had received from the son of the cowherd. His
father took him to the king and showed his son's
shoulders, and said: 'This insult we have received
from thy servant, the son of the cowherd.' Astyages
summoned Mithradates and his son. When Astyages

---

[1] Herod. 1, 112, πιστοτάτους τῶν δορυφόρων, while in the recapitula-
tion, 1, 117, we have πιστοτάτους τῶν εὐνούχων.

asked the latter how he dared so to insult the son of
a man in such high favour with the king as Artembares, the lad maintained that he was right in acting
as he did, but if he was to blame he was ready to
bear the penalty. Astyages was surprised by the
likeness of the boy to his own family, and the freedom
of his reply. After applying the torture to Mithradates, he soon discovered the truth. He was more
enraged at Harpagus than at Mithradates, but concealed his resentment. When Harpagus at his request
had acknowledged what he had done, Astyages said:
'The boy was alive, and all that had been done was
well. Let Harpagus send his own son to join the
new-comer, and also come himself to the banquet.' As
soon as the son of Harpagus, a boy of thirteen years,
was in the palace, Astyages caused him to be slain,
and the dismembered limbs were boiled and roasted,
while the head, hands, and feet, were put in a covered
basket. At the banquet Harpagus was served with
the flesh of his own son, while the other guests ate
the flesh of sheep. When Harpagus had eaten,
Astyages inquired whether he had enjoyed the meal,
and when he replied that he had enjoyed it greatly,
the servants of the king brought him the basket, bade
him uncover it and take what he would. Harpagus
controlled himself, and said that whatever the king
did was best. Then Astyages took counsel with the
Magians who had interpreted the dreams : they were
to consider everything, and give him the advice best
for himself and his house. The Magians declared that
they had it much at heart that the dominion of Astyages should continue ; for if the throne passed to the
boy who was a Persian, the Medes would be governed
by others, 'but if thou remainest king we are rulers in
our degree, and have great honour from thee.' But as

the boy had already been king in the game, the dream
was fulfilled; the king might send him back to Persia
to his parents. Astyages did so. When Cyrus came
to the house of Cambyses, his parents received him
with great joy, when they found who he was, since
they believed that he was already dead, and desired
to know how he had been preserved. He told them
that he had been supposed to be the son of the
cowherd, but on the way he had ascertained everything from the convoy which Astyages had sent with
him. He related how the wife of the herdman had
brought him up, and praised her much, and Spako
(the dog) was always on his lips. His parents seized
on the name in order that the preservation of the
boy might appear to be the work of the gods, and
laid the foundation for the legend that a dog had
suckled Cyrus when exposed."

"When Cyrus came to manhood and was the
bravest and best-beloved of his comrades, Harpagus
sought to win him by presents with a view to vengeance on Astyages, for he regarded the injury done to
Cyrus as no less than that done to himself. He
had already prepared his revenge. As Astyages was
severe towards the Medes, he had secretly persuaded
the chief men among them, one by one, that an end
must be put to the rule of Astyages, and that Cyrus
must be raised to the throne. When this was done
and all was ready, he wished to discover his views to
Cyrus, who was then in Persia. As the roads were
guarded, he invented the following stratagem : he
prepared a hare by cutting open the belly without
further injury to the skin, inserted a letter, and then
again closed the opening. This hare he gave with
some nets to the most faithful of his slaves, and sent
him, as though he were a hunter, to Persia, with a

command to take the hare to Cyrus, and at the same
time to tell him that he must open it himself and
let no one be present at the time.   Cyrus opened the
hare, and found written : ' Son of Cambyses, the gods
regard thee with favour, or thou hadst not attained to
such good fortune.   Avenge thy death on Astyages,
for dead thou art in his intention ; it is through the
gods and me that thou livest.   Long ago thou hast
learnt all that befell thee, and what I have suffered at
the hands of the king because I did not slay thee, but
gave thee to the cowherd.   If thou wilt follow my
counsel, thou shalt rule over all the land over which
Astyages was ruler.   Persuade the Persians to revolt,
and march against Media, and if I or any other chief
man among the Medes is appointed by Astyages to
lead the army against thee, all will be as thou wilt.
They will revolt from the king, and by passing over
to thee attempt to dethrone him.   All is ready here ;
act therefore, and act quickly.'

  " Cyrus considered in what way he could best
persuade the Persians to revolt, and when he discovered what he believed to be the best plan, he
wrote down his intentions in a letter and summoned
an assembly of the Persians.   In their presence he
opened the letter, and read out, that Astyages had
appointed him general of the Persians ; then he
added : ' I command that every one of you appear with
a sickle.'   And when they were all assembled, furnished
with sickles, Cyrus bade them clear a bushy tract of
land about twenty stades in length and breadth, and
make it fit for cultivation in a single day.   When
they had done this, he bade them assemble on the
next day ; every one was to come bathed.   Then he
caused all the goats, sheep, and oxen of his father to
be got together, slaughtered and dressed, and prepared

in addition wine and other excellent food, and entertained the whole of the Persians in a meadow; after
the meal he asked them which they preferred, the
entertainment of that day, or the work of the day
before? They replied that the difference was great:
yesterday they had nothing that was good, to-day
nothing that was bad. Cyrus took up this reply, and
discovered his aims, saying: 'O Persians, thus it is
with you. If ye will follow me, ye shall have these
blessings and many others, without any service; if
ye will not, ye will have troubles without number
like those of yesterday. Follow me, and ye will be
free. I believe that I was born by the favour of
heaven to take this work in hand, and I do not count
you as less than the Medes, in war or any other
service. Since this is so, revolt at once from Astyages.'
The Persians were quite ready to liberate themselves;
they only required a leader, and had long borne the
yoke of the Medes with dissatisfaction."

"When Astyages found what Cyrus had done, he
summoned him into his presence by a messenger.
Cyrus bade the messenger reply that he would come
before Astyages wished. Then the king armed all the
Medes, and, as though blinded by the gods, he named
Harpagus as general, entirely forgetting the injury he
had done to him. When the Medes and Persians
met, some of the Medes, who were not in the con-
spiracy fought, but the greater part made no resistance
and fled. Thus the Median army was shamefully
put to rout. But Astyages threatened Cyrus and
said, that even so he should not accomplish his
purpose. The interpreters of dreams among the
magicians who had advised him to let Cyrus go he
impaled, and then armed all who had remained in the
city, young and old, and led them out. He was

defeated, lost those whom he commanded, and was himself taken captive. Harpagus spoke harsh words to him, and asked how he liked slavery instead of monarchy with reference to that banquet. Astyages replied by asking, whether the insurrection was his own work or that of Cyrus. Harpagus answered that he had written the letter, and the insurrection was therefore his doing. Then Astyages said that he was the most foolish and unjust of men ; the most foolish because when he might have been king, if what had been done had been his doing, he had given up his power to another ; the most unjust because in revenge for that banquet he had brought the Medes into slavery ; if the throne must pass to another it would be more just that it should go to a Mede than a Persian, but now the innocent Medes were slaves instead of masters, and the Persians, who had previously been the servants of the Medes, were their masters. Thus Astyages lost the throne, after a reign of thirty-five years, and in consequence of his cruelty the Medes became subject to the Persians. Cyrus did no injury to Astyages, but kept him with him till his death."

In the Persian history of Ctesias the narrative of the fall of Astyages occupied more than one book. But we only know that it contradicted the story of Herodotus, that the daughter of Astyages was not called Mandane but Amytis, that she was married to the Median Spitamas, not to the Persian Cambyses, and that it was not the Median Harpagus but the Persian Oebares who was Cyrus' counsellor.[1] The loss of these books of Ctesias is compensated by a fragment of Nicolaus of Damascus, which seems to give the narrative in a compressed form. It is only

[1] Ctesias, " Fragm. Pers." 2, 5.

in a few unimportant points at the close that the
fragment differs from the excerpt of Ctesias which has
come down to us.

" Astyages," so we are told in Nicolaus, " was the
noblest king of the Medes after Arbaces.   In his reign
occurred the great revolution by which the dominion
passed from the Medes to the Persians ; and the cause
was as follows :—It was a law among the Medes that
a poor man who went to a rich man to gain a livelihood, and gave himself up to him, should be fed and
clothed and kept as a slave ; if the rich man did not
do his duty in this respect, the poor man might go on
to another.   In this way a boy named Cyrus, a Mardian
by birth, came to the servant of the king who was
placed over the sweepers of the palace.   He was the
son of Atradates, whose poverty forced him to live by
plunder, and Argoste his mother lived by keeping
goats.   He gave himself up to the servant for bread,
and assisted in cleaning the palace, and as he was
industrious the overseer gave him better clothing, and
brought him from among those who swept outside to
those who cleaned the interior, and put him under their
overseer.   This man was severe, and often whipped
Cyrus.   Cyrus left him, and went to the lighter of the
lamps, who showed him kindness, and brought him
nearer to the king by placing him among those who
bore the lights.   As Cyrus distinguished himself there
also, he came to Artembares, the chief butler, who
gave the king his wine.   He gladly received Cyrus,
and allowed him to wait on those who ate at the
king's table.   Ere long Astyages remarked how deftly
Cyrus waited, and with what a stately air he handed
the goblets, and asked Artembares whence the youth
came who waited so well.   ' O king,' he replied, ' he
is thy slave, a Persian by race, of the tribe of the

Mardians, who has given himself over to me in order to
gain a livelihood.' Artembares was old, and once,
when suffering from a fever, he entreated the king to
be allowed to remain at home till he was cured ; 'in
my place the youth, whom thou didst praise, will
hand the wine, and if he find favour in thy eyes as
cupbearer, then will I, a eunuch, adopt him as my
son.' Astyages consented, and Artembares gave much
advice to Cyrus, as if to his own son. Cyrus now
stood at the side of the king, and served him by
day and by night, and showed much good sense and
skill. And Astyages allowed him as the son of
Artembares to receive his income, and gave him many
gifts in addition, and Cyrus became great, and his
name was heard everywhere."

" Astyages had a very noble and beautiful daughter,
whom he gave to Spitamas the Mede, adding the
whole of Media as a dowry. Then Cyrus caused his
father and mother to come from the land of the
Medians, and they rejoiced at the greatness of their
son, and his mother told him the dream which she
had while he was yet an unborn child. She had
fallen asleep in the sanctuary when tending her goats,
and in her dream water flowed from her in such
quantities that it became a great stream, and inundated all Asia, and flowed down to the sea. When
the father heard this, he ordered the dream to be laid
before the Chaldæans in Babylon. Cyrus sent for the
most skilful of them and laid the dream before him.
He declared that the dream portended great good
fortune for Cyrus, and the highest place in Asia ;
Astyages was to know nothing of it, ' otherwise he
will put you to death in some shameful manner, and
me also,' the Babylonian said. They mutually swore
to impart to no one this great and unparalleled

vision. Cyrus afterwards came to yet greater honours, and made his father satrap of Persia, and his
mother one of the first among the women in Persia
in wealth and position."

"The Cadusians were at enmity with Astyages.
Their leader was Onaphernes, who was a traitor to his
people in the interests of Astyages, and he despatched
a messenger saying, that he must send a trusty person
with whom to confer about the surrender. Astyages
sent Cyrus to arrange everything with Onaphernes,
bidding him be back again in Ecbatana on the fortieth
day. The interpreter of dreams urged Cyrus to go to
the Cadusians, and filled him with confidence. Cyrus,
who was of a noble and ambitious nature, intended,
with the help of heaven, to bring the Persians to
revolt, to attempt the overthrow of Astyages, and
place confidence in the Babylonian, who was better
acquainted than others with the will of heaven. They
consulted with each other; the Babylonian told
Cyrus that it was destined that he should overthrow
Astyages and his dominion, he knew this for certain;
and Cyrus promised the Babylonian that if this turned
out to be true and he became king, he would make him
a great reward. Cyrus remembered how Arbaces had
previously overthrown Sardanapalus, and obtained his
dominion, and yet the Medes, by whom he was supported, were not stronger than the Persians. Arbaces
was not stronger than himself, and to him, as to
the other, his fortune had been foretold. With such
thoughts Cyrus passed the boundaries of the land of
the Cadusians. Here he was met by a man who had
been whipped, and carried dung in a basket. Cyrus
took this for a sign, and inquired of the Babylonian,
who told him to ask the man who he was and whence
he came. The man replied that he was a Persian of

the name of Oebares. Then Cyrus was greatly
pleased; for Oebares signifies one who brings good
news. And the Babylonian told Cyrus that the other
signs were most favourable — both that he was a
countryman of Cyrus, and that he was carrying horse-
dung, which portended dominion and power. Cyrus
without delay took the man with him."

"Then he came to Onaphernes, and when the
treachery had been arranged by mutual concessions,
he set out on the way back to Persia. He had given
Oebares a horse and Persian clothing, and being con-
vinced of his friendly disposition he often conversed
with him. Once he said : ' How hard it is to see the
Persians ill-treated by the Medes, and yet they are as
good as they!' 'O Cyrus,' replied the other, 'there
is no great-hearted, high-minded man, to put an
end to the dominion of the Medes over better men
than themselves.' 'Why should there not be such
a man?' asked Cyrus. 'Perhaps there is such an
one,' Oebares replied, 'but want of courage does not
allow him to do it, though he could.' Cyrus pushed
his questions further : 'If such a venturesome man
should appear, how might he accomplish his aim?'
'The first step,' Oebares answered, ' would be to unite
with the Cadusians, who would be willing to join him,
for they love the Persians, and hate the Medes; then
he must rouse the Persians, who are about 40,000 in
number, and arm them; their treatment by the Medes
will prepare them for this. Their land also is most
suitable, being full of mountains and rocks, and even
if the Medes should invade it, they will be driven
back with loss.' Then Cyrus asked: 'Suppose that
this man should appear, would you join in the danger
with him?' Oebares replied : 'Most readily. if you
were the man to take the matter in hand; your father

is the ruler of Persia, so that you have the best place of refuge, and are the strongest. If not you, who is it to be?' As Cyrus saw from this that Oebares was a cautious and brave man, who placed all his hopes in him, he revealed his plan and consulted him. Oebares encouraged him, and gave him good counsel to guide him. He urged Cyrus to send to his father Atradates and entreat him to arm the Persians, apparently to aid the king against the Cadusians, but in truth to revolt against Astyages; then he must ask Astyages for permission to visit Persia for some days, in order to offer the sacrifice which he had vowed for the safety of the king, and at the same time for his father who was sick. If he obtained his request he must set manfully to work; when a man ventures in a great enterprise it is no hardship to venture his life, and if need be to lose it, for this happens even to those who do nothing. Cyrus was pleased at the man's resolute frame of mind, and now told him his mother's dream and the interpretation of the Babylonian. Oebares then inflamed his spirit yet more, but cunning as he was, he bade him take care that the Babylonian did not tell the dream to the king—'if you will not permit his death, which would be the safest thing.' 'That be far from me,' said Cyrus. Filled with alarm that the Babylonian would betray the dream to Astyages, Oebares gave out that according to ancestral custom he would offer sacrifice to the goddess of the moon at night, and obtained of Cyrus all that he required for the purpose—incense, wine, and pillows— and arranged that Cyrus should take no part in the sacrifice. In his tent he dug a deep trench, put thick pillows over it, and invited the Babylonian to a banquet, and made him intoxicated. When he sank down on the pillows, he threw him into the trench,

and his servants with him. In the morning, Oebares
went quietly on with Cyrus, who soon inquired for
the Babylonian. Oebares acknowledged what he had
done; he could find no other way of escape for Cyrus
and his children. Cyrus was deeply distressed, and
even more angry, and would not see Oebares any more,
but at length he again placed his confidence in him."

"When Cyrus was again with Astyages, Oebares
reminded him of his advice. Cyrus followed it, sent
to Persia, and when he found that all was ready, asked
Astyages, under the pretext that Oebares had sug-
gested, for permission to go to Persia. The king would
not let him go. Then Cyrus betook himself to the
most trusty of the eunuchs; when a favourable
moment came, he was to obtain permission for the
journey to Persia. One day when Cyrus found the
king in the best of humours and cheered with wine,
he gave the eunuch a sign, and the latter said to the
king: 'Cyrus asks to perform the sacrifice, which
he has vowed for thee in Persia, that thou mightest
continue gracious to him, and for permission to visit
his sick father.' The king called for Cyrus, and with
a smile, gave him permission of absence for five
months; in the sixth month he was to return. Cyrus
bowed in gratitude before the king, appointed Tiridates as butler to the king during his absence, and
early on the next morning he set out to Persia."

"In vain had the wife of the slain Babylonian
waited for his return to Ecbatana; Oebares told her
that robbers had killed him. Then she became the
wife of the brother of her husband, and when she
heard that Cyrus had gone to Persia, she remembered
that her first husband had once confided to her the
dream of the mother of Cyrus, and its interpretation. She related this to her husband, who at once

went to Astyages, told him all, and added that Cyrus
had obviously gone to Persia with a view of pre-
paring for the execution of that which the dream had
portended. The king was seized with great anxiety,
and the Babylonian advised him to put Cyrus to death
as soon as he returned. Towards evening Astyages
caused his concubines to dance and play before him
while drinking wine. One of the players sang : ' The
lion has let the boar which he had in his power go
forth to the pasture. There he will become strong and
give great trouble to the lion, and at length he, the
weaker, will overcome the stronger.' Astyages applied
this song to himself and Cyrus, and on the spot sent
300 horsemen to bring him back ; if he would not
obey they were to cut off his head and bring that.
When the horsemen brought to Cyrus the commands
of Astyages, he answered cunningly, perhaps on the
advice of Oebares : ' Why should I not return as my
lord summons me ? To-day we will feast ; to-morrow
morning we will set out.' This met with their
approval. After the manner of the Persians, Cyrus
caused many oxen and other animals to be slain in
sacrifice, feasted the horsemen, and made them intoxicated ; at the same time he sent a message to his
father to send at once 1000 cavalry and 5000 foot-
soldiers to the city of Hyrba which lay on the way,
and to arm the rest of the Persians as quickly as
possible in such a way that it should seem to be done
by command of the king. His true aims he did
not communicate to him. In the night he and
Oebares took horse, just as they were, hastened to
Hyrba, armed the inhabitants, and drew out those
whom Atradates had sent in order for battle. When
the horsemen of Astyages had slept off their debauch
on the following morning, and found that Cyrus had

disappeared, they pursued him and came to Hyrba.
Here Cyrus first displayed his bravery, for with his
Persians he slew 250 of the horse of Astyages. The
remainder escaped, and brought the news to Astyages.
'Woe is me!' cried the king striking his thigh, 'that
I, well knowing that we should not do good to the
evil, have allowed myself to be carried away by clever
speeches, and have raised up this Mardian to be such
a mischief to me. Still, he shall not succeed.' He
called his generals and bade them assemble the army,
and led out against the Persians nearly 1,000,000
foot-soldiers, 200,000 horse, and 3000 chariots."

"Meanwhile the army under Atradates, who was
now fully instructed, was collected: 300,000 infantry,
50,000 horse, and 100 chariots. Cyrus encouraged
the Persians, and Oebares seized the passes of the
mountain and the heights, built lines, and brought
the people from the open cities into such as were
well fortified. Astyages burned down the abandoned
cities, summoned Atradates and Cyrus to submission,
and taunted them with their former beggary. Cyrus
replied that Astyages did not recognise the power of
the gods, which forced them, goat-herds as they were,
to accomplish what was destined to be done. As he
had done them kindness, they bade him lead back the
Medes, and give their freedom to the Persians who
were better than the Medes. Thus it came to a battle.
Astyages, surrounded by 20,000 of his body-guard,
looked on: among the Persians Atradates had the
right, and Oebares the left, wing; Cyrus, surrounded
by the bravest warriors, was in the centre. The Persians defended themselves bravely, and slew many of
the Medes, so that Astyages cried out on his throne:
'How bravely these "terebinth-eaters" fight!' But at
length the Persians were overpowered by numbers, and

driven into the city before which they fought. Cyrus
and Oebares advised to send the women and children
to Pasargadae, which is the loftiest mountain, and re-
new the battle on the next day : ' If we are defeated
we must all die, and if that must be so it is better to
fall in victory and for the freedom of our country.'
Then all were filled with hatred and anger against the
Medes, and when the morning came and the gates were
opened, all marched out ; Atradates alone remained
with the old men in the city to defend the walls. But
while Cyrus and Oebares were fighting in the field,
Astyages caused 100,000 men to go round and attack
the Persian army in the rear. The attack succeeded.
Atradates fell covered with wounds into the hands of
the Medes. Astyages said to him : ' An excellent
satrap are you ; is it thus that you thank me, you and
your son, for what I have done for you ? ' Atradates,
almost at the last gasp, replied : ' I know not, O king,
what deity has roused this frenzy in my son ; put me
not to the torture, I shall soon die.' Astyages had
compassion on him and said : ' I will not put you to
the torture ; I know that if your son had followed
your advice, he would not have done such things.'
Atradates died, and Astyages gave him an honourable
burial. Meanwhile Cyrus and Oebares after a brave
struggle had been compelled to retire to Pasargadae.
The mountain was very high and with steep sides, and
the way to it led through narrow passes, which were
here and there overtopped by high walls of rock.
Oebares defended the passes with 10,000 heavy-armed
men. As it was impossible to force a way through,
Astyages gave command that 100,000 men should go
round the mountain, and seek for a pass there and
climb the mountain. This movement compelled Cyrus
and Oebares to seek shelter during the night on a

lower hill for the army, together with the women and
children. Astyages followed quickly, and his army
was already between the two mountains, and bravely
attacked that held by the Persians, the approach to
which, lying through deep gorges, thick oak forests,
and wild olive trees, was very difficult. The Persians
fought still more bravely; in one place Cyrus dashed
forward, and in another Oebares, who urged them not
to let their wives, mothers, and old men be massacred
and tortured by the Medes. So they rushed down
with a cry, and when their javelins failed, they threw
down stones in great numbers. The Medes were
driven back, and Cyrus chanced to come to the house
in which he once lived with his father as a boy, when
he pastured goats. He kindled a fire of cypress and
laurel-wood, and offered the sacrifice of the man who
is distressed and in desperate circumstances. Then
followed thunder and lightning, and when Cyrus sank
down in prayer, birds of good omen settled on the
roof, as a sign that he would again reach Pasargadae.
So the Persians remained for the night on the
mountain, and when on the following morning the
Medes renewed the attack, they fought yet more
bravely, relying on the happy omens. But Astyages
placed 50,000 men at the foot of the mountain behind
those who were attacking, and bade them slay all who
came down. Thus pressed, the Medes fought more
zealously than on the previous day, and the Persians
retired to the top of the mountain on which were
their women and children. These ran to meet the
fugitives, and cried out to them, 'Cowards, whither
would ye fly, will ye creep back into the bosoms that
bore you?' Seized with shame, the Persians turned,
and in one onslaught drove the Medes down the
mountain, and slew sixty thousand of them."

" But Astyages did not retire from the siege of the mountain. Cyrus had still need of much cunning and bravery before he succeeded in defeating Astyages and taking the camp of the Medes. On that day, Cyrus went into the tent of Astyages, seated himself on his throne, and took the sceptre amid the acclamations of the Persians; and Oebares put the king's kidaris on his head with the words: 'Thou art more worthy to bear it; the gods give it to thee for thy virtue, and grant the Persians to rule over the Medes.' The treasures of Astyages, which the Persians found in the camp of the Medes, were brought to Pasargadae under the care of Oebares; but even those which they found in the tents of the other Medes were enormous. It was not long before the intelligence of the defeat and flight of Astyages spread abroad, and nations as well as individuals deserted him. First of all Artasyras, the chief of the Hyrcanians, came, with 50,000 men, and recognised Cyrus as king; afterwards came the chiefs of the Parthians, Sacæ, Bactrians, and other nations, each seeking to arrive before the other. Only a few faithful men remained with Astyages, and when Cyrus marched against him he was easily overcome. Then Cyrus gained possession of Ecbatana. There the daughter of Astyages and her husband Spitamas were taken captive with their two sons. But Astyages could not be found; Amytis and Spitamas had hidden him in the palace in the woodwork of the roof. Then Cyrus commanded that Amytis, her husband, and her children should be tortured that they might confess where Astyages was, but he came forward of his own will to prevent the torture. Spitamas was beheaded, because he had lied, and said that he did not know the hiding-place of Astyages; Amytis Cyrus took for his wife. He loosed from Astyages the heavy chains which Oebares had put upon him, honoured him as a father, and made him satrap of the Barcanians."[1]

According to Deinon, who wrote in the first half of the fourth century B. C., Cyrus was first governor of the staff-bearers of Astyages, and then of his body-guard. In a dream he had thrice seen the sun at his feet, and thrice stretched out his arms to grasp it, and the magicians had interpreted this dream to the effect that he would reign for thrice ten years. When Astyages had given Cyrus leave to go to Persia, and he had availed himself of it, the king sent for Angares, the most famous of the Median minstrels, in order to sing before him and his company at the banquet. After reciting the usual songs, Angares at last said : "The great beast of prey, more mighty than a wild boar, is let loose in the swamps ; when he is master of his land, he will with ease fight against many." And when Astyages asked, "What wild beast is this ?" Angares answered : "Cyrus the Persian." Then Astyages, regarding the suspicion as well-founded, sent to fetch Cyrus back, but failed to recover him.[2]

The narrative of Pompeius Trogus has been pre-served in excerpts only. Astyages had a daughter, but no male heirs. From her bosom, he saw, in a dream, a vine growing, of which the branches over-shadowed all Asia. The interpreters of dreams de-clared that this vision portended the greatness of the grandson whom his daughter would bring forth, but it also involved the loss of the empire to him. To be rid of this fear, Astyages had not given his daughter to any eminent man, nor even to a Mede

---

[1] Nicol. Damasc. fragm. 66 ; Ctes. "Fragm. Pers." 2, 5 ; Tzetz. "Chil." 1, 1, 82 ff.   [2] Athen, p. 633 ; Cic. "de Divin." 1, 23.

—that there might not be rank on the father's side
as well as on the mother's, to excite the ambition of
his grandson—but to Cambyses, a man of middle
station, in the then unknown nation of the Persians.
Even this did not remove the alarm of Astyages;
when his daughter was pregnant he sent for her in
order to have her child put to death before his
eyes. When a boy was born he gave him to Harpagus, his trusted friend, to be put to death. But
Harpagus, fearing that the daughter of Astyages if
she should come to the throne would avenge on him
the death of her son, gave the child to the herdman
of the king, and bade him expose it. The herdman
obeyed, but when his wife heard of the matter, she
urged her husband to fetch the child and show it to
her. Wearied by her entreaties, the herdman went
back into the forest, and there found a dog beside the
child, suckling it, and defending it from the beasts of
prey. He took it up and carried it to his fold, while
the dog followed in much distress. When the herdman's wife took it in her arms, the child smiled on
her as though it had known her, and it was so full
of life and sweet smiles that the woman induced her
husband to expose her own child in place of the
grandson of the king. After this the excerpt goes
on to relate, like Herodotus, the game of the boys,
the answer of Cyrus, the revenge of Astyages on
Harpagus, the letter in the hare's belly, in which
Harpagus imparts to Cyrus his plan for the desertion
of the Medes to the Persians. When Cyrus had
received and read this letter in Persepolis, a dream
also urged the enterprise upon him, but at the same
time bade him take as his associate the man whom
he met first on the following day. Next day, before
dawn, Cyrus went on a journey, and met a slave of

the name of Oebares, belonging to the house of a
Mede.   When Cyrus found that he was a Persian by
birth, he took his chains off and turned back with him
to Persepolis.   Cyrus then assembled the Persians.
On the first day he made them cut down a wood on
the way, and on the second he entertained them.
Astyages sends Harpagus against them, and he
passes over to their side with the army entrusted to
him.   Astyages now marches out in person, after sum-
moning all his forces, against Persia.   The struggle
was severe.   Astyages placed a portion of his army
in the rear of his forces, and told the latter that they
must try whether they could not break through the
ranks of the enemy in battle more easily than through
the ranks behind them in flight.   The Medes attacked
with great spirit; the Persians were forced back to
their wives and children, by whom they were again
driven into the battle with the cry: Would they fly
for refuge into the bosoms of their mothers and wives?
They put the Medes to flight.   Here the excerpt of
Justin breaks off, though he represents Astyages as
having been taken prisoner in this battle after the
rout.   Cyrus merely took the government from him;
he treated him as his grandfather, and made him
satrap of the Hyrcanians; Oebares he made ruler of
Persia, and gave him his sister in marriage.[1]

Polyaenus repeats the narrative of Herodotus about
the manner in which Cyrus induced the Persians to
revolt.   Then followed a war between the Medes and
Persians, and Cyrus was three times defeated.   As the
women and children of the Persians were at Pasargadae, Cyrus was compelled to risk another battle in the
neighbourhood of this place.   The Persians were again
put to flight; Oebares was retreating when the women

[1] Justin, 1, 4—7 ; cf. 44, 4.

met the fugitives, with the cry already quoted. The
Persians halted; and as the Medes were pursuing
without order, the Persians gained such a victory that
no further battle was needed to decide the question of
the throne.[1] Anaximenes of Lampsacus also relates
that Cyrus had built Pasargadae at the place where
he had overcome Astyages in battle. Strabo tells us:
"Cyrus held Pasargadae in honour, for it was there
that he conquered Astyages in the final battle, and
became ruler of all Asia in his place, and he built
a city and a palace in remembrance of the victory."[2]
Plutarch tells us: When Cyrus revolted from Astyages
and the Medes he was three times conquered in battle,
and when the Persians fled into the city, the enemy
had almost succeeded in forcing an entrance with them,
when the women came out to meet them. The cry of
the women brought about a change in the battle, and
for this reason Cyrus made a law that as often as the
king came into the city of Pasargadae, every woman
should receive a piece of gold. Ochus marched past
the city to evade the law; but Alexander twice
entered Pasargadae, and gave double to all the women
that were with child.[3] In all these narratives the
land of the Persians is the scene of the decisive
conflict.

Only a few short fragments remain of the account

---

[1] Polyæn. "Strat." 7, 6; 7, 45. But he also explains the change of
fortune at Pasargadae in another way. When Cyrus fled to that place
after his retreat, and many Persians deserted to the Medes, he spread
abroad a report that on the following day 100,000 enemies of the
Medes (Cadusians?) would come to his assistance; every man was to
prepare a bundle of faggots for the allies. The deserter told this to
the Medes, and when Cyrus in the night caused all the bundles to be
lighted, the Medes, thinking that the Persians had received substantial
assistance, deserted.

[2] Strabo, p. 727, 730. Steph. Byzant. Πασσαργάδαι.

[3] "De mulier. virtute," 5.

given by Diodorus of the overthrow of Astyages. With
him Cyrus is the son of Mandane, the daughter of
Astyages, and Cambyses. His father brought him
up as a king, and inflamed him with a desire for
the mightiest achievements. As a young man he displayed a capacity in advance of his years, and clearly
showed that he would undertake the most important
enterprises. He was the first man of his time in
bravery, wisdom, and all other virtues. Another fragment obviously comes after the defeat, which, according to Nicolaus, Astyages suffered in the final battle
at Pasargadae. When defeated, Astyages, though he
had himself disgracefully turned and fled, showed
ferocious anger against his army. He deposed all the
commanders and elected others in their place. Those
who were to blame for the flight, he executed one
and all, thinking that he should thus compel the
others to show themselves brave men in danger.
" For he was cruel and harsh in character. But he
did not terrify the multitude by this severity; on the
other hand, by the exasperation which such violence
and caprice excited in every one, he roused them to a
desire for revolution and deposition. The troops met
in their divisions; treasonable speeches were uttered,
and the majority urged each other to vengeance." [1]

Xenophon, it is true, has not written a history of
Cyrus, but has given a description of his life from
his knowledge of the Persian life and character,
and the conclusions he deduced therefrom, as to the
possible origin of the empire, in order to explain and
realise to the Greeks the difficulty which they found
it so hard to solve — the manner in which great
nations could form one community and be governed
by one person. With him Cyrus is the son of

[1] Diod. "Ex. de virt. et vit." p. 552, 553 (= 9, 24); cf. 4, 30.

Cambyses, who is the king of the Persians, and Mandane the daughter of Astyages of Media, whom Xenophon represents as reigning before Cyaxares. When Cyrus was twelve years of age, his mother went with him to Media, in order to show him to his grandfather, whom the boy astonished by his apt answers. At the age of sixteen, Cyrus performs his first deeds of arms. When Astyages died, he was succeeded on the throne by his son Cyaxares, the brother of Mandane. He entreats Cambyses to aid him against the Assyrians; Cambyses sends Cyrus, by whose services the Medes are defeated. After this he conquered the Lydians, who had come to aid the Assyrians against the Medes, and took Babylon; and his uncle Cyaxares, whom Xenophon does not describe as a pattern ruler, gives him his daughter in marriage, and Media as a dowry, for he was without male children. Cambyses and Mandane assented to this arrangement. After the death of Cambyses, Cyrus became king of Persia, and on the death of Cyaxares, Media also became his.

The Armenians also narrate the fall of Astyages. Moses of Chorene (I. 513) tells us that he only related the stories of the Persians to please his patron Sahak (Isaac) Bagratuni, and gave them a meaning which they did not possess. Biurasp Asdahag lived at the time of Nimrod, and the person whom the Persians in their stories call the child of Satan, served him; and with regard to the dragon, or the changing of Asdahag into a dragon, the truth was that he sacrificed men in infinite numbers to the dragon, till the multitude grew weary, overpowered him, and threw him into a trench filled with bitumen. Moses further tells us: The ninth descendant of Baroir of Armenia (I. 515), King Tigran, was the

mightiest of all the princes of Armenia, and helped
Cyrus to overthrow the kingdom of the Medes.
Tigran was pledged by treaties to Asdahag (Astyages)
the king of the Medians, and when he united with
Cyrus, Astyages had an evil dream. He saw a high
mountain surrounded by snow and ice, as in the land
of the son of Haikhs (I. 513). On the summit of the
mountain, a woman in purple, covered with a sky-blue
veil, brought forth three heroes at once: one, carried
on a lion, dashed toward the west; the second, on a
leopard, to the north; the third, on a monstrous
dragon, to Media. With this Asdahag fought in the
dream: they shed a sea of blood, and pierced each
other with their lances. Asdahag explained this
dream to mean that he had to expect an attack from
Tigran, the king of Armenia. To prevent this, and
secretly to destroy Tigran, Asdahag sought Tigran's
sister, Tigranuhi, in marriage, obtained her, and held
her in great honour. Then he asked for a meeting with
Tigran. But Tigranuhi had perceived the duplicity of
Asdahag, and warned her brother. He collected the
best warriors of great and little Armenia, and marched
against the Medes. The war continued for four
months, till Tigran in a hand-to-hand conflict pierced
the iron armour of Asdahag with his lance. The death
of Asdahag put an end to the battle and the war,
and Tigran led his sister back to Armenia, where she
became the ancestress of the race of Osdan. Anuish
(Aryanis), the first wife of Astyages, and a number of
young princesses and boys, more than 10,000 in all,
Tigranes brought to Armenia, and settled there to
the east of the great mountain, towards the land of
Koghten, in the plain of Ajtnayan, as far as Nakh-
jevan. In the songs of the people of Koghten, the
descendants of Astyages are spoken of in an alle-

gorical manner, as the descendants of the dragon; for Astyages (Asdahag) in our language means the dragon."[1] As has been shown, the Armenians were closely allied to the people of Iran in language, character, and religious worship. It cannot therefore astonish us that the legends of Iran are known to them. What Moses tells us of Biurasp Asdahag and his serpents rests on the myth in the Avesta of the serpent Azhi dahaka, the Zohak of the later form of Iranian legend (p. 250). The epithet which Moses gives to Asdahag, Biurasp, is also of Iranian origin; Baevaraçpa means the lord of 10,000 horses. That the descendants of Astyages are spoken of in the national legend of Armenia as the descendants of the dragon, shows that the Armenians had confounded Astyages of Media with Azhi dahaka or Zohak. The Armenians can only claim as their own the legend of King Tigran, who overcomes and slays Asdahag of Media. They ascribe to their princes the overthrow of the Medes. As already remarked, the Armenian legend of Tigran must come down from an early date. Xenophon makes Tigran the son of the king of Armenia, the most faithful helper and associate of Cyrus.[2]

Leaving out of sight the romance of Xenophon, and the Armenian tradition, which involve special hypotheses, the accounts in the West of the fall of

[1] Moses Choren. 1, 24—30, and appendix to the first book, according to Le Vaillant's translation.

[2] The form and explanation of the legend of Asdahag in Moses, as well as the mention of Rustem Sakjig, who has the strength of ten elephants (2, 8), i.e. of Rustem of Sejestan, prove that the East-Iranian legend, as we find it in Firdusi, must have been current in Western Iran in the fourth century at the latest, if it came into Armenia in the fifth century. I do not think it probable that Moses took the legend of Tigran from Xenophon's narrative. The vision in a dream and the duel point to Armenian tradition.

Astyages go back to two distinct versions, one of which we have in the narrative of Herodotus, the other in the narrative of Ctesias-Nicolaus, which is presupposed in Deinon and Polyaenus. In Trogus we have a third version, which combines the two. So far as Justin's excerpt allows us to form an opinion, this version, and the fragments of Diodorus, are based upon the Persian history of Deinon. The introduction is distinguished from the account of Herodotus by the fact that only one dream of Astyages is mentioned; that Cyrus is already exposed, and a dog is suckling him before the herdsman's wife, whose name was "dog," brings him up; then follows the story of Herodotus, including the letter, which Harpagus sends to Cyrus in the hare's belly. At this point Trogus passes into the account of Nicolaus; he represents Cyrus as receiving in a dream the exhortation to rise against Astyages, and to take the first man he meets as his associate. Cyrus meets Oebares, though not, it is true, on the borders of the Cadusians. The place of the horse-men, who in Nicolaus are first sent by Astyages, is taken in Trogus by the march of Harpagus, and his desertion to Cyrus; then follows the narrative of the war, which in the most essential traits agrees with the · version of Ctesias-Nicolaus. From Deinon's frag-ments we shall add to the excerpt from Trogus, that Cyrus before his rebellion had served at the court of Astyages as overseer of the staff-bearers, and then of the body-guard; that Astyages was warned by Angares; and, finally, the defection of the Medes after the battle of Pasargadae, as given in the fragments of Diodorus.

The detail and liveliness of the traits in the accounts of Herodotus and Ctesias-Nicolaus, in the fragment of Deinon, and the narrative of Trogus—the warnings and portents—the dialogues and speeches of the action—the letter :—all these point to poetical sources. We found that the accounts of Ctesias of the foundation, rise, and fall of Assyria, and of the rise of Media, were based upon poems, and here also, beyond doubt, poetic traditions form the groundwork.   Herodotus, at the beginning of his narrative, tells us :   " I write these matters from the accounts given by some of the Persians, who do not exaggerate the life of Cyrus, but wish to narrate the order of events ; I am aware that three other different accounts of the life of Cyrus are in existence." [1]   Xenophon tells us that Cyrus "is even now the theme of song among the barbarians." [2]   In Deinon's fragment it is Angares, the most famous of the Median minstrels, who, while singing at the table of Astyages, warns him in a poetical figure against Cyrus (p. 354) ; in the account of Nicolaus it is one of the singing women, from whom, at the same time and in a similar figure, this warning comes.   At the court of the Sassanids there were singing women who sang to the kings the achievements of old days.   Ibn-al-Hareth brought women of this kind from the court of Chosru Nushirvan to the Koreishites, and they sang the deeds of Rustem. [3] According to these statements and indications we may regard it as certain that the elevation of Cyrus and the fall of Astyages was celebrated in song among the Persians and Medes.   In spite of the differences between the three narratives, certain traits are common to all.   In all dreams announce the future greatness of Cyrus; in Herodotus these appear to Astyages; in Nicolaus, to the mother of Cyrus; in Deinon and Trogus, to Cyrus also.   In Herodotus

---

[1] 1, 95.   [2] " Cyri Instit." 1, 2, 1.
[3] J. Mohl, " Livre des rois," Introd. p. 29.

Cambyses is rich in flocks, in Nicolaus the mother of
Cyrus tends goats ; in Herodotus Cambyses is of a
quiet disposition, in Nicolaus he is driven by his son
to revolt, and finally disowns the enterprise. All three
narratives lay stress on the warnings given to Astyages
against Cyrus, though in different ways; all mark
strongly the early personal valour of Cyrus, which
Xenophon also celebrates. Artembares the Mede is
found both in Herodotus and Nicolaus, though in a
different relation to Cyrus. In all three accounts a
counsellor—Harpagus in the one case, Oebares in the
other—exercises the greatest influence on the resolutions
of Cyrus. Herodotus and Nicolaus mark the cunning
of Cyrus as opposed to Astyages ; in both Cyrus gives
out that he is carrying out the king's orders in arming
the Persians. In Herodotus Cyrus tells the Persians
that he does not consider them worse men than the
Medes, and they revolt "because they have now got a
leader in Cyrus." In Nicolaus Cyrus asks whether
there is not a leader who can put an end to the rule
of the Medes over better men than themselves. In
both the dominion of the Medes has long been hated
by the Persians. In both before the beginning of
the struggle Astyages commands Cyrus to appear
before him. In Herodotus Astyages says, when
Harpagus has passed over to Cyrus and the Median
army has broken up, that "he shall not succeed ;"
and in Nicolaus he uses the same words after the
first defeat of his horsemen. In Herodotus it is the
cruelty of Astyages to Harpagus, and his severity
towards the Medes, which cost him his throne ; in
Diodorus the army revolts, even after brave fighting,
from Astyages because he cruelly revenges upon
them the defeat at Pasargadae. In all three accounts
Cyrus does no harm to Astyages after his victory.

Let us set aside the poetical colours in the account of Herodotus in order to test its coherence. What alarm could Astyages, who was without male heirs, feel at the announcement that his daughter's son would one day rule over all Asia, *i. e.* would still further extend the dominion of the Medes? In the second dream, which portends no more than the first, a reason is given for the alarm; the interpreters declare that the dream signifies that Astyages will lose his throne. If Astyages had reason to fear the yet unborn child of his daughter, the obvious remedy was not to allow her to marry. Nevertheless she is married, not to a Mede, but to a man of the subject races, a Persian of a good family, *i. e.* of noble descent, wealthy, but "quiet in his disposition." This was equivalent to taking the Persian into the royal family, giving up to him or his son the right of succession, bringing the crown of Media into the possession of a stranger, and allowing the kingdom to pass from the Medes to the Persians. Even if such perversity could occur to Astyages the Medes were not likely to permit it, when the Magians tell Astyages, in Herodotus, how anxious they are that the dominion should not fall into the hands of a Persian. It is true that Herodotus represents Harpagus some twenty or thirty years later as persuading the chief Medes, and persuading them singly, that Astyages must be overthrown, and the Persian made king, but this is simply incredible. After this marvellous marriage of the heiress to the throne with a Persian, Cambyses is not brought to Ecbatana to the court, but remains in Persia, and no harm is done to the dreaded son of the marriage, even when his real origin has been discovered. Nay, more, the boy who at an early age discovers high aims, and a resolute will, is not even brought to the court to be under the eye of Astyages, but is sent back to Persia to his father, and by his means Harpagus is able to bring Persia to revolt. The letter hidden in the hare's belly obviously arose from an anticipation of the supervision of the great roads which was introduced at a later time by the Achæmenids. But what reason had Cyrus to cause the Persians to revolt? According to Herodotus Cambyses is the son-in-law, and hence the heir, of Astyages. Cyrus will succeed his father as heir to the Median throne, why then should he rebel against his aged grandfather?—why should he seek by hazard, danger, and bloodshed, a crown which by inheritance must soon come to Cambyses or Cyrus?[1]

In the narrative of Herodotus Cyrus is no more than an instrument in the hands of Harpagus. The crime of Astyages against Harpagus; the well-merited punishment of this crime by his own imprisonment and loss of empire, form the hinge of the narrative, which at the same time brings into prominence the doctrine that no one, even though warned, can escape his doom. It is not probable that there were songs among the Persians or Medes, which illustrated Herodotus' view of the unavoidable *Nemesis* which governs the actions and fortunes of men; or that Persian poems would represent Cyrus as the son of a Median mother. In them the Persians merely glorified the

[1] It has been objected to this analysis that the marriage with the heiress may not have conveyed the throne *ipso facto* to the husband; it may have been open to the chieftains to elect a king out of the members of the royal family. This may be correct for the election of the Afghan chiefs at the present day by the heads of the families. How the succession to the throne was arranged among the Medes we do not know in any detail, or whether their chiefs had any importance at all; but we do see that the crown went from father to son from Deioces downwards. In any case, even under that hypothesis, the husband of the heiress had a nearer claim.

founder of their freedom and supremacy, of whom, as we know, they cherished the most grateful memories. But the Medes might possess poems in which the change of empire was treated from their point of view; they might attempt to make the loss of empire appear less painful, the dishonour of defeat by the Persians less degrading. To be overthrown by a man belonging to the subject race was bitter. Hence the Medes could avail themselves of a change frequent in the East, and represent Cyrus as a scion of their own royal house. The Egyptians maintained that Cambyses, the son of Cyrus, who reduced them to subjection, was the son of Cyrus and the daughter of their own Pharaoh Hophra.[1] This was mere invention; and the Medes must have found their version the more easy to maintain, because Cyrus spared Astyages after the defeat, and took his daughter into his harem. And if it was not the arms of the Persians, but rather the treachery of a distinguished Mede, the discontent of the chiefs of Media with a cruel king, that decided the struggle between the Persians and Medes, the submission became thus less intolerable to the pride of the Medes. If a distinguished Mede had been at variance with Astyages, and in the last moment of the battle had gone over to Cyrus,—much could be made of the desertion in Median poems. If after his victory Cyrus reposed great confidence in an eminent Mede, this might be made a ground for previous treachery to Astyages. A few years after his victory Cyrus entrusted to the Mede Harpagus, the leadership of the army, the subjugation and maintenance of far distant regions. If the legend of the Persians represented Achæmenes,

---

[1] Herod. 3, 2. So Deinon and Lyceas of Naucratis in Athenaeus, p. 560.

the ancestor of their princely race, as being fed by
an eagle (p. 327), their poems would speak of the
founder of their dominion as distinguished by divine
honours, and surround his birth and youth with
happy omens of the future. These traits the Medes
could use for their own purposes as warnings vouchsafed to Astyages. If the Persians represented Cyrus
as suckled by a dog, the favoured creature of Auramazda, the Medes carried the subject further, and
spoke of the exposing of Cyrus, which was then
brought into combination with the enmity of Harpagus to Astyages; the origin of this was the refusal of Harpagus to put the Persian boy to death,
which Astyages punished by the Thyestean banquet.
Thus owing to the crime of Astyages, Harpagus
their own countryman became filled with desire for
vengeance; he is the counsellor of Cyrus, the author
and leader of the revolt.

Median poetry of this kind has been followed by
Herodotus. He has told us already that he would
narrate the life of Cyrus as it was given by the
Persians, who had no desire to exaggerate their
account, but these Persians are undoubtedly the
Medes. The Median origin of his story is placed
beyond doubt by the words which the captive Astyages addresses to Harpagus, and by the fact that
with him it is a Mede who is the decisive counsellor
and guide of Cyrus, while in the other version it is a
Persian. Beside the reason given by Herodotus himself for choosing this version, others no doubt had
influence. The Delphian oracle bade Crœsus take to
flight " whenever a mule should govern the Medes."
According to the Medes Cyrus was the son of a
Persian father and Median mother. The sufferings
and acts of Harpagus formed the centre of the Median

version, and he was only too well known to the
Greeks on the west coast of Asia Minor. With the
warning portents, and the exposure of Cyrus, the
Median version brought Herodotus on the familiar
ground of Greek legend, in which similar oracles,
futile exposing of children, and deceptive explanations
were common. Finally, the vengeance which overtook Astyages suits the ethical feeling of Herodotus.
We may assume therefore that his narrative faithfully
represents the contents of Median poems. These
could already have changed the dog which was
said to have suckled Cyrus into the herdman's wife,
who was called by the name of "dog." But inasmuch as Herodotus does not "intend to exaggerate,"
as he observes that "the dog was everything in
the mouth of Cyrus," and "his parents caught this
up in order to represent the preservation of Cyrus
as a work of the gods,"—as he further remarks "that
Cyrus owing to his origin was regarded as more than
human,"[1]—this rationalising turn may have proceeded
from the historian himself. In the Persian tradition
Cyrus was certainly suckled and guarded by the dog,
and this trait is retained in the account of Deinon-
Trogus, though united with the story of the exposure. But Deinon has at the same time proved the
exposure impossible, for he states that Cyrus came
to the throne in his fortieth year, and lived till his
seventieth.[2] If this were true, the exposure and the
command of Astyages respecting it would fall to the
ground, for Cyrus would have seen the light in the
year 599 B.C., i. e. some years before the accession of
Astyages, even if we allow the latter the longer reign
which Eusebius assigns to him.

If the story of Herodotus is governed by the

[1] Herod. 1, 207; 3, 75; 7, 11.   [2] Cicero, "de Divin." 1, 23.

conception of the unavoidable punishment of crime, the connecting clue in the story of Nicolaus is the rise of a beggar-boy of the lowest origin by skill and industry, by cunning and bravery, by endurance in the greatest danger, and final victory in the most severe struggles. Cyrus is the son of humble parents; his father is driven by want to robbery, his mother tends goats; they belong to the lowest tribe of the Persians, the marauding Mardians whom we have found in the mountains of south-western Persia (p. 323). Hunger drives the boy from the goat-pasture to Ecbatana. Beginning as a sweeper of the palace, he works his way step by step upwards by address and industry to the highest offices at the court, so that he can make his father satrap of Persia and his mother the most distinguished lady in Persia. Then the dream of his mother, and the interpretation given of it by the Babylonian, plant ambition in his soul, which is strengthened by the happy portent, vouchsafed to him on his mission to the chief of the Cadusians, and the advice of Oebares. He succeeds in persuading Astyages to grant him permission to visit his parents in Persia; when too late, Astyages is warned by the wife of the Babylonian, and the words of the singing-woman (Angares in Deinon). A fierce war breaks out. The father of Cyrus is taken captive, and in his last moments disavows the attempt of his son. Defeated again and again, the Persians in their last refuge at Pasargadae are reduced to the greatest distress. Then fortune turns; the Medes are driven back and defeated in numerous engagements, and Oebares can at length place the crown on the head of Cyrus in the tent of Astyages.

If Xenophon in his book on Cyrus sought to make it clear to the Greeks, by what personal and material

means Cyrus was able to conquer Asia, Ctesias or
Nicolaus will show pragmatically how a beggar-boy
rose step by step to be lord of the continent. He says
nothing of the relationship of Astyages and Cyrus, or
of the princely origin of Cyrus, or of his exposure, or
of the dog: Cyrus owes his successes to himself and
the gods. However impossible it may be that this
introduction and the whole tendency of the narrative
can be borrowed from the tradition of the Persians;
however certain that Cyrus the beggar-boy is an
invention of the Greeks, to point the contrast between
beginning and end, and make the subject more in-
teresting; yet if only we give another turn to the
introduction, we have the Persian account before us in
the narrative of Nicolaus, as we have the Median in
the account of Herodotus—and a mixture of the two
in the excerpt from Trogus. The Persian version is
from the first marked in Ctesias and Nicolaus by the
fact that they do not represent Cyrus as the descendant of Astyages. Moreover, the parallel between the
fall of the Assyrians and the fall of the Median empire
cannot be mistaken. "We must narrate the great
change brought about by the transition of the dominion to the Persians"—such is the beginning of the
account of Nicolaus. This parallel can only have
arisen from Persian minstrels. They had to show
that the task of Cyrus was great, and more difficult
than that of Arbaces. They had to lay the greatest
stress on the personal excellence of Cyrus in order
to raise him above the level of Arbaces. The latter,
guided by the advice of the viceroy of Babylon and
aided by the Babylonians, had proved the conqueror.
The arts of the Chaldæans were certainly respected
and used in Iran; they must have been sought after
and employed as a poetic motive. It was to carry

out the parallel that the Persian songs gave Cyrus
a Babylonian adviser; yet they represent the counsel
and influence of this Babylonian as entirely removed
by a Persian of far greater importance, and utterly
thrown into the shade. The emphasis which the
Persian songs laid on the personal virtue of Cyrus
misled the Greeks into making an attempt at the
biography of the beggar-boy, and so rendered this
change easier. Atradates, the name given by Nicolaus
to the father of Cyrus, is no doubt taken from an
epithet of Cyrus himself. Strabo tells us that Cyrus
was originally called Atradates; the word is the
old Persian *atriyadata*, old Bactrian, *ataredata*; the
Avesta recommends the name as good and saving.
The parents of Cyrus are said to belong to the tribe of
the Mardians, but later on Nicolaus himself shows
that Cyrus' ancestral home is at Pasargadae (p. 352).
In contempt the Medes might unite the whole Persian nation under the name of their poorest tribes.
"Why have I raised up these Mardians for such
mischief?" Astyages asks in Nicolaus. The goat-
tending of the mother of Cyrus is due to the same
cause. In the account of Herodotus Cambyses is
said to be rich in herds; among the Persians the
care of flocks occupied a large place, and at a later
time the tending and protection of the flocks was one
of the means employed for strengthening and hard-
ening the Persian youth. Cyrus himself, in the narrative of Nicolaus, calls himself and his father goat-
herds. When Arsaces of Armenia visited the court
of the Sassanid Shapur II. one of the first officers
at the court of Shapur insolently said: "Will the
king of the goats pasture on our slopes?"[1] Such
traits as these in the Persian poems, connected with

[1] St. Martin on Lebeau, "Bas Empire," 2, 221.

the poverty and simplicity of the life of the "terebinth-eating" Persians (which Nicolaus also, following the tradition, brings into such prominence), supplied the Greek revision with the necessary support for changing Cyrus into a Mardian goat-herd and beggar-boy. Yet the true position of the parents of Cyrus breaks through in the statement that the father of Cyrus was satrap of Persia, and his mother the first lady in the land, a position which also appears in the statement in Herodotus of the noble descent and wealth of Cambyses, and is even more plainly marked in other passages in which the taunt is hurled at Cyrus: that the son of Cambyses ought not to give way to a woman,—and traces the lineage of Cyrus back to Achæmenes, though in the account of the rebellion of Cyrus he calls his grandfather also Cyrus.

The rise of Cyrus at the court of Astyages was borrowed from another trait in the Persian poems. The custom of the East, that the sons of distinguished princes and nobles should perform certain courtly and honourable services at the gate of the king, must have been current in Media also. The Persian poems must have proudly declared how Cyrus distinguished himself there in his youth in the duties of the court or of arms. This description was changed into the series of stages by which the beggar-boy rose to the highest office at the court of the king. The Persian account is obviously preserved here in Deinon's narrative—like the suckling and protection of Cyrus by the dog—in which Cyrus before the rebellion is chief of the staff-bearers and the body-guard of the king. When Cyrus had won the favour of Astyages, Nicolaus is obviously more true to the Persian account. In old days the chaff of horses announced his elevation to Arbaces, and to Cyrus it is announced by horse-dung,

which is carried to him by a Persian, the slave of a
Mede, who has been recently whipped; and as to
Arbaces, so to Cyrus, a Babylonian announces that
the throne is destined for him. As Arbaces is in-
stigated and encouraged by Belesys, so is Cyrus by
the interpreter of dreams from Babylon, and Cyrus
promises him great rewards if he reaches the throne,
as Arbaces had promised Belesys. The conversations
of Arbaces with Belesys correspond exactly to the
conversations of Cyrus with the Babylonian and
Oebares. In Nicolaus Cyrus says, that Arbaces who
overthrew Sardanapalus was not wiser than himself,
nor were the Medes better warriors than the Persians.
But if the Median empire was founded with the help
of the Babylonian, the Persian must rise without such
assistance. Arbaces had to concede to Belesys and
his successors the hereditary dominion over Babylonia; on this occasion Oebares takes care that in the
future empire of the Persians, Babylonia shall not be
in the way as an hereditary monarchy given in reward
of services; he removes the Babylonian against the
wishes of Cyrus. If the Medes had formerly been
able to conquer Assyria with the aid of the Babylonians, the Persians now defeat the Medes unaided,
and if Sardanapalus was effeminate, Astyages, according to Nicolaus, is the bravest king of the Medes after
Arbaces. To treat the struggle so briefly as Herodotus
does was impossible for Nicolaus, as the object of his
narrative was to bring out the valour of Cyrus. So
we may assume that the Persian songs gave similar
prominence to the contests before Nineveh and Pasargadæ. Arbaces is thrice defeated before Nineveh, and
inclined to retire. Astyages leads against Cyrus the
whole forces of his kingdom—more than a million
soldiers. In spite of the excellent arrangements of

Oebares and the utmost bravery, Cyrus is three times defeated :—he is already reduced to extremities in the fourth conflict, when the cry of the women restores the fight. At length Oebares is able to place the Median crown on the head of Cyrus in the tent of Astyages. With such servants the throne and kingdom of the Persians is more firmly established than that of the Medes.

This inquiry enables us to reconstruct in its main outlines the tradition of the Persians. Cambyses, the descendant of Achæmenes, was the chief of the Persians. Before the birth of Cyrus his wife had a dream that so much water came from her " that it was like a great river which inundated all Asia, and flowed into the sea." We know what reverence the Avesta pays to the dog, and the importance it ascribes to its glance (p. 207). The suckling of the boy Cyrus by a dog is the sign of the most bounteous favour and most secure protection on the part of the gods. Herodotus told us above that owing to his origin Cyrus counted himself as more than a man, and Xenophon represents him as begotten by gods, springing from a line of kings, and practised from his youth up in bravery and virtue.[1] In accordance with the custom of the Persians the son of the prince grows up among the flocks. Mithradates, which Herodotus gives as the name of the herdsman with whom the boy is brought up, means "given by Mithra ;" the favourite of the god, who increases the flocks of the farms where men worship him, and gives victory in battles, is the protector of Cyrus. In the game of the boys he shows by cleverness and unbroken resolution the great destiny to which he was called. Then he goes into service at the court of the Median king ;

[1] " Cyri instit." 7, 3, 24.

where the Persian poems have already shown us
Parsondes at the time of Cyaxares, who subsequently
made the Cadusians enemies of the Medes.[1] Eminent
in every position, Cyrus wins the confidence of Astyages, and becomes the chief of his bodyguard. Then
according to Deinon's fragments he sees the sun in a
dream thrice inclining towards him. It was the
brilliance or majesty of the king which Cyrus is
represented as beholding. In the Avesta Thraetaona
and Kereçaçpa seize the majesty when it departs
from Yima, and the Turanian Franghraçyan seeks
thrice to grasp the glance of the majesty.[2] Then a
Persian, the slave of a Mede, brings a new sign of
good fortune to Cyrus when far from his fatherland
on the borders of the Cadusians. Oebares (Hubara,
the good bearer) is the first Persian whom Cyrus
liberates from the service of the Medes ; and thus he
has gained his most faithful helper. Angares the
Mede, who warns Astyages, calls Cyrus " more mighty
than a wild boar." The singing girl also calls Cyrus
a " boar." We saw above that the victorious god
Verethraghna appears in the form of a boar, and in
that shape accompanies the chariot of Mithra.[3] The
battle in the mountains of Persia, as described by
Nicolaus, belongs in all essential traits to the Persian
legend. It is precisely at Pasargadae, at the house
of Cyrus, i. e. of Achæmenes, that the fortune of arms
changes. The proclamation of Cyrus in the tent of
Astyages, and his coronation by the Persians, which
first made him a free man instead of a Median slave,
is throughout in accordance with the meaning and
tendency of the Persian legend. The gentleness of

[1] Above, p. 299 ff.   [2] Above, p. 34, 35, 36, 256.
[3] Above, p. 110. Cf. Windischmann, "Zoroastrische Studien," s.
277.

Cyrus towards Astyages is the counterpart of the generosity which the Median king who conquered Nineveh once displayed towards Belesys. Oebares undoubtedly belongs to the Persian Epos; he is the faithful servant who upholds the interest of the kingdom even against the will of the king, and sacrifices himself for it. The Persians of the best time held it a duty to sacrifice themselves for the king.

The overthrow of the Parthian empire is explained in the same way as the overthrow of the Medes. Papak, the prince of Fars, sees in a dream the sun illuminating the world from the head of his herdman Sassan. His daughter brings forth Ardeshir to Sassan; Ardeshir serves at the court of the Parthian king Artaban, and shoots wild asses better than anyone else. On an announcement of the interpreters of stars, Ardeshir flies from the court and arms the Persians. Artaban abuses him as an impudent Kurd, and sends the prince of Susiana to fetch him, but this prince, and then Artaban himself, are overcome. Shapur, the son of Ardeshir, is restored to life against his command, and his grandson Auharmazdi is brought up secretly, and recognised by his conduct in the play of the boys. In both, dreams and letters and the inborn majesty of the royal children play their part. [1]

Astyages, who ascended the throne in the year 593 B.C., ruled over the Median empire for more than 30 years; he had already reached a great age when the Persians rebelled against him. Aristotle remarks that his effeminate life and the carelessness of his government inspired Cyrus with courage.[2] The daughter of

----

[1] Nöldeke, "Tabari," p. 12; Karnamak, s. 68.
[2] "Politic." 5, 10, 24.

Alyattes of Lydia, whom he had married in his youth,
had brought him no son; both the Median version
of Herodotus, and the Persian in Trogus and Ctesias,
allow Astyages a daughter only—Mandane in the
one case, in the other Amytis, the name of the sister
of Astyages, whom Nebuchadnezzar married. This
daughter, according to Ctesias and Nicolaus, Astyages
marries to Spitamas, the Mede (Çpitama, _i. e._ the
excellent) and at the same time gives him "all Media
as a dowry." Marriage with the heiress to the throne
gave her husband the claim and right to succession. The daughter of the king bore two sons to
Spitamas: Spitaces and Magabernes.[1] About the
origin of Cyrus there is no doubt. He was the son
of Cambyses, the grandson of Teispes, the great-grandson of Achaemenes, who united the Persian tribes
under his leadership, and recognised the sovereignty
of Phraortes the Median king. As Cyaxares and
Astyages followed Phraortes on the throne of Media,
so did Teispes and Cambyses follow Achaemenes as

---

[1] If Astyages was married to the daughter of Alyattes in the year
610 B.C. he must have been 18 or 20 years old at that time; between
610 and 558 the year of his fall there are 52 years. Moreover, according to Ctesias, Astyages outlived his fall at least ten years (" Fragm.
Pers." 5). If this were the case, and Astyages did not die till 548, he
cannot well have been born before 630 B.C. In Herodotus and Pompeius Trogus it is expressly said that Astyages had no son, and this is
the motive which induces Harpagus not to put Cyrus to death, as he
would in that case expose himself to the vengeance of the mother, the
heiress to the throne. In Nicolaus also the daughter comes distinctly
forward, and in Ctesias she is also the heiress (_e. g._ " Pers." 2); in the
history of the overthrow and the death of Astyages, we hear of her
constantly. At the death of Cyrus, her sons by the first marriage
receive satrapies. In Ctesias, it is true, a brother of Amytis is inci-
dentally mentioned, on the occasion of a later war of Cyrus (" Pers."
3). But as Ctesias is here following a Median version, and after the
death of Astyages the husband of Amytis and not her supposed
brother is removed out of the way, no importance can be attached to
this.

his viceroys or vassal kings over Persia. It may have been the case that, as already remarked, after the consolidation of the Median empire, the sovereignty became more oppressive for the Persians, and the links of their dependence were drawn closer. According to the previous custom, the viceroyalty of Persia would descend, at the death of Cambyses, to his son Cyrus. If the custom which subsequently prevailed in the Persian kingdom was current among the Medes, and the sons of the satraps or princes of the subject lands had to wait at the king's gate, and perform courtly or martial service as hostages for the fidelity of their fathers, and at the same time to learn obedience and submission in order to find favour with the king when in his immediate presence and covered by the splendour of his power—Cyrus must also have served at the court of Astyages, and may have filled the office of the staff-bearer, body-guard, or of butler, an honourable position at the court of the Medes and Persians. In Ecbatana he had no doubt an opportunity of comparing the simple manners, the capacity and vigour of his Persians, with the splendour of the court, and the luxurious life of the Median chiefs. Moreover, the great advantage which Spitamas had gained by marriage with the daughter of the king must have excited the jealousy and ambition of other Medes who considered themselves to have a better claim, or even raised their eyes to the throne. In the account of Herodotus, Harpagus is said to be akin to the family of Astyages. It is possible that Cyrus contemplated a breach between Persia and Media on the death of Astyages, when he would find his opportunity in a contested and previously disputed succession. It may be a fact that Astyages had his suspicions, that he summoned Cyrus who had already left the court before him, and Cyrus was thus compelled to break with him sooner than he intended. It seems more certain that Cambyses was still alive, than that the Persians took up arms against Astyages at the instigation of Cyrus, who was, as we have remarked, at that time in his fortieth year.[1]

It follows from the position of affairs that the Persians awaited the attack of the Medes in their own country. It was only in the defence of the passes of their mountains that they could hope to make a stand against the overwhelming power of their enemies. In this we may put confidence in the Persian tradition, as well as in all that it has to say of a character unfavourable to the Persians ; above all, in the fact that the war was long and severe. As a fact the Medes appear to have twice penetrated into the heart of the Persian land. Not only Nicolaus, Pompeius Trogus, and Polyaenus tell us that the struggle took place at first in Persia, and that the battle which saved the country was fought at Pasargadae, but also an authority of importance, Anaximenes of Lampsacus, the contemporary of Aristotle and Strabo (p. 357). "In reward for the services which the women rendered in that battle," says Nicolaus, "the women of Persia each received, when the king came to Pasargadae, a gold coin of the value of twenty Attic drachmas." Plutarch, as has been observed,[2] confirms this statement, on the ground of the accounts of the companions of Alexander, in a very definite way. We must assume, therefore, that Cyrus maintained the independence of Persia in a very severe struggle. When success had been obtained, he went on to

[1] Above, p. 369.
[2] Above, p. 357. Nicol. Dam. Fragm. 66 ; Plut. "Alex." c. 69 ; Plut. "De Mul. virt." 5.

attack Media, whether it was that he did not consider the freedom of Persia secure without the overthrow of that country, or that he at once formed
the most ambitious designs. After a battle in Media
had given Cyrus the victory in this new war, the
chiefs of the nations subject to the Medes, the Hyrcanians, Parthians, Sacæ, and Bactrians, and finally
a part of the Medes, must have abandoned Astyages,
who, after a second defeat, fell into the hands of
Cyrus either in the encounter itself or at the capture
of Ecbatana. The walls of Ecbatana and the seven
rings round the citadel could not avert his fate
(558 B. C.).[1]

[1] According to the canon of Ptolemy, Cyrus dies 529 B.C. We arrive
at the same year if we reckon back from the death of Darius. This
took place five years after the battle of Marathon (Herod. 7, 1—4),
i. e. 485 B.C. Darius reigned 36 years according to Herodotus and the
canon of Ptolemy. An Egyptian pillar gives the year 34, a demotic
contract the year 35 of his reign : he ascended the throne therefore in
521 B.C. Before him the Magian reigned for seven months, Cambyses
for seven years and five months (Herod. 3, 66, 67). The canon of
Ptolemy omits the Magian and gives Cambyses eight years, because it
reckons by complete years ; hence Cambyses ascended the throne in
529. As Cyrus, according to Herodotus, reigned 29 years after his
accession (1, 214), the beginning of his reign over Media must be
placed in 558. If Ctesias gives Cyrus a reign of 30 years ("Pers." 8),
like Deinon (p. 369), and Justin (1, 8), and Eusebius a reign of 31
years, these statements may be reconciled by the fact that Cyrus may
have taken up arms against Media 30 or 31 years before his death, and
reigned 29 years after the overthrow of Astyages. Diodorus puts the
beginning of Cyrus : Olymp. 55, 1 = 560 B.C. Africanus in Euseb.
"Præp. Evang." 10, p. 488.

CHAPTER V.

THE Median empire was not of long duration. Little more than a century had passed since Phraortes succeeded Deioces in the government of the land of Ecbatana, little more than eighty since Phraortes had united the tribes of the Medes under his leadership, about sixty since Cyaxares had expelled the Scythians, and not quite fifty since Nineveh had succumbed to the arms of the Medes and Babylonians.

In the overthrow of so mighty a power, Cyrus had achieved a great, and, so far as we can tell, an unexpected, success. Scanty as our information is, we can still perceive that he used the victory with circumspection and moderation. Herodotus told us that he did no injury to the captive Astyages, and kept him with him till his death. Ctesias relates that at the command of Cyrus, the heavy chains, which Oebares had put on Astyages, were quickly taken off; that he honoured him as a father; and entrusted him with the government of the Barcanians. According to the statement of Pompeius Trogus, Cyrus allowed him to be viceroy of the Hyrcanians. The same nation may be meant by these two names; in the inscriptions of Darius Hyrcania is called Varkana, in the Avesta Vehrkana.[1]

[1] Ctes. "Pers. Ecl." 5; Tzetz. "Chil." 1, 1, 83; Justin, 1, 6. Yet Diodorus mentions the Barcanians together with the Hyrcanians (2,

Ctesias further tells us that Cyrus put to death the
Mede Spitamas, whom Astyages had married to his
daughter Amytis, and then made his successor, and
that after treating Amytis for some time as his mother
he subsequently made her his wife. No harm was
done to Megabernes and Spitaces, the sons of her
marriage with Spitamas; on the contrary, the first
was placed by the wish of Cyrus in the satrapy of
the Barcanians, the second in the satrapy of the
Derbiccians.

Cyrus must have made it his object to reconcile the
Medes to their defeat and loss of empire. If he could
make the house of Astyages his own, and take his
daughter to wife, the edge of the change was softened,
and the more apparent it was that this marriage had
the consent of Astyages, the more legitimate would
his rule be in the eyes of the Medes, the less could
they regard it as the dominion of a stranger. It was
of importance to gain the assent of the Medes to the
new kingdom, and support this if possible on the
united power of Medes and Persians. Moreover, the
relations of alliance in which Astyages stood to the
princely houses of Lydia and Babylonia made it
advisable to deal carefully with Astyages and his
kindred. Astyages was still alive in 549 B.C.,[1] according to Herodotus and Ctesias. Whatever may be
the case as to the connection of Cyrus with Amytis,
his legitimate wife was Cassandane, the daughter of
the Persian Pharnaspes, who according to Herodotus
was an Achæmenid, and was in fact one of the
six tribal princes. Cassandane bore Cyrus two sons,

2); Curtius (3, 2) represents the Barcanians as providing 12,000 men
for the last Darius; Stephanus of Byzantium (Βαρκάνιοι) puts them
beside the Hyrcanians. Yet all these statements may rest on the
same misconception.

[1] Herod. 1, 73; above, p. 378, note.

Cambyses and Bardiya, whom Herodotus calls Smerdis; Ctesias, Tanyoxarkes; and Xenophon, Tanaoxares. The death of Cassandane was a great grief to Cyrus; he caused the whole kingdom to go into mourning for her.[1]

With respect to the position which Cyrus took up in regard to the royal family of Media, and Amytis more especially, Ctesias has preserved a somewhat incredible story. This narrative, which again is obviously taken from a poetical source, ascribes the death of Astyages to Oebares, to whom, according to Trogus, Cyrus had given the government of Persia and his sister in marriage, as a reward for his services, who in the beginning of his reign had been his associate in all his dangers, and whom, according to Ctesias, he had afterwards to thank for the capture of Sardis. The motive of this act, according to the drift of these poems, can only have been anxiety on the part of Oebares lest the influence of Astyages and his friends should endanger the succession of the house of Cyrus in the Persian kingdom and the dominion of the Persians. Oebares had previously murdered the Babylonian who possessed the secret which controlled the future of Persia, against the wishes and without the knowledge of Cyrus (p. 347), and he now acts in a similar manner towards Astyages. Cyrus, so we are told in our excerpt,[2] after the Lydian war sent the eunuch Petesaces to bring Astyages from the Barcanians, as both he and Amytis wished to see him. Oebares advised Petesaces to abandon Astyages on the way in some desert place, to perish by starvation.

---

[1] Herod. 2, 1; 3, 2; 7, 11.

[2] Ctesias, "Pers." 8. The narrative of the death of Astyages follows the narrative of the wars against the Bactrians and Sacæ, and against the wars against the Derbiccians.

This was done. The crime was revealed by dreams,
and Cyrus, on the repeated entreaty of Amytis, gave
Petesaces up to her for punishment. She caused
him to be blinded, flayed, and crucified. Oebares,
fearing that a similar lot was in store for him,
though Cyrus assured him that he should not permit
anything of the kind, refused all nourishment for ten
days, and so put an end to his life. The corpse
of Astyages received a splendid burial. Lions had
guarded it in the desert place in which it had been
abandoned, until Petesaces returned and carried it
away. In the poem in which the singing woman
warns Astyages against Cyrus he is compared to a
lion (p. 349). Whether the lions performed this
service to the corpse of Astyages in the source from
which Ctesias copied—it could scarcely by such an
incident exhibit him as a man favoured by heaven—
or whether the lions dealt with the corpse in a
manner more in accordance with the views of Eastern
Iran, we must leave out of the question. What is
more certain is, that the most zealous Persian could
have no real reason for putting Astyages to death, for
after the Lydian war he would be in his eightieth
year. The importance ascribed to Amytis points to
a Median version ; the death of Oebares is accounted
for in a manner suitable to his life and his fidelity.

In Herodotus the Persians, on the instigation of
Artembares, one of their tribesmen, say to Cyrus :
"Since Zeus gives the sovereignty to the Persians,
and above all to thee, Cyrus, who hast overthrown
Astyages, so let it be thy care that we leave our land
and obtain a better, for our country is small and wild.
Many better regions are close at hand, many at a
distance, and if we gain one of them, we shall be
more admired in the eyes of men. To do this is

proper for men who possess the dominion, and when
can it be done better than now, when we have so
many men, and rule over all Asia?" When Cyrus
heard this he expressed no astonishment, but said
simply: they might do so, but they must be prepared
to be rulers no longer, but subjects; the same land
could not produce the noblest fruits and warlike men.
The Persians saw that Cyrus' view was the better,
and chose to inhabit and rule over a scanty land,
rather than be the slaves of others.[1] The distinct
opposition of Cyrus and Artembares seems to carry
us back to Persian poems, otherwise the narrative is
less likely to belong to the tradition of Persia than
to arise out of the necessity which the Greeks felt
for explaining how the Persians succeeded in founding
so mighty an empire from a mountain country so
moderate in extent.

In any case the Persians, after the overthrow of
Media, were far from possessing the dominion over
Asia. In Nicolaus, it is true, when the news is spread
abroad that Astyages has retired from Persia and
has fled before Cyrus in the first battle in Media,
the chief of the Hyrcanians comes with 50,000 men,
to pay homage to Cyrus as king; he is followed by
the chiefs of the Parthians, Sacæ, and Bactrians, and
then by the remaining nations. But as a fact the
course of things seems to have been different. If the
princes and natives who were subject to the Medes
were ready to throw off their dominion as soon as
they were defeated by the Persians, they were hardly
inclined to recognise Cyrus as sovereign in the room
of Astyages. Herodotus tells us that Cyrus subjugated the Bactrians and Sacæ, and Upper Asia, one
nation after the other, and puts these conquests after

[1] Herod. 9, 122.

the Lydian war.[1] Xenophon represents the Hyrcanians
as joining Cyrus at an early date, and the Cadusians
follow their example, which harmonises with the view
taken in the Persian poems of the hatred of the
Cadusians to the Medes. In Xenophon and Ctesias
the Sacæ are the allies of Cyrus as early as 549 B.C.[2]
If Astyages receives the satrapy of the Hyrcanians
in Justin, this nation and the Parthians, who were
still nearer neighbours of Media, must have been
among those who were subject to Cyrus.

In Ctesias, Cyrus after the conquest of Astyages
marches against the Bactrians; the battle was undecided. But when they found that Astyages was
the father and Amytis the wife of Cyrus, the Bactrians voluntarily submitted to Amytis and Cyrus.
Then Cyrus conquered the Sacæ, and took their king
Amorges captive. We remember that, according to
Herodotus' statement, the proper name of the Sacæ was
Amyrgians, and in the inscriptions of Darius we found
the Çaka Humavarka. The name Amorges seems to
be borrowed from the Amyrgians. When Amorges
had been defeated and taken captive by Cyrus, his
wife Sparethra, as she is called in Ctesias, collected
the Sacæ and took the field with them. Zarinaea,
a princess of the Sacæ, had previously fought with
great bravery against the Medes, but her achievements are far surpassed by those of Sparethra. With
300,000 men and 200,000 armed women, she went
against the Persians, and defeated Cyrus, taking many
captives, among whom were Medes of distinction. As
a ransom for these Amorges was restored to Sparethra,
and there was friendship between Cyrus and the king
of the Sacæ, and the latter marched with him to the
war against the Lydians. Strabo also speaks of a

[1] Herod. 1, 177.   [2] "Cyri instit." 5, 3, 22.

c c 2

battle in which Cyrus was defeated by the Sacæ.
Being hard pressed on his retreat he abandoned his
camp with large stores of every kind, especially of
wine. When the Sacæ had enjoyed their spoil,
Cyrus fell upon them and massacred nearly all.[1]

Trogus following Deinon tells us that the nations
who were subject to the Medes did not submit to
Cyrus. Hence arose many wars. The greater part of
these nations he had already overpowered, before he
marched against the Lydians, i. e. in the first eight
years after the overthrow of Astyages. We may assume
that Cyrus, immediately after the dethronement of
Astyages, was occupied with bringing the neighbours
of Media on the east, north, and west into obedience
to the new kingdom. So long as the Parthians,
Hyrcanians, Armenians, were independent or in arms
against Cyrus, the Medes must be strongly tempted
to recover their lost dominion. The Cadusians in
Ghilan were subjects of Cyrus; at any rate the name
of the city Cyropolis on the Caspian Sea, on the
coast of the Cadusians, is a proof that Cyrus placed a
fortress there, in order to keep them or their neighbours in check; and under the successors of Cyrus
the Cadusians are always mentioned as subjects.[2]
Then he took the same line towards the west, on
which Cyaxares of Media had advanced sixty years
previously after driving out the Scythians; he gained
Armenia and Cappadocia, and made the Halys the
border of his kingdom towards Lydia. In his narrative of the events of the year 549 B.C., Herodotus
remarks that the Cappadocians were subject to Cyrus,

[1] Strabo, p. 512.
[2] Ptolem. 6, 2; Ammian, 23, 6. The rebellion of the Cadusians at
a later time was mentioned by Xenoph. "Hellen." 2, 1, 13: Plut.
"Artaxerx." 24; Diod. 15, 8; Justin, 10, 3. They fought with the
last Darius at Arbela; Arrian, "Anab." 3, 11.

having previously been subjects of the Medes. It is clear from repeated statements that at this time the Halys was the western border of the empire of Cyrus.[1] Xenophon reckons the subjugation of the Armenians, who had been subjects of the Medes, among the earliest achievements of Cyrus; he tells the story in his own manner, and places after this the subjection of the neighbours on the south, the Chaldæans (Gordyæans) who dwelt in the mountains which separate the table-land of Armenia from the hilly country of Assyria. The legends of the Cappadocians conceal their subjugation to Cyrus under supposed links of alliance; Cambyses, the father of Cyrus, had given his own sister Atossa in marriage to Pharnaces, the king of the Cappadocians.[2] The extension of the Persian dominion to the east over Parthia and Hyrcania, the subjugation of the Drangians, Gedrosians, and Arachoti, must, in consideration of the observation of Herodotus, that in 548 B.C. Cyrus was intent on military preparations against the Bactrians and Sacæ, and the urgent difficulties which at that time summoned him to the east, be placed in the later years of his reign; in fact, they cannot come earlier than the second decade; which does not, however, make it impossible that Cyrus should have fought against the Bactrians and Sacæ in the first decade.[3]

Cyrus must have arranged his court and state after the pattern of Media, which in its turn was a copy

[1] Crœsus, when he has crossed the Halys, is at once in Persian territory; Herod. 1, 72, 73.

[2] Xenoph. "Cyri instit." 3, 1; 3, 2, 1, 2; 7, 2, 5; Diod. 31, 19.

[3] The serious difficulty of Cyrus is shown by his rapid march back from Sardis with much the larger part of his army before the Greek cities, the Lycians and Carians were reduced. Cp. Vol. VI. chapters 8 and 9

of the court of the kings of Asshur and Babylon.
Ctesias asserts that Petesaces, the eunuch, and after
his death Bagapates, another eunuch, had great influence with Cyrus.[1] The abode of Achæmenes,
Teispes, and Cambyses, the ancient place of assembly
and metropolis of the tribe of the Pasargadæ, was
changed by Cyrus into a city and fortress ; there he
built his palace, in which he deposited the spoil of
his wars, and collected his treasures.[2] The new
kingdom rested on the power of the Persians ; they
alone had to pay no tribute to the king ; they formed
the nucleus of the army ; the leaders and satraps
were mainly chosen from them. But Cyrus was
obviously anxious to reconcile the Medes, next to
the Persians, with the change in affairs, and win
their aid. This design lay at the base of his treatment
of Astyages and the marriage with his daughter, and
scarcely ten years after the fall of the Median kingdom, we find Medes at the head of the army of
Cyrus. The clemency of Cyrus towards the other
subject nations is also extolled. Herodotus vouches
for the fact that he laid no fixed tribute upon them,
but left it to themselves to fix the amount of their
yearly contributions. Of all men, Xenophon says,
Cyrus made the largest presents, and exhibited the
greatest liberality towards those who had done him
good service, and in this the subsequent kings of
Persia followed his example.

According to Xenophon's description, Cyrus was
of a kindly disposition, eager to instruct himself, and

[1] " Persic." 9.
[2] Strabo, p. 730 ; Curt. 5, 6, 10 ; Arrian, "Anab." 3, 16, 18. The
observation in Xenophon ("Cyri instit." 5, 2, 1), that Cyrus whenever
he trod the soil of Persia gave a piece of gold to each Persian man and
woman, may have arisen from the presents to the women of Pasargadæ.

so ambitious that he shrank from no effort and no danger.[1] With the Greeks he passes not only for the founder of the dominion of the Persians, but for the author of excellent arrangements in the kingdom. From this point of view Xenophon wrote his treatise on Cyrus. By his example he wished to prove to the Greeks how the empire over nations could be gained, how a great kingdom could be founded and maintained, how a ruler could command obedience even among those who had never seen him and were separated by great distances. It is a historical romance which he has written on Cyrus; but he knew the Persian empire, and could not advance anything absolutely in contradiction to the current opinion of the Greeks about Cyrus. According to him the relation of Cyrus to the Persians rested on a kind of compact. When his son had subjugated the nations far and wide, Cambyses collected the elders of the Persians and the officers who held the highest places, and told them the Persians had elected Cyrus to be their general, and given him the army; Cyrus had extended their power over Asia, and gained glory among all men; he had made the bravest men in the army rich, and found pay and food for all the soldiers. If this relation were maintained it would be for the advantage of both parties; if, on the other hand, Cyrus sought to rule over the Persians with the same caprice as over other nations, or the Persians should attempt to take the command from him, each would do the greatest harm to the other. Let Cyrus, therefore, undertake to protect Persia and uphold the Persian laws, and the Persians to render Cyrus any service that he needed against rebellion and enemies. "After

[1] "Cyri instit." 1, 2, 1.

me," Cambyses concludes, " Cyrus will be king, and
whenever he comes to Persia he will offer for you
the sacrifice which I am offering now. If he is
in a foreign land, it will be best for the noblest
of our family to offer sacrifices to the gods." " What
Cambyses proposed was approved by Cyrus and the
Persians with invocations to the gods, and the arrangement is still observed on both sides." [1] Plato
even puts Cyrus on the same level as Lycurgus,
the founder of the constitution of Sparta. He gives
Dion the choice of rivalling the ancient Lycurgus or
Cyrus, or any one else who may be distinguished
by moral excellence and political wisdom.[2] According to the Laws, Cyrus, brought up from his youth
in the camp and surrounded by danger, became a
skilful general, and as a ruler kept before his eyes
the prosperity of the state. In the same book we
are told that the monarchical form of government
attained its most complete state among the Persians,
and the democratic among the Athenians. But as
the Persian state pursued absolute dominion, and
the Attic uncontrolled freedom, neither discovered
the correct limit; though in ancient times they had
observed due moderation. At the time of Cyrus the
Persians were midway between slavery and freedom.
At first they were free, then they became the lords
of others. But while ruling they had given the
subjects a share in freedom, and treated them on
an equal footing. For this reason the warriors were
devoted to their general and ready to plunge into
danger. And if an intelligent man appeared, who
could give wise counsel, Cyrus gave him liberty to
speak; and as he honoured those who knew how

---

[1] "Cyri instit." 8, 5, 21 ff.
[2] Plato, "Epp." 4, p. 320. Cf. "Menexen." p. 239.

to give advise, every opinion was made use of for the common good, and the Persians of that day succeeded in everything by freedom, concord, and common deliberation.[1]

[1] "Legg." p. 693, 694. Cicero, ("de Republ." 1, 27, 28), calls Cyrus the most just, wise, and amiable of rulers.

END OF VOL. V.